Literacy in the United States

Literacy in the United States

Readers and Reading since 1880

Carl F. Kaestle

Helen Damon-Moore, Lawrence C.

Stedman, Katherine Tinsley, and

William Vance Trollinger, Jr.

Yale University Press

New Haven and London

Published with assistance from the
Louis Stern Memorial Fund.

Designed by James J. Johnson.
Set in Century Schoolbook type by The
Composing Room of Michigan, Inc.
Printed in the United States of America
by Vail-Ballou Press, Binghamton, New
York.

The paper in this book meets the
guidelines for permanence and
durability of the Committee on
Production Guidelines for Book
Longevity of the Council on Library
Resources.

*Library of Congress Cataloging-in-
Publication Data*

Kaestle, Carl F.
    Literacy in the United States :
readers and reading since 1880 /
Carl F. Kaestle ; Helen Damon-
Moore . . . [et al.].
        p. cm.
    Includes bibliographical references
(p.   ) and index.
    ISBN 0-300-04946-3 (cloth)
        0-300-05430-0 (pbk.)
    1. Literacy—United States—
History. I. Damon-Moore, Helen
(Helen M.) II. Title.
LC151.K32   1991
302.2′244—dc20   90-46716
                                    CIP

A catalogue record for this book is
available from the British Library.

10 9 8 7 6 5 4 3

Contents

List of Figures   ix

List of Tables   xi

Preface   xiii

Acknowledgments   xxi

PART ONE: Historians and Literacy

1. Studying the History of Literacy   CARL F. KAESTLE   3
2. The History of Readers   CARL F. KAESTLE   33

PART TWO: Americans' Reading Abilities

3. Literacy and Reading Performance in the United States from 1880 to the Present
   LAWRENCE C. STEDMAN AND CARL F. KAESTLE   75
4. The Great Test-Score Decline: A Closer Look
   LAWRENCE C. STEDMAN AND CARL F. KAESTLE   129

PART THREE: Americans' Reading Activities

5. Literacy as a Consumer Activity
   LAWRENCE C. STEDMAN, KATHERINE TINSLEY,
   AND CARL F. KAESTLE   149
6. Surveying American Readers   HELEN DAMON-MOORE
   AND CARL F. KAESTLE   180

7. Highbrow and Middlebrow Magazines in 1920   WILLIAM
   VANCE TROLLINGER, JR., AND CARL F. KAESTLE   204

   PART FOUR: Literacy and Diversity in
   American History

8. Autobiographies and the History of Reading: The
   Meaning of Literacy in Individual Lives   KATHERINE
   TINSLEY AND CARL F. KAESTLE   225

9. Gender, Advertising, and Mass-Circulation Magazines
   HELEN DAMON-MOORE AND CARL F. KAESTLE   245

10. Standardization and Diversity in American Print
    Culture, 1880 to the Present   CARL F. KAESTLE   272

Appendix   295

Bibliography   299

About the Authors   333

Index   335

Figures

3.1. Survival Literacy Study, Form 3: Application for Driver's License

3.2. Sample Items from the Reading Difficulty Index Study

3.3. Sample Items from the English Language Proficiency Survey

3.4. Sample Item from the Adult Functional Reading Study

3.5. Sample Item from the Adult Functional Reading Study

3.6. Sample Item from the Adult Functional Reading Study

3.7. Sample Item from the Brief Test of Literacy

5.1. Total Reading Expenditures, 1929–1986, in 1982 Dollars

5.2. Reading Expenditures per Person 18+, 1929–1986, in 1982 Dollars

5.3. Reading Expenditures as a Percentage of Total Expenditures, 1929–1986

5.4. Reading Expenditures as a Percentage of Recreation Expenditures, 1929–1986

5.5. Reading Expenditures as a Percentage of Mass-Media Expenditures, 1929–1986

5.6. Reading Expenditures as a Percentage of Other Expenditures, 1929–1986

5.7. Newspapers, Magazines, and Books as a Percentage of Reading Expenditures, 1929–1986

5.8. Recreation Expenditures as a Percentage of Total Expenditures, 1929–1986

5.9. Media Expenditures as a Percentage of Recreation Expenditures, 1929–1986

5.10. Print Expenditures versus Electronic Expenditures, as a Percentage of Mass-Media Expenditures, 1929–1986

7.1. "The Play": Tree Structure of a Story Excerpted from the *Saturday Evening Post,* April 3, 1920 (Young-Miller Analysis)

7.2. "The Ghost": Tree Structure of a Story Excerpted from the *Atlantic Monthly,* April 1920 (Young-Miller Analysis)

7.3. "The Play": Event Chain of a Story Excerpted from the *Saturday Evening Post,* April 3, 1920 (Kemper Analysis)

7.4. "The Ghost": Event Chain of a Story Excerpted from the *Atlantic Monthly,* April 1920 (Kemper Analysis)

Tables

3.1. Local Then-and-Now Studies of Reading Achievement

3.2. Statewide and National Then-and-Now Studies of Reading Achievement

3.3. Functional Illiteracy Rates

3.4. Results of Reading Difficulty Index Study

5.1. Percentage of People Buying Various Reading Materials in the United States, 1888–1983

5.2. Stepwise Regression: Expenditures on Books and Newspapers by U.S. Industrial Workers, 1888–1890

5.3. Stepwise Regression: Expenditures on Books and Newspapers by Families of Workers in Selected Industrial Occupations, 1888–1890

5.4. Percentage of Americans Buying Newspapers, Magazines, and Books by Income Class, 1918–1972

5.5. Household Expenditures, by Income Class, 1918–1982 (in Dollars)

6.1. Frequency of Reading Newspapers, Magazines, and Books, 1937–1985

6.2. Percentage of Readership by Age: Chicago, 1923

6.3. Book Readership by Age, 1949–1984

6.4. Percentages of Estimated Daily Newspaper Reading, by Respondent Cohorts, 1946–1977

6.5. Percentage Who Read Books, Magazine, and Newspapers, by Education: Chicago, 1923

6.6. Percentage of American Adults Who Read Books, by Education, 1949–1984

6.7. Readership by Sex: Chicago, 1923

6.8. Active Book Readership by Sex, 1949–1984

6.9. Respondents Who Read a Book Last Month, by Income and Education, 1945

6.10. Frequency of Reading Three Print Forms, by Education: Baltimore
     Women, 1961
7.1. Flesch Readability Ratings of 1920 Reading Materials
9.1. Top Ten Paid-Circulation Magazines, 1900–1980

Preface

Literacy is a hot topic in the United States today. In the past few years measurement experts have documented low functional-literacy skills among young adults, educators have decried falling test scores, humanists have argued about the need for more "cultural literacy," books by reformers have warned us of an "illiterate America," and legislators have submitted bills to "eliminate illiteracy." Television networks, newspaper chains, business councils, and prominent political figures have joined the campaign. It is an issue with considerable staying power.

Meanwhile, the history of literacy has become a very visible and productive subfield within academic circles. Although historians' interest in literacy is a relatively new development, already there are several shelves of books on the subject. A collection of interesting works on the introduction of writing and its effects on early civilizations has recently been joined by a burgeoning literature on the history of literacy in the modern West, focusing on trends in basic literacy rates, their causes, and their consequences. Literacy has played a role in such major social transformations as the Reformation, the creation of nation-states, and industrialization; literacy has in turn been influenced by these developments. The distribution and functions of literacy have been shaped by systems of class, status, and ethnic relations; in turn, literacy has played a role both in maintaining and in changing such structures. Different actors, in different settings, have seen literacy as an entrée to opportunity, as a powerful tool of dissent, and as an instrument of conformity and assimilation.

In the early flowering of work on the history of literacy, twenty-five years ago, most historians concentrated on tracing how many people were nominally literate. They investigated how their social characteristics differed from those who were illiterate, treating literacy as a dichotomous variable. Recently, more historians have become interested in different levels of literacy and in the uses of literacy, drawing difficult connections between literate people and the things they read, and linking the history of literacy to such topics as the history of the book, the history of education, of the press, and of popular reading tastes.

This exciting turning point in historical studies of literacy—when historians took up the challenge to bring together the study of readers and printed texts—marks the point of departure for our research. One might imagine, given the urgency of literacy as a policy issue in the United States today, and given the exciting new work in the history of literacy, that a body of work on the history of literacy in America's recent past would already exist. Strangely, though, we know very little about the distribution and uses of literacy over the past century. Nor is it easy to learn about trends in literacy and their meaning. Sources are sparse, data are often not comparable over time, and precise definitions are elusive. Literacy is all around us and is immensely important, but measuring it and assessing its meaning are hard and tracing its progress in earlier decades is even harder. Because literacy has a cultural as well as an economic dimension, personal as well as collective importance, psychological as well as social meanings, the theoretical insights that might help the historian grapple with this unwieldy subject are as scattered and diverse as the sources themselves.

In a research effort beginning in 1983, I have addressed many of these issues, along with four young scholars, each of whom served as a research assistant on the project at some time during the past six years. Given the scattered nature of the evidence and the relative paucity of previous studies on which to build, our work is necessarily exploratory. To investigate levels of literacy and its uses, we turned to studies of the production and distribution of newspapers, magazines, and books, to studies of reading-achievement testing, to studies of reading habits, to government surveys, and to personal life-history materials. Chapter by chapter we explore different sources and different levels of analysis.

The topic is vast; this book is only a beginning. We do relatively little with the history of libraries and nothing with the uses of literacy beyond the major print forms. Government pamphlets, church bulletins, grocery lists, and love letters have an important place in the history of literacy, but they fall outside the scope of this volume. Building on the foundation provided by these research studies, I plan in the coming few years to write a book-length essay on the history of the American reading public.

In the hope of providing historical perspective on current debates about literacy in the United States, we focus here mostly on the development of the American reading public over the past century. We begin in

1880, when the population was broadly if not highly literate, and the nation was on the verge of a rapid expansion of popular printed material and a slower but steady expansion of secondary education. We take the analysis to the present, when print literacy faces stiff competition from electronic media and many commentators worry that we are experiencing a literacy crisis and that the very future of print is in doubt.

To set our efforts in the context of existing historical studies of literacy, however, we must start with a broader canvas. Other scholars have focused heavily on Europe before 1900 and, to a lesser degree, on early American literacy; the two chapters of part 1 assess the state of the art. The first chapter presents the major issues and findings in the field, commenting on problems of evidence and definition. It summarizes historians' principal conclusions about the relationship of literacy rates to urbanization, industrialization, Protestantism, and nationalism. However, the best recent studies depart from literacy rates and inquire into the uses of literacy. Chapter 2, therefore, looks at diverse studies of readers, print production, and the reading public, concentrating on the American case. Chapter 2 also considers theories that may be helpful in interpreting the evidence on this messy topic. It discusses briefly the comprehensive theoretical perspectives of Harold Innis and of Raymond Williams, but argues for a more eclectic approach to theory. We look at both readers and texts in these essays; this effort to join readers and texts finds support in recent developments in literary theory, communications research, and reading research. The second half of chapter 2 turns from theory to historical trends, summarizing what recent historians have learned about the American reading public in the early and mid-nineteenth century.

Part 2 turns to the period 1880–1980 in the United States. Rejecting the notion of literacy as an either-or trait, we look at varying levels of reading skill over time. Chapter 3 takes a long technical look at how well people could read over the past century. The data are sparse for the early decades, so most of our attention is on the past thirty or forty years. This chapter charts the immense expansion of schooling and analyzes reading-achievement scores over time. Next, chapter 4 looks more closely at the much-publicized test-score decline of the late 1960s and early 1970s—its magnitude, its causes, and its policy implications.

Having established in part 2 the contours of an impressive but uneven expansion of literacy in the United States over the past century, we turn in part 3 to the uses of literacy. Chapter 5 uses family-budget studies conducted by the government to assess the purchase of reading materials, looking at changes over time and across social groups. Given the expected differences by income, the study reveals a quite robust commitment to reading by people in lower-income groups over the long term.

Recently, however, it seems that the influential McCombs Constancy Hypothesis (which asserts level amounts of reading purchases over time) has been overturned by downward trends, lending support to apprehensions about declining popular reading.

Chapter 6 gets at the same trends from different sources: Studies of the reading public in which self-reported reading activities are tabulated, mostly focusing on how frequently people read magazines, newspapers, and books. The most substantial additions to the reading public had probably occurred by the 1930s, when these studies by pollsters and reading researchers began. Since then, proportions of the population who regularly read magazines and newspapers have been level or declining. The data on book reading are less clear; different pictures emerge from different sources. The family-budget data reveal that the proportion of households in which someone purchased a book continued to rise to a high point of 60 percent in 1972, after which it began to decline (to 47 percent in 1983); but the proportion of people who told pollsters they read books regularly was steady at about 20 to 25 percent from the 1950s to the 1980s; if anything, the sketchy data suggest a slight rise. Having begun at the national aggregate level, chapter 6 moves to differences among Americans by age, sex, and other characteristics and then to local studies, for a more in-depth look at reading habits. These studies go beyond data on the frequency of people's reading to information about people's uses of literacy and their attitudes about reading. Chapter 6 ends by stressing the differences between elite highly educated readers and a more popular reading public who read books less frequently.

Chapter 7 ventures to combine knowledge of the reading publics of 1920 with an analysis of highbrow and middlebrow prose. It reports on an experiment in which we applied the latest readability tests to stories published in 1920, one from an elite magazine (*Harper's*) and one from a mass-circulation magazine (the *Saturday Evening Post*). Although we don't expect other researchers to emulate this rather elaborate use of computer analysis on historical materials, it helped us to think about what sort of mental processes are involved in reading "more difficult" and "less difficult" prose. Like reader-response theory in literary studies, this is a way to connect reader and text through the analysis of text, not through actual empirical observation of the reader. Rather, one imagines what is going on in an "implied" or generalized reader's head, at a very microscopic level of prose processing. We concluded that there were substantial differences in the difficulty of the prose in highbrow and middlebrow magazines in 1920, that the reading skills required of the highbrow prose were probably limited to a small minority of the population, and that this probably reinforced other factors that tended to stratify the reading public.

Part 4 explores the diverse uses of literacy in America, against a backdrop of capitalist consolidation and cultural assimilation. In chapter 8 we examine the autobiographies of women in the late nineteenth and early twentieth centuries. What were the functions of literacy in these women's lives? What was at stake? What were their strategies regarding the uses of literacy? This small-scale study does not develop a predictive model; the analysis of autobiography is not a scientific enterprise, but it humanizes the analysis yielded by more exact data on trends and large populations. We use the concept of cultural capital to think about what was at stake for young readers from different family situations. For the children of affluent parents, especially native-born and highly educated parents, the culture of their family and the culture of their school were quite compatible, and the payoff from learning the culture of the school was clear. For the children whose parents were poorer, less educated, or outside the cultural mainstream (or all three), the stakes were quite different. The payoff from learning school culture was less certain, and the young readers had to bridge a gap between family culture and school culture. Some of the children of "outsiders" became alienated radicals or union activists, whereas others became zealous assimilationists, thus underscoring the diverse uses of literacy. Although individuals' strategies differed in unpredictable ways, the stakes for these outsiders were similar, and different from the stakes faced by youths from the middle-class mainstream.

In the last two chapters of the book, we leave behind the data on actual readers and look at the production side of the print world, still with an eye toward diversity. The production of magazines, newspapers, and books is important to the history of the reading public. These major print forms provide opportunities and set limits for readers. Reading cannot serve the purpose of maintaining diversity if diverse views are not printed; conversely, it cannot serve the purpose of cultural consolidation if common information and values are not widely disseminated. Those who produce printed material are heavily influenced by their notions about their readers—readers as students, as citizens, and most important, readers as consumers, that is, as people who will buy books, magazines, and newspapers and who will read advertisements. Part of the history of the reading public is thus the history of the production of our major print forms and the study of the forces that influenced that cultural production. There is a mountain of historical writing about the book trade and journalism, about the leading characters in those enterprises—publishers, editors, and writers—and about the content of many individual publications and genres. The last two chapters of the book synthesize some of this material, with a view toward diversity. Chapter 9 looks at a major divide in the history of the reading public, the gap between men and women. The chapter explores why women's magazines were an enduring and prominent part of the high-circulation lists, whereas men's magazines were more problematic. Starting with a detailed comparison of the *Ladies' Home Journal* and the *Saturday Evening Post* in the early twentieth century, the chapter moves through the decades to the present, considering how gender works in relating magazine content to capitalism.

Chapter 10 looks at the role of the major print forms in promoting both cultural consolidation and diverse subcultures. Although the long-term drift is toward consolidation of production and thus standardization of content, there are periods when standardization predominates and periods when renewed diversity predominates. The intersection of culture and technology in the production of print thus is complex and not entirely one-directional. The common "pendulum" metaphor is not apt either, however, because there are underlying forces of consolidation that are not reversed when culture and technology periodically invigorate diversity in the world of published reading material. Chapter 10 wrestles with this complexity and anticipates some of the themes of the subsequent book planned in this research effort.

In this volume we address basic questions about the history of the American reading public—how well people could read, how much they read, what types of things they read, what functions the reading served, what factors influenced the availability of reading materials for people, what social characteristics attached to people with different reading habits, and how these patterns changed over time during the past century. Because this is largely uncharted territory, we sought to explore the possibilities by concentrating on different types of primary sources in different chapters. The book attempts to sort out methodological problems that arise when historians ask difficult questions of incomplete and imperfect sources. It then attempts, little by little, to find out what trends existed, and what we can say about the causes and meanings of the trends.

Some themes emerge. There has been a huge expansion of literacy in America over the past century, against which the modest skill declines of the 1970s seem insignificant. Second, however, the expansion of literacy has been very uneven. Levels of literacy have been correlated with gender, race, ethnicity, and income throughout our history. As we closed the gap on rudimentary literacy of women, black Americans, and immigrants, new gaps appeared at higher levels, as we raised our literacy expectations. Americans tried to meet these higher expectations through increased years of schooling. Whether that strategy for meeting literacy gaps is sufficient today is doubtful, though schools continue to be the major arena for training in literacy.

Third, paralleling the rise of literacy abilities, there has been a tremendous expansion of the availability, purchase, and use of printed materials, and they have become increasingly standardized, exposing more and more people to common syndicated newspaper features, popular fiction, and mass-circulation magazines. Fourth, control of the press has nonetheless been contested; people have used print to maintain their differences, and diversity has been renewed in various ways at various times, depending upon the interplay of cultural, marketing, and technological factors. Fifth, literacy has leveled off and even declined recently in some areas of reading, such as daily newspaper reading, apparently in response to the expansion of electronic communication. It is thus a propitious time to contemplate both the recent trends in literacy and the social policies that might encourage not only high-level literacy abilities but also the production of high-quality, diverse reading materials in our society.

The volume offers various perspectives on contemporary nervousness about the state of American print literacy. We argue that in the 1960s and 1970s the electronic media did not have a dramatic negative impact on reading habits and that the test-score decline of the 1970s has been exaggerated and misunderstood. Yet newspaper reading *has* declined over the past two decades, and there was a decline in reading abilities during the 1970s. These trends are a matter of legitimate concern. Furthermore, the proportion of our population that has even middle-level critical reading skills is (and probably always has been) quite low.

Even though this volume musters the data on reading habits and trends in reading ability more thoroughly than any previous efforts, we are not as concerned with arguing about the magnitude of increases and decreases as we are in providing a perspective on the present moment in the history of American literacy. We are impressed by the importance of reading in giving individuals a sense of political agency, in connecting them to cultural traditions, and in enhancing their opportunity to succeed in the job market. High levels of literacy are also crucial to our collective political and economic fate. Given the record of the past century, we argue that the United States is at another important turning point and that Americans must raise their literacy expectations and their literacy skills, across the whole population. We hope that this volume of research essays will contribute not only to historical perspective but also to a sense of urgency about literacy problems in our society.

Acknowledgments

I began working on the history of literacy during a year's leave-of-absence in 1982–83 at the Center for Advanced Study in the Behavioral Sciences at Stanford, and I am happy to express my gratitude to the Center's then director, Gardner Lindzey, and to its wonderful staff. Funds supporting my year at the Center came from the National Endowment for the Humanities and from the Graduate School Research Committee of the University of Wisconsin at Madison. I had the privilege of being at the Center during a year when a number of wonderful historians were in residence, including Albert Camarillo, Richard Dunn, Elizabeth Eisenstein, and James McPherson, as well as a number of scholars in other disciplines interested in language and literacy, among them Bob Crowder, Kenji Hakuta, Nancy Stein, and Tom Trabasso, so it was an ideal group of colleagues for my interests in the social history of literacy and reading. Upon my return to Madison in the fall of 1983, this research was supported first by the National Institute of Education (Grant No. NIE-G-84-0008) for two years, and since then by the Spencer Foundation, to whom I owe my greatest debt; in particular I am grateful for the support, friendship, and advice of Spencer's vice president, Marion Faldet, and its former president Lawrence A. Cremin. Larry's untimely death in September 1990 was a great loss to the education research community. I shall miss his intellectual energy and his wit.

Research grants for this project were made to me in my capacity as a faculty associate at the Wisconsin Center for Education Research, another marvelously supportive environment for scholarship. To its former director, Marshall Smith, its present director, Andrew Porter, and to the many staff members at WCER who make complex, collaborative research projects work, I owe thanks for countless acts of help and encouragement—in particular to Karen Donnelly, Deborah Stewart, Jerry

Grossman, Sandra Treptow, Al Divine, Ed Frederick, and, with special gratitude, Lois O'Brien Opalewski.

In addition to my four coauthors, four other graduate assistants have contributed to the research for this volume, and to my ongoing further work in the history of American literacy: JoAnne Brown, Anne Durst, Marc Goulden, and Dina Stephens. My thanks to them for hard work, bright ideas, and continual graciousness.

During the last stages of preparing this volume I was named to a William F. Vilas Professorship at the University of Wisconsin-Madison. This is an honor for which I am very grateful; in particular, I am grateful to my colleagues in the Department of Educational Policy Studies and its then chair, Michael Olneck, to colleagues in the Department of History and its chair, John Cooper, to Dean of Education John Palmer, to then Dean of Letters and Science E. David Cronon, to then Vice-Chancellor for Academic Affairs Bernard Cohen, and to the Chancellor of the University of Wisconsin-Madison, Donna Shalala, for their support. Support from the Vilas Professorship has helped in the later stages of preparing this book.

I have given earlier versions of some of this research as lectures or seminar papers at other universities, and I have benefited from these opportunities to receive constructive criticism of my work. In particular, I am grateful to Bengt Ankarloo of the History Faculty of Lund University, Sweden, John Briggs of the Department of Cultural Foundations of Education at Syracuse University, Roger Farr of the Program in Reading of Indiana University, Lawrence Stone, director of the Shelby Cullom Davis Center at Princeton, and Richard Venezky of the Department of Educational Studies at the University of Delaware. Informal conversations with colleagues around the country have, of course, challenged my ideas and enriched my sources; these have included discussions with Richard Anderson, Bernard Bailyn, Robert Gross, Shirley Brice Heath, Irwin Kirsch, Larry Mikulecky, Jennifer Monaghan, David Nord, Daniel Resnick, Thomas Sticht, Andrew Sum, David Tyack, Richard Venezky, Maris Vinovskis, and others. At Wisconsin, many colleagues have suffered my preoccupation with literacy matters for eight years and provided endless good advice; in particular these have included Michael Apple, Paul Boyer, Merle Curti, Jim Dankey, Sterling Fishman, Linda Gordon, Jurgen Herbst, Herbert Kliebard, Gerda Lerner, David Myers, Michael Olneck, Francis Schrag, David Ward, and Wayne Wiegand.

Paul DiMaggio of the Department of Sociology at Yale University read an earlier version of the manuscript and made extensive comments; his expertise and his encouragement were crucially important. He and all other scholars who made suggestions are absolved of responsibility for the failings of our book.

Gladys Topkis, our editor, has been enthusiastic, supportive, and helpful from beginning to end, making all the more pleasurable the privilege of publishing this book with Yale University Press. Editorial assistance came from Diane Paley and Deborah Stewart of the Wisconsin Center for Education Research and from Cynthia Carter Ayres and Laura Jones Dooley of Yale University Press.

Some chapters or parts of chapters have appeared elsewhere and were substantially revised and updated for this volume. Specifically, portions of chapters 1 and 2 appeared as "The History of Literacy and the History of Readers," in *Review of Research in Education,* ed. Edmund Gordon, vol. 12 (Washington, D.C.: American Educational Research Association, 1985); an earlier version of chapter 3 appeared as "Literacy and Reading Performance in the United States, from 1880 to the Present," in *Reading Research Quarterly* 22 (Winter 1987); an earlier version of chapter 4 appeared as "The Test Score Decline Is Over: Now What?" in *Phi Delta Kappan* 67 (November 1985); and portions of chapter 10 appeared as "Literacy and Diversity: Themes from a Social History of the American Reading Public," in *History of Education Quarterly* 28 (Winter 1988). These materials are adapted here by permission of the publishers.

I was involved in the research and the writing of all the chapters, and I brought them together and revised them for this volume. Authorship of the individual chapters is indicated at the beginning of each chapter. Each of the coauthors also read and commented on the entire volume, and much informal discussion took place during the course of the project. I am grateful to them for their research, their insights, their contributions to the text, and their friendship.

They join me in thanking our various spouses, friends, children, and parents for providing encouragement and welcome distractions along the way.

Carl F. Kaestle

I Historians and Literacy

1 Studying the History of Literacy

CARL F. KAESTLE

The history of literacy is a lively and often controversial field, full of surprises, contradictions, and reinterpretations. Not only the explanations but even the basic facts about literacy trends remain uncertain. As with other topics in the history of ordinary people, historians of literacy have tangled with problems of inadequate data and fuzzy definitions. The term *literacy* appears straightforward, but because it can refer to a wide range of reading and writing activities, historians' definitions vary. Even if restricted only to reading, the term literacy may imply a wide range of abilities.

In this chapter we define literacy as the ability to decode and comprehend written language at a rudimentary level—that is, the ability to say written words corresponding to ordinary oral discourse and to understand them. Most historians of the subject appear to have such rudimentary literacy ability in mind when they estimate literacy rates. It should be noted, however, that defining literacy as low-level reading ability may give a false sense of clarity to the research problem, for the practice of using literacy as a dichotomous variable is itself an oversimplification. The categories "literate" and "illiterate" are neither precise nor mutually exclusive. Some individuals learned to read but then forgot how. Some were literate but read only rarely. Some perceived themselves to be literate but were perceived by others as illiterate, or vice versa. Furthermore, individuals who were unable to read participated in literate culture by listening to those who could read; the worlds of literacy and oral communication are interpenetrating.

Nonetheless, there are good reasons to explore the expansion and consequences of rudimentary literacy rates over time, as long as we remember that literate people have a wide range of abilities and that illiterate people are not wholly isolated from the influence of print. Lacking more direct evidence, historians began by counting the people who signed their names on documents and comparing them to those who marked an X. This may seem a simplistic beginning, but it soon fed essential debates about the probable relation between signing ability and reading ability. Over the last fifteen years scholars have developed considerable consensus that signing ability and modest reading ability are roughly correlated.

Major Interpretive Questions

In addition to the problem of evidence, several interpretive issues have shaped recent studies in the history of literacy, four of which are particularly relevant to our interests in this volume. The first issue is whether literacy is uniformly and unequivocally tied to progress. Even for ancient cultures some scholars question this hypothesis. Eric Havelock, for example, argued that in view of the artistic and political achievements of preliterate Greece, we should not equate cultural sophistication with literacy.[1] Some twentieth-century historians bemoan the erosion of an authentic indigenous folk or working-class culture due to the proliferation of mass commercial print matter.[2] Apart from its effect on folk and oral culture, does print literacy have a liberating or a constraining effect on individuals? The answer, obviously, is both, but the relative emphasis on these twin potentials does much to define a historian's interpretation and is itself shaped by ideology as well as evidence. In Lawrence Cremin's view, literacy is liberating and enlightening; similarly, modernization theorists have emphasized literacy's role in widening mental horizons and bolstering rationality.[3] Meanwhile, Lee Soltow and Edward Stevens, along with Harvey Graff, have seen literacy as an ideology of middle-class schooling. Their work is in keeping with

1. Eric Havelock, *Origins of Western Literacy* (Toronto: Ontario Institute for Studies in Education, 1976), 3–6.

2. Richard Hoggart, *The Uses of Literacy* (London: Chatto and Windus, 1957), chaps. 7–8; Oscar Handlin, "Comments on Mass and Popular Culture," *Culture for the Millions? Mass Media in Modern Society,* ed. Norman Jacobs (Princeton, N.J.: D. Van Nostrand, 1961), 63–70; see also Patrick Brantlinger, *Bread and Circuses: Theories of Mass Culture as Social Decay* (Ithaca: Cornell University Press, 1983).

3. Lawrence A. Cremin, *American Education: The National Experience, 1783–1876* (New York: Harper and Row, 1980); Cremin, *American Education: The Colonial Experience, 1607–1786* (New York: Harper and Row, 1970); Cremin, *American Education: The Metropolitan Experience, 1876–1980* (New York: Harper and Row, 1988); Alex Inkeles and David Smith, *Becoming Modern: Individual Change in Six Developing Countries* (Cambridge: Harvard University Press, 1974).

the trend in revisionist educational history toward viewing schooling as an imposition.[4]

The second background question is whether literacy, for good or for ill, is always expanding. Is the alleged recent decline in literacy skills in the United States unprecedented? This second concern recalls the problems of defining and measuring literacy, for if we cannot agree on how to define and measure it, we cannot determine whether it is declining or increasing. The issue is not settled by arbitrary definitions of literacy as an either-or condition. There are many levels of literacy, and deficiencies may demand policy makers' attention not only at the lowest skill level but also at the middling and upper levels. In chapters 3 and 4 we discuss levels of literacy historically and as a policy matter, with the debate over the test-score declines in the 1970s as a backdrop.

The third question has to do with causation. Were changes in literacy principally causes or effects of other social changes? It is an issue that has been much debated. Elizabeth Eisenstein staked out a bold argument for the printing press as a neglected agent of cultural change, but she met much resistance from other scholars.[5] Jack Goody and Ian Watt decided after some criticism that what Goody had earlier called the "consequences" of literacy in traditional societies should be toned down to "implications."[6] Harvey Graff argued that literacy's efficacy in improving individual life chances was a "myth."[7] The relevance to current policy is obvious: if illiteracy is largely a symptom of other disadvantages, it doesn't make much sense to focus on it as a fulcrum of reform and an equalizer of opportunity. Of course, to ask whether literacy is principally cause or principally effect is to oversimplify the problem because the relationship is reciprocal and ongoing: increases in literacy lead to changes in the work force, education, and social relations that breed further changes in literacy. For analytical purposes we can focus on the causes of literacy at a given historical moment, or on its consequences, but the real relationship is always dynamic and circular.

The fourth question centers on the relationship between literacy and

4. Lee Soltow and Edward Stevens, *The Rise of Literacy and the Common School in the United States: A Socioeconomic Analysis to 1870* (Chicago: University of Chicago Press, 1981); Harvey Graff, *The Literacy Myth: Literacy and Social Structure in the Nineteenth-Century City* (New York: Academic Press, 1979).

5. Elizabeth Eisenstein, *The Printing Press as an Agent of Change: Communications and Cultural Transformations in Early-Modern Europe* (Cambridge: Cambridge University Press, 1980).

6. Jack Goody, ed., *Literacy in Traditional Societies* (Cambridge: Cambridge University Press, 1968), 4; Goody and Ian Watt, "The Consequences of Literacy," *Comparative Studies in Society and History* 5 (1963):304–45.

7. Graff, *Literacy Myth,* 19, 52, 223.

schooling. Schools are doubtless the most important mediating institutions in the development of literacy, that is, they translate economic, political, and religious mandates for literacy into actual training. And, as we shall see, literacy rates are generally correlated with school enrollment rates. Still, we need to be reminded periodically that the workplace, the church, the family, and the printing press also have affected levels and uses of literacy, and that scholars today continue to debate the importance of these institutions relative to the school. Some historical and social science research suggests that it is a mistake to equate literacy with schooling, in spite of their intimate connections. Questions about the fit between schooling and literacy are relevant both for contemporary policy discussions and for historical understanding.

The remainder of this chapter is organized chronologically, from the invention of the alphabet to the policy debates of the 1980s. Answers to the four major issue questions are woven into the chronological review and are summarized at the end of the chapter.

From Oral to Written Culture

The invention of writing was a gradual process. Scholars have identified several stages, not only in the evolution of writing systems but also in the diffusion of literacy to different groups in society. Mnemonic symbols evolved into word-syllabic systems among the Sumerians, and later the Babylonians, the Hittites, and the Egyptians, as commerce necessitated more abstract symbols that could record different products and individuals. From these word-syllabic systems evolved various syllabic systems and ultimately, through the Phoenicians, the alphabetic writing of the Greeks.

Beyond these technical stages of writing development, the early history of literacy may be roughly periodized according to the level at which literacy was diffused among the population. For some centuries after the introduction of alphabetic writing, literacy was restricted to a small elite and limited to a few functions, chiefly religion, accounting, genealogy, and, sometimes, political administration. Historians have called these centuries a time of "craft," or restricted, literacy. As writing eventually gained a foothold in more and more areas of activity, it prompted more general literacy among the elite. At the same time, the diffusion of writing tended to consolidate and standardize vernacular language.[8]

8. On the technical aspects of the history of writing, the standard authorities are Ignace J. Gelb, *A Study of Writing*, 2d ed. (Chicago: University of Chicago Press, 1963), and David Diringer, *The Alphabet: A Key to the History of Mankind*, 3d ed. (New York: Funk and Wagnalls, 1968); but see also Denise Schmandt-Besserat, "The Earliest Precursor of Writing," *Scientific American* 238 (June 1978):50–59.

Some qualifications to the concept of stages in literacy are in order. First, not all societies move through all stages; for example, nonliterate societies can adopt alphabetic writing from abroad, skipping the earlier stages. Second, although the stages of diffusion are generally sequential, they are sometimes reversible; for example, in Europe the literate population narrowed during the medieval period, and in Greece, between the twelfth and the ninth century B.C., writing utterly vanished.[9] Third, the stages are not mutually exclusive; they express gradual and overlapping developments.

These early developments took place in the context of mass illiteracy and pervasive oral culture. Oral culture did not atrophy in contact with written culture; rather, the written word modified and extended communication networks. Not only has the great majority of the earth's population been illiterate throughout history, but the great bulk of communication in literate societies is still oral. Nonetheless, writing is a technology and, as such, it allowed new modes of communication, administration, and record keeping, as well as innovations in economic, political, and cultural activities. Most profoundly, it allowed and encouraged new modes of thinking.

Did the introduction of writing mark a great watershed in the history of culture and consciousness? For a long time, the shift to writing seemed to correspond with the shift from "traditional" to "modern" society or from "primitive" to "advanced" cultures. These dichotomies no longer seem adequate and are out of fashion among anthropologists and historians. Still, some fundamental changes can be associated with the advent of writing. Plato saw them coming, and he criticized writing; in the *Phaedras* he has Socrates argue that writing encourages forgetfulness, has only the appearance of wisdom, cannot answer questions or clarify itself, and can be misunderstood and misused.[10] Later observers were a good deal more enthusiastic, associating literacy with progress. Recently, anthropologists and historians of language have attempted a more balanced view. Jack Goody criticized Claude Lévi-Strauss's dichotomy between the "savage" and "domestic" minds, but argued that we must be

9. On the extinction of pre-alphabetic writing in Greece, see John Chadwick, *The Mycenaean World* (Cambridge: Cambridge University Press, 1976), 15–34; on the introduction of alphabetic writing in Greece, see L. G. Jeffery, "Greek Alphabetic Writing," in *The Cambridge Ancient History,* ed. John Boardman et al., vol. 3, 2d ed. (Cambridge: Cambridge University Press, 1982), 819–33. For a thorough review of the origins of Greek writing, see Barry B. Powell, *Homer and the Origin of the Greek Alphabet* (Cambridge: Cambridge University Press, 1990), and for the functions of literacy in the Greco-Roman world from the return of literacy to the fifth century A.D., see William V. Harris, *Ancient Literacy* (Cambridge: Harvard University Press, 1989).

10. Eric Havelock, *Preface to Plato* (Oxford: Basil Blackwell, 1963), 39–49; Harris, *Ancient Literacy,* 30, 91–92.

willing to chart the historical evolution of cognitive processes and acknowledge the central role of writing, because, as he had written earlier, writing "changed the whole structure of the cultural tradition."[11] Walter Ong was careful to emphasize the overlap of oral and written cultures, and he expressed considerable admiration for oral traditions; nonetheless, he argued that "without writing, human consciousness cannot achieve its fuller potentials."[12] There is, then, a high degree of consensus about the technical capacities released by the invention of writing. The more difficult job of interpretation is determining the conditions under which these capacities are translated into fundamentally new forms of cultural enterprise and social organization. Both the timing and the inevitability are at issue when scholars assert the "consequences" of written culture.

As a technology, writing has facilitated a broad array of activities in communication. Among the most important are the replication, transportation, and preservation of messages, the back-and-forth scanning of written material, the study of sequence, the deliberation of word choice, and the construction of lists, tables, recipes, and indexes. Writing fosters an objectified sense of time, and it separates the message from the author, thus "decontextualizing" language. It allows new forms of verbal analysis, like the syllogism, and of numerical analysis, like the multiplication table. The long-range developments made possible by this technology have been profound, leading eventually to the replacement of myth by history and the replacement of magic by skepticism and science. Writing has fostered bureaucracy, accounting, and legal systems with universal rules. It has replaced face-to-face governance with depersonalized administration. On the other hand, it has allowed authorship to be recorded and recognized, thus contributing to the development of individualism in the world of ideas.[13]

The initial assertion of these consequences by Goody and Watt, Havelock, Ong, and others in the 1960s prompted case studies to test

11. Jack Goody, *The Domestication of the Savage Mind* (Cambridge: Cambridge University Press, 1971), 67.

12. Walter Ong, *Orality and Literacy* (New York: Methuen, 1982), 14.

13. On the intellectual and social consequences of the shift from oral to written culture, the most imaginative recent works are Goody and Watt, "Consequences of Literacy," 304–45; Havelock, *Preface to Plato;* Goody, ed., *Literacy in Traditional Societies;* Goody, *Domestication of the Savage Mind;* Sylvia S. Scribner and Michael M. Cole, *The Psychology of Literacy* (Cambridge: Harvard University Press, 1981); Ong, *Orality and Literacy;* Ong, *The Presence of the Word* (New Haven: Yale University Press, 1967); Michael Clanchy, *From Memory to Written Record: England, 1066–1307* (Cambridge: Harvard University Press, 1979); and Brian Stock, *The Implications of Literacy: Written Language and Models of Interpretation in the Eleventh and Twelfth Centuries* (Princeton, N.J.: Princeton University Press, 1983).

whether they occurred predictably and universally. Goody edited a sampling of such studies, the most interesting of which was reported in an article by Kathleen Gough on literacy in traditional China and India, in which she qualified some aspects of the Goody and Watt formulation. For example, a clear distinction between the supernatural and the natural did not occur in China and India until long after the appearance of writing. Also, the emergence of history as distinct from myth was true for China but very weak in India. Skepticism was also stronger in China but was tempered in both countries by strong traditional forces. Although in both countries there was evidence of literate people striving for objective, scientific truth, Gough doubted that the specialization of knowledge and consequent alienation Goody and Watt had hypothesized were typical of preindustrial literate societies.[14]

As a result of such modifications, literacy scholars began to emphasize various "brakes" on the expansion of literacy, and thus on the processes of objectification and bureaucratization in traditional societies. Writing materials were costly, and religious officials guarded their monopoly on literacy. Instead of wondering why literacy did not develop quickly, urged Michael Clanchy, "we should be asking 'Why did it develop at all, considering the obstacles in its path?'"[15] In his analysis of oral and written culture in England from 1066 to 1307, Clanchy portrayed a society that made a gradual but important transition from restricted clerical Latin literacy to more widespread secular, vernacular literacy, laying the groundwork for the print revolution of the sixteenth century, more than two thousand years after the invention of alphabetic writing.[16] As a technology, writing had transforming potential, but its impact was neither automatic nor sudden.

From Script to Print

The distinction between script writing and print has prompted debate. Some of the most important alleged consequences of writing for science, secularization, and bureaucratization seem to have emerged substantially only after the spread of printing. Given this, should the development of printing, and not writing, be considered the great technological and psychological turning point in the history of literacy? The issue is one of emphasis, but marvelously complex nonetheless. Recent

14. Kathleen Gough, "Implications of Literacy in Traditional China and India," in *Literacy in Traditional Societies,* ed. Goody, 70–84.

15. Michael M. Clanchy, "Looking Back from the Invention of Printing," in *Literacy in Historical Perspective,* ed. Daniel Resnick (Washington, D.C.: Library of Congress, 1983), 19.

16. Clanchy, *From Memory to Written Record.*

works of Elizabeth Eisenstein and Michael Clanchy illustrate this dialogue. Clanchy, a medievalist, saw trends of secularization and the expansion of script literacy as necessary antecedents to print, while Eisenstein, an early modernist, saw a decisive turning point in print technology.[17] Furthermore, Eisenstein was interested not in the role of printing in expanding literacy, but in how printing transformed modes of thinking and the uses of literacy among those already literate. In Eisenstein's judgment, scholars had underestimated the impact of the printing press as an agent of change; they had overlooked a communications revolution. Among the intellectual activities made possible by printing was the exact duplication of technical work, which allowed the expansion of data pools in astronomy, botany, and geography. Printing allowed the spread and preservation of Renaissance scholarship, so that it did not disappear like its counterparts in earlier revivals. Spawning cataloging, indexing, cross-referencing, and other aids to analysis, printing also spread vernacular language and helped standardize language across dialects. Some of the consequences of print were contrasting or even paradoxical. Although standardized print made reading more impersonal, for example, the development of authorship made individual celebrities possible. Print had a bridging, unifying effect in science, but a divisive, fragmenting effect in religion, fostering pamphlet wars and doctrinal polarization. Within religion, print fostered both modern criticism and resistant fundamentalism.[18]

Trends in Rudimentary Literacy Rates

Printing launched the modern era of literacy. Although Eisenstein was principally interested in intellectual changes among the literate, most scholars who have studied literacy after 1600 have been preoccupied with the expansion of literacy, its causes, and its consequences. Between 1600 and 1900 the countries of Western Europe moved from restricted to mass literacy, with profound consequences for education, social relations, and communications. The exact trends, however, are difficult to trace, as the evidence is skimpy and its validity suspect. Because national averages mask variation that could reveal causal relationships, the need for further studies is almost endless. Thus, even after

17. Eisenstein, *Printing Press as an Agent of Change;* Clanchy, "Looking Back from the Invention of Printing"; Clanchy, *From Memory to Written Record.*
18. Some reviewers argued that Eisenstein made the advent of printing too revolutionary; see A. T. Grafton, "The Importance of Being Printed," *Journal of Interdisciplinary History* 11 (1980): 265–86; and Paul Needham, review of *The Printing Press as an Agent of Change,* by Elizabeth Eisenstein, *Fine Print* 6 (1980):23–35.

we have estimated the trends in rudimentary literacy, it is difficult to move beyond them to the causes, the quality, and the meaning of literacy.

Signatures and Reading Ability

Very little evidence is available about the extent of literacy before 1850 except that provided by people's ability to sign such documents as marriage registers, army rolls, and wills. Because the relationship of signing ability to reading ability remains uncertain, the validity of the measure is one of the most frequently discussed methodological problems in the history of rudimentary literacy rates. Roger Schofield, a leading expert, has argued for the equivalency of signature rates with the proportion of people who could read. He based his judgment on surveys that compared the self-reported reading and writing abilities of English working-class groups in the 1830s and 1840s.[19] Schofield concluded that signing ability overestimates the number who could actually write but underestimates the number who could read at the most rudimentary level; thus he decided that signing ability conveniently approximated the proportion of people who could read "fluently." Many scholars who have relied on signature counts for their literacy studies have concurred in and cited Schofield's arguments.[20] Theodore Hamerow, how-

19. Roger S. Schofield, "The Measurement of Literacy in Pre-industrial England," in *Literacy in Traditional Societies,* ed. Goody, 311–25. The surveys were analyzed in R. K. Webb, "Working Class Readers in Early Victorian England," *English Historical Review* 65 (1950):333–51.

20. Kenneth Lockridge, citing Schofield and others, stated confidently: "Scholars agree" that signing ability corresponds to fluent reading ability. Lockridge, *Literacy in Colonial New England: An Enquiry into the Social Context of Literacy in the Early Modern West* (New York: W. W. Norton, 1974), 7. François Furet and Jacques Ozouf found a "spectacular proximity of the variables 'ability to sign the *acte de mariage*' and 'able to read and write' for both men and women" in nineteenth-century samples that included both sorts of evidence. Furet and Ozouf, *Reading and Writing: Literacy in France from Calvin to Jules Ferry* (Cambridge: Cambridge University Press, 1982), 15, originally published as *Lire et écrire: L'alphabétisation des français de Calvin à Jules Ferry* (Paris: Editions de Minuit, 1977). Citing Schofield and Furet and Ozouf, David Cressy concluded that "the statistical study of literacy over the last decade has been on the right track."Cressy, *Literacy and the Social Order: Reading and Writing in Tudor and Stuart England* (London: Cambridge University Press, 1980), 55. Walter Stephens declared that "contemporary opinion and recent research appear to indicate that signature literacy was a good indication of ability to write" and that "certainly more people could read to some extent than could sign for their names." Stephens, *Education, Literacy and Society, 1830–70: The Geography of Diversity in Provincial England* (Manchester: Manchester University Press, 1987), 3–4. Other useful discussions of signature literacy include Geoffrey Parker, "An Educational Revolution? The Growth of Literacy and Schooling in Early Modern Europe," *Tijdschift voor Geschiedenis* 93 (1980):210–20; William J. Gilmore, "Elementary Literacy on the Eve of the Industrial

ever, was more skeptical. Citing German data on reading and writing ability, he concluded that "the usual definition of literacy as the ability to sign one's name includes a large number, often half or more, of those whose mastery of the 3 R's was so inadequate that they should properly be classified as functional illiterates."[21]

What can we say, then, about signature counting, the basis of most literacy studies for the period 1600 to 1850? Signing may correlate with "fluent" reading ability, as Schofield argued, but confidence on that score must be guarded. One might argue that whatever the absolute levels, at least over time the trends in signing should parallel trends in other literacy skills; but even this common-sense notion must be qualified. The relationship between signing and reading may vary by gender, by class, by place, and by period. For example, if schools taught reading earlier than writing, poorer children who had to work as they got older might have learned to read but not write.[22] On the other hand, where the skills were taught together, the signing and reading abilities of adults would be more closely correlated. If elite providers of education promoted reading skill but feared writing instruction, many adults who could read might have been unable to sign; conversely, where reading and writing were equally encouraged, the two rates must have been closer.[23] If historians of literacy are cautious about such possibilities, they can reasonably use signature counts as a rough indicator of the minimum number of people who had rudimentary reading skills. There may have been many who made an X and could nonetheless read and others who could sign their names but could not read. The leading scholars of literacy rates, however, believe that signing rates are closely tied to minimum rudimentary reading rates.

Rudimentary Literacy Rates in Europe, 1600–1850

With the spread of vernacular print matter during the sixteenth century, rudimentary literacy rose in Europe. In 1600 an estimated 35 to 40

Revolution: Trends in Rural New England, 1760–1830," *Proceedings of the American Antiquarian Society* 92 (1982):81–178; and Richard L. Venezky, "The Development of Literacy in the Industrialized Nations of the West," in *Handbook of Reading Research,* ed. P. David Pearson (Newark, Del.: International Reading Association, in press).

21. Theodore Hamerow, *The Birth of a New Europe* (Chapel Hill: University of North Carolina Press, 1983), 182.

22. Margaret Spufford, "First Steps in Literacy: The Reading and Writing Experiences of the Humblest Seventeenth-Century Spiritual Autobiographers," *Social History* 4 (1979):410–14.

23. Carl F. Kaestle, "'The Scylla of Brutal Ignorance and the Charybdis of a Literary Education': Elite Attitudes toward Mass Education in Early Industrial England and America," in *School and Society,* ed. Lawrence Stone (Baltimore: Johns Hopkins University Press, 1976), 177–91.

percent of Europeans were literate, according to Carlo Cipolla, but the rate of literacy varied by locale. More than 50 percent of town dwellers could read, but in rural areas, where most people lived, literacy rates dropped well below the 50 percent mark. The progress of literacy was not linear. Wars, depressions, and disease disrupted much of seventeenth-century Europe, and in the nineteenth century the early stages of industrialization actually discouraged education because of the market for unskilled labor and the use of children in industry. By 1850, overall literacy in Europe had not risen much above 50 percent, though there was much variation.[24]

In general, literacy rates were biased in favor of the upper classes, males, and urban dwellers. Higher literacy also was associated with northern areas of Europe and with Protestant areas. How uniform were these biases and what caused them? About the first three, there is little doubt. Literate people were disproportionately male, upper status, and urban, consistently and for fairly obvious reasons. Literacy was associated with power and was restricted by the powerful. High-status and male occupations demanded literacy more than did the jobs open to the poor and women. Cities provided concentrations of population to support schools and printing presses, and they were the site of jobs that required literacy.

The north-south bias, usually explained by Protestantism, industrialization, or both, is more complex. There is no doubt that literacy rates in southern Europe were lower than in northern Europe and that this discrepancy coincided generally with a Protestant-Catholic split. From Portugal and Spain, across southern Italy to Greece and the Balkans, literacy rose slowly in comparison with Prussia, the Lowlands, Scandinavia, and Britain. But the southern tier was not just Catholic; it was also poorer and more rural than the north. Such socioeconomic factors may have outweighed the religious factor. For example, Bavaria and the Rhineland were highly literate and predominantly Catholic areas, perhaps because of economic factors and generally high German school support. Northern France was more literate than southern France, though equally Catholic. In a fascinating regional study of schooling comparing the Vaucluse in southern France with northern Baden in Ger-

---

24. The starting point for a quick survey of European literacy rates has long been Carlo Cipolla, *Literacy and Development in the West* (Harmondsworth, England: Penguin Books, 1969), though we now also have Harvey Graff's detailed and comprehensive synthesis, *The Legacies of Literacy: Continuities and Contradictions in Western Culture and Society* (Bloomington: Indiana University Press, 1987), which summarizes much of the detailed evidence, and Rab A. Houston, *Literacy in Early Modern Europe: Culture and Education, 1500–1800* (New York: Longman, 1988), which is less detailed than Graff's book but relates the development of literacy to education and culture more generally and now supersedes Cipolla's book.

many, Mary Jo Maynes showed that the culture and customs of a region may affect people more than their own religion or even the religion of their community. Protestant communities in the Vauclase, a predominantly Catholic region, had lower school-enrollment rates than Catholic communities in Baden, a predominantly Protestant region, principally because traditional means of supporting schoolmasters were widespread and successful in Baden.[25]

In spite of these interesting exceptions, Catholics within a given country generally had lower literacy rates than Protestants. In 1871, 93 percent of Prussian Protestants were literate, whereas 85 percent of Prussian Catholics were. In the same year 90 percent of Irish Presbyterians could read, compared with 60 percent of Irish Catholics.[26] Neither the Prussian nor the Irish data control for differences in economic activity, the supply of schools, or rural-urban residence. In nineteenth-century Quebec, though, communities that were predominantly French Catholic had dramatically different literacy rates from those that were predominantly English Protestant, even when controlling for urban-rural status. In 1844, for example, 12 percent of the people in French-speaking communities and 60 percent in English-speaking communities in rural areas could read and write.[27] Higher literacy rates for Protestants are sometimes interpreted as evidence that in spite of Catholics' Counter-Reformation support of schooling and vernacular Bible reading, their efforts lacked the intensity of Protestant concern for lay reading. Rab Houston expresses nicely the manner in which religious differences entailed larger cultural and historical experiences in the Netherlands, which, Houston believes, "encapsulates" the experience of Europe: "In the northern provinces, the Protestant tradition of education and personal religious involvement through the Bible produced signing ability one and a half times greater than in the Catholic southern areas where the visual culture of the Baroque enhanced the power of oral culture and made custom and collective memory more significant than the written forms which prevailed in the north."[28] In some historical settings, says Houston, differences in literacy rates that correlate with

25. Mary Jo Maynes, "Virtues of Archaism: The Political Economy of Schooling in Europe, 1750–1850," *Comparative Studies in Society and History* 21 (1979):611–25. See also Maynes, *Schooling for the People: Comparative Local Studies of Schooling History in France and Germany, 1750–1850* (London: Holmes and Meier, 1984).

26. Cipolla, *Literacy and Development in the West,* 73.

27. Allan Greer, "The Pattern of Literacy in Quebec, 1745–1899," *Histoire sociale* 44 (1978):293–335.

28. Houston, *Literacy in Early Modern Europe,* 115. See also Gerald Strauss, "Lutheranism and Literacy: A Reassessment," in *Religion and Society in Early Modern Europe, 1500–1800,* ed. Kaspar von Greyerz (Boston: George Allen and Unwin, 1984), 109–23.

religion narrow or vanish when other explanatory factors are known; in other settings, religion remains important after controlling for other factors.[29] In sum, it is difficult to disentangle religion from other factors; the data alone cannot clinch an argument about attitudes and commitment.

Two nations whose high literacy is often attributed to Protestantism are Sweden and Scotland. For Sweden there can be no doubt that the impetus was religious. The big surge in Swedish literacy occurred between 1660, when the national rate was about 35 percent, and 1720, when it reached a remarkable 90 percent. At this time Sweden was overwhelmingly agrarian. The literacy campaign was initiated by the church and implemented with little emphasis on schools. Families were directed to instruct children or to have them instructed. Ministers monitored progress closely, and church sanctions were levied against illiterates. The Swedish campaign is unique and extremely well documented: An activist Protestant church, prior to industrialization, effected a dramatic rise to nearly universal literacy in a span of about sixty years, mainly through family and clerical instruction.[30]

The Scottish case is less clear. Historians have long cited Scotland as an example of high preindustrial literacy resulting from an interventionist Calvinist church. Recently, however, Rab Houston has challenged this view, softening the contrast between Scotland and England and highlighting regional differences within Scotland. He found rural illiteracy to be very high in mid-seventeenth-century Scotland, and the national literacy rate to lag at least 5 percent behind England at that time. In the next 150 years of literacy trends, Houston concluded, "the role of education and religion was severely tempered by identifiable socio-economic constraints."[31] Calvinist strongholds displayed literacy rates identical to those of otherwise similar areas. Houston was doubtful about the importance of state schools, because the northern counties of England, without state intervention and without intense Protestantism, achieved rates similar to the Scottish average. Houston reasserted the primary importance of socioeconomic factors, both for regions and individuals, in the acquisition of literacy, and he minimized the importance of religion and schooling. In a rejoinder to Houston, T. C. Smout adduced evidence from the rural town of Cambuslang, the scene of a religious revival in the 1740s, to challenge the value of Houston's signature count-

29. Houston, *Literacy in Early Modern Europe,* 147–50.

30. Egil Johansson, "The History of Literacy in Sweden," in *Literacy and Social Development in the West: A Reader,* ed. Harvey Graff (Cambridge: Cambridge University Press, 1981), 152–53.

31. R. A. Houston, "The Literacy Myth? Illiteracy in Scotland, 1630–1760," *Past and Present* 96 (1982):89.

ing. Many of Cambuslang's 110 converts, chronicled in detailed interviews, could read well but could not write, especially the women. Reading, furthermore, was normally learned at school, though it was a skill that could be acquired elsewhere. The converts' interviews depicted a society in which reading was expected and was widespread, even among those whom Houston's figures had labeled as illiterate. Houston responded that the Cambuslang converts were unrepresentative.[32] Thus literacy studies proceed: scholars conduct careful regional studies of signature rates to revise national generalizations; others use local studies to go beyond simple signature rates, challenging the regional statistics with evidence about how individuals actually acquired and used literacy.

Just such a dialogue has been going on among scholars studying English literacy during the same period. In a detailed study using traditional signature-counting methods, David Cressy charted trends in English literacy during the Tudor and Stuart periods.[33] Because his literacy rates were so highly stratified by occupational group, Cressy doubted the importance of radical Protestantism and concluded that increased literacy was driven by "pull" factors, that is, by demand, which differed by class. Cressy devoted a great deal of energy to mustering the complicated data and charting successive waves of expansion and recession in signature literacy rates. His is one of the best books in the signature-counting tradition. Margaret Spufford, critical of Cressy's approach, analyzed the autobiographies of 141 seventeenth-century men. Although these were accounts of religious conversion, and thus not typical of all Englishmen, their detailed descriptions of education revealed that many of the writers' contemporaries were literate nonwriters, some of whom were in the lower occupational groups that Cressy had identified as predominantly illiterate. Because reading was taught in families and in the earliest school years, Spufford argued that it was more widespread among all classes than Cressy had concluded. Although grammar school attendance and university training were socially restricted, Spufford perceived "a murky and ill-defined world" in which people commonly acquired some reading ability and frequently came into contact with print.[34]

32. T. C. Smout, "Born Again at Cambuslang: New Evidence on Popular Religion and Literacy in Eighteenth-Century Scotland," *Past and Present* 97 (1982):114–27; R. A. Houston, *Scottish Literacy and the Scottish Identity: Illiteracy and Society in Scotland and Northern England, 1600–1800* (Cambridge: Cambridge University Press, 1985), 189–90.

33. Cressy, *Literacy and the Social Order.*

34. Spufford, "First Steps in Literacy," 409; see also Spufford, *Small Books and Pleasant Histories: Popular Fiction and Its Readership in Seventeenth-Century England* (Cambridge: Cambridge University Press, 1981).

The effort to trace literacy rates has become a minor industry among British historians. Much of the discussion has centered on the relationship between literacy and industrialization. In his now-classic article on literacy in England from 1600 to 1900, Lawrence Stone pointed out that the two great periods of expanding literacy, the seventeenth century and the late nineteenth century, coincided with cultural and political ferment, whereas the industrial revolution of the late eighteenth and early nineteenth centuries began during a time of stagnant literacy rates. Roger Schofield, mustering a more thorough sample, found somewhat higher rates of literacy than Stone, but agreed that economic growth did not depend on increased literacy. Not only did British industrialization take off during a lull in literacy growth, but also the immediate local impact of industrialization upon education and literacy was negative.[35] This view has been pressed by Michael Sanderson, who discovered declining school enrollment and literacy rates in industrializing Lancashire. Early factory work did not require literacy for most workers, and child labor interfered with education. National rates showing increases during industrialization are misleading, argued Sanderson. When disaggregated, the data for the areas of industrial development show deteriorating literacy and schooling.[36] Reanalyzing the same data, Thomas Laqueur suggested that Sanderson's Lancashire decline started too early to be accounted for by industrialization and that an upturn in literacy had begun by the early nineteenth century, when the effects of industrialization should have been in full force. Contradicting Sanderson's argument, Laqueur attributed the eighteenth-century decline to massive population increases and the lack of adequate institutional apparatus for education; the reversal of the downtrend Laqueur attributed to schooling efforts arising from industrialization and urbanization.[37] From this debate an understanding began to emerge that although the long-run impact of industrialization on a region was to increase literacy, the short-run effect in factory towns was socially disruptive and inhibited the acquisition of literacy.

François Furet and Jacques Ozouf explored in detail the relationship between literacy and industrialization in France. In early modern France, Protestantism and then the Counter-Reformation tended to de-

35. Lawrence Stone, "Literacy and Education in England, 1640–1900," *Past and Present* 42 (1969):102–26, 137; Roger S. Schofield, "Dimensions of Illiteracy, 1750–1850," *Explorations in Economic History* 10 (1973):437–54.

36. Michael Sanderson, "Literacy and Social Mobility in the Industrial Revolution in England," *Past and Present* 56 (1972):75–104.

37. Thomas W. Laqueur, "Literacy and Social Mobility in the Industrial Revolution," *Past and Present* 64 (1974):96–107. See also Stephens, *Education, Literacy and Society,* chap. 2.

mocratize literacy, and these impulses initiated the diffusion process. In the long run, however, the expansion of literacy ran along socially stratified lines and corresponded with the growth of the market economy. For purposes of the history of literacy, therefore, France can be divided into two great regions—the north, which achieved mass literacy in the seventeenth and eighteenth centuries, and the south, where literacy was quite restricted until the 1800s. Within these regions, of course, there was great variety. In general, towns had higher literacy rates because they had concentrations of literate occupations and educating agencies. But the nineteenth century brought a decline in urban literacy, due in large part to major economic upheavals. Industrialization encouraged child labor, the in-migration of uneducated workers, and rapid population expansion that outstripped the capacity of schools and other social agencies. Furet and Ozouf thus distinguished between the higher-literacy old commercial towns and the lower-literacy new industrial towns. They also distinguished between agricultural areas with new supplementary industries, which had the same inhibiting effect on literacy as industrialization in the cities, and traditional agricultural areas with seasonal labor patterns allowing more school and family education. Often such agricultural areas registered higher literacy rates than towns affected by industrialization.[38]

The emerging picture, then, is one in which literacy is correlated with economic growth in a region but depressed temporarily by industrialization. Commerce, the professions, schooling, and gradual population concentration all were associated with rising literacy rates. Child labor, rapid population growth, and the stress and insecurity of early industrialization inhibited the expansion of literacy. In short, literacy was boosted by the commercial aspects of urbanization, not the industrial aspects.

The Literacy Rise in Europe, 1850–1900

Literacy expanded rapidly again in Europe in the second half of the nineteenth century, for both men and women. National consolidation, state intervention, and wider male suffrage combined with expanding capitalism to establish school systems and encourage literacy. As Theodore Hamerow noted, in Hungary, Austria, England, France, and Prussia, school reform closely followed political independence or election reform.[39] But these reforms only reinforced trends already in progress. England moved from about 69 percent male literacy in 1850 to 97 percent

38. Furet and Ozouf, *Reading and Writing*, chaps. 1 and 5.
39. Hamerow, *Birth of a New Europe*, chap. 6.

in 1900, and the national average for women rose from one-third in 1850 to equal the male rate by the turn of the century.[40] In France male literacy moved from 68 percent to 96 percent in the same years, and the female rate rose from 53 percent to 94 percent.[41] In Belgium, the number of army recruits who could write increased from 56 percent to nearly 88 percent.[42] Most major social changes in this period fostered increased literacy. Reformers had responded to the social disruptions of early industrialization by creating schools as a moral reform; trade continually demanded more literate workers; women went to work outside the home and took on greater educational responsibilities for children in schools and at home; nation-states strove to instill loyalty and to create national identity; rising productivity provided governments with resources for the development of institutions; and an expanding male franchise created pressures for education from above and below.

The Renaissance, the printing press, and the Reformation had planted seeds for the democratization of reading, but those impulses had not been universally accepted. In the nineteenth century, another watershed was passed: The old conservative argument against popular literacy waned, and the governing classes began to encourage the spread of universal reading ability.[43] In urban-industrial societies, states moved to shape and consolidate popular belief by promoting state schooling. Popular demand for practical, recreational, and devotional reading material also increased. The motives and purposes of early school advocates have been the topic of much debate. The problem of causation still engages historians of nineteenth-century schooling, but there is no doubt about the rising rates of literacy and school enrollment during this period. In surveying the history of American literacy, we shall touch upon the question of whether the expansion of literacy and schooling were positive developments and, if so, for whom.

Literacy in America, 1600–1900

Literacy rates in colonial British America were quite high, and America's rise to nearly universal white literacy was earlier than Europe's. But many of the same research questions are relevant: how to interpret signature rates, whether literacy should be associated with progress,

40. Schofield, "Dimensions of Illiteracy"; Stone, "Literacy and Education in England."
41. François Furet and Jacques Ozouf, "Literacy and Industrialization: The Case of the Départment du Nord in France," *Journal of European Economic History* 5 (1976):5–44.
42. Cipolla, *Literacy and Development in the West*, 117–18.
43. Kaestle, "'Scylla of Brutal Ignorance,'" 181.

whether there have been declines as well as increases in the history of literacy, how literacy functions as both cause and consequence of social change, and how literacy was related to schooling.

Samuel Eliot Morison noted in the 1930s that American literacy measured by signature counting was high compared to Europe, and that a particularly large percentage of New England immigrants could sign their names.[44] Kenneth Lockridge later made a more extensive study of signatures and marks on more than three thousand New England wills from 1640 to 1800. He confirmed that British America had high signature literacy by European standards and that the rate in New England was higher than in the South and the Middle Atlantic. Still, Lockridge found signature literacy to be lower in seventeenth-century New England than Morison had claimed. Beginning at about 60 percent in 1650 and rising slowly to 70 percent by about 1710, male signature literacy took off in the eighteenth century. By the time the Founding Fathers signed the Constitution, 90 percent of white males who signed documents were signing their names. Female signature literacy paralleled male rates in the seventeenth century, rising slowly from 30 percent in 1650 to 40 percent around 1710, but then tapered off, remaining below 50 percent through the late eighteenth century—"stagnant," to use Lockridge's phrase.[45]

Lockridge argued that Protestantism, and particularly the Puritan version of Calvinism, was the driving force behind New England literacy, that the expansion of literacy was accomplished chiefly through schools, and that its purpose was conservative. Although Calvinism may have "paved the way to modernity," it was intensely traditional in the seventeenth century.[46] Their religious concerns prompted New England Puritans to demand that their towns provide schools, but sparse population during the seventeenth century made the laws difficult to enforce. In the 1700s, however, these laws worked to advance literacy as population became more concentrated, argued Lockridge. His view departed from three other recent interpretations. He contended that the reliance upon schooling was not a result of family breakdown in the face of the wilderness environment, as Bernard Bailyn had argued; that literacy in the eighteenth century was not "liberating," as Lawrence Cremin had argued; and that it was not associated with modern attitudes, as Alex

44. Samuel E. Morison, *The Intellectual Life of Colonial New England* (Ithaca: Cornell University Press, 1956), 82–85, originally published as *The Puritan Pronaos* (1936).

45. Lockridge, *Literacy in Colonial New England*, 38.

46. Ibid., 45.

Inkeles and David Smith and other modernization theorists had argued.[47]

As for the first challenge, Bailyn's disruption hypothesis was more subtle than Lockridge allowed. Bailyn was not writing as a simple environmentalist when it came to the transfer of culture in the seventeenth century. Customary English life was disrupted in the New World not only by wild land, sparse population, physical hardship, and contact with native Americans, but also by selective migration, the shift to Puritan religious dominance in New England, new governing arrangements, and the separation from European institutions. The stresses of this situation, coupled with the Puritans' concern about religious decline, produced a public focus on schooling in colonial New England. This focus was reinforced, as Cremin pointed out, by the colonists' traditional reliance on schools, a custom they brought with them from England. Nonetheless, schooling did not have a dramatic effect on expanding literacy in seventeenth-century New England. Although Cremin and Bailyn correctly emphasized the important educational roles of the family, the church, and the workplace, they both acknowledged a growing role for schools as the colonial period progressed. Whatever roles an expanding press and a resurgent evangelical Protestantism may have played in the second half of the eighteenth century, the expansion of literacy also coincided with the establishment of more district schools, closer to people's homes.

As for Cremin's interpretation that eighteenth-century literacy was "liberating" rather than conservative, this reflects his optimistic general conviction that "on balance, the American educational system had contributed significantly to the advancement of liberty, equality and fraternity."[48] There is, of course, evidence on both sides of the issue, which has animated historical debate about American education over the last fifteen years. The enduring contribution of Lockridge's New England study is its warning against an automatic equation of literacy with a liberating modernity. His emphasis on the conservative function of Puritan literacy may be exaggerated, but it serves as a useful reminder that literacy can serve many purposes, sometimes traditional and constraining, sometimes innovative and liberating.

Like their counterparts in England, American historians have tested generalizations with local studies. Alan Tully discovered a nearly constant level of male signature literacy for Chester County (around 72

47. Bernard Bailyn, *Education in the Forming of American Society* (Chapel Hill: University of North Carolina Press, 1960); Cremin, *American Education: The Colonial Experience;* Inkeles and Smith, *Becoming Modern.*

48. Lawrence A. Cremin, *Traditions of American Education* (New York: Basic Books, 1977), 127.

percent) and Lancaster County (around 63 percent) in southeastern Pennsylvania during the eighteenth century, and he concluded that there had been no educational revolution or expansion of "liberating" literacy in that rural setting.[49] Ross Beales, testing Lockridge's generalizations on rural Grafton, Massachusetts, in the midst of the 1748 religious revival, found levels slightly higher (98 percent males, 46 percent females) than Lockridge's figures would have led one to predict. Beales did not find any relationship between literacy and conversion among women.[50] Attempting to reconcile these contrasting findings, we may speculate that rudimentary literacy rates in eighteenth-century America were lower in some places than Cremin's interpretation would suggest and higher, particularly for women, than in Lockridge's samples. Moreover, the salient influence of revival religion or political ferment cannot be predicted when one focuses on the local level. In any case, one should not expect uniformity.

On the issue of female literacy, however, evidence is mounting to suggest that the eighteenth and early nineteenth centuries were important years of increased rudimentary literacy. Suspicions that some women who could not write could nonetheless read seem well-founded; furthermore, some fragmentary local evidence shows a more dynamic increase in women's signature ability in the eighteenth century than Lockridge found. Tully found a sharp eighteenth-century rise in female signature literacy in his small Pennsylvania samples, and Linda Auwers charted increasing female signature writing in Windsor, an old Connecticut town, from 21 percent in the 1660s birth cohort to 94 percent in the 1740s birth cohort.[51] Auwers's late-seventeenth-century data for female signing ability correlated not with wealth but with parental literacy and parental church membership; in contrast, the eighteenth-century literacy data correlated with wealth but not with church membership, leading Auwers to remark that Windsor may have been enacting a cultural shift from "Puritan" to "Yankee." Windsor, Auwers admitted, was at the high-literacy end of the spectrum, but it foreshadowed more general eighteenth-century developments. A family's proximity to a school also increased the chances of a daughter's acquiring literacy in Windsor, providing support for Lockridge's emphasis on schools. Literacy was associated with schools, and both were associated with capitalism. William

49. Alan Tully, "Literacy Levels and Education Development in Rural Pennsylvania, 1729–1775," *Pennsylvania History* 39 (1972):302–12.

50. Ross W. Beales, Jr., "Studying Literacy at the Community Level: A Research Note," *Journal of Interdisciplinary History* 9 (1978):93–102.

51. Tully, "Literacy Levels and Education Development"; Linda Auwers, "Reading the Marks of the Past: Exploring Female Literacy in Colonial Windsor, Connecticut," *Historical Methods* 13 (1980):204–14.

Gilmore, studying more than ten thousand signatures and marks on various documents for a Vermont county from 1760 to 1830, found almost universal male signature literacy throughout the countryside. Female rates, however, ranged from 60 percent to 90 percent, varying with the level of commercial involvement of the community.[52]

Not all literacy was acquired in schools. Gerald Moran and Maris Vinovskis recently redirected attention back to the family, arguing that the changing gender dynamics of instruction within the family generated pressure for more female education in the eighteenth century. In the late seventeenth century, they reasoned, church membership shifted strongly toward females. Thus, the catechizing role within the family fell increasingly to women, who were at a relative disadvantage in terms of literacy. The resolution of this tension was a rhetorical emphasis on pious, educated women in early-eighteenth-century New England and increased female access to schools by the late eighteenth century.[53]

By 1850 the rudimentary literacy rates of white men and women, self-reported to U.S. Census marshals, were nearly equal.[54] The biggest gaps in literacy rates were between native whites, foreign-born whites, and nonwhites, but regional, income, and rural-urban disparities also persisted. Lee Soltow and Edward Stevens, who made the most thorough investigation of these nineteenth-century developments, considered first whether male literacy was "nearly universal" by 1800. Some studies of signatures that report such high rates admit that a significant portion of the population never signed documents, like deeds or wills, and thus perhaps as much as one-fifth of the population is not included in the sample.[55] Soltow and Stevens studied petitions and army enlistment lists and concluded that male literacy as high as 25 percent was common in the early years of the Republic. They also showed that the inability to sign remained widespread among certain groups of white males. Throughout the period 1800 to 1840, 30 percent of merchant seamen could not sign their enlistment papers. Signature illiteracy in the enlistment rolls of the U.S. Army, at 42 percent in 1800 and 35 percent in the

52. Gilmore, "Elementary Literacy on the Eve of the Industrial Revolution."
53. Gerald F. Moran and Maris A. Vinovskis, "The Great Care of Godly Parents: Early Childhood in Puritan New England," in *History and Research in Child Development,* Serial no. 211, vol. 50, ed. Alice Boardman Smuts and John W. Hagen (Chicago: University of Chicago Monographs of the Society for Research in Child Development, 1986), 24–37. See also E. Jennifer Monaghan, "Literacy Instruction and Gender in Colonial New England," in *Reading in America: Literature and Social History,* ed. Cathy N. Davidson (Baltimore: Johns Hopkins University Press, 1989), 53–80.
54. Maris A. Vinovskis and Richard Bernard, "Beyond Catharine Beecher: Female Education in the Antebellum Period," *Signs* 3 (1978):856–69.
55. Gilmore, "Elementary Literacy on the Eve of the Industrial Revolution," 157.

1840s, declined to 25 percent in the 1850s, to 17 percent in the 1870s, and to 7 percent in the 1880s.[56]

In 1840 the U.S. Bureau of the Census added a question on literacy to its survey form. Given the problems inherent in interpreting signature rates, this might be expected to have greatly improved the validity of the available evidence on literacy. Unfortunately, however, the census marshals never administered any literacy test, so the data represent only the self-reported literacy and illiteracy of household residents. Furthermore, the questions differed from decade to decade; over time the census changed the age group questioned, changed the wording of questions on reading and writing, and, finally, added a question on foreign-language literacy. At worst, census illiteracy statistics measure nothing more than people's willingness to admit illiteracy; at best, they indicate a minimal estimate of illiteracy.

Soltow and Stevens analyzed the aggregate rates in this census data and, through samples of individual family schedules, investigated the correlation of literacy with other factors. In general, they concluded that nation building, economic development, and population density all favored the provision of schools and fostered the development of an "ideology of literacy." Literacy rates correlated most strongly with school enrollment rates, with average family wealth in one area, and with the population density of a community. Not surprisingly, high literacy rates were biased toward the North and toward urban areas, but by 1870 the common-school movement, the circulation of print matter, and improved transportation had reduced these biases.[57]

Nonetheless, social-class biases persisted. Like David Cressy's work on seventeenth-century England, Harvey Graff's work on three Ontario cities in 1861 emphasized that social status was highly correlated with literacy, that is, the higher one's social status, the more likely one was to be literate. This is not to suggest the converse, that increased literacy brought improved social status. In fact, Graff concluded that literacy did not affect income and occupational status as much as did ethnicity and family conditions. Although these results were not very surprising, it is useful to be reminded that illiteracy is more a symptom than a cause of disadvantage. The opposite and fallacious view, according to Graff, is what he called the "literacy myth," the belief that literacy by itself improved the careers of nineteenth-century urban dwellers. However, only 10 percent or less of the population were labeled illiterate in his three Ontario cities; he could draw no conclusions about the relative reading abilities of the great majority of people or about the impact literacy had

56. Soltow and Stevens, *Rise of Literacy,* 50–52.
57. Ibid., 22–23, 53, 56, 159–60.

on their lives. Graff's position placed him squarely in the revisionist camp of educational historians but went beyond what can be proved by the census's crude literacy variable.[58]

Although Soltow and Stevens's work is the most detailed study of U.S. Census literacy information for the nineteenth century, the most convenient discussion of the trends in aggregate rates over a longer period is the brief book by John Folger and Charles Nam. According to their analysis, white illiteracy in the census, male and female combined, declined from 10.7 percent in 1850 to 6.2 percent in 1900. Whereas only 4.6 percent of native-born whites admitted illiteracy in 1900, 12.9 percent of foreign-born whites did. Among nonwhites the reported illiteracy rate in 1900 was 44.5 percent.[59] At the turn of the century, concern about illiteracy was focused on black Americans and, to a lesser degree, upon recent European immigrants. The big story in nineteenth-century American literacy is the development of common-school systems and the near elimination of self-reported outright illiteracy among native-born whites.

Twentieth-Century Literacy: The American Case

The early twentieth century witnessed rapid urbanization, black migration northward, pressure for immigration restriction, and a resurgence of racist social theories. Given the white-black and native-foreign gaps in rudimentary literacy, therefore, it is not surprising that census monographs reflected anxieties about illiteracy among black people and European immigrants. Actually, immigrant illiteracy was concentrated among the century's first arrivals and declined rapidly after the restriction of immigration in 1921; black illiteracy decreased dramatically in the late nineteenth and early twentieth centuries, an impressive trend in light of the discrimination, hostility, poor resources, and meager job incentives for black Americans. Higher-order literacy skills are a different matter, of course, and these are not indicated in the census data. Even at the level of rudimentary literacy, gaps remained between native and foreign born, white and nonwhite, North and South, urban and rural, but overall, the twentieth century has been an era of declining illiteracy and convergence of literacy rates across social groups. Today, although the percentage of outright illiterates is small, the absolute number of illiterates remains great. In 1979, only .6 percent of all persons fourteen years of age and older reported that they were illiterate, but this equaled nearly one million people.

58. Graff, *Literacy Myth,* chap. 2.
59. John K. Folger and Charles B. Nam, *Education of the American Population* (Washington, D.C.: Government Printing Office, 1967), 113–14.

As the reported rudimentary illiteracy rates declined among all groups, commentators and analysts turned their attention to higher-order skills. The term "functional literacy" gained popularity in the 1930s. Initially it was applied simply to a level of schooling deemed sufficient to ensure a person's ability to read most everyday print matter, usually the fourth or fifth grade. Later the term came to be associated with performance on actual tests of practical reading tasks encountered outside of schools. In view of the achievement testing that pervaded schools by the 1930s and educators' growing concern about functional literacy, one would expect that our knowledge about the history of literacy skills over the past fifty years would be familiar and precise. On the contrary, there is little historical work on the subject and the sources are riddled with problems. Chapter 3 of this book takes on the task of assembling and critiquing the available data. We have better measures of students' higher-order literacy abilities over the past twenty years, from college entrance examination trends, from the National Assessment of Educational Progress, and from renorming exercises by the producers of standardized achievement tests. These data are the evidence at issue in the tangled test-score decline debate. They have their own deficiencies, which we review in chapter 4.

From a long-range perspective one sees not decline but a great expansion of literacy skills in America during the twentieth century, evidenced by increasing educational attainment and increased circulation of print matter. The slight declines of recent years pale by comparison.[60] The problems of today's illiterates, the dearth of writing activity in the schools, the absence of critical reading skills in the workplace, and the negative effect of the electronic media on reading activities are all matters of legitimate concern. They should not lead us to invent a golden age of literacy in some earlier decade.

Most historians of literacy have focused on the social differences between nominally literate and nominally illiterate people, on the relationship of literacy to schooling, and on the correlation of literacy rates with other social indicators. They have produced detailed and rigorous work; there are excellent studies available in English about literacy in England, France, Sweden, Canada, and New England. Nonetheless, it is still difficult to make confident generalizations about the causes or the consequences of literacy, and historians have persuasively challenged

60. John R. Bormuth, "The Value and Volume of Literacy," *Visible Language* 12 (1978):118–61; Martin Trow, "The Democratization of Higher Education in America," *Archives européennes de sociologie* 3 (1962):231–62; and Trow, "The Second Transformation of American Secondary Education," *International Journal of Comparative Sociology* 2 (1961):144–66.

some of the old, simple correlations. Writing about literacy in English communities, Walter Stephens concluded, "We can discern no 'iron law,' no easy categorization, but only a tendency against which to set the unique history of each particular town."[61] Yet Stephens himself has done much to sort out the patterns of local variation and the reasons for them.[62]

I return now to the four broad background questions posed in the beginning of the chapter, in the light of the trends, correlations, and interpretations surveyed in the literature review. On the vexed question of whether literacy is a sign of progress and an unquestionable benefit to its possessors, a cautious, critical viewpoint is warranted. The benefits of literacy should be analyzed in specific historical circumstances for various historical actors. Modernization theorists generally argue that literacy is necessarily correlated with modernization and that modernization is a Good Thing. Although literacy has indeed generally proceeded along with other indicators of development used by modernization theorists, literacy also can be used for culturally intolerant or politically repressive purposes.

The uses of literacy are various. As a technology, it gives its possessors potential power; as a stock of cultural knowledge within a given tradition, literacy can constrain or liberate, instruct or entertain, discipline or disaffect people. Princeton historian Lawrence Stone once remarked that if you teach a man to read the Bible, he may also read pornography or seditious literature; put another way, if a man teaches a woman to read so that she may know her place, she may learn that she deserves his. These are the Janus faces of literacy. Although for purposes of public policy, increased literacy is assumed to benefit both individuals and the society as a whole, the association of literacy with progress has been challenged under certain circumstances. Paolo Freire has questioned whether literacy is a good thing for oppressed people if the content and conduct of literacy training are not under their control.[63] From a variety of political viewpoints, American and British culture critics of the 1950s questioned whether mass culture, including popular reading materials, was debilitating to its consumers. Furthermore, throughout history the distribution and maintenance of differential literacy skills have been associated with class, race, ethnicity, and gender. Given these considerations, the answer to the first question—whether literacy is

61. Walter Stephens, "Illiteracy and Schooling in the Provincial Towns, 1640–1870," in *Urban Education in the Nineteenth Century,* ed. David Reader (London: Taylor and Francis, 1977), 47.

62. Stephens, *Education, Literacy and Society.*

63. Paolo Freire, *Pedagogy of the Oppressed,* trans. Myra Bergman Ramos (New York: Herder and Herder, 1971), chap. 1.

synonymous with progress—must be: It depends upon who is judging, whose literacy is at issue, and whose benefit is being considered.

The answer to the second question—whether literacy is always expanding—is: Usually, but not always. In general, the history of literacy is characterized by expansion, both in the number of people who are literate and in the quality of their literacy skills. But history also provides some examples of declining literacy: in ancient Greece, in medieval Europe, in early industrial towns, possibly among American blacks subjected to harsh slave codes before the Civil War, and allegedly among American schoolchildren in the 1970s. We take up this last example in chapter 4.

In spite of these examples of decline, the expansion of literacy rates has been the norm since the invention of writing. Historians have found it more difficult to explain the surges and plateaus in this history than to chart them. Our third background issue addressed this difficult causal question: What conditions have fostered the expansion of literacy? The causes of literacy are generally inferred from correlations, and despite much local variation, some correlations persist. Higher literacy rates have generally been associated with people of higher social status, males, Protestants, industrializing regions, and dense population. These generalizations stand up fairly well for the modern West. The correlation of literacy with higher social status, a persistent theme, is hardly surprising, although the correlation can be stronger at some times than at others. The relationship between literacy and industrialization has occasioned heated debate, which can be resolved as follows: Defined as a long-term process in a region or nation, industrialization has been associated with rising literacy; in the short turn, at the local level, the onset of factory production often inhibited literacy training—and thus reduced literacy rates—because of child labor and immigration patterns. Among specific urban communities, rising literacy has been more clearly correlated with commerce than with industry. Although it is difficult to disentangle religion from other factors, earlier rises in literacy also correlated with Protestantism. Male rates of estimated rudimentary literacy were consistently higher than those of women until the twentieth century, if we accept signature signing as a proxy for reading ability. However, as we have seen, there is reason to be skeptical about the illiteracy of some who marked with an X. Finally, in spite of interesting short-run exceptions, rising literacy has been associated with the expansion of schooling. The most durable patterns in rudimentary literacy, then, are the least surprising.

One of the "causes" of higher literacy rates, in a sense, is higher literacy rates. For example, as more people become literate, the amount of fiction circulating commercially will increase and newspapers will become cheaper; in a society where more reading material is available, there is more motivation for people to learn to read and to use their skills. If schools turn out more highly literate people, this will, in turn, affect the job structure, which can affect the future demands placed on schools. Thus one of the effects of literacy at the societal level is that it fosters more literacy.

But what do we know about the concrete effects of literacy on the lives of individuals? There is only scant empirical evidence on the subject. Educators often have associated literacy with economic advancement, but historians have done little to probe the connection. A few works on industrialization in nineteenth-century America touch upon the subject. Alexander Field argued that skill requirements declined rather than increased during the initial shift to factory labor in the United States, so there would have been little real advantage to the educated industrial laborer sometimes hailed by manufacturers.[64] Stephan Thernstrom documented the importance of child labor in the family economies of Newburyport shoe laborers and concluded that sending children to school would have been counterproductive for workers' families.[65] Thomas Dublin found that literacy correlated with higher wages among Lowell's female textile workers, but not when controlling for ethnicity; he thus concluded that literacy was incidental to higher status in the mills.[66] Harvey Graff, relying on census data, also found that literacy had little weight in overcoming the ethnic bias of the social structure in Ontario cities.[67] Maris Vinovskis, taking as his point of departure Horace Mann's claim that education contributed to greater industrial productivity, pointed out that Mann's evidence was biased, his motives political, and his estimates of the value of education greatly exaggerated.[68] Nonetheless, as Vinovskis has recently reminded us, education was not without economic benefit in nineteenth-century America.[69] It was, however, more valuable to some groups than others. Sketchy evidence suggests

64. Alexander Field, "Industrialization and Skill Intensity: The Case of Massachusetts," *Journal of Human Resources* 15 (1980):149–75.

65. Stephan Thernstrom, *Poverty and Progress: Social Mobility in a Nineteenth-Century City* (Cambridge: Harvard University Press, 1964), 154–57; but see Joel Perlmann, "Working Class Homeowning and Children's Schooling in Providence, R.I., 1880–1925," *History of Education Quarterly* 23 (Summer 1983):175–93.

66. Thomas Dublin, *Women at Work: The Transformation of Work and Community in Lowell, Massachusetts, 1826–1860* (New York: Columbia University Press, 1979), 149–51.

67. Graff, *Literacy Myth,* 190–91.

68. Maris A. Vinovskis, "Horace Mann on the Economic Productivity of Education," *New England Quarterly* 43 (1970):550–71.

69. Maris A. Vinovskis, "Quantification and the History of Education: Observations on Antebellum Education Expansion, School Attendance and Educational Reform," *Journal of Interdisciplinary History* 14 (1983):856–69.

that early high schools assisted middling-status white males (sons of both lower white-collar workers and skilled craftsmen) in maintaining or improving intergenerational status.[70] For women, education became an entrée to teaching, and by the late nineteenth century female students predominated in America's public high schools.

The available evidence on the issue of the returns to education may be summarized as follows. First, education paid off better for those in the middle reaches of society than it did for laborers. Second, there was a greater return for education in the twentieth century than in the nineteenth; skill levels were upgraded, education expanded, the clerical and service sectors burgeoned, and a tighter fit developed between an individual's level of schooling and later occupational fate. Third, the benefits to literacy for members of oppressed groups were often more apparent collectively than individually, and in the long run rather than the short run. The Irish shoe worker of 1840 was probably correct in thinking that there would be little benefit in a high-school education for his son, but Irish people as a group have benefited from increased education in the long run. Similarly, expanded education for blacks may have gained them little access to status in white society in the 1890s, but in the long run, education has helped to narrow racial inequalities. The same argument can be made for the history of women. What is implied, of course, is a history of frustration and bitterness for individuals who face a discriminatory world but who recognize the necessity of acquiring literacy, and then higher education, as resources in confronting economic and occupational inequality.

Literacy is discriminatory with regard to both access and content. Problems of discrimination are not resolved just because access is achieved; there is a cultural price tag to literacy. Thus, whether literacy is liberating or constraining depends in part on whether it is used as an instrument of conformity or of creativity. Chapter 8 of this volume analyzes individuals' uses of literacy through a study of autobiographies; chapter 10 discusses the contrasting functions of published reading material—for cultural consolidation and for the expression of alternatives.

On the fourth background question—the relationship of literacy to schooling—expanding literacy persistently correlates with expanding schooling. This suggests a causal relation, but the history of efforts by outsiders to acquire literacy suggests the relevance of family and group values. For example, white women in America closed the gap in rudimentary literacy between the mideighteenth and midnineteenth centuries. In a complicated set of realignments, women became more important in

70. Carl F. Kaestle, *Pillars of the Republic: Common Schools and American Society, 1780–1860* (New York: Hill and Wang, 1983), 121.

organized religion and in the education of children, both at home and in school; they therefore pressed for and received more access to formal schooling themselves. The relative contributions of schooling and of the family are impossible to estimate; increased female literacy resulted from the combined effects of enhanced educational opportunity and higher literacy expectations for girls in the home. The same combination was at work in narrowing the huge literacy gap between white and black Americans. In the 1870 census, shortly after emancipation, 81 percent of black Americans reported themselves to be utterly illiterate, compared with 11 percent of whites. Twenty years later, the black rate was down to 57 percent, compared with 8 percent of whites. Booker T. Washington once described freed slaves as an entire nation wanting to go to school, and they did so, their efforts sustained by family values that were nurtured during the antebellum slavery years, when literacy became associated with power and freedom. Today, the rudimentary literacy rates for all American racial and ethnic groups are very high, above 98 percent, but at higher skill levels gaps persist; both the family and the school remain relevant. The most recent and most thorough study of literacy abilities, the Young Adult Literacy Assessment of the National Assessment of Educational Progress, provided rich background information on gaps in functional literacy among racial, ethnic, and income groups. It reinforced the notion that schools cannot do the job alone. Reading abilities correlated with a wide variety of family factors—not just race, income, and parents' educational level, but also the number of publications that enter the home and how often children read them.[71] Although the policy implications of these findings are problematic, there are ways in which the government can affect the literacy potential of families. This has become one of the themes in the recent campaign against low literacy skills in the United States (see chapter 10).

Our review of the literature revealed a healthy dialogue in which national studies and even larger syntheses have aimed to discover general tendencies over long periods of time, and in which local studies have tested the generalizations, suggesting refinements and new variables, and integrating the story of literacy into the texture of local culture. It takes a certain maturity in a historical subfield to make possible such large-scale syntheses of research as Graff's *Legacies of Literacy* and Houston's *Literacy in Early Modern Europe*. But to suggest new directions and answer new questions we also need studies focused on single communities or more specific topics, studies that address such questions as educational opportunity and the uses of literacy among adults. As

71. Irwin S. Kirsch and Ann Jungeblut, *Literacy: Profiles of America's Young Adults: Final Report* (Princeton, N.J.: National Assessment of Educational Progress, Educational Testing Service, 1986), chap. 7.

more historians become skeptical of the literate-illiterate dichotomy and of the equation of signing ability or census responses with actual reading ability, we will see more studies that deal centrally with the acquisition and uses of literacy and only incidentally with literacy rates. As we move from literacy rates to the uses of literacy, the history of literacy becomes the history of readers. Chapter 2 turns to this approach.

2 The History of Readers

CARL F. KAESTLE

A broad history of literacy must look beyond the labels of "illiterate" and "literate" to study the functions of reading in adults' lives; that is, it must move beyond the reader to the production and distribution of printed materials and the situations in which they are read. Conversely, an improved history of popular literature must go beyond the texts to the readers. In short, to understand the functions of literacy over time we must reach out to more general histories of education, culture, publication, and communication, as well as theoretical works in these areas. Broadening the history of literacy to consider the functions of reading by adults may seem to diffuse the subject hopelessly. In the first part of this chapter, I consider what guidance we can expect from theoretical works.

The Relevance of Theory

Historians use theory at various levels. Some, though not many, operate within the framework of a general social theory, such as Marxism or modernization theory, or they develop a general theory of their own. Others have a middle-level theory or a model of how the particular phenomenon they are studying works. Still other historians find even such models too constraining but incorporate narrower aspects of theory in shaping their questions and interpretations. In sorting out the theoretical possibilities, let us consider first two historians of literacy who developed comprehensive theories that guided their research and provided their themes.

Two Comprehensive Theories

Harold Innis anchored social change in technological developments in communication. A student of Robert Park and a mentor to Marshall

McLuhan, Innis saw communication as power and believed that technology expressed itself most saliently through the communications media. He developed a dichotomous scheme in which "time-biased" media, such as heavy clay tablets, favored local government, oral tradition, and a monopoly of literacy; "space-biased" media like papyrus or paper, favored empire, innovation, and the expansion of literacy. Throughout history the two kinds of media have been in tension, Innis argued, each conferring power to different groups and structuring society and culture in different ways. Although modern history has favored space-biased media, any society that did not achieve a balance between the two communication worlds was unstable.[1] Innis's theory featured not only broad, predictive generalizations but also an element of nostalgia for the village, where oral communication, religion, and tradition were central.

Innis argued that the space-biased print and electronic media have dominated communications in the twentieth century, making the individual a passive recipient, whereas oral traditions fostered participation, dialogue, and understanding. Although Innis saw a few historical moments of balance between space and time biases—especially classical Greece—the drift throughout history was toward space-biased communication, which eroded true democracy. This, of course, was just the opposite argument from that of modernization theorists, who associated increasing literacy with increasing democracy in the long run. Although Innis believed in the possibility of a revival of oral forms of participation in his own day, his global history was driven by a pessimistic technological determinism. Space-biased media were thoroughly entangled with the production and distribution of material goods. In spite of sporadic resistance, elites associated with space-based media successfully centralized power and subordinated marginal groups.

For Raymond Williams the fulcrum of history was the economy, not technology. Whereas Innis was a technological determinist, Williams developed a theory of cultural materialism, more or less in a Marxist framework. In Williams's historical drama, Western history witnessed three great revolutions—a democratic revolution, an industrial revolution, and an expansion of culture, which Williams called "the long revolution." The expansion of culture has been governed by the other two revolutions. The democratic revolution dictated continually widening audiences for culture, and the industrial revolution ensured that the production of culture would take a commercial form. New forms of popu-

1. Harold A. Innis, *The Bias of Communication* (Toronto: University of Toronto Press, 1951). See also James W. Carey, "Harold Adams Innis and Marshall McLuhan," *Antioch Review* 27 (1967):5–39; William H. Melody, Liora Salter, and Paul Heyer, eds., *Culture, Communication, and Dependency: The Tradition of H. A. Innis* (Norwood, N.J.: Ablex, 1981).

lar culture often have been viewed by elite commentators as threats to the quality of print culture. Some of these, like the daily newspaper and the novel, seem in retrospect to have represented cultural gains, Williams argued. Still, the most worrisome cultural problem of the twentieth century, according to Williams, was the expansion of the worst aspects of culture, due to the profit motive. The alternative to this historical tendency would be more governmental support and regulation of culture, with the particular pitfalls of that system. Williams urged new modes of analysis and creative thinking to move the long revolution into "a new and constructive stage."[2]

Innis and Williams both argued for policy changes they derived from their historical analyses. We are more particularly interested, however, in their historical theories, rather than their policy positions. How useful are their comprehensive theories? Innis's technological determinism is more persuasive when thinking about the global sweep of civilizations and nations than for determining how the process works out in the short run. For understanding the details of the relationship between technology, culture, and social structure in the short run, some historians have developed more interactive models. Writing about the advent of electric lights and telephones in the United States, Carolyn Marvin emphasized that communication practices in modern societies are always in tension and always changing: "existing groups perpetually negotiate power, authority, representation, and knowledge. . . . Old habits of transacting between groups are projected onto new technologies. . . . New practices do not so much flow directly from technologies that inspire them as they are improvised out of old practices that no longer work in new settings."[3] Innis's moral blend of conservative nostalgia and democratic anxieties tended toward a blanket condemnation of print, rather than considering the diverse uses of literacy by different groups. Nonetheless, his work is important; it was a counterweight to the bland, progressive view of communication history that predominated at the time he wrote.[4] Furthermore, his focus on the themes of centralization and cultural consolidation now seems inescapable, as does his theme

2. Raymond Williams, *The Long Revolution* (London: Chatto and Windus, 1961), 354; see also Williams, *Marxism and Literature* (Oxford: Oxford University Press, 1977).

3. Carolyn Marvin, *When Old Technologies Were New: Thinking about Communications in the Late Nineteenth Century* (New York: Oxford University Press, 1988), 5. On the interaction of culture and technology, see Lewis Mumford, *Technics and Civilization* (New York: Harcourt, Brace, 1934); for examples from the history of American newspapers, see Richard Z. Schwarzlose, "Historical Dynamics of Technology and Social Values," *Prospects* 11 (1987):135–55.

4. James W. Carey, "The Problem of Journalism History," *Journalism History* 1 (Spring 1974):3–5, 27.

of the tension between democratic participation and the passive reception of modern media.

As for Williams, the most prominent critic of *The Long Revolution* was E. P. Thompson, who charged that Williams had distanced himself from socialism too successfully, that he focused too reverently on conservative traditions of thought, that he depersonalized conflict, and that he homogenized the reading public.[5] Still, Williams's theme—the subordination of cultural democratization to the needs of capitalism—is one that must be addressed by anyone writing on the history of the reading public. *The Long Revolution* remains a succinct and forceful example of the use of comprehensive theory to integrate various aspects of the history of literacy. Chapter 10 of this volume considers whether these themes drawn from Innis and Williams—cultural consolidation and centralization—explain American developments from the 1880s to the 1980s.

Models

For those who believe that comprehensive theories are more constraining than illuminating in historical work there remains a range of theoretical possibilities. Some historians of print and literacy use midrange theories or models. Models often help classify the phenomena under investigation, suggesting what the researcher should examine. Commenting on the complexity of book history, Robert Darnton wrote, "the questions could be multiplied endlessly because books touched on such a vast range of human activity—everything from picking rags to transmitting the word of God. They were products of artisanal labor, objects of economic exchange, vehicles of ideas, and elements in political and religious conflict."[6] Darnton proposed a spatial model for integrating the research on these diverse topics, based on the metaphor of a circuit. Beginning with a book's author, the model moved in a circular fashion to examine the connections between authors and publishers, then between publishers and printers, then on to printers, shippers, booksellers, and finally readers. At each point in the circuit, Darnton argued, researchers must relate text transmission to the political, economic, and intellectual context of the period.[7] He left the important but murky connection be-

5. E. P. Thompson, "The Long Revolution," *New Left Review* 9 (May–June 1961):24–33, and 10 (July–August 1961):34–39.

6. Robert Darnton, *The Business of Enlightenment* (Cambridge: Harvard University Press, 1979), 1.

7. Robert Darnton, "What Is the History of Books?" *Daedalus* 111 (1982):65–83. This and other essays by Darnton are collected in Darnton, *The Kiss of Lamourette: Reflections in Cultural History* (New York: W. W. Norton, 1990).

tween readers and authors as a dotted line, not quite completing the circuit.

In an earlier use of the circuit metaphor, Robert Escarpit had argued that within the "cultured circuit" of the educated middle-class book buyers in France in the 1950s, the circuit from reader back to writer was completed through bookstore owners, who relayed readers' comments to authors and publishers; whereas in the "popular circuit" of tobacco stores and newsstands selling tabloids and mysteries, "all initiative is firmly in the hands of the wholesale distributor."[8] Escarpit's cultured and popular circuits were quite separate, with little overlap between the books carried by the two different kinds of distribution outlets and little overlap in their clientele.[9]

Models can determine a scholar's research focus. In the case of Escarpit and Darnton, the circuit model turns our attention to connections between authors and other people in the production and distribution process, possible feedback from readers to producers, and the amount of overlap between different circuits. Models can also shape an analyst's thematic conclusions and policy concerns. If we look at America in the 1980s, in Escarpit's terms, the shift to franchise bookstore chains like B. Dalton's and Waldenbooks involves two changes from the situation Escarpit described in France in the 1950s, a system of separate popular and high culture book circuits that also prevailed in the United States until recently. In the franchise outlet of the 1980s, the two book-market circuits are combined to a greater extent. Harlequin romances appear on the shelf alongside *New York Times* best sellers. But the combined distribution circuit has the one-way feature of Escarpit's popular circuit: there is no feedback loop for consumers. Franchise bookstores are provided with books according to national sales figures; bookstore managers have little control over the titles they receive, so the stores cannot respond to individual readers' interests.[10] The circuit model focuses our

8. Robert Escarpit, *The Sociology of Literature,* trans. Ernest Pick (Painesville, Ohio: Lake Erie College Press, 1965), 64–67, originally published as *Sociologie de la littérature* (Paris: Presses universitaires de France, 1958). Even earlier, Harold Lasswell had used the same metaphor, noting that although mass communications are predominantly one-way, "audiences do 'talk back'" and thus there are "circuits of two-way contact." Lasswell, "The Structure and Function of Communication in Society," in *The Communication of Ideas,* ed. Lyman Bryson (New York: Institute for Religious and Social Studies, 1948).

9. Robert Escarpit, *The Book Revolution* (London: George Harrap, 1966), 138–42, originally published as *La Révolution du livre* (Paris: UNESCO, 1965).

10. "Waldenbooks: Countering B. Dalton by Aping Its Computer Operations," *Business Week,* October 8, 1979, 116–21; Bruce Porter, "B. Dalton: The Leader of the Chain Gang," *Saturday Review,* June 9, 1979, 53–57; N. R. Kleinfield, "The Super-

attention on this process of standardization and centralization; such an analysis reinforces contemporary concerns about the decline of bookstores responsive to the individualized and highly educated tastes of the highbrow reading public.

The Incidental Use of Theory

Some scholars use theory in incidental ways, to inform their research on some particular aspect of the history of literacy. Robert Kelly, pondering the value of fiction as historical evidence, turned to anthropology for a definition of culture and to Peter Berger and Thomas Luckmann for ideas about the sociology of knowledge. Armed with these theoretical perceptions, Kelly sorted out the possible cultural meanings of juvenile fiction. We cannot infer anything about readers' reactions to text solely from the text, he concluded, nor can we use the text itself as a description of actual social conditions. But we may take the authors of such fiction to represent the values of a certain segment of society, expressing their goals and anxieties through didactic fiction.[11]

Displaying the interdisciplinary thrust of the new history of literacy, Shirley Brice Heath explored the relationship between sociolinguistics and the social history of reading.[12] She combined sociolinguists' theoretical propositions about stereotypical verbal routines, such as greetings, with empirical work on 350 etiquette books of the nineteenth century. Contrary to what one might expect, Jacksonian-era etiquette books laid great stress on class distinctions. This emphasis became muted later, an illustration of cultural lag in the dissemination of egalitarian ideals. The role of class was suggested by sociolinguistic theorists interested in etiquette; the historical data, Heath suggested tentatively, might in turn be used to test theories about how etiquette changed over time.

---

marketer of Books," *New York Times Magazine,* November 9, 1986, 44–47, 59–61, 65–66, 70. For a recent optimistic forecast about the revival of independent bookstores, see Jason Epstein, "The Decline and Rise of Publishing," *New York Review of Books,* March 1, 1990, 8–12, and for the thriving condition of university presses, which play an important role in diverse, regional publications, see Roy Reed, "From the Campuses: Adventures in Publishing," *New York Times Book Review,* September 24, 1989, 1, 61–62.

11. Robert G. Kelly, "Literature and the Historian," *American Quarterly* 26 (1974):141–59; Peter Berger and Thomas Luckmann, *The Social Construction of Reality* (Garden City, N.Y.: Doubleday, 1966).

12. Shirley Brice Heath, "Social History and Sociolinguistics," *American Sociologist* 13 (1978):84–92.

Theories Relevant to Our Analysis

We present no grand historical theory about the history of literacy in this volume, but our work is influenced by theories at the different levels described above: at the general level, we try to join texts and readers in our analysis when possible, an orientation that is informed by theoretical developments in various fields; at the level of models, I propose a model for understanding what is at stake socially when individuals acquire and use literacy; and, at the incidental level, we also borrow or test bits of various theories to understand specific processes better.

Our effort to get at real readers' activities echoes theoretical developments in several fields of research. During the early 1980s, developments in the study of communication, reading comprehension, and literature converged on the notion of the reader as an active interpretive agent and therefore as a necessary research focus.

The Uses and Gratifications Approach

In communication theory this focus is seen most prominently in the "uses and gratifications" approach. Uses and gratifications research has its roots in the studies of media impact, or media effects, that were begun in the 1930s. The first wave in this genre emphasized the potency of the media. Readers and listeners were characterized as passive, helpless victims of propaganda and advertising.[13] In the 1940s empirical research cast doubt upon the potency of the media and emphasized their multiple functions. Paul Lazarsfeld and others detailed the important mediating influences of personal contact between highly informed and less informed individuals. Bernard Berelson discovered that newspaper reading has many functions, including its value as an enjoyable habitual activity per se, apart from content. Communications researchers thus moved in the 1950s toward a view of the media as less powerful in its impact and more diverse in its functions than earlier theorists had depicted it.[14] By 1960 Joseph Klapper could announce a general shift from

13. See Jack M. McLeod and Lee B. Becker, "The Uses and Gratifications Approach," in *Handbook of Political Communications,* ed. D. Nimmo and K. Sanders (Beverly Hills, Calif.: Sage, 1981), 67–99; Michael R. Real, "Media Theory: Contributions to an Understanding of American Mass Communications," *American Quarterly* 32 (Bibliography issue, 1980):240–44; and James W. Carey and Albert Kreiling, "Popular Culture and Uses and Gratifications: Notes toward an Accommodation," in *The Uses of Mass Communications: Current Perspectives on Gratifications Research,* ed. Jay G. Blumler and Elihu Katz (Beverly Hills, Calif.: Sage, 1974), 223–48.

14. Paul F. Lazarsfeld, Bernard Berelson, and Hazel Gaudet, *The People's Choice*

the powerful "hypodermic needle" effects that researchers asserted before World War II to the "functional" approach of the 1950s, with its emphasis on factors that limited the direct effects of media messages.[15] In the 1960s, effects research was rather dormant; a revival in the early 1970s, prompted in part by work done in Europe, resulted in 1974 in an influential summary volume on uses and gratifications research, edited by Jay Blumler and Elihu Katz.

The uses and gratifications approach rests on several assumptions. First, the audience is active and goal directed; individuals seek to satisfy needs and therefore have definite expectations from the media. Second, the initiative is with the audience member; thus, effects cannot be inferred from content in a simple way. Third, needs that can be met by media often can also be met by other sources of gratification. Fourth, the research assumes that audience members are sufficiently self-aware that they can report their needs and interests. Fifth, unlike popular culture critics, uses and gratifications researchers take a neutral stance toward the value of media content and experiences.[16]

This approach places an interactive model of producers and audiences at the center of media research. Researchers have asserted two different kinds of interaction. One concerns readers as interpreters, the other as consumers. In the first kind of interaction, the interpretation of a text (or other media message) is the product of the content of the text combined with the interests, prior experiences, critical abilities, and values of the reader (or listener, or viewer). This interpretive interaction is also stressed in recent cognitive research on reading and in recent literary theory, as we shall see below. The second kind of interaction is not interpretive but social; it concerns communication from the audience back to the producers of text. Through such audience measures as opinion polls, purchasing power, and selective television viewing, the audience influences that which is subsequently produced. This is the kind of interaction Escarpit had in mind when he talked about a feedback circuit. Both kinds of interaction in this uses and gratifications approach invest the audience with more autonomy and influence than previous approaches did.

One can thus view the uses and gratifications approach as a way of

(New York: Harper and Row, 1944); Elihu Katz and Paul F. Lazarsfeld, *Personal Influence* (New York: Free Press, 1955); Barnard Berelson, "What 'Missing the Newspaper' Means," in *Communication Research, 1948–9,* ed. Paul F. Lazarsfeld and Frank N. Stanton (New York: Duell, Sloan and Pearce, 1949), 111–28.

15. Joseph T. Klapper, *The Effects of Mass Communication* (Glencoe, Ill.: Free Press, 1960), 8.

16. Elihu Katz, Jay Blumler, and Michael Gurevitch, "Utilization of Mass Communication by the Individual," in *Uses of Mass Communications,* ed. Blumler and Katz, 21–22.

rescuing the audience from its stereotypical role as a group of mindless victims. A theoretical orientation that asserts the agency of individuals against impersonal institutions and shifts the emphasis from elites' intentions to ordinary people's intentions is consistent with recent trends in social and cultural history and is certainly not inherently a conservative orientation. But the uses and gratifications research tradition has its roots in the functionalist social theory and social psychological concerns of the 1940s and 1950s. Its devotees generally address nondisruptive and personal purposes of communication like cognitive growth, diversion, relaxation, and habit; the bias, therefore, leans toward a quest for equilibrium. This makes it vulnerable to the criticism leveled at functionalists: that they take the status quo as a given. In the case of media studies, this means that one accepts the range of communication messages and products offered and does not question the productive system that lies behind them. In emphasizing the motives and choices of the audience, uses and gratifications researchers have overlooked the power of the producers to constrain and limit such choices. Thus, critics of uses and gratifications research, from the mid-1970s to the mid-1980s, have called for renewed attention to the production and transmission of communication and for more attempts to relate uses and gratifications research to theories about culture and society.[17] Some uses and gratifications researchers accept these criticisms; they believe that the basic model can be retained, while being more self-consciously theoretical and shedding the functionalist origins of the approach.[18] But in practice, most uses and gratifications researchers have been optimistic functionalists who didn't worry much about dysfunctions of the system as a whole.

Whatever the future relationship between uses and gratifications research and critical social theory, this line of inquiry has drawn attention to the audience as a group of active interpreters, assigning importance to the audience member's frame of mind, motives, interests, and values. In this regard, communications researchers have been drinking from the same trough as the cognitive scientists who study reading. The

17. Among the many valuable critiques are Carey and Kreiling, "Popular Culture and Uses and Gratifications"; McLeod and Becker, "Uses and Gratifications Approach"; Jay G. Blumler, Michael Gurevitch, and Elihu Katz, "Reaching Out: A Future for Gratifications Research," in *Media Gratifications Research: Current Perspectives,* ed. Karl E. Rosengren, Lawrence A. Wenner, and Philip Palmgreen (Beverly Hills, Calif.: Sage, 1985), 255–74; and David L. Swanson, "Political Communication Research and the Uses and Gratifications Model: A Critique," *Communication Research* 6 (1979):37–53.

18. Philip Palmgreen, Lawrence A. Wenner, and Karl E. Rosengren, "Uses and Gratifications Research: The Past Ten Years," in *Media Gratifications Research,* ed. Rosengren, Wenner, and Palmgreen, 15–18.

strong similarity of their models is evident in the statements of their leading researchers. James W. Carey and Albert Kreiling, two communications researchers, have argued that perception is not "a passive registering process but an active organizing and structuring process," and Richard Anderson, a psychologist who directs the Center for the Study of Reading, has written that "in interpreting a text, readers draw on their store of knowledge . . . to fill in gaps in the message and to integrate the different pieces of information in the message. That is to say, readers 'construct' the meaning."[19]

The Psychologists' Interactive Reading Model

Over the past fifteen years, reading research has attracted the attention of cognitive psychologists interested in mental processes. Many have studied actual readers to explore the process of reading; others have remained text-based in their analysis but have nonetheless become more sophisticated in their attention to the strategies and processes that go on when readers try to comprehend and interpret a text. As in uses and gratifications research on media, this focus on what the reader brings to the task results in a recognition of the great variation in individuals' interpretations. Marianne Amarel, reviewing the field, summarized this consensus: "Children bring a varied, individually differentiated set of resources to reading, such as interests and stylistic preferences, which significantly influence the course of their reading history."[20] Teun van Dijk and Walter Kintsch elaborated: "Not only the comprehender's knowledge, but also beliefs and goals play a crucial role in this process. . . . A reader of a text will try to reconstruct not only the intended meaning of the text—as signaled by the writer in various ways in the text or context—but also a meaning that is most relevant to his or her own interests and goals."[21] This "constructivist" concept, wrote Nancy Nelson Spivey, "has dramatically changed theory and research in reading during the past fifteen years."[22]

The notion that we can study reading comprehension only as an interactive process is now a commonplace. But in reading research, as in

19. Carey and Kreiling, "Popular Culture and Uses and Gratifications," 227; Richard C. Anderson et al., *Becoming a Nation of Readers: The Report of the Commission on Reading* (Washington, D.C.: National Institute of Education, 1985), 9.

20. Marianne Amarel, "Reader and the Text—Three Perspectives," in *Reading Expository Materials,* ed. Wayne Otto (New York: Academic Press, 1982), 243–57.

21. Teun A. van Dijk and Walter Kintsch, *Strategies of Discourse Comprehension* (New York: Academic Press, 1983), x, 11.

22. Nancy Nelson Spivey, "Construing Constructivism: Reading Research in the United States," *Poetics* 16 (1987):169–92.

communications research and literary criticism, we sometimes need to analyze the text without the presence of a real audience. Reading researchers, like researchers in the other fields, have benefited from interactive models even when they do text-based analysis. They have moved away from the surface analysis of traditional readability measures, for instance, to examine the overarching rhetorical and logical structure of prose passages and such underlying features as the density of arguments, the number of inferences required of the reader, the amount of memory recall demanded, and the amount of reorganization of material involved. Although a text-based analysis can never predict the meanings that readers will derive from a text, it can incorporate models of the processes they go through as they arrive at those meanings (see chapter 7 below).[23]

The Reader-Response Approach in Literary Criticism

If reading is the construction of meaning by a reader interpreting a text, and if many interpretations are possible, then presumably a literary critic cannot determine the meaning of poetry or prose fiction by looking exclusively at the text. In a development parallel to that in reading research, one influential group of literary critics came to just such a conclusion in a flurry of theoretical activity around 1980. Although the major thrust in recent literary theory had been deconstruction, theorists within that school and others, including feminist, psychoanalytic, and structuralist critics, began calling attention to the importance of the reader. Some became closely associated with reader-response theory; although they came to it from different theoretical orientations, this group included Stanley Fish, Wolfgang Iser, Jonathan Culler, and Norman Holland.[24]

23. Walter Kintsch and Douglas Vipond, "Reading Comprehension and Readability in Educational Practice and Psychological Theory," in *Perspectives on Memory Research,* ed. Lars-Goran Nilsson (Hillsdale, N.J.: Lawrence Erlbaum, 1979), 329–65; van Dijk and Kintsch, *Strategies of Discourse Comprehension,* ix, 4.

24. For an introduction to reader-response criticism, see Jane P. Tompkins, ed., *Reader-Response Criticism: From Formalism to Post-Structuralism* (Baltimore: Johns Hopkins University Press, 1980); Susan R. Suleiman and Inge Crossman, *The Reader in the Text: Essays on Audience and Interpretation* (Princeton, N.J.: Princeton University Press, 1980); Jonathan Culler, *On Deconstruction: Theory and Criticism after Structuralism* (Ithaca: Cornell University Press, 1980); and Elizabeth Freund, *The Return of the Reader: Reader-Response Criticism* (London: Routledge, Chapman and Hall, 1987). On the evolution of Stanely Fish's theories, see Fish, *Is There a Text in the Class? The Authority of Interpretive Communities* (Cambridge: Harvard University Press, 1980), and Fish, *Doing What Comes Naturally: Change, Rhetoric, and the Practice of Theory in Literary and Legal Studies* (Durham, N.C.: Duke University Press, 1989). On Wolfgang Iser's evolution, and his disputes with Fish, see Iser, *Prospecting:*

Reader-response critics share a focus on the reader's role in interpreting literature. The reader is a cocreator of meaning, in conjunction with the text. This viewpoint is often seen as a revolt against the New Criticism, which reigned in the 1950s and 1960s. New Critics asserted that neither the author's intentions (which were unknowable) nor the readers' responses (which were infinitely variable) were relevant to determining the meaning of a literary work. According to reader-response theory, text has no meaning independent of the reader; thus, the text lost the stability and timelessness imagined by New Critics. In Germany a related focus on the reader, called reception theory, was seen as a reaction not only against the New Criticism but also any other literary theory that ignores the reader.[25] In both Germany and the United States, critics have suggested that changes in modern fiction itself reinforced the shift of focus to the reader. The modern novel guarantees no clear message, and the reader's role becomes problematical. The more "open" or "indeterminate" text of some modern works leaves more interpretive latitude and responsibility to the reader.[26]

That literary critics are interested in the variable interpretations of readers may seem like a welcome, kindred development for historians interested in popular culture and the uses of literacy. But within literary criticism it causes extraordinarily difficult theoretical and methodological problems; furthermore, the ways in which the reader-response critics tried to solve these problems underscore their distance from social historians. The New Critics had warned that taking account of readers' responses would lead to a chaos of limitless interpretations. How did the reader-response critics rescue themselves from this chaos? First, they didn't concentrate very much on real readers; instead, they imagined what readers go through in trying to interpret a work. They thought about process, about ambiguity, about conflict resolution, about impediments to understanding, and about other experiences the reader might have. Different critics called this imagined reader by different names, such as the "ideal" reader, the "informed" reader, and the "intended"

From Reader Response to Literary Anthropology (Baltimore: Johns Hopkins University Press, 1989), 3–69, 262–84.

25. On the New Criticism, see Fish, *Is There a Text,* 2–3, and Culler, *On Deconstruction,* 17–30. On German reception theory, see Hans R. Jauss, "Literary History as a Challenge to Literary Theory," in *New Directions in Literary History,* ed. Ralph Cohen (Baltimore: Johns Hopkins University Press, 1974), 11–41; Peter U. Hohendahl, "Introduction to Reception Aesthetics," *New German Critique* 10 (1977):29–64; and Robert C. Holub, *Reception Theory: A Critical Introduction* (London: Methuen, 1984).

26. Hohendahl, "Introduction to Reception Aesthetics," 37; Culler, *On Deconstruction,* 37; Wolfgang Iser, *The Act of Reading: A Theory of Aesthetic Response* (Baltimore: Johns Hopkins University Press, 1978), 205–6.

reader. The "ideal" reader, it seems, would share virtually all of the author's knowledge and instincts. The "informed" reader was quite linguistically competent and strove to use all of her or his knowledge to interpret texts. The "intended" reader was the reader the author had in mind, which might be indicated in the text in various ways.[27] Reader-response theorists did indeed think about the processes that readers go through, but they protected themselves from the chaos of countless readers' interpretations by hypothesizing a generic reader.

In a second common tactic most reader-response critics found some way to reintroduce text-based interpretation into the analysis. Although Iser emphasized the role of the reader as cocreator of meaning and wrote in detail about the process of reading, he emphasized the "repertoire" and the "potential" established by the text. For example, the reader "finds himself obliged to work out why certain conventions should have been selected for his attention."[28] Iser used the concept of an "implied" reader who is "invited" by the author to make a particular interpretation of the text. The reader fills in certain "gaps," but the gaps are presented in the text. "The implied reader as a concept has his roots firmly planted in the structure of the text; he is a construct and in no way to be identified with any real reader."[29]

Stanley Fish started out strenuously asserting the autonomy of the reader; then, as his work developed, he allowed certain common elements across different readers, by talking about "primary" or shared interpretations and "secondary" or idiosyncratic interpretations, and by positing certain shared assumptions of "interpretive communities" of readers. Later, however, he went back in the other direction, declaring that all constraints on interpretation were in the reader, not the text.[30]

Steven Mailloux also wrote during the formative years of reader-response theory, but not from a berth in the pantheon where the warring gods Iser and Fish resided. Nonetheless, he restored textual criticism to reader-response theory in a way that seems very relevant to a social historian. Building on Fish's notion of interpretive strategies and Jonathan Culler's notion of reading conventions, Mailloux tried to construct a "social" model of reading response. Although much of the theoretical wrangling involved in this debate seems to be no more than jargon-building, Mailloux did apply his scheme to historical examples of

27. See Iser, *Act of Reading*, 27–34, and Steven Mailloux, *Interpretive Conventions: The Reader in the Study of American Fiction* (Ithaca: Cornell University Press, 1982), 203–4.

28. Iser, *Act of Reading*, ix, 61. For discussions of Iser, see Tompkins, ed., *Reader-Response Criticism*, "Introduction," xv, and Mailloux, *Interpretive Conventions*, 44–45.

29. Iser, *Act of Reading*, 34.

30. Fish, *Is There a Text*, 16–17, 268.

literary reception. One category of "interpretive conventions" is people's expectations about genre, and one of Mailloux's examples is about the different responses Melville's *Moby Dick* received from critics in England, in contrast to its reception in America. In England, according to Mailloux, critics were much more guided by genre conventions, and *Moby Dick* didn't seem to fit in any genre, a confusion that influenced their generally negative reviews. American critics, less concerned about literary traditions, generally celebrated the book for its mongrel quality, calling it "an intellectual chowder" and a "salmagundi of fact, fiction and philosophy."[31]

Mailloux's "social" theory of reading is social only in the sense that it tries to connect text with groups of people who might share some of the same literary conventions. It is not sociological; indeed, reader-response theory has been justly criticized for ignoring class, gender, race, and other variables that divide society and thus shape readers' interests and predispositions.[32] If historians of literacy wish to understand the uses of literacy, they will have to take account of these factors. Also, as Norman Holland has pointed out, when one studies different readers reading the same text in the real world, their interpretations are shaped by all manner of concerns and understandings that seem illogical or irrelevant to others, but turn out to be central to their unique, subjective understanding.[33]

Because of these and other problems, reader-response theory per se has essentially run its course among literary critics. It has been abandoned by some, incorporated and modified by others.[34] Nonetheless, reader-centered critical theories survive among feminist, psychoanalytic, semiotic, and other critics. These critics have demonstrated the benefit of thinking about the process of reading when trying to explicate a particular text. In doing so, they have added their voices to the general chorus that favors paying attention to the reader.

31. Mailloux, *Interpretive Conventions*, 173–78. For a thorough study of American reviewers' responses to fiction at the time of Hawthorne and Melville, see Nina Baym, *Novels, Readers and Reviewers: Responses to Fiction in Antebellum America* (Ithaca: Cornell University Press, 1984).

32. See Mailloux, *Interpretive Conventions*, 41; Terence Hawkes, "Taking It as Read," *Yale Review* 69 (1980):560; and Patrocinio P. Schweickart, "Reading Ourselves: Toward a Feminist Theory of Reading," in *Gender and Reading: Essays on Readers, Texts, and Contexts*, ed. Elizabeth A. Flynn and Patrocinio P. Schweickart (Baltimore: Johns Hopkins University Press, 1986), 35–39.

33. Norman Holland, *Five Readers Reading* (New Haven and London: Yale University Press, 1975).

34. See Freund, *Return of the Reader*.

Reader Responses: Stalking the Real Reader

The reader-centered perspective seems very relevant to a broadened history of literacy, but at the same time it is a frustrating source of theory for historians. Historians are not interested in idealized or generalized readers, and it is difficult to match real readers to particular texts in the past. Nonetheless, some historians have done it, and with interesting results. At the individual level, many memoirs of highly educated people—authors, journalists, professors, and the like—include comments about what they read and how it influenced them. Werner Sollors, for example, uses the autobiography of Ludwig Lewisohn to argue that ethnic identities are socially constructed, deliberate, and shaped by a person's reading. A German Jew who grew up in the American South, Lewisohn tried hard to be as much like an Anglo-Protestant as he could, until he encountered modern German poetry at Columbia University in graduate school. Then his "real" self emerged; the poetry called up "deep things, the true things of which I had been ashamed. . . . [These poets] spoke my thoughts, they felt my conflicts; they dared to be themselves. . . . They made me free."[35] Perhaps Lewisohn indulged in some reshaping when he reminisced about this reading; but it certainly is self-conscious and articulate historical testimony about a reader's own understanding of his reaction to a text.

Of even greater interest to social historians are the unusual cases of less socially privileged people who have left behind detailed records of what they read and what it meant to them. In sixteenth-century Italy, in the small town of Montereale, a miller named Menocchio was accused of heresy. Working with the transcripts of Menocchio's interrogations, historian Carlo Ginzburg created a fascinating picture of this man's contact with the printed word and his uses of it. Though Menocchio had read widely and had cited various sacred works in defense of his religious opinions, Ginzburg discovered that he couldn't trace Menocchio's ideas directly from the texts he cited. Instead, Menocchio seems to have gone to the texts with strong opinions formed through the oral culture of mid-sixteenth-century rural Italy, and he found confirmation in books, but, according to Ginzburg, often only through a skewed reading of the text. Ginzburg makes a watershed of this single case, presenting Menocchio as a dramatic example of the juncture between oral and printed culture. Menocchio "had experienced in his own person the historical leap of incalculable significance that separates the gesticulated, mumbled,

35. Ludwig Lewisohn, *Up Stream: An American Chronicle* (New York: Boni and Liveright, 1922), 114. See Werner Sollors, *Beyond Ethnicity: Consent and Descent in American Culture* (New York: Oxford University Press, 1986), 194–206.

shouted speech of oral culture from that of written culture, toneless and crystallized on the page." But Ginzburg also reminds us that printed culture encountered and interacted with oral culture: "In Menocchio's talk we see emerging, as if out of a crevice in the earth, a deep-rooted cultural stratum so unusual as to appear almost incomprehensible."[36]

Robert Darnton, a leading historian of France and of the book, discovered another watershed in the late eighteenth century, dramatized by a single individual who recorded his responses to his reading. Darnton discovered forty-seven letters from a bourgeois merchant in La Rochelle to a publisher, ordering books and commenting on what he had read. Wealthy but otherwise unremarkable, Jean Ranson was an avid reader with particularly animated reactions to Rousseau, especially *La Nouvelle Héloïse*. Citing Iser, Hans Jauss, Fish, and others as his theoretical guides, Darnton tackles the reader-response analysis with delightful results. In this case, the "intended" reader is quite clearly defined, because Rousseau was very intrusive, commenting liberally on how he expected his readers to read him. Ranson dutifully conformed, so the real reader matched the intended reader. According to Darnton, this was a matter of some importance, for Rousseau required a new kind of reader—one who was emotionally involved, who related the imaginative prose to problems in real life, who was looking for sentiment over plot: in short, the romantic reader. *La Nouvelle Héloïse,* a collection of six volumes of sentiment and advice, was immensely popular; Jean Ranson epitomized the new reader, a role that persisted in French literature at least until the work of Flaubert, according to Darnton, and then faded. Darnton has used this extensive testimony by a single reader to humanize the history of reading, to give it texture. Depending upon one's methodological bent, questions about the typicality of the single case either impugn the analysis or pale next to its inventiveness. As Ginzburg said about qualitative versus quantitative research, "it must be emphasized that, as far as the history of the subordinate classes is concerned, the precision of the latter cannot do without (cannot *yet* do without, that is) the notorious impressionism of the former."[37]

The identification of major shifts in the uses of literacy is an ambitious and exciting undertaking. The major technological shifts are more obvious; but even the invention of alphabetic writing and the printing press have prompted scholarly debate about the nature, the pace, and

36. Carlo Ginzburg, *The Cheese and the Worms: The Cosmos of a Sixteenth-Century Miller,* trans. John and Anne Tedeschi (New York: Penguin Books, 1982), 58–59.

37. Ginzburg, *Cheese and the Worms,* xxi. In a personal communication Robert Darnton noted with approval that while some scholars are working at the case-history level, exploring the "inner processes of reading," as his study so elegantly exemplifies, others lean toward the macrosocial level, the focus of most of the chapters of this book.

the generalizability of the changes that are observed. With these intermediate watersheds—Ginzburg's, about the consequences of print invading the countryside, or Darnton's, about new forms of fiction requiring new kinds of readers—we move into even more difficult interpretive matters. But the concept of shifts in the nature of reading is pertinent for two reasons. First, it warns us that reading has not always been what it is today—that the process, the functions, and the modes of reading may have been very different in past times. Second, there is a certain poignancy to the notion of watersheds in the history of reading, given contemporary claims that we are undergoing such a change in our own time due to the changing relationship of print to television and computers.

Basing such a shift on a single case study, however, is only suggestive. How do we move to a higher level of generality? The next step would be to study a group of individuals, such as those whom Margaret Spufford analyzed from the sixteenth century, or the group of women in late-nineteenth- and early-twentieth-century America whose autobiographies we discuss in chapter 8. Even here, of course, there may be qualms about the typicality of the group, but if we have several cases before us, we can at least look for what is common and what is distinctive in people's uses of literacy. At a higher level of aggregation one can study the production and uses of reading materials aimed at particular groups in the society, like the sentimental middle-class novel of the 1820s, or German socialist newspapers in Chicago around 1900, or the Spanish-language press in El Paso in the 1920s, or fundamentalist Christian books in the Midwest in the 1970s. At this level, one loses individual readers' responses. Instead, attention turns to issues like the importance of print in creating a community of readers, efforts to create demand for a certain kind of publication, and the frequent contests among producers vying for readers' minds and readers' patronage. At an even higher level of generality, we can muster survey data on the frequency of reading, types of reading, and the level of expenditures on reading materials of various groups in the society, or of the society as a whole over time. This we do in chapters 5 and 6, exploring the varying levels of detail one can achieve using local data and national data.

Connecting Readers and Texts to Society

All of the efforts to link texts and readers at various levels will ultimately be useful in pursuing a broader history of literacy. These links are consistent with the interactive theories I have reviewed in communication theory, cognitive psychology, and literary criticism. Even though the focus on readers and texts derives from theories about the process of reading, it does not constitute a theory about the uses of literacy in society. The reader-text emphasis may be embedded in different theories or sets of assumptions about reading, social change, and social structure, and these need to be made as explicit as possible. Yet it is extraordinarily difficult to fashion a theoretical context for the study of readers and texts in the past. The very phenomenon we wish to explore is both empirically elusive and conceptually complex. There is little evidence of detailed responses by readers in the past, especially among ordinary people, so some of the work is necessarily speculative or indirect. Conceptually, it is difficult to articulate a single theory about reading in society because reading is both so ubiquitous and so multipurpose. Any theoretical orientation that restricts its focus to socioeconomic structures invites complaints that it ignores the symbolic, psychological, and aesthetic aspects of reading. Thus in discussions of uses and gratifications research, or reader-response literary criticism, one hears frequent pleas for balance. Reading has cultural, symbolic, ritualistic aspects as well as its instrumental, ideological, economic, educational, casual, and playful sides. Michael Denning writes that the "economics of the dime novel must be complemented by a poetics of the dime novel."[38] In criticizing the uses and gratifications emphasis on audience choices, Blumler and his colleagues argue that "choices are less free and less random than a vulgar gratificationism would presume," and they urge uses and gratifications researchers to "work toward convergences with other paradigms."[39] Carey and Kreiling, however, warn against too quick a shift to determinism, not wishing to trade an optimistic functionalism for a pessimistic one. "Popular culture should not be studied in relation to predefined sociological categories, but as a cultural process in which persons create shared expressive and conceptual models that supply common identities and apprehended realities," they write.[40] Peter Hohendahl echoes this appeal for balance: "Reception studies can hardly be relegated to the position of an appendix for the capitalist market," but, he writes, "they can hardly do without a sociological basis."[41] Balance is needed, it seems, not only between the reader and the text, but between the interpretive act and the social context, between the autonomous individual and the predisposing situation, between cultural meaning and social function.

38. Michael Denning, *Mechanic Accents: Dime Novels and Working-Class Culture in America* (London: Verso, 1987), 66.

39. Blumler, Gurevitch, and Katz, "Reaching Out," 260, 271.

40. Carey and Kreiling, "Popular Culture and Uses and Gratifications," 237, 246.

41. Hohendahl, "Introduction to Reception Aesthetics," 66–67.

A Model: Reading and the Creation of a Cultural and Political Identity

With these pleas for balance and nondeterministic theories in mind, I suggest the following model. People act individually to develop identities, choose allegiances, form beliefs, and conduct their day-to-day lives, but they do so within the constraints of cultural inheritances and economic relationships. Some of these constraints act systematically and are rooted in the social structure. Applying this model of agency and constraints to the world of reading, we can acknowledge the unpredictable responses of individuals within an analysis of how social forces shape the content of reading material and the distribution of literacy skills. Studies of the uses of literacy at various levels will reveal great variation among individual cases—some people use literacy to assimilate, others to preserve differences; some to rise socially, others to rebel; some to work, others to relax; some for long-term growth, others for short-term utility. But we shall also see patterns over time in levels of literacy and its uses. For example, the distribution of literacy mirrors power relationships, and reading materials encourage assimilation and conformity more than differences and critical thinking. Ultimately, studying the uses of literacy among various groups should teach us something about the limits of agency within the constraints of the market, the constraints of tradition, and the constraints of an imperfect educational system. The history of the uses of literacy is also eminently suited for—indeed cannot escape—reflections upon the tensions between modern capitalism and political democracy. This model constitutes an agenda; it informs the essays of this volume. Chapter 8 applies the model to autobiographical accounts of reading, and chapter 10 explores some of the cultural and technological factors that constrain readers' choices.

The model must be understood against a backdrop of the themes previewed in the Preface. First, there has been an impressive expansion of literacy skills over the past century, drawing ever-increasing numbers of people into the ranks of book readers and high-school graduates. Second, the expansion has been uneven. The acquisition of literacy skills continues to be very unequal today, and the gaps correlate with income, ethnicity, and parents' education levels. Third, paralleling this impressive but uneven expansion of literacy skills has been an expansion of reading materials, which have become increasingly standardized, drawing more and more people into a shared culture of syndicated newspaper features, popular fiction, and mass-circulation magazines. Fourth, control of the press has nonetheless been contested; diverse groups have used print to maintain their differences, and diversity has been stifled or renewed in various ways at various times, depending upon the interplay of cultural, marketing, and technological factors. Fifth, literacy has leveled off and even declined in some ways during the past ten to twenty years, due to various social factors and to the expansion of the electronic media; this trend has caused a major period of reassessment, anxiety, and reform.

The Secondary Literature: Nineteenth-Century America

I now turn to recent efforts by American historians to broaden the history of literacy and to carry on the dialogue between theory and new research findings. The most extensive research along these lines has focused on the late eighteenth and early nineteenth centuries. Historians of literacy, historians of the book, and historians of popular literature are studying the uses of literacy, exploring new ways to connect readers and texts. Some themes are emerging.

An American Reading Revolution?

The first theme is that a "book revolution" took place in the late eighteenth and early nineteenth centuries in America.[42] Before that time, books were relatively scarce, new imprints were relatively infrequent, literacy was uneven, and information circulation was slow. In the late eighteenth and early nineteenth centuries, schooling escalated, literacy expanded (especially for women), the number of titles and books increased rapidly, the speed of communications increased dramatically, and literacy penetrated into the countryside.[43] Commerce seems to have been at the root of the transformation, but once the take-off began, the causal relationships became reciprocal. Commerce encouraged literacy, and literacy encouraged commerce. The mediating institutions became mutually supportive. Commerce bred schooling, which bred literacy,

42. The phrase ("Leserrevolution") comes from Rolf Engelsing, who applied it to eighteenth-century Germany. See Engelsing, *Der Burger als Leser: Lesergeschichte in Deutschland, 1500–1800* (Stuttgart: Metzlersche, 1973).

43. David D. Hall, "The Uses of Literacy in New England, 1600–1850," in *Printing and Society in Early America,* ed. William L. Joyce et al. (Worcester: American Antiquarian Society, 1983), 1–47; Cathy Davidson, *Revolution and the Word: The Rise of the Novel in America* (New York: Oxford University Press, 1986); William Gilmore, "Literacy, the Rise of an Age of Reading, and the Cultural Grammar of Print Communications in America, 1735–1850," *Communication* 11 (1988):23–46; Gilmore, *Reading Becomes a Necessity of Life: Material and Cultural Life in Rural New England, 1780–1835* (Knoxville: University of Tennessee Press, 1989).

which bred a demand for print, which bred a demand for literacy, which bred a demand for schooling. According to Lawrence Cremin, "in an expanding literary environment, literacy tends to create a demand for more literacy." In the words of Richard D. Brown, there was "a self-intensifying spiral of growth in the production, distribution, and consumption of print."[44]

Rolf Engelsing argued that the increases in literacy and in available reading materials changed the very nature of reading. Prior to the book revolution, reading was "intensive," that is, literate people usually owned only a few books and they read them over and over. As a result, reading performed more of a devotional or ritualistic function than an informative one. Such intensive reading could be revolutionary if the text was revolutionary, but given the preponderance of Bibles and books about mainstream religion, traditional literacy tended to be conservative. In the new world of more plentiful books there were more competing ideas; the subject matter expanded into new secular areas and new kinds of fiction, and the periodical and newspaper trade expanded. Reading in this world was "extensive," that is, more diverse, quick, information oriented, and superficial.

Engelsing presented this interpretation with some negative overtones; he regretted the "commodification" of reading matter. Other scholars, while accepting the theme of a book revolution, have questioned the intensive-extensive dichotomy and its qualitative consequences for the reading process. Cathy Davidson argued that reading more books was compatible with reading some of them carefully and intensely. She also believed that the literacy promoted by the book revolution was potentially emancipating. "Extensive reading—and I emphasize novel reading here—served for many early Americans as the bridge from elementary to advanced literateness, a transition in mentality the importance of which cannot be overstated." Novel reading, she concluded, "could be emotionally intense, psychically fulfilling, imaginatively active, socially liberalizing, and educationally progressive—quite the opposite of the merely consumptive, passive repetitive act" that Engelsing pictured.[45]

Robert Darnton reinforced the notion that reading the new fiction could be intensive. Speaking of his late-eighteenth-century bourgeois merchant, Darnton said, "One could hardly find a more intensive reader than Ranson, and his reading became more intense as he did more of it."

44. Cremin, *American Education: The National Experience,* 493; Richard D. Brown, "From Cohesion to Competition," in *Printing and Society,* ed. Joyce et al., 305.
45. Davidson, *Revolution and the Word,* 72–73.

Thus Darnton rejected the qualitative revolution that Engelsing had proposed.[46] Meanwhile, Cremin's work supports Davidson's emphasis on the liberating potential of expanded reading material. He characterized the watershed as a shift from "a more traditional inert literacy in which people read the Bible and a few other works of devotion and instruction but not much else, to a more liberating literacy in which they reached out to an expanding world of print for information and guidance on private and public affairs." Literacy did not guarantee liberation; as Cremin said, "literacy cannot confer agency, in and of itself; but literacy does hold the makings of agency, insofar as it helps people to see beyond the boundaries of household, parish, and neighborhood . . . [and] facilitates the self-conscious individualization of belief and behavior."[47] Still, the subversive tendencies of expanded literacy did not pass unnoticed by the guardians of tradition. Various efforts at channeling literacy (what some historians call "social control") arose to challenge the worrisome diversification and expansion of print. Schools and newspaper editorialists extolled virtuous reading and inveighed against reading trash, while librarians resisted the inclusion of popular romances and story papers in their collections.[48]

The first theme shared by historians of literacy and popular literature, then, is that there was a major expansion of the reading public in the late eighteenth and early nineteenth centuries, accompanied by an expansion and diversification of printed matter. Newspapers and books became cheaper and more diverse. Five times as many books were published in the twenty years after 1830 than in the previous sixty.[49] The newspaper-reading public was far from universal, however, and the book-reading public had expanded only from a tiny minority to a more substantial minority of all adults. So we should not let the high rates of signature literacy and talk of a book revolution encourage us to imagine a nation in which everyone read extensively every day. In spite of the market's penetration of the countryside, the expansion of schooling, and the diversification of the book trade, a majority of Americans were probably not regular readers of newspapers and certainly not of books, other than religious works, which had long been the staples of traditional

46. Robert Darnton, "Readers Respond to Rousseau," in *The Great Cat Massacre and Other Episodes in French Cultural History* (New York: Vintage Books, 1974), 251.

47. Cremin, *American Education: The National Experience,* 492–93.

48. Soltow and Stevens, *Rise of Literacy,* chap. 3; Denning, *Mechanic Accents,* chap. 4; Robert A. Gross, "Much Instruction from Little Reading: Books and Librarians in Thoreau's Concord," *Proceedings of the American Antiquarian Society* 97 (1987):129–87.

49. Helen Waite Papashvily, *All the Happy Endings: A Study of the Domestic Novel in America, the Women Who Wrote it, the Women Who Read It, in the Nineteenth Century* (New York: Harper and Row, 1956), 35.

literacy. William Gilmore, whose book about Windsor township, Vermont, is the most intricate case study of literacy and print culture in this period, says that he prefers the concept of "the rise of an age of reading," instead of a "reading revolution." He points out also that the median number of volumes in personal libraries in Windsor was only three in the early nineteenth century, and that a majority of families appeared to read predominantly in what Engelsing called the "intensive" mode.[50] Still, there was an expansion of literacy between 1750 and 1850, evidenced by an upswing in signature literacy and in schooling, an expansion of the book trade, a popularization of newspapers, and the development of new forms of fiction, chiefly the sentimental novel and the story paper.

Divergent Reading Publics

A second theme shared by several of the new historians of reading is fragmentation, or the divergence of different reading publics. This theme is more difficult to summarize than the theme of expansion, for several reasons. First, the timing is tricky; society is apparently *always* coming apart at the seams, so historians tend to hypothesize coherence at the beginning of any time period and fragmentation at the end of it. Second, the extent to which different reading publics coincided with different social-class groups remains a major research dilemma. It is impossible to get systematic data on who read various works and genres; we can muster only impressionistic evidence. Third, the metaphors of fragmentation and cohesion are never quite adequate to the reality. They suggest polar opposites when in reality both processes can and usually are going on simultaneously. An expansion of literacy can draw more people into reading the same things (for example, McGuffey's *Readers* or syndicated newspaper columns) but at the same time encourage the development of distinctive reading materials that serve different groups. Fourth, there is a risk of comparing New England in 1700 with the entire nation in 1840, or a homogeneous elite of the seventeenth century with the larger reading public of the nineteenth century. Part of the phenomenon of fragmentation of print culture is inherent in the social structure. When reading expanded, it spread to classes and groups that had long had different interests and styles, but whose understandings and modes of expression had not been so visible before they appeared in print. This is not to suggest, however, that new forms of reading material were direct expressions of the culture and interests of increasingly literate groups, for the expansion of literacy was accompanied by the increasing commer-

50. Gilmore, "Literacy," 25–26; Gilmore, *Reading Becomes a Necessity,* 264–82.

cialization of reading material. Thus, we face the further challenge of interpreting literature that was written *for* a given social group but not necessarily *by* members of that group.

In spite of the interpretive problems it poses, diversification is part of the history of literacy and must be addressed. Indeed, at the time the cracks in the reading public were developing, contemporaries reacted to the threat of social fragmentation by trying to govern reading habits. This is a major theme in the history of literacy, and it helps tie literacy to the socioeconomic context, not only because the divergent reading publics were identified with social classes, but because the new popular reading materials emerged as popular culture became commercialized. The logic of capitalism increasingly came into play in the production of reading matter.

The theme of fragmentation is prominent in recent writings on the history of reading. David Hall traced the evolution of literacy from cohesion in early British America to discordant conflict in the early nineteenth century. He viewed the process as contrapuntal, however; in reaction to the threatening diversity of the early nineteenth century, guardians of American culture asserted a new synthesis, American Victorianism, with some success.[51] Richard D. Brown reinforced the fragmentation theme. With the American Revolution as a catalyst, the expanded world of print offered diverse values. "Where printing had once been an instrument of cultural cohesion, it had now become a principal agent of cultural fragmentation and competition."[52]

Among literary scholars, the notion that different literatures emerged for different groups of people in the nineteenth century has been around for a long time. In the form of the "highbrow-lowbrow" distinction, it was argued by Van Wyck Brooks in 1915, picked up by Russell Lynes in the 1940s, adopted by Edward Shils and others in the 1950s debate on popular culture, and repeated by Henry Nash Smith in the 1970s. This older interpretation of literary stratification paid little explicit attention to class and was rather derogatory about popular fiction. According to Smith, highbrow fiction was alienated and critical, challenging social conventions, whereas popular fiction "was designed to soothe the sensibilities of its readers by fulfilling expectations and ex-

51. Hall, "Uses of Literacy," 20, 43, 46.
52. Brown, "From Cohesion to Competition," 308. The theme is now elaborated in his *Knowledge Is Power: The Diffusion of Information in Early America, 1700–1865* (New York: Oxford University Press, 1989). Rhys Isaac made the same case for Virginia between 1750 and 1800, attributing the fragmentation to religious revivalism as well as competing political ideologies. Isaac, "Books and the Social Authority of Learning: The Case of Mid-Eighteenth-Century Virginia," in *Printing and Society*, ed. Joyce et al., 228–49.

pressing only received ideas, and to provide channels for the unimpeded discharge of strong but crude feelings."[53]

More recent interpreters of this diversification of literary culture have expressed a more positive view of popular reading material. Cathy Davidson sees sentimental novels as a clear diversification in the early nineteenth century. Not only were the novels accessible to a different group (people who were not trained in the collegiate classical culture, especially women), but also the message of the novels was distinctive. Contrary to Smith's opinion, Davidson sees the novels as promoting subversive messages and aspirations contrary to those expressed in school textbooks and in church.[54]

In a recent book about dime novels, Michael Denning attacks two traditional stereotypes about those works, which sold in great volume in the 1870s and 1880s: that they were read mainly by middle-class adolescent boys and that they were harmless adventure tales that reinforced mainstream values. Denning argues that the popular culture category should be split along class lines, that the "middlebrow" level was for middle-class readers, whose main staples were magazines and sentimental novels, and that the "lowbrow" level was for working-class readers, who mainly read story papers and dime novels. Whereas Henry Nash Smith had argued that the "notorious vagueness of class lines in the United States" precluded any "close linkage between brow levels and the actual social structure," Denning makes a plausible case that dime novels were characteristically, if not exclusively, read by working-class readers. There is little hard evidence about the class position of readers of dime novels (or of sentimental novels, or Steinbeck, or *Peyton Place* for that matter), but Denning argues that common schooling for working-class people expanded prior to the heyday of the dime novel, that labor papers carried stories similar to dime novels or offered dime novels themselves as subscription bonuses, and that some working-class autobiographers mentioned that they had read dime novels.[55] The case is

53. Henry Nash Smith, "The Scribbling Women and the Cosmic Success Story," *Critical Inquiry* (September 1974):50; and Smith, *Democracy and the Novel: Popular Resistance to Classic American Writers* (New York: Oxford University Press, 1978), 8–9; Van Wyck Brooks, "America's Coming of Age" (written in 1915), in *Three Essays on America* (New York: E. P. Dutton, 1934). Russell Lynes and Edward Shils added a "middlebrow" category, which is followed by Smith in his 1978 book. Lynes, *The Tastemakers* (New York: Grosset and Dunlap, 1949), chap. 17. Shils, who was considered a defender of popular culture, called the highbrow level "superior," the middle level "mediocre," and the lowbrow level "brutal." At the "brutal" level "the depth of penetration is almost always negligible, subtlety is almost entirely lacking, and a general grossness of sensitivity and perception is a common feature." Shils, "Mass Society and Its Culture," in *Culture for the Millions?* ed. Jacobs, 6.

54. Davidson, *Revolution and the Word*, 11–13.

55. Smith, *Democracy and the Novel*, 9; Denning, *Mechanic Accents*, 27–31.

hardly conclusive, as Denning himself acknowledges. The evidence from contemporaries' comments about the readership of dime novels is mixed—some suggest readership across class lines, others a predominantly working-class readership—but Denning's corrective of the middle-class stereotype is viable.[56]

His argument about the message of the dime novels is even more speculative. Although the dime novels were not generally written by working-class authors, Denning argues that they were somewhat responsive to working-class concerns and values, displaying the artisan version of republican ideology, which rejected the individualism typical of the sentimental novels. Denning focuses on excerpts from dime novels that offered sympathetic depictions of working-class life, acknowledgment of the dreadful working conditions of such workers as miners, criticism of irresponsible capitalists, and ambivalent attitudes about strikes.[57]

Much must be taken on faith in this analysis, and the argument that working-class readers read dime novels in an "allegorical" mode requires a faith that borders on the mystical. Denning's argument that the text is "contested terrain" is also fuzzy. The dimes were not written by working-class authors and were "perhaps not the self-representation of any class," yet in them, Denning argues, concepts of class were "alternately claimed, rejected, and fought over."[58] The battle metaphor doesn't really clarify the claim of conflict. Was the battle just between conflicting ideas, or also between people? If it was people, who was fighting whom? In spite of these problems, Denning's methodological discussions are good, and his summaries of the dime novel's themes should be required reading for anyone who believes that dime novels were unmitigated endorsements of middle-class values.

Denning and Davidson offer the best recent examples of the efforts of literary historians to move from text to readers; together they illustrate both the potential and the limitations of such attempts. Both authors reserve textual analysis for the second half of their works. In the first half they discuss the conditions of the readers and the development of the genre, including such matters as education, literacy, contemporary commentary about reading habits, autobiographical comments about reading, and controversies within the book trade or reform circles about popular reading. Denning's theoretical guide is Antonio Gramsci, who rejected the "escapist" interpretation of formula genres and enumerated various purposes of popular fiction in workers' lives: The continuation of storytelling traditions, the provision of conversation topics, the depiction

56. Denning, *Mechanic Accents,* 29.
57. Ibid., 73, 79, 128, 133.
58. Ibid., 77.

of heroes, and the interpretation of various social problems. Denning rejects reader-response theory because of its indifference to real historical readers, but in his textual analysis he clearly keeps his asserted working-class reader firmly in mind. In the end, Denning's innovative analysis is limited because he can neither prove who read the dimes nor prove that working-class readers heard the "mechanic accents" over the noise of the main messages: the heroics of cowboys, detectives, and upwardly mobile office boys. Critics and historians of popular culture will continue to struggle to connect text and reader.

Davidson pulls out all the theoretical stops, citing reader-response theory, Robert Darnton's *histoire du livre,* Janice Radway's feminist interpretation of romance novels, Hans Jauss's German reception theory, and Clifford Geertz's "thick description." She boldly asserts that "one can construct an ethnography of the early American novel reader." In her attempt to do so, she relies on diaries and letters, clues in the texts, and controversies about novel reading.[59] But Davidson's most direct and intriguing links between texts and readers are the marginalia and inscriptions she found when she examined multiple copies of early novels in archives. Unfortunately, the execution cannot live up to the promise of this method; the marginalia are less revealing than one might hope, and Davidson's analysis of them is highly speculative, closer to archaeology than ethnography. Having made this valiant effort to document the responses of historical readers in a very concrete way, Davidson, like Denning, moves in the second half of her book to textual analysis, with an eye toward women readers' possible interpretations of the novels. In one case, she notes, an author provided her readers "the opportunity to see" a view of women like themselves in print, dealing with real-life problems; in another case, Davidson elucidates "two radically different stories . . . latent within the text" of a novel.[60] Like Denning, Davidson has pressed her evidence energetically to bring texts and historical readers closer together; both do so in a methodologically self-conscious way that allows us to judge each step of the argument.

In spite of the limitations of their evidence, each historian makes an interesting case that a new popular literary form offered dissenting viewpoints to a particular social group. Both books thus present a positive view of literacy, as well as a positive view of the diversification of popular genres. But not all analysts tell such a tale of beneficial differentiation. The most provocative recent treatment of this theme bemoans

59. Davidson, *Revolution and the Word,* 4–5, 10. On the necessity of using ethnographic methods in studying the uses of literacy, see John F. Szwed, "The Ethnography of Literacy," in *Variation in Writing: Functional and Linguistic-Cultural Differences,* ed. Marcia Farr Whiteman (Hillsdale, N.J.: Lawrence Erlbaum, 1981), 13–23.
60. Davidson, *Revolution and the Word,* 144, 252.

the stratification of culture. Written by one of our finest cultural historians, it is not about print culture but about drama, music, and the visual arts.

In *Highbrow/Lowbrow* Lawrence Levine documents a world of popular culture in the early and mid-nineteenth century in which knowledge of Shakespeare was shared across classes, in which socially mixed audiences often went to Shakespeare plays together, a world in which instrumental music, art museums, and opera were more commonly shared. In the second half of the nineteenth century, these shared art forms became "sacralized" (worshiped, given the trappings of religion) and restricted to more homogeneous, elite audiences. Levine's documentation of the large and diverse audience for these art forms in the early decades is solid and interesting, as is his evidence for the rhetoric and behavior associated with their sacralization. The parallels he draws across Shakespearean plays, symphony concerts, and museum operations are impressive. The sacralization metaphor is apt. It arises from the sources themselves rather than merely as the historian's invention. Also, the metaphor works in an extended sense: there were gods, priests, sacred texts, rituals, and vestments in the religion of high culture.

Levine doesn't spend a lot of time explaining this shift to sacralized high culture, but when he does touch briefly on the causes, he mentions American Victorians' desire for order and their consequent distaste for the mixed, boisterous audiences characteristic of Jacksonian America, in combination with the increasing prestige of the expert, who rendered the amateur performer incompetent. The claim to special stewardship of sacred art, not only by the artists but also by their elite audiences, seems tied to Anglo-Americans' nervous efforts to maintain their cultural hegemony.[61]

Levine overlooks some aspects of shared high culture today that might challenge his thesis, like Luciano Pavarotti's appearances on Johnny Carson, favorite classical melodies on mail-order LPs, and the Hollywood film version of *Romeo and Juliet*. In his analysis of the development of symphony orchestras, Levine overlooks the persistence of concert bands today, especially at high schools and colleges, and the increasing popularity of "pops" orchestras, both of which play popular repertoires to mixed audiences and thus run counter to the major trend Levine is out-

61. Lawrence W. Levine, *Highbrow/Lowbrow: The Emergence of Cultural Hierarchy in America* (Cambridge: Harvard University Press, 1988), 56–64, 211, 221. A similar argument is made for orchestras and art museums in Paul DiMaggio, "Cultural Entrepreneurship in Nineteenth-Century Boston: The Creation of an Organizational Base for High Culture in America," and "Cultural Entrepreneurship in Nineteenth-Century Boston, Part II: The Classification and Framing of American Art," *Media, Culture and Society* 4 (1982):33–50, 303–22.

lining. Nonetheless, he offers appropriate caveats, and his defense on this issue seems sufficient: "to say that sacralization remained an ideal only imperfectly realized is not to deny that it became a cultural force."[62]

But there are some other problems with this fascinating book. When Levine argues that the nonelite majority, having been excluded from these art forms, took to jazz, blues, musical comedy, movies, and comics to satisfy their aesthetic urges, he implies that these popular art forms now belonged to the hoi polloi alone. But very few elites utterly reject the popular arts; most highly educated people share popular culture variously and selectively. Levine's ambitious claim that "the United States in the first half of the nineteenth century did experience greater cultural sharing" than it does today thus seems to rest upon an assumption that the only cultural sharing that counts is the sharing of the cultural forms that have become high culture today. Levine's argument about the stratification and sacralization of Shakespearean drama, opera, orchestras, and art museums is persuasive and interesting. But if we examine different art forms at different points in time, and if we include all cultural sharing in our analysis, we must conclude that there is more shared culture in the 1980s, considering the extent to which Americans have shared Louis Armstrong, the Beatles, Fred Astaire, Indiana Jones, and the Ghostbusters. Thus one can read the twentieth-century history of popular culture as a story not of increasing segregation but of increasing consolidation and inclusion.

As an example of the Victorians' distaste for disorder, Levine cites their desire to exclude rowdy working-class people from Central Park, and he says a similar impulse was involved in the effort to make vaudeville and movies more respectable for middle-class patrons. But this process actually conflicts with Levine's central point. As Kathy Peiss and others have documented, the early twentieth century witnessed successful efforts by commercial promoters to make dance halls, vaudeville, movies, and amusement parks more respectable in order to attract middle-class patrons.[63] Thus, whereas high culture in the fine arts was becoming sacralized and segregated, working-class amusements were becoming more respectable and generalized across class lines. Furthermore, the expansion of public schooling, particularly high schools, was instrumental in disseminating a watered-down version of sacred culture. Levine says that Shakespeare was regularly included in school texts of the nineteenth century, but relatively few children ever reached the

62. Levine, *Highbrow/Lowbrow*, 168.

63. Kathy Peiss, *Cheap Amusements: Working Women and Leisure in Turn-of-the-Century New York* (Philadelphia: Temple University Press, 1986), 103–4, 127–29, 161; also see Lewis A. Erenberg, *Steppin' Out: New York Nightlife and the Transformation of American Culture, 1890–1930* (Westport, Conn.: Greenwood Press, 1981), 146–58.

higher grade levels, where most of these textbook allusions were presented. It was in the twentieth century, when high-school attendance became
a majority experience, that most children were introduced to Shakespeare in print, albeit often in a tiresome, undramatic manner. Levine is
on stronger ground discussing the decline of live Shakespeare in popular
theater than when he turns to popular culture in general. Education,
entertainment, and media exposure were becoming more common in the
twentieth century, despite the stratification of some cultural forms into
high-, middle-, and lowbrow categories.

Nor does Levine sufficiently consider the converse point: there was
considerable cultural stratification in the early nineteenth century. For
example, the classical culture of American colleges was restricted to a
small minority of men, mostly of upper status, even in the Jacksonian
period; later, higher education became less stratified, not more. Meanwhile, antebellum working-class people had saloons, fire companies,
lodges, and other institutions that generated their own distinctive cultural expressions.

Does Levine's thesis about shared culture in antebellum America
apply to reading materials? He briefly suggests that it does, citing the
large audience for Twain and Dickens. Yet during the antebellum period
Hawthorne and Melville complained about indifference to their work
from the new popular audience that preferred middlebrow sentimental
novels. Perhaps the stratification simply occurred earlier in fiction than
in drama, art, and orchestral music. Or perhaps the history of popular
reading material is substantially different from the history of the fine
arts. The expansion of reading material may have exposed more people to
the same things at the very same time that it allowed the production of
more diverse materials for segregated audiences. Chapter 10 of this volume returns to this question as it pertains to the period after 1880. In the
meantime, Levine stands as an interesting counterpoint to Davidson and
Denning. All three see stratification of culture taking place, but Davidson and Denning, looking at popular art forms, see it as a healthy expression of counterhegemonic ideas; Levine, focusing on high culture,
sees it as developing elitism. Despite his protestations to the contrary,
Levine evokes some nostalgia that I think is misplaced. Still, Levine's is a
smart, provocative book, and its relevance to the history of readers must
be pondered.

Other Nineteenth-Century Studies: Journalists and Novelists

Works from many historical subfields help to elucidate the emergence
of reading publics and their choices in the nineteenth century. At least
two merit discussion: the history of journalism and the history of au-

thorship. Some historians of journalism have of late moved from the traditional interest in technology, the media industries, and newspaper content to a new interest with evolving reading publics, journalists' social values, and the functions of the press. Michael Schudson and Dan Schiller both have written about the rise of penny newspapers in pre–Civil War America and the emergence of the press's claim to objectivity. Their interest in the history of readers is incidental to their interest in developing a critical history of journalism's myths. Still, Schudson argues that the new audience was middle-class, whereas Schiller argues it stretched across merchant and artisan lines.[64] The evidence on readership is murky (as usual), but the debate draws them into the arena where the uses of literacy are explored.

In literary history much attention is still paid to authors' values and intentions. Because the production of reading materials is an essential aspect of the history of literacy, literary history that explores the social status, values, and working conditions of authors remains important. One of the livelier debates has been about the values contained in the domestic novels of the period 1830 to 1880. Ann Douglas's quirky, judgmental, and influential book, *The Feminization of American Culture*, argues that tough-minded Calvinist orthodoxy was gutted by anti-intellectual Victorian sentimentalism. The former she associates with the intellectual rigor of Jonathan Edwards's and Melville's "masculine vision of history," the latter with women novelists and liberal Protestant ministers, who, to Melville's horror, were trying to replace his views with "a feminine view of social and biological process." Douglas notes with some satisfaction that feminized sentimentalism fell to "lowbrow" status in the twentieth century.[65]

Douglas is certainly not the first to write disapprovingly of nineteenth-century domestic novelists, but she does it with the most verve.[66] In contrast to Douglas, the most sophisticated sympathetic view of these authors comes from Mary Kelley in *Private Woman, Public Stage*. Kelley sees the authors of domestic novels as frustrated and sometimes angry,

64. Michael Schudson, *Discovering the News: A Social History of American Newspapers* (New York: Basic Books, 1978); Dan Schiller, *Objectivity and the News: The Public and the Rise of Commercial Journalism* (Philadelphia: University of Pennsylvania Press, 1981).

65. Ann Douglas, *The Feminization of American Culture* (New York: Alfred A. Knopf, 1977), 7–9, 87, 313.

66. See also, for example, Leslie Fiedler, *Love and Death in the American Novel* (New York: Criterion Books, 1960), and Smith, *Democracy and the Novel*. An oft-cited exception is Papashvily, *All the Happy Endings*, which argued that these novels were reassuring handbooks on how to control men and marriages. Nina Baym takes a similar stance in *Women's Fiction: A Guide to Novels by and about Women in America, 1820–1870* (Ithaca: Cornell University Press, 1978).

but unable to escape the confines of women's prescribed role, which they had internalized to a large degree.[67] In Kelley's hands these novelists are more serious, complex, and worthwhile than in Douglas's. Kelley makes a good case that such authors as Augusta Evans Wilson were working out preoccupying problems about women's intellect and women's roles in their novels.[68]

Such discussions of authorial intent and the possible meanings of text are important in imagining the functions of literacy in a given period. But were the readers preoccupied with the same problems as the authors? That Ann Douglas and Mary Kelley can construct such opposite arguments about the meaning of domestic novels may illustrate the limitations of textual criticism as a tool; still, a broadened history of literacy cannot do without textual criticism. We need studies that try to persuade us about the social and psychological messages available in various popular print forms.

Several themes are emerging in the history of American literacy in the Revolutionary and antebellum periods. Literacy expanded more rapidly from the mid-eighteenth to the mid-nineteenth century than in previous hundred years. Reading materials were becoming cheaper and more diverse, and they and their audiences were differentiating into something like highbrow, middlebrow, and lowbrow categories, although it is difficult to discern how much overlap and common reading occurred. Due to the expansion of reading materials, America changed from a society of scarce books and newspapers, in which reading was intensive and repetitive, to a society in which people used their literacy in different modes. Traditional, intensive reading of authoritative texts like the Bible continued; new forms of intensive reading developed around such genres as political pamphlets and sentimental novels; and the expansion of the printing industries created newer, faster styles of reading for the people closest to the centers of the "reading revolution."

The Secondary Literature: 1880 to the Present

Nothing that approaches this emerging consensus has developed for the history of American reading publics after 1880. No history of literacy abilities during this period exists, and only a handful of sketchy attempts to summarize the historical trends can be found in the voluminous social science studies of people's reading activities and interests. Historical works abound on the producers of print—publishers, editors,

67. Mary Kelley, *Private Woman, Public Stage: Literary Domesticity in Nineteenth-Century America* (New York: Oxford University Press, 1984), 187–88, 206, 335.
68. Kelley, *Private Woman,* 104–5.

and authors—as do books on the themes, values, and heroes of fiction. But nothing like the recent works about the reading publics of early and mid-nineteenth-century America is available to describe the twentieth century.

There is, nonetheless, a huge amount of material relevant to a history of the uses of literacy over the past century. We can sample the available types of studies by ranging them along a circuit, to use Robert Darnton's term. The circuit moves from the industry to the author, from the author to the text. Very few works attempt to move from the text to the reader. Still, works on industries, authors, and texts can be used to situate ordinary people's reading activities in the context of the social structure and the economic system.

Studies of Industries and Markets

A survey of industry-based studies must begin with the comprehensive histories of the three major sectors of publishing: books, magazines, and newspapers. Sometimes dull, sometimes celebratory, generally vague about audiences, these studies nonetheless are full of details about technological developments, the evolving economic organization of the industries, competition among the major producers, access to authorship, and how decisions were made about changing format and content.[69] There are also countless studies of particular topics or episodes in publishing history. Raymond Shove, for example, chronicled the production of cheap reprints of English and European books during the 1870s and 1880s, including such series as Harper's Franklin Square Library and George Munro's Seaside Library, before the 1891 copyright law made these unfeasible.[70] Kenneth Davis, writing about the 1950s paperback revolution, emphasized the diversity of books available by the mid-1950s. These titles ushered out the sleepy Eisenhower years with a wave of salacious covers, political dissent, reprinted classics, and contemporary reportage, with

69. John Tebbel, *A History of Book Publishing in the United States,* 4 vols. (New York: R. R. Bowker, 1972–81); Charles A. Madison, *Book Publishing in America* (New York: McGraw-Hill, 1966); Hellmut Lehmann-Haupt, Lawrence C. Wroth, and Rollo G. Silver, *The Book in America: A History of the Making and Selling of Books in the United States,* 2d ed. (New York: R. R. Bowker, 1951); Alfred M. Lee, *The Daily Newspaper in America: The Evolution of a Social Instrument* (New York: Macmillan, 1937); Edwin Emery, *The Press and America: An Interpretive History,* 3d ed. (Englewood Cliffs, N.J.: Prentice-Hall, 1972); Theodore Peterson, *Magazines in the Twentieth Century,* 2d ed. (Urbana: University of Illinois Press, 1975); Frank Luther Mott, *A History of American Magazines,* 5 vols. (Cambridge: Harvard University Press, 1930–68).

70. Raymond H. Shove, *Cheap Book Production in the United States, 1870 to 1891* (Urbana: University of Illinois Library, 1937).

Mickey Spillane next to *Ivanhoe,* and with Dr. Spock nestled on the shelf next to the Kinsey Report, all at the corner drugstore.[71]

Industry studies also include analysis of distribution. Relevant secondary sources include works on best sellers, book clubs, and other aspects of the market.[72] Because a sizable percentage of all books that are read come from libraries, a broad history of the uses of literacy must eventually incorporate some history of the uses of libraries. Until now, historians of libraries have focused more on internal professional development than on readers or the circulation of books. Several studies of the expansion of libraries in the United States, however, do provide information on regional variation, private philanthropy, and the effects of government assistance.[73]

Studies that focus on the publishing industries often emphasize consolidation, beginning with the early wire services, the penetration of the countryside by city papers, the development of newspaper and bookstore chains, and finally, the development of conglomerates that have absorbed media companies as subsidiaries. Most journalism history textbooks review these developments, and historical monographs concentrate on particular aspects.[74] The theme has been pursued with vigor in

71. Kenneth C. Davis, *Two-Bit Culture: The Paperbacking of America* (Boston: Houghton Mifflin, 1984); see also Frank L. Schick, *The Paperbound Book in America: The History of Paperbacks and Their European Background* (New York: R. R. Bowker, 1958), and Thomas L. Bonn, *Heavy Traffic and High Culture: New American Library as Literary Gatekeeper in the Paperback Revolution* (Carbondale: Southern Illinois University Press, 1989).

72. Alice Payne Hackett, *80 Years of Best Sellers, 1895–1975* (New York: R. R. Bowker, 1977); James D. Hart, *The Popular Book: A History of America's Literary Taste* (New York: Oxford University Press, 1950); Frank Luther Mott, *Golden Multitudes: The Story of Best Sellers in the United States* (New York: Macmillan, 1947); Joan Shelley Rubin, "Self, Culture, and Self-Culture in Modern America: The Early History of the Book-of-the-Month Club," *Journal of American History* 71 (March 1985):782–806.

73. Angus Campbell and Charles Metzner, *Public Use of the Library and Other Sources of Information* (Ann Arbor: University of Michigan, Institute for Social Research, 1950); Louis R. Wilson, *The Geography of Reading* (Chicago: University of Chicago Press, 1938); H. Daniel, *Public Libraries for Everyone: Growth and Development of Library Services in the United States, Especially since the Passage of the Library Services Act* (Garden City, N.Y.: Doubleday, 1961); George S. Bobinski, *Carnegie Libraries: Their History and Impact on American Public Library Development* (Chicago: American Library Association, 1969). For further bibliographical and historiographical information, see Stephen Karetzky, *Reading Research and Librarianship: A History and Analysis* (Westport, Conn.: Greenwood Press, 1982), and Michael H. Harris and Donald G. Davis, Jr., *American Library History: A Bibliography* (Austin: University of Texas Press, 1978).

74. See, for example, Elmo S. Watson, *A History of Newspaper Syndicates in the United States, 1865–1935* (Chicago, 1936); Richard A. Schwarzlose, *The American Wire Services: A Study of Their Development as a Social Institution* (New York: Arno

the recent past, often by media critics troubled by the "bottom line" and "blockbuster" mentalities encouraged by corporate consolidation. One prominent critic, Ben Bagdikian, has written extensively about the woes of blandness, homogenization, and bias that have accompanied media conglomeration.[75] Thomas Whiteside has written of similar problems in book publishing—decisions made by precise calculations of profits, pressure for big sellers, preoccupation with "tie-in" products, and intense marketing of formulaic sequels.[76] The extent of such pressures is a matter of debate, but their existence and impact have certainly been major themes in the recent history of print media. The effects of all these developments upon America's reading publics can be considered at different levels. At a concrete level of supply, these trends suggest that more readers will be exposed to the same publications, that new authors will find it increasingly difficult to break into print, and that faddish sequels will be a prominent feature of the book market; blandness seems to be the major drawback to newspaper consolidation, because it discourages competition and the expression of distinctive, contrasting viewpoints. The cumulative effects on people's world view and level of information, however, are a much more speculative matter.

Industry studies include biographies of publishers and editors, and three recent works suggest a range of approaches. Ronald Steel's biography of Walter Lippmann focuses largely on Lippmann's career in journalism, as well as on the elite circles of politicians and academics with whom Lippmann associated. It is a fresh, meticulous, readable biography, but it does not aim to analyze who read Lippmann, probably the most influential journalist of the century.[77] James Baughman's new biography of Henry Luce, the founder of *Time* and *Life,* doesn't focus on audiences either, but it makes an implicit argument about those who read Luce's magazines. Luce is often faulted as a leading propagandist for cold

Press, 1979); W. Carl Masche, "Factors Involved in the Consolidation and Suspension of Daily and Sunday Newspapers in the United States since 1900" (M.A. thesis, University of Minnesota, 1932); Raymond B. Nixon, "The Problem of Newspaper Monopoly" (1948), reprinted in *Mass Communications,* 2d ed., ed. Wilbur Schramm (Urbana: University of Illinois Press, 1960), 241–50; and John W. Kitson, "Profile of a Growth Industry: American Book Publishing at Mid-Century, with an Emphasis on the Integration and Consolidation Activity between 1959 and 1965" (Ph.D. diss., University of Illinois, 1968).

75. Ben H. Bagdikian, *The Media Monopoly,* 3d ed. (Boston: Beacon Press, 1990). Compare the more sanguine view in Benjamin M. Compaine et al., *Who Owns the Media? Concentration of Ownership in the Mass Communications Industry* (New York: Harmony Books, 1979).

76. Thomas Whiteside, *The Blockbuster Complex: Conglomerates, Show Business, and Book Publishing* (Middletown, Conn.: Wesleyan University Press, 1980).

77. Ronald Steel, *Walter Lippmann and the American Century* (Boston: Little, Brown, 1980).

war imperialism, but Baughman stresses the extent to which he reflected his audience's views rather than shaped them.[78] In her book on William Allen White and the *Emporia (Kansas) Gazette,* Sally Foreman Griffith situates White and his paper thoroughly in the context of a single small Midwestern town. One basic source of conflict is nicely highlighted and documented in the book: that between the local values of Emporia and the encroaching national, commercial, cosmopolitan values that White had to interpret, embrace, or resist. Another conflict, at which Griffith only hints, lay within Emporia itself. Although Griffith stresses that the *Gazette* was responsive to Emporia because White was surrounded by his audience every time he walked down the street, she also suggests briefly that White knew little about the immigrants across the tracks, and that the *Gazette's* local allegiances were very selective, ignoring Catholic working-class folks and Democratic party activists. At times, Griffith equates Emporia with the *Gazette's* acquiescent, conservative Republican readers, and, indeed, they probably comprised a majority of the town's population. But she also presents evidence supporting her minor theme, that there was "little room in White's conception of community journalism for genuine diversity of opinion."[79] Griffith's thoughtful consideration of such issues makes hers a particularly relevant book, given our interest in the social history of literacy.

Studies of Authors

It seems a small step from the biographies of editors and publishers to the biographies of authors. But when we take that step, we find that the emphasis has shifted from newspapers and magazines to books. Studies of authors are traditional in literary history, often combining biography with analysis of the author's works, social beliefs, and literary theories. These matters are only of tangential interest to the historian of popular literacy; they tell us something of the content and possible meanings of popular reading material. Authorship is nonetheless an interesting juncture on the literacy circuit. Studies of the conditions of authorship can tell us something about the difficulties of getting into print, the biases that operated, the resources that were required, the constraints authors faced due to background or training, and the constraints placed upon them in terms of socially acceptable subject matter and style. A small literature illuminates these issues for the nineteenth century,

78. James L. Baughman, *Henry R. Luce and the Rise of the American News Media* (Boston: Twayne, 1987).

79. Sally Foreman Griffith, *Home Town News: William Allen White and the Emporia Gazette* (New York: Oxford University Press, 1989), 177.

when an increasingly profitable reading audience gave rise to the profession of authorship.[80] For the twentieth century, many works on pulps and other formula fiction discuss the extent to which authors had to acquiesce in editorial demands about plot and values. Christopher Wilson argues that even less formulaic writers like Jack London and Upton Sinclair were shaped by the developing market of American publishing.[81]

Studies of Texts

Works about authors inevitably delve into the content of the works, and thus we have moved in our circuit to the text itself. Here again, there is a mountain of work, most of which displays only an occasional interest in real readers and their reactions to the text. We can organize our examples under two headings: works on popular formula fiction and works about the literature of special groups. Works under the first heading, including books about Westerns, detective mysteries, romances, and science fiction, are vague about audience or acknowledge only in passing the conventional impressions of the typical reader. The second heading, including works on such reading matter as foreign-language newspapers, the black press, and the feminist press, gets us much closer to our interest in the uses of literacy by particular groups. These reading materials also seem to carry the heavier weight of cultural and political purpose that formula fiction lacks. But all reading materials embody ideological and cultural messages, no matter how diffuse their target audience or how devoted they seem to entertainment. And formula fiction is of interest to us for another reason. The romance, the Western, and the hard-boiled detective novel follow carefully prescribed patterns or formulas. Sometimes this is noted with condescension, but we are not interested here in comparisons with high culture or with the canons of literary history. We are interested in what people read and what it might have meant to them. The more "closed" the text—that is, the more its characters, plot, and values are predictable and unambiguous—the more we can say about what the reader was probably experiencing. We cannot

80. William Charvat, *The Profession of Authorship in America, 1800–1970* (Columbus: Ohio State University Press, 1968); see also E. Jennifer Monaghan, *A Common Heritage: Noah Webster's Blue-Back Speller* (Hamden, Conn.: Archon Books, 1983), for Webster's formative influence on text and reference book markets, and Kelley, *Private Woman,* discussed above, for the position of women as authors.

81. Christopher P. Wilson, *The Labor of Words: Literary Professionalism in the Progressive Era* (Athens: University of Georgia Press, 1985). On the conditions of authorship in the past few decades, see Lewis A. Coser, Charles Kadushin, and Witter W. Powell, *Books: The Culture and Commerce of Publishing* (New York: Basic Books, 1982).

know how reading materials fit into a reader's life, nor can we predict what an individual reader's interpretation of a work was, no matter how formalized. But the conventions of these formula genres do provide us with knowledge of the expectations of the readers as a group, and we therefore have more basis for asserting that the readers of a given formula genre were a community with regard to those conventions. By this logic, textual analysis of formula fiction can move us closer to the reader's experience than textual analysis of Joyce's *Ulysses*.

Dime novels, beginning in the 1860s, were the first highly profitable mass-market fiction, and Westerns were the predominant genre among the dimes. Two prominent works on Westerns suggest the value of genre approaches to the history of popular literacy, as well as their limitations. John Cawelti, the most influential analyst of formula conventions, emphasized the continuities in the Western formula, all the way from James Fenimore Cooper to the recent Western novel, although he did trace various minor cultural adjustments in tone and subject matter. The defining characteristic of the Western is not a particular plot structure but the setting: the frontier, where advancing civilization meets nature. The tension of the formula comes from this central drama in the American experience, the tension between order, culture, and civilization on the one hand, and natural virtue, expanse, and freedom on the other. The hero adjudicates a battle between Indians and settlers, between ranchers and farmers, or between other symbolic representatives of the frontier antinomy. Whatever the plot variation, the hero resolves this conflict, usually through an act of violence.[82] Cawelti's emphasis on continuities over a long period of time seems somewhat ahistorical, and he paid little attention to the question of who really read Westerns at any given point in time.[83] But his insistence on multiple functions seems sound, and his insights about the possible meanings of the durable Western formula are helpful.

Christine Bold's recent book is an interesting contrast to Cawelti. She acknowledges the constraints of the formula, but emphasizes that different authors reacted differently to the demands of the "fiction factory." Bold thus reveals variety in the genre not only across time, as larger cultural styles and values changed, but also among individual authors at a given time. Much more historically specific than Cawelti, she gives us more detail about the conditions of authorship, about the procedures of editors, and about the shifts from dime novels to pulps, from pulps to

82. John G. Cawelti, *Adventure, Mystery, and Romance* (Chicago: University of Chicago Press, 1976), chap. 8. See also Cawelti, *The Six-Gun Mystique* (Bowling Green, Ohio: Bowling Green University Popular Press, 1971).

83. For a critique along these lines, see Fredric Jameson, "Ideology, Narrative Analysis, and Popular Culture," *Theory and Society* 4 (1977):543–59.

"slicks" (like *Munsey's, McCall's,* and *Collier's*), and from slicks to the more recent Western novels.[84] Bold's book suggests a more long-term dynamic between readers and producers: as editorial conformity became more and more rigid, a formula could simply wear itself out, and readers or authors deserted it in favor of other pursuits or other forms. But the formula could revive (as the Western certainly has, several times), through a new twist, a new format, or a new audience. In each new situation, the level of editorial conformity might be negotiated differently. Thus, the Western stories in the slicks, with their purportedly more sophisticated middle-class audience, were less regulated than those in the pulps and the modern Western novel was even less constrained, though still within the basic paradigm that Cawelti so aptly described.[85]

Genre fiction carried social messages and was sometimes targeted at particular groups, such as women, working-class readers, and adolescents. Many other publications were aimed at such perceived reading publics, and there is a large literature that directly addresses the history of publications for special groups, including useful works on the black press, the immigrant press, the religious press, the radical press, and the feminist press.[86] But there are many gaps, and we need more analysis of the degree of segmentation and overlap of readership among and between these different social groups. Nonetheless, these works are an essential part of the history of the uses of literacy, and they play an

84. Christine Bold, *Selling the Wild West: Popular Western Fiction, 1860–1960* (Bloomington: Indiana University Press, 1987).

85. Space does not permit a review of works about other formulas, but relevant historical works with similar limitations exist for British spy thrillers, hard-boiled detective stories, science fiction, fantasy tales, and romances. See, for example, Bruce Merry, *Anatomy of the Spy Thriller* (London: Gill and Macmillan, 1977); David Geherin, *The American Private Eye: The Image in Fiction* (New York: Frederick Ungar, 1985); Ron Goulart, *The Dime Detectives* (New York: Mysterious Press, 1988); Lester del Rey, *The World of Science Fiction, 1926–1976: The History of a Subculture* (New York: Garland, 1980); Brian W. Aldiss, with David Wingrove, *Trillion Year Spree: The History of Science Fiction* (New York: Atheneum, 1986); L. Sprague de Camp, *Literary Swordsmen and Sorcerers: The Makers of Heroic Fantasy* (Sauk City, Wis.: Arkham House, 1976); and Carol Thurston, *The Romance Revolution: Erotic Novels for Women and the Quest for a New Sexual Identity* (Urbana: University of Illinois Press, 1987).

86. Walter C. Daniel, *Black Journals of the United States* (Westport, Conn.: Greenwood Press, 1982); Donald F. Joyce, *Gatekeepers of Black Culture: Black-Owned Book Publishing in the United States, 1817–1981* (Westport, Conn.: Greenwood Press, 1983); Joshua Fishman et al., *Language Loyalty in the United States: The Maintenance and Perpetuation of Non-English Mother Tongues by American Ethnic and Religious Groups* (The Hague: Mouton, 1966); Robert E. Park, *The Immigrant Press and Its Control* (New York: Harper and Brothers, 1922); Mary L. Reilly, *A History of the Catholic Press Association, 1911–1968* (Metuchen, N.J.: Scarecrow Press, 1971); Laureen Kessler, *The Dissident Press: Alternative Journalism in American History* (Beverly Hills, Calif.: Sage, 1984); Elizabeth Fox-Genovese, "The New Female Literary Culture," *Antioch Review* 38 (Spring 1980):193–217.

important role in the analysis in chapter 10 of this volume, which addresses diversity and standardization of reading materials.

The history of the uses of literacy is more fully developed for the nineteenth century than for the twentieth. For the nineteenth century common themes have emerged, and some scholars have begun to synthesize the existing work on the history of the book, the history of reading abilities, and the history of the publishing industries in ways that illuminate the history of readers. For the period after 1880 we are at a less-developed stage. A wealth of primary sources are available, as well as the background provided by the secondary literature discussed above. The remainder of this book, relying largely on primary sources, lays the groundwork in three areas: in part 2 we explore readers' literacy levels over time; in part 3 we muster data for time series on the basic reading activities of the population as a whole and of various subgroups within it; and in part 4 we reflect on the diverse uses of literacy amid pressures for assimilation and cultural standardization.

II Americans' Reading Abilities

3 Literacy and Reading Performance in the United States from 1880 to the Present

LAWRENCE C. STEDMAN AND CARL F. KAESTLE

Two objectives motivate our efforts to examine trends in reading abilities over the past one hundred years. First, if the history of literacy is to expand its focus from the simple "head counts" of who is literate and who is not to a more sophisticated analysis of the uses of literacy, we need to know more about the range of literacy abilities among America's population and how those have changed over time. Second, current discussions about literacy focus on an alleged decline in reading abilities and an epidemic of functional illiteracy. Better knowledge of long-term trends can set the recent figures in a more appropriate context. As we attempt to establish these long-term trends, we shall grapple with some technical difficulties in measuring literacy and in comparing rates over time. These difficulties not only make life challenging for the historian of literacy, but also bedevil current policy debates.

Estimates of the magnitude of the literacy problem vary wildly. In 1982, for example, Congressman Paul Simon opened a congressional hearing on literacy by declaring that "10 to 25 million Americans are unable to read and write." Furthermore, he reported, "an additional 35 million Americans can read only at the fifth grade level."[1] Concurring, Secretary of Education Terrel Bell testified that "in 1975, you have 63 million Americans that aren't proficient in meeting the educational requirements of every day adult life."[2] By 1982, Bell noted, the number had risen to 72 million, or half of the adult population.

1. U.S. Congress, House, *Illiteracy and the Scope of the Problem in This Country: Hearing before the House Subcommittee on Post Secondary Education and Labor,* 97th Cong., 2d sess., 1982, 1.
2. Ibid., 5.

The public and many scholars have blamed the schools, arguing that test scores have been in decline for nearly twenty years, writing skills have atrophied, and permissive schooling and electronic media have dulled the reading abilities of our nation's youth. After reviewing the evidence, the President's National Commission on Excellence in Education concluded in 1983 that the very security of the nation was "at risk."[3] In March 1986, Senator Edward Zorinsky, Democrat of Nebraska, charging that "the schools are creating illiterates," concluded, "we cannot leave reform up to the educators."[4]

Findings by other experts suggest that these claims may have been greatly exaggerated. The U.S. Bureau of the Census, for example, reported in 1979 that fewer than 1 percent of the population considered themselves illiterate.[5] In a reexamination of functional literacy studies for the National Institute of Education, Donald Fisher concluded that "few if any functional illiterates were actually awarded high school diplomas."[6] Some scholars emphasize that educational attainment has risen steadily during this century, in response to the rising literacy demands of a highly technological, information-laden society.[7] Research by Roger Farr and his colleagues seems to confirm that each succeeding generation has been better educated than the last. When given the same tests that had been administered in 1944–45, Indiana students in 1976 outperformed their predecessors.[8] A comprehensive review of then-and-now studies also suggested that students' reading skills have improved over the course of the century.[9] The authors commented that "anyone who says that he *knows* that literacy is decreasing is . . . at best unscholarly and at worst dishonest."[10]

3. National Commission on Excellence in Education, *A Nation at Risk: The Imperative for Educational Reform* (Washington, D.C.: Government Printing Office, 1983).

4. U.S. Congress, House, *Oversight on Illiteracy in the United States: Hearing before the House Subcommittee on Elementary, Secondary, and Vocational Education,* 99th Cong., 2d sess., 1986, 3.

5. U.S. Bureau of the Census, *Educational Attainment in the United States: March 1979 and 1978,* Current Population Reports, ser. P-20, no. 356 (Washington, D.C.: Government Printing Office, 1980).

6. Donald L. Fisher, *Functional Literacy and the Schools* (Washington, D.C.: National Institute of Education, 1978), 7.

7. Daniel Resnick and Lauren Resnick, "The Nature of Literacy: An Historical Exploration," *Harvard Educational Review* 43 (1977):370–85; Bormuth, "Value and Volume of Literacy," 7.

8. Roger Farr, Leo Fay, and Harold Negley, *Then and Now: Reading Achievement in Indiana (1944–45 and 1976)* (Bloomington: Indiana University, School of Education, 1978).

9. Roger Farr, Jaap Tuinman, and Michael Rowls, *Reading Achievement in the United States: Then and Now* (Bloomington: Indiana University, Final Report to the Educational Testing Service, 1974).

10. Ibid., 140.

What is the interested nonexpert to believe? Is illiteracy a serious problem or a relatively minor one? Are the trends up or down? Are the people with the apocalyptic visions and those with the rose-colored glasses looking at the same information differently, or is each commentator mustering the data selectively?

The purpose of this review is to set recent debates on adult literacy and school reading performance in the longer-range perspective of the past hundred years. Writers engaged in policy debates rarely have projected literacy trends back more than twenty years. Some imply that before the test-score decline of the 1960s and 1970s there was a golden age of literacy, a high plateau of impressive test scores, rigorous standards, and old-fashioned academic schooling. Most have focused on an alleged decline of standards in the rebellious 1960s and the deleterious effects of television.

Historians have been little help in providing perspective on this issue. As we noted in chapter 1, they have concentrated on the advent of printing in sixteenth-century Europe and the expansion of literacy in late-eighteenth- and nineteenth-century industrial societies, including the United States. For the twentieth century, there exist only a few summary articles about United States literacy trends. This chapter is a first step toward a history of reading ability in the United States since 1880. It takes a hard look at the quality of the data and the arguments of previous scholars, and it concludes that much of the available data is unreliable, unrepresentative, or noncomparable over time. The attempt to determine trends is therefore perilous, but there is much to learn and the answers are important to contemporary policy debates.

People often think of literacy as a hierarchical, measurable skill, but recent work by linguists and anthropologists suggests otherwise. Literacy is elusive, complex. Its study requires careful definitions. Because this chapter reviews previous measurement efforts, we are to some degree prisoners of previous definitions. But we can clarify literacy trends by categorizing earlier measurement efforts under different concepts of literacy.

We distinguish between literacy skills as they are taught and measured in schools (usually called "reading achievement") and literacy skills that are practiced outside of schools (usually called "functional literacy"). The relationship between these two sets of skills is particularly difficult to define. Some commentators assume that there is an obvious, direct relationship: if the schools don't teach students how to read effectively, the students will not be able to read as adults. Other writers, however, have argued that school literacy and out-of-school literacy are quite different. School reading is embodied in a sequential curriculum, and children are tested frequently as they move up through a hierarchy of graded skills and content. At the lowest level—which we call rudimentary literacy—the student learns to read and understand simple words already in his or her speaking vocabulary. At higher levels, the school reader learns not only more vocabulary and concepts but also more complex inferential and interpretive skills. Functional literacy outside the school is less structured, less hierarchical. It involves a greater variety of materials and settings and is often used to accomplish practical tasks.[11]

In spite of these clear differences, reading tasks required in school overlap a great deal with those presented in everyday life. Reading achievement thus has an important bearing on the functional literacy of adults. In this chapter we discuss both, using a spatial metaphor to organize our review. We treat the acquisition of initial literacy and subsequent grade-level achievement—the focus of the school—as the "vertical" dimension; the measurement of diverse reading tasks from everyday life—functional literacy—is characterized as the "horizontal" dimension. This metaphor is useful because the two dimensions intersect: at any given grade-level ability of reading achievement, the application of those skills can be traced horizontally out into some nonschool situations. Conversely, in any real-world setting, one can ask how demanding the reading tasks are on a vertical scale.

Later in this chapter we address briefly the differences in literacy that correlate with gender and race. For most of the chapter, however, we forgo analysis of literacy by groups, not because the differences are unimportant, but because the conceptual and measurement problems involved in rating literacy over time at the aggregate level are so complicated that they demand our primary consideration. Also, this chapter and chapter 4 address the current debate about declining literacy skills, which has also focused on national averages, not group differences.

The Entry Level

Attempts to study rudimentary literacy rates in the United States began with the Census Bureau. In each decennial census from 1840 through 1930 and in sampling surveys since, individuals were asked whether they could read and write in any language. The bureau

11. David R. Olson, "The Languages of Instruction: The Literate Bias of Schooling," in *Schooling and the Acquisition of Knowledge,* ed. R. C. Anderson, R. J. Spiro, and W. E. Montague (Hillsdale, N.J.: Lawrence Erlbaum, 1977); James T. Guthrie and Irwin S. Kirsch, "The Emergent Perspective on Literacy," *Phi Delta Kappan* 65 (1984):351–55; Larry Mikulecky and Jeanne Ehlinger, "The Influence of Metacognitive Aspects of Literacy on Job Performance of Electronics Technicians," *Journal of Reading Behavior* 18 (1986):41–62; Shirley Brice Heath, "The Functions and Uses of Literacy," *Journal of Communication* 30 (1980):123–33.

generally classified as illiterate those who said they were "not able both to read and to write a simple message either in English or any other language."[12] This simple-message definition comes close to our definition of rudimentary literacy, that is, the ability to read and understand simple words that are already in the reader's spoken vocabulary. The record shows a tremendous reduction in self-reported illiteracy over the past century. In 1870, 20 percent of the population considered themselves illiterate, whereas in 1979 only .6 percent did. Among youths aged fourteen to twenty-four, the self-reported illiteracy rate in 1979 was only .19 percent.[13] Self-reported illiteracy, then, had declined to very low percentages, although the absolute numbers of self-reported illiterates remained large—822,000 of those fourteen and older.[14]

What are we to make of the validity of this record? For more than one hundred years, the Census Bureau did not administer literacy tests. It relied instead upon respondents describing their own literacy status, although the census never defined precisely what the bureau meant by literacy.[15] This self-reporting is clearly the fundamental weakness of the U.S. Census literacy data. As a 1919 *New York Times* editorial stated, "nothing could be more inexact or humorous."[16] Writing for the Census Bureau in 1967, however, John Folger and Charles Nam claimed that individuals' self-reporting mirrors their performance on literacy tests. On the basis of two studies, they concluded that census reports of literacy are "generally accurate."[17] It should be noted, however, that both studies were conducted abroad, not in the United States, and that one actually demonstrated the inaccuracy, not the accuracy, of self-reporting.[18]

Part of the problem is deliberate misreporting. Understandably, illiterate people have difficulty admitting their inability to read and write.

12. U.S. Bureau of the Census, *Illiteracy in the United States: November 1969*, Current Population Reports, ser. P-20, no. 217 (Washington, D.C.: Government Printing Office, 1971), 5.

13. U.S. Bureau of the Census, *Ancestry and Language in the United States: November 1979*, Current Population Reports, ser. P-23, no. 116 (Washington, D.C.: Government Printing Office, 1982), 17.

14. Ibid., 5.

15. See Census Instruction, in Folger and Nam, *Education of the American Population*, 249–52; U.S. Bureau of the Census, *Illiteracy in the United States: October 1947*, Current Population Reports, ser. P-20, no. 20 (Washington, D.C.: Government Printing Office, 1948); U.S. Bureau of the Census, *Literacy and Educational Attainment: March 1959*, Current Population Reports, ser. P-20, no. 99 (Washington, D.C.: Government Printing Office, 1960); Bureau of the Census, *Illiteracy in the United States: November 1969;* and Bureau of the Census, *Ancestry and Language in the United States: November 1979.*

16. Editorial, *New York Times,* February 19, 1919, p. 12, col. 4.

17. Folger and Nam, *Education of the American Population,* 129 n. 1.

18. Gerald S. Coles, "U.S. Literacy Statistics: How to Succeed with Hardly Trying," *Literacy Work* 5 (1976):47–70.

In some cases they have developed elaborate methods of concealment and will even hide their illiteracy from other illiterates.[19] Given that reading levels and literacy demands have increased greatly during this century, the stigma attached to illiteracy also may have increased, making false reporting more likely.

Nevertheless, some recent tests of functional literacy suggest that the level of outright, utter illiteracy is now very low. Educational improvements of the past one hundred years support this finding. Extensive basic literacy training through New Deal agencies and the military, plus continually expanding public schooling and programs in adult basic education, created major gains in the attainment of literacy. These efforts helped eliminate much of the nation's illiteracy, as the census record suggests. Although the percentage of self-reported totally illiterate people is small, the *number* of people remains high, and as we will discuss, millions of other people still have trouble with simple reading tasks. What, then, are the trends in reading performance among the literate? Our information comes from then-and-now studies and standardized test-score trends.

The Vertical Dimension

Then-and-Now Studies

Then-and-now studies aim to satisfy our curiosity as to whether students today are performing better than their grade- and age-level counterparts of yesterday. Such studies involve giving a group of students today the same test that was given to a comparable group of students years earlier. This is not a new idea; one of the first then-and-now studies was performed in 1906, when John Riley gave all ninth-grade students in Springfield, Massachusetts, the same tests that had been administered to ninth graders in 1846. Students in 1906 did much better on these tests, which covered spelling, arithmetic, and geography.[20]

Previous reviewers used then-and-now studies as evidence for their claim that reading performance steadily improved from the early part of the century through the mid-1960s.[21] The historical record, however, is

19. Howard E. Freeman and Gene G. Kassenbaum, "The Illiterate in American Society: Some General Hypotheses," *Social Forces* 34 (1956):372–73; Jonathan Kozol, *Illiterate America* (New York: Anchor/Doubleday, 1985).

20. The Riley study is described in Farr, Tuinman, and Rowls, *Reading Achievement in the United States*, 17.

21. Paul Copperman, *The Literacy Hoax: The Decline of Reading, Writing, and Learning in the Public Schools and What We Can Do about It* (New York: William Morrow, 1978), 32–34; Farr, Tuinman, and Rowls, *Reading Achievement in the United States*.

ambiguous. Of the thirteen local then-and-now studies that measured reading during this period, seven did not indicate any clear-cut improvement. Of the seven, two showed declines (Boss; Burke and Anderson) three exhibited statistically insignificant gains (Krugman and Wrightstone; Finch & Gillenwater; Bradfield), and two showed mixed results (Grant, Parlow) (see table 3.1). Eight of the eleven state and national then-and-now studies provided more support, but three showed no improvement. One had declines, one mixed results, and one lacked comparable data (see table 3.2).

Researchers also used then-and-now studies to argue about the seriousness of the test-score decline of the late 1960s and early 1970s. Some claimed that, in spite of this decline, the 1970s students were doing as well as those of the 1940s and 1950s, whereas others argued that the decline was so marked that modern-day students had fallen seriously behind. One study supported the optimistic viewpoint;[22] two studies were more pessimistic.[23] Even superficially, therefore, then-and-now studies provide weak evidence for sweeping claims about changes in national performance. More important, their execution was so poor that conclusions about rises and declines are unwarranted. There are several problems.

First, then-and-now studies are riddled with problems of comparability. Because few researchers investigated the social composition of their tested groups, we cannot rule out the possibility that the higher achievement of one group was due to its higher social-class background. This problem is particularly acute in local then-and-now studies, which usually focused on reading achievement in only one city. With ten to twenty years between testings, the chances are great that a city's social composition had, in fact, changed. In only two local studies did researchers ensure that the two groups had similar socioeconomic status, but both of these involved such small groups that generalizations were unjustified.[24]

State studies, with one exception, spanned even more time than did the local studies, from twenty to thirty-two years, yet none of the researchers matched their groups for social class. Given the population migrations and economic transformations that have occurred during this century, this longer time span virtually ensured that a state's composi-

22. Farr, Fay, and Negley, *Then and Now.*
23. Jane Elligett and Thomas S. Tocco, "Reading Achievement in 1979 vs. Achievement in the Fifties," *Phi Delta Kappan* (June 1980):698–99; Alvin C. Eurich and Gayla A. Kraetsch, "A Fifty-Year Comparison of University of Minnesota Freshmen's Reading Performance," *Journal of Educational Psychology* 73 (1982):660–65.
24. See table 3.1 and the studies cited there, which are discussed in Farr, Tuinman, and Rowls, *Reading Achievement in the United States,* chap. 1.

Table 3.1. Local Then-and-Now Studies of Reading Achievement

Study	Then	Now	Grade	Location	Number of Students		Academic Areas	Results (in Months)
					Then	Now		
Reading Skills								
Grant	1916	1949	—	Grand Rapids, Mich.	5 schools	5 schools	Comprehension, oral reading, speed of silent reading	+, =, =
Boss	1916	1938	1–8	St. Louis, Mo.	8,923	1,156 "Measured Sample"	Oral and silent reading	—
Woods	1924	1934	6	Los Angeles, Calif.	33 elementary schools	33 elementary schools	Reading	+6
Worcester & Kline	1921	1947	3–8	Lincoln, Neb.	5,690	5,106	Silent reading	+
Davis & Morgan	1927	1938	6	Santa Monica, Calif.	Grade 6	Grade 6	Reading	+2
Krugman & Wrightstone	1935–41	1944–46	6–9, 11	New York City	> 290,000	> 242,000	Reading	+, but n.s.
Tiegs	Before 1945	After 1945	4–11	6 communities in 7 states	115,000	115,000	Vocabulary, reading comprehension, total reading	−1, +1.3, +1.7

Finch & Gillenwater	1931	1948	6	Springfield, Mo.	144	198	Reading	+, but n.s.
Burke & Anderson	1939	1950	1–6	Ottawa, Kans.	162	216	Reading (+5 other subjects)	−
Miller & Lanton	1932	1952	3–5, 8	Evanston, Ill.	1,828	1,828	3d: reading completion, paragraph meaning, vocabulary; 4th, 5th, 8th: reading comprehension, vocabulary	Ranged from +2.5 to +8
Partlow	1933	1953	5–8	St. Catharines, Ont.	All pupils in city	All pupils in city	Reading completion, vocabulary	5th–8th reading: +, +, =, = Vocabulary: +, −, −, −
Fridan	1940	1956	1–7	Lafayette, Ind.	All pupils in one parochial school	All pupils in one parochial school	Reading	1st–5th, 7th: +1.1 to +6 6th: −8.5
Bradfield	1928	1964	5	Rural Calif.	35	51	Reading	+, but n.s.

Sources: Data for the studies are from Farr, Tuinman, and Rowls, *Reading Achievement in the United States,* and Grant, *Comparative Study of Achievement.*

Notes: − means decrease; + means increase; = means same; n.s. means not significant. If no numeral is given, the amount of change was unspecified.

Table 3.2. Statewide and National Then-and-Now Studies of Reading Achievement

Study	Then	Now	Grade	Location	Number of Students		Academic Areas	Results
					Then	Now		
Statewide								
Tyler (1930)	1924	1930	HS	Ohio	Selected high schools	Same	Physics, math, English	Mixed
In Witty & Coomer (1951)	1915	1947	HS	New York	Statewide	Same	NY Regents	+: 71% pass rate to 84%
Sligo, in Armbruster (1977)	1934	1954	HS	Iowa	Selected high schools	Same	Algebra, general science, English, history	—
In Farr, Tuinman, & Rowls (1974)	1940	1965	3–8	Iowa	38,000	Similar	Reading	+ .2 of a grade to 1 grade or more
Farr, Fay, & Negley (1978)	1944	1976	6, 10	Indiana	Volunteer schools 15,206 11,424	Stratified sample 8,000 7,000	Reading (average of various subtests)	6th: −2 months 10th: −2 percentile pts.; after age adjustment: +8 months, +10 pts.
Eurich & Kraetsch (1982)	1928	1978	First year college	Univ. of Minnesota	1,313 First-year students 4,191 HS seniors	865 incoming students	Paragraph comprehension subtest; vocabulary, reading comprehension & rate	—

					National			
Gates (1961)	1937	1957	1–6	National	107,000	31,000 EQ: 12 school districts	Reading (average of various subtests)	−.1 to −.3 grades; after age adjustment, 4th-6th: +4 to +6.7 months
Tuddenham (1948)	1918	1943	Young men	National	WWI large sample of white recruits	WWII representative draftee sample	Army Alpha	+33 percentile pts.
Yerkes (1921), Gray (1956)	WWI	WWII	Young men	National	Millions of draftees	Millions of draftees	Rejection rates, illiteracy, years of schooling	Noncomparable
Bloom (1956)	1943	1955	12	National	See text	EQ	English composition, social studies, natural science, literature, math	+2 to +8 percentile pts.
Elligett & Tocco (1980)	1950s	1979	6	Pinellas Co., Fla.	—	18 6th-grade classrooms EQ: 1 school district	Reading	−5 to −10 months

Note: − = decrease; + = increase; EQ = Equating Study.

tion had changed. Farr, Fay, and Negley, for example, found that between 1944 and 1976 Indiana's population had become more urban, workers were increasingly likely to hold service as opposed to laboring jobs, adults had become better educated, and the proportion of blacks and Hispanics had doubled.[25] Even national then-and-now studies may have involved noncomparable groups. Immigration could have increased the number of linguistic-minority students, for example, which might lower scores. In spite of this possibility, none of the researchers checked the nativity or language status of the groups they compared.

Comparability also was affected by changing educational policies. As states raised the legal school-leaving age, for example, the proportion of teenagers who stayed in school to graduate steadily increased. One might presume that this increased the proportion of lower-achieving students, thus making a maintenance or increase in scores more impressive. On the other hand, dropping out of school was more acceptable before the raising of mandatory school-attendance age, and some students did so for nonacademic reasons, such as helping to support their families, joining the military, or getting jobs and being independent.[26] Researchers conducting high school then-and-now studies failed to consider the net effect of these patterns.

The second major problem with then-and-now studies is that they are not nationally representative. Mary Fridan, for example, studied one parochial elementary school in Indiana; H. R. Partlow studied schools in one Canadian city; Robert Bradfield studied one fifth-grade class in a rural California town. The state studies are hardly more representative, coming mostly from Midwestern rural or semirural states with few minorities and no major cities. Even the national studies are not completely representative. Benjamin Bloom, for example, administered the General Educational Development (GED) test to 1943 and 1955 high-school seniors during their final two months of school.[27] With high school graduation rates at only around 50 percent in the 1940s, this meant that many students were not included.[28] Nor did Bloom sample technical, vocational, private, or black high schools.[29] His report of a slight increase in achievement from 1943 to 1955 must be viewed as a measure of the performance of white students who attended public schools and completed their senior year.

25. Farr, Fay, and Negley, *Then and Now*, 81.

26. Ibid., 85–86.

27. Benjamin S. Bloom, "The 1955 Normative Study of the Tests of General Educational Development," *School Review* 64 (1956):110–24.

28. U.S. Bureau of the Census, *Historical Statistics of the United States, Colonial Times to 1970: Part 1* (Washington, D.C.: Government Printing Office, 1975), 379.

29. Bloom, "1955 Normative Study," 111.

A third limitation of then-and now studies, for our purposes, is that they often measured skills other than reading comprehension. Although the first six local studies listed in table 3.1 included grammar and spelling, they emphasized such subjects as arithmetic and geography. The Indiana study included speed-reading tests, "comprehension" tests better described as short-term memory tests (students had to answer ten questions in two minutes about reading passages they could no longer see), and sentence-meaning tests that included questions testing prior knowledge or requiring a moral judgment. Among these questions were the following: "Is treason to one's country punishable by death?" "Is it necessary for the President of the United States to be a citizen?" "Does allegiance to one's country imply loyalty?"[30] These unusual questions make overall results from that study suspect. Read Tuddenham's comparisons of World War I and II draftees based on the U.S. Army Alpha test, which included mathematical word problems, number-pattern guessing, and questions testing general knowledge and "common sense."[31] The test's cultural and class biases are apparent to even the casual reader. For example, although its creator, Robert Yerkes, said that the Alpha test measured "native intellectual ability," it required responses to such statements as: "Rosa Bonheur is famous as a poet, painter, composer, or sculptor"; and "The Wyandotte is a kind of horse, fowl, cattle, or granite."[32]

A fourth major problem in then-and-now research was whether results should be presented by age or grade. We illustrate this problem by discussing one of the better-known studies, in which Arthur Gates renormed his 1957 reading test in order to compare students in 1957 with those who took the test in 1937.[33] A renorming study—or "equating" study, as it is better described—differs from a traditional then-and-now study in that two different tests are involved. In equating, a researcher presents both the old and the new version of a test to a group of present-day students. Their performance on the tests establishes a scale for converting scores from one test to the other. Using this scale, researchers can convert the nation's average score on the current test to its equivalent score on the old one to see whether it is higher or lower than the old national average. (Thus the Elligett and Tocco study is classified as a

30. Farr, Fay, and Negley, *Then and Now,* 35–36.
31. Read D. Tuddenham, "Soldier Intelligence in World Wars I and II," *American Psychologist* 3 (1948):54–56.
32. Clarence S. Yoakum and Robert M. Yerkes, *Army Mental Tests* (New York: Henry Holt, 1920), 16, 206, 218. See also Stephen J. Gould, *The Mismeasure of Man* (New York: W. W. Norton, 1981), 199–200.
33. Arthur I. Gates, *Reading Attainment in Elementary Schools: 1957 and 1937* (New York: Teachers College, 1961).

national study [table 3.2] even though the researchers only tested students in one school district.)

Using such a procedure, Gates converted 1957 norms to their 1937 equivalents. He found that the 1937 students outperformed their 1957 counterparts by as much as 4.5 months, with margins increasing as grade level increased. Initially, these results suggested that reading performance was better in the 1930s, but Gates noted that students in 1937 were older at each grade level due to stricter promotion policies. When he compared students of the same age, he found the 1957 students outperformed those of 1937. Gates argued that the proper comparison is by age, not grade, because a student's grade is an artifact of the time period's educational policies, particularly those relating to school-entering age and retention policies. We agree. By this standard, then, reading performance was better in 1957 than in 1937, at least for the elementary grades. But no sweeping conclusions should be reached. Even after age adjustments, first and second graders showed no difference in performance, and third graders differed by only 1 to 1.5 months. Furthermore, because there could have been dips or peaks in the scores between the two testings, any assertion of steady improvement was unsupported by available evidence. Our reservations about using equating studies to determine national trends are described in a later section.

Farr, Fay, and Negley also explored the age issue in their then-and-now study (see table 3.2).[34] They found that in Indiana sixth and tenth graders scored about the same in 1944 and 1976, yet analysis of census data showed that sixth graders in 1970 were ten months younger and tenth graders fourteen months younger than their 1940 counterparts. After adjusting scores for the age difference, Farr, Fay, and Negley concluded that reading performance was better in 1976. Their age adjustment, however, was arbitrary. The researchers simply added ten months to the scores of the 1976 sixth graders, presuming that they would have gained one extra month for every additional month in school. This was unlikely. Sixth graders in 1976 were already near the top of the performance spectrum, so such large improvements were improbable. Finally, on the one test that measured what most educators now think of as reading comprehension, the paragraph-comprehension subtest, tenth graders in 1976 showed no gain in performance even after Farr, Fay, and Negley adjusted for age.[35] The best that can be concluded from this study is that Indiana students in the 1970s were probably scoring about the same as Indiana students did in the 1940s.

34. Farr, Fay, and Negley, *Then and Now.*
35. Ibid., 27.

Given all of these difficulties, what can one conclude from then-and-now studies about reading trends? If one takes age into account, more of the tests showed gains than declines, whereas many others showed approximately equal performance rates. But few of the studies were nationally representative. And the magnitude of the changes, up or down, was usually half a school year or less—a shift that can easily be attributed to the margin of error caused by the problems we have described.

Our educated guess is that schoolchildren of the same age and socioeconomic status have been performing at similar levels throughout most of the twentieth century (we consider the 1970s in detail in chapter 4). But we also caution that then-and-now studies are fraught with design and interpretation problems; reliance upon them to support arguments about literacy trends is unjustified.

Achievement-Test Score Trends

Six major reviews of test-score trends were published in the mid- to late 1970s.[36] Most reviewers concluded that twentieth-century reading performance had improved steadily until the mid-1960s, but that since then, for all grades above the third or fourth, it had been declining dramatically.[37] The declines were considered greater at higher grade levels.[38] Two of the six studies offered different conclusions. Frank Armbruster suggested that reading performance had dropped somewhat in the early 1920s and 1940s before declining steeply after 1965, whereas Farr, Tuinman, and Rowls suggested that the post-1965 decline was only slight and not the dramatic decrease that others had suggested.[39]

The first claim, that of a steady improvement to the mid-1960s, was based on an uncritical acceptance of then-and-now studies, test renormings of the early 1960s, and state trends in achievement tests. As we have

36. Farr, Tuinman, and Rowls, *Reading Achievement in the United States;* Annegret Harnischfeger and David Wiley, *Achievement Test Score Decline: Do We Need to Worry?* (St. Louis: CEMREL, 1975); T. A. Cleary and S. A. McCandless, "Summary of Score Changes (In Other Texts)," in Advisory Panel on the Scholastic Aptitude Test Score Decline, *On Further Examination* (New York: College Entrance Examination Board, 1977), appendix; Frank E. Armbruster, *Our Children's Crippled Future: How American Education Has Failed* (New York: Quadrangle Books, 1977); Copperman, *Literacy Hoax;* Copperman, "The Achievement Decline of the 1970s," *Phi Delta Kappan* (June 1979):736–39.

37. Copperman, *Literacy Hoax,* 29; Armbruster, *Our Children's Crippled Future,* 4.

38. Harnischfeger and Wiley, *Achievement Test Score Decline,* 115; Cleary and McCandless, "Summary of Score Changes," 1; Copperman, *Literacy Hoax,* 44, 49; Armbruster, *Our Children's Crippled Future,* 40.

39. Farr, Tuinman, and Rowls, *Reading Achievement in the United States,* 139.

seen, the poor quality of the then-and-now studies does not substantiate the reviewers' claims of a general rise in United States achievement.

Furthermore, William Schrader's comprehensive study of the early 1960s renorming data provided only equivocal support for a mid-1950s to mid-1960s rise in achievement. For grades five through eight Schrader found an increase of eight percentile points, which he described as "small, but by no means trivial."[40] He noted, however, that the test publishers had excluded private schools in their 1950s testing, but included them in the 1960s. Given the selectivity and higher achievement of private schools, Schrader suggested, this may account for as much as half of the apparent improvement.[41] At the high-school level, he found mixed results. On the School and College Ability Tests (SCAT) he found a nine percentile point improvement between 1957 and 1967, but private schools had again been added to the second norming group. By contrast, the renormings of the Preliminary Scholastic Aptitude Test (PSAT), 1960 and 1966, and the Iowa Tests of Educational Development (ITED), 1957 and 1962, which covered the same types of schools in both years, showed stable scores over time.

Finally, the reviewers' data were too sketchy to support any firm conclusions. Paul Copperman, for example, cited only three states to demonstrate that achievement rose from the mid-1950s to the early 1960s. Undermining his case further, Idaho and New Hampshire provided data for only one grade, and most of West Virginia's data collecting did not begin until 1964 or 1965. Annegret Harnischfeger and David Wiley cited studies of only two states, Minnesota and Iowa, focusing on only one grade in each.

The case for a major test-score decline beginning in the mid-1960s is also problematic. The socioeconomic profile of students taking the SATs was changing, a factor that undoubtedly contributed to the decline. On some achievement tests, however, scores remained stable or improved in the 1960s, particularly at the high-school level. The period 1970 to 1978 does show a dramatic downturn in junior-high and high-school scores on most major tests. Yet even in the 1970s several important tests showed no declines, and some of the decline in the other tests can be explained by changing demographics. A popular interpretation of the test-score decline is that faced with the disruptions of the late 1960s, students lost their motivation, teachers lost their nerve, and schools across the country abandoned their academic standards, a trend that undermined achievement. Recovery in the 1980s, according to this interpretation, resulted from renewed high standards.

40. William B. Schrader, *Test Data as Social Indicators* (Princeton, N.J.: Educational Testing Service, 1968), 18.

41. Ibid., 22.

However, as we shall argue in more detail in the next chapter, the timing does not support the "permissive 1960s" interpretation. High-school students didn't start to earn lower scores until after the worst of the disruptions were over, and that trend continued into the late 1970s, well after the permissive reforms had been abandoned and back-to-basics embraced. Furthermore, we question how widespread permissive educational practices actually were, and how widespread their influence; the empirical evidence suggests that elective courses, open campuses, and open classrooms were in limited use and had a limited effect on national test scores. Although the standards and attitudes of educators may have influenced trends, other nonschool factors, such as television, drugs, and divorce, may also have played a role in declining school achievement, where it occurred.

The evidence for a massive, consistent skill decline, then, is more mixed than some critics claimed; the contradictory evidence is not easily explained; and the causes of test-score declines appear to be more complex than the permissive-schooling thesis suggests. We must also put the decline into its historical context. When interpreted in terms of the tremendous gains that have been achieved in educational attainment during the past several decades, the decline seems much less substantial. The median educational level of the adult population (twenty-five years and older) rose two full years between 1960 and 1980, from 10.5 to 12.5. Between 1940 and 1980 the median level rose nearly four full years, from 8.6 to 12.5.[42] Even if one accepts the notion of a skills decline, a decline of half a year in certain subjects on certain tests at certain grade levels is minor compared to these tremendous gains in educational attainment—more children getting more years of schooling.

In any case, the test-score decline ended in the late 1970s and early 1980s. Scores leveled off or began rising about 1978 on standardized reading and math tests and on college entrance exams, such as the SAT and American College Test (ACT). In spite of rising test scores, there still is a pressing need to improve the basic reading skills of many children and the critical reading skills of all students. Before educators compliment themselves on recent improvements in test scores, they must examine how these reading skills—taught and measured in schools—translate into performance on tasks outside of school. Are the failure rates on real-world reading performance tests more alarming than those on school achievement tests? Have society's demands for literacy skills overwhelmed the schools' ability to produce readers who can be effective workers and citizens?

42. W. V. Grant and L. J. Eiden, *Digest of Educational Statistics* (Washington, D.C.: Government Printing Office, 1982), table 10, 16.

The Horizontal Dimension

Functional literacy outside the school has been estimated in four ways: by using school attainment as a proxy, by administering tests of applied reading skills, by comparing a population's reading grade level to that of common materials, and by investigating job literacy requirements. In describing these four approaches, we pay attention to how functional literacy was defined and how accurately it has been measured. We are interested in answering two major questions: What proportion of the population has attained functional literacy in the United States today, and how has this changed over time?

By functional literacy we mean the reading and writing skills necessary to understand and use the printed material one normally encounters in work, leisure, and citizenship. We distinguish functional literacy from functional competency, which also includes the problem-solving and mathematical skills needed to complete everyday societal tasks.

Educational Attainment as a Proxy for Functional Literacy

The Civilian Conservation Corps seems to have coined the term "functional literacy" in the 1930s.[43] They defined it as three or more years of schooling, reasoning that a person with that much schooling could read the essential printed material of daily life. The level of education considered necessary to be functionally literate has risen steadily since then. During World War II the army used the term to refer to a fourth-grade educational level and, until manpower demands became overwhelming, rejected recruits with less schooling. In 1947, the Census Bureau applied the term "functional illiterates" to those with fewer than five years of schooling and ceased questioning those with more schooling about rudimentary literacy.[44] In 1952, the bureau raised the functional-literacy definition to the sixth grade,[45] and by 1960, the U.S. Office of Education was using eighth grade as the standard.[46] Finally, by the late 1970s, some noted authorities were describing functional literacy in terms of high-school completion.[47]

43. Folger and Nam, *Education of the American Population,* 126.

44. Bureau of the Census, *Illiteracy in the United States, October 1947,* 3; Eli Ginzberg and Douglas W. Bray, *The Uneducated* (New York: Columbia University Press, 1953).

45. U.S. Bureau of the Census, *School Enrollment, Educational Attainment, and Illiteracy: October, 1952,* Current Population Reports, ser. P-20, no. 45 (Washington, D.C.: Government Printing Office, 1953), 6, 9. 10.

46. Fisher, *Functional Literacy and the Schools,* 38; David Harman, "Illiteracy: An Overview," *Harvard Educational Review* 40 (1970):226–43.

47. Carmen St. John Hunter and David Harman, *Adult Illiteracy in the United States: A Report to the Ford Foundation* (New York: McGraw-Hill, 1979), 27; John B. Carroll and Jeanne C. Chall, (New York: McGraw-Hill, 1975), 8.

Each of these successively steeper criteria assumed that people who reach a certain grade have acquired enough reading skills to function in society. This is a shaky generalization when applied to individual cases, but it seems reasonable that a substantial increase in school attainment would raise the average reading ability of a population. Indeed, school-attainment rates have risen continuously. In 1910, for example, 23.8 percent of the population over twenty-five had completed fewer than five years of schooling, whereas in 1980, only 3.3 percent had.[48] Among those aged twenty-five and twenty-nine in 1980, the rate was only .7 percent, indicating that functional illiteracy by this 1910 standard had been virtually eliminated among the younger generation.

However, following the same grade-level standard over the course of the century makes little sense. The literacy skills demanded in 1980 are more complex than in 1910. If we accept the government's changing grade-level definitions of functional literacy, we discover that school-attainment levels may not have risen fast enough to keep pace with rising functional-literacy demands. In 1930, about 88 percent of the adult population had attained a third-grade education or more; in 1950, 88.9 percent had a fifth-grade education or more; by 1960, only 78 percent had at least an eighth-grade education; and by 1980, only 68.7 percent had completed high school.[49] However, if we use a more conservative standard for 1980—an eighth-grade education—functional literacy has increased slightly in the past fifty years—from 88 percent (completing third grade) in 1930 to 90.3 percent (completing eighth grade) in 1980.

There are three limitations to this approach to estimating functional literacy. First, the line between functional literacy and illiteracy is drawn somewhat arbitrarily, and authorities rarely explain why they chose a particular cutoff. Second, drawing a line means that functional literacy is conceptualized in dichotomous terms: a person is either functionally literate or illiterate. This makes little sense. A person who has completed eighth grade is not suddenly able to function effectively in society while the person with only seven years of schooling is unable to cope. There are gradations in the ability to function, and a person's performance varies by setting and task. Finally, setting educational attainment as a measure of functional literacy equates schooling with learning. Many people, however, perform at a level below the grade they reached, so the number who are functionally illiterate may be greater than the school-attainment figures suggest. A proper assessment of

48. Folger and Nam, *Education of the American Population,* 133; Grant and Eiden, *Digest of Educational Statistics,* table 10, 16.
49. Folger and Nam, *Education of the American Population,* 133; Grant and Eiden, *Digest of Educational Statistics,* table 10, 16.

functional literacy requires testing the population on functional-literacy tasks.

Direct Tests of Functional Literacy

Guy Buswell at the University of Chicago made the pioneering effort in testing functional literacy in 1937.[50] Buswell tested 897 Chicago-area adult residents on such tasks as finding prices in a mail-order catalog and telephone numbers in a directory, and he concluded that their performance varied by education and reading habits. Following Buswell's effort, work in the area lapsed until the 1970s, when five major national studies with scientifically drawn samples were conducted.[51] Investigators tested such skills as reading a map, using a dictionary, understanding classified ads, deciphering train schedules, and comprehending product labels. Since then, two additional national assessments have been conducted. The U.S. Department of Education reported in 1986 the results of a 1982 study, and the National Assessment of Educational Progress published in 1986 an investigation of the functional literacy of young adults based on 1985 data.[52]

The functional-illiteracy rates reported in these seven national studies ranged from 3 percent to 54 percent and prompted a decade of debate about the magnitude of America's literacy problems. The variations in findings resulted from differences in the tasks that were tested and in the levels at which functional literacy was set. The lowest rate, 3 percent, which corresponded to 4.3 million functionally illiterate adults, was derived from a series of exercises in which participants were asked to fill out such application forms as that for a driver's license.[53] A relatively relaxed standard was set, one that allowed individuals to make several mistakes before being labeled functionally illiterate. The highest rate, 54 percent, was derived from a test of functional "competency," not just literacy, and included "marginally competent" adults as well as those

50. Guy T. Buswell, *How Adults Read,* Supplementary Educational Monographs, no. 45 (Chicago: University of Chicago, Department of Education, 1937).

51. Louis Harris and Associates, Inc., *Survival Literacy Study* (Washington, D.C.: National Reading Council, 1970); Louis Harris and Associates, Inc., *The 1971 National Reading Difficulty Index: A Study of Functional Reading Ability in the United States, for the National Reading Center* (Washington, D.C.: National Reading Center, 1971); Charles J. Gadway and H. A. Wilson, *Functional Literacy: Basic Reading Performance* (Denver, Colo.: Education Commission of the States, 1976); Richard T. Murphy, *Adult Functional Reading Study* (Princeton, N.J.: Educational Testing Service, 1973); Adult Performance Level Project, *Final Report: The Adult Performance Level Study* (Washington, D.C.: U.S. Office of Education, 1977).

52. U.S. Department of Education, *Update on Adult Illiteracy* (Washington, D.C.: Government Printing Office, 1986); Kirsch and Jungeblut, *Literacy: Final Report.*

53. Harris and Associates, *Survival Literacy Study.*

deemed functionally "incompetent."[54] This result was the basis for Secretary of Education Bell's testimony to Congress in 1982 that as many as 72 million adults were not literate enough to function effectively in society.[55]

The seriousness of the functional-literacy problem obviously depends upon the estimate one chooses to accept. Some critics argued that the estimates of people not functionally literate were greatly exaggerated, others that they were too low. In the section that follows, we describe the seven tests and their results, explore the major criticisms, and, finally, review the scant evidence concerning historical trends.

Descriptions of the Functional-Literacy Tests

The first national study of functional literacy in the 1970s was conducted in 1970 by Louis Harris and Associates for the National Reading Council, a group appointed by President Richard Nixon.[56] Called the Survival Literacy Study, it tested the ability of people sixteen years and older to read, understand, and complete application forms. Of the five forms, one requested personal identification information, and the others were applications for a driver's license, a bank loan, public assistance, and Medicaid (see figure 3.1). The researchers established three criterion levels. Those who answered 70 percent or less correctly, the "low survival" group, were considered functionally illiterate. Those who answered 90 percent or more correctly, the "likely survival" group, were considered functionally literate. In between were the "questionable survival" (70 to 80 percent correct) and "marginal survival" (80 to 90 percent correct) groups. The intermediate categories softened the problem of arbitrary and dichotomous definition.

The Survival Literacy Study showed that an average of 3 percent of the population over age sixteen were functionally illiterate, that is, they scored below 70 percent correct on each of the five forms. The percentages ranged from less than .5 percent on the public assistance form to 9 percent on the Medicaid form. In absolute numbers, this meant that 4.3 million people sixteen years of age and older were functionally illiterate. On average, 13 percent fell short of the functional-literacy level of 90 percent correct. In absolute numbers, this translated into an average of 18.5 million people who were in the low, questionable, or marginal survival categories.

The 1971 National Reading Difficulty Index, also conducted by Harris and Associates for the National Reading Council, was similar to the Survival Literacy Study. Researchers asked a national sample of people

54. APL Project, *Final Report*, 31.
55. Congress, House, *Illiteracy and the Scope of the Problem*, 5.
56. Harris and Associates, *Survival Literacy Study*.

1. What is your name? _____
2. What is your weight? _____
3. What is your height? _____ feet, _____ inches
4. What is the color of your eyes? _____
5. List any visual, physical, or mental conditions that
   might impair your ability to drive safely: _____
6. List any previous driver's license issued to you:
   State _____ Year _____
7. How many times have you previously been examined for
   a driver's license? _____
8. What day of the week would be most convenient for you
   to take the driver's examination? _____
9. What hour of the day would be most convenient for you
   to take the driver's examination? _____

PLEASE MAKE SURE ALL QUESTIONS HAVE BEEN
ANSWERED. IF YOU ARE NOT SURE OF AN AN-
SWER TO ANY ITEM, DRAW A LINE THROUGH THE
SPACE PROVIDED FOR THE ANSWER.[a]

Figure 3.1. Survival Literacy Study, Form 3: Application for Driver's License

Source: Harris and Associates, *Survival Literacy Study,* 36.
[a]Drawing a line through the space was considered a correct answer.

sixteen years and older to fill out various official forms, such as application forms for a passport, a driver's license, and a credit card. Researchers
also tested the population's ability to read three types of materials: telephone dialing and rate information, classified housing ads, and classified employment ads (see figure 3.2 for examples).

After weighing the items for difficulty, researchers found that 4 percent of the sample was unable to answer at least 80 percent of the test
correctly, a proportion that amounted to 5.7 million people aged sixteen
years and older nationwide. The researchers concluded that these people
"suffer from serious deficiencies in functional reading ability." Another
11 percent (15.5 million) scored below 90 percent correct, and researchers
concluded that these individuals would need to make a "serious effort" to
handle real-life reading situations.[57]

The third study was conducted by the National Assessment of Educational Progress for the U.S. Office of Education's National Right to Read
Effort.[58] This test, the Mini-Assessment of Functional Literacy, assessed

57. Harris and Associates, *1971 National Reading Difficulty Index,* 57.
58. Gadway and Wilson, *Functional Literacy.*

Example #1: From Telephone Dialing Station

Subjects were given a card with the following information on it:

AREA CODES FOR SOME CITIES

Place	Area Code
Evansville, Indiana	812
Oakland, California	415
Harrison, New York	914
Williamsport, Pennsylvania	717
Austin, Texas	512

Subjects were then asked two questions:
1. Please look at this card and see if you can tell me the area code for Williamsport, Pennsylvania.
2. Please look at the card again and tell me which city you would reach by dialing area code 812.

Example #2: From Housing Ads Section

Subjects were given a card on which was printed the following:

"Attractive house in excellent condition. Three floors. Full basement. Large living room. Backyard with garden. Two-car garage."

Subjects were then asked three questions:
a. Would you tell me how the ad describes the living room of the house?
b. How does the ad describe the backyard?
c. How does the ad describe the basement?

Figure 3.2. Sample Items from the Reading Difficulty Index Study

Source: Harris and Associates, *1971 National Reading Difficulty Index,* 10–12.
 The employment section was similar in nature to the housing ads section; the application form was similar to the Survival Literacy example presented in figure 3.1.

the ability of seventeen-year-old students in 1971, 1974, and 1975 to read word passages, reference materials, and graphic materials, including charts, maps, pictures, coupons, and forms. Mini-Assessment researchers chose the 75 percent correct level as the functional-literacy threshold. They found that 12.6 percent of the nation's seventeen-year-old students did not reach this level and were thus considered functionally illiterate. In the spring of 1983, the President's National Commission on Excellence in Education used this 13 percent teenage illiteracy rate as one of its indicators that the future of the nation was at risk.

 The Adult Functional Reading Study, the fourth test, was organized by the Educational Testing Service.[59] It measured the ability of the population aged sixteen and older to read and understand advertisements, legal documents, instruction, and such listings as telephone directories and train schedules. Because researchers were leery of choosing an arbitrary criterion and recognized the widespread disagreement over what constitutes functional literacy, they decided instead simply to report the average percent correct on each item.[60] Irwin Kirsch and John Guthrie, however, reanalyzed the Adult Functional Reading Study data for two groups of tasks. They found that the average "maintenance" item (items relating to common signs, schedules, or recipes) was answered incorrectly by 18 percent of the population. An average of 25 percent could not handle the occupational items, which dealt with sick leave, discrimination information, and employment applications.[61]

The fifth study, the Adult Performance Level Project, was conducted in 1974 by researchers at the University of Texas sponsored by the U.S. Office of Education.[62] It differed from earlier studies in three major ways. First, it was a study of functional competency rather than functional literacy, so it assessed writing, computation, and problem solving as well as reading. Second, the test designers conceived of competency partly in terms of knowledge, and thus tested information as well as skills. Third, the test was deliberately designed to distinguish between those who were successful in society, that is, those who had completed high school and held white-collar or professional jobs, and those who were unsuccessful, that is, who had fewer than eight years of schooling, were unskilled or unemployed, and lived in poverty. Researchers reported scores in terms of three competency groupings. Adult Performance Level 1 described the group of adults who were "by and large, 'functionally incompetent'"; those in APL 2 were described as "marginally competent"; and those in APL 3 were "most competent."[63] Researchers used a complex statistical analysis to determine the proportion of the population in each category, but they never provided full details. They found that 19.7 percent of the adult population aged eighteen to sixty-five, representing 23 million people, was in the APL 1 category and concluded: "approximately one-fifth of the U.S. adults are 'functionally

59. Murphy, *Adult Functional Reading Study;* Richard T. Murphy, "Assessment of Adult Reading Competence," in *Reading and Career Education,* ed. Duane M. Nielsen and Howard F. Hjelm (Newark, Del.: International Reading Association, 1975).

60. Richard T. Murphy, *Adult Functional Reading Study: Supplement to Final Report* (Princeton, N.J.: Educational Testing Service, 1975); Murphy, "Assessment of Adult Reading Competence."

61. Irwin S. Kirsch and John T. Guthrie, "The Concept and Measurement of Functional Literacy," *Reading Research Quarterly* 13 (1977–78):501.

62. APL Project, *Final Report.*

63. Ibid., 17.

incompetent.'"[64] An additional 33.9 percent of the adult population was categorized in APL 2, or marginally competent. Considering both groups, one could estimate that 53.6 percent of the adult population, or as Secretary Bell estimated for 1982, 72 million adults, had difficulty functioning.

The sixth test of functional literacy, the English Language Proficiency Survey, was conducted in 1982 by the Census Bureau at the behest of the Department of Education.[65] The test, administered to 3,400 persons twenty years or older, was designed to judge how well they could read official notices and applications for public assistance written in English. Twenty-six items were presented in two formats. In the first format individuals had to pick a synonym or an equivalent phrase for each of eight underlined words or phrases. The other format, choosing the best word or phrase to complete a sentence, included eighteen items (see figure 3.3). Using a cutoff of twenty correct answers for literacy, researchers found that 13 percent of the adult population was illiterate. The illiteracy rate for those whose native language was English was 9 percent, whereas among those for whom English was a second language, it was 48 percent.[66]

The seventh study, the Young Adult Literacy Assessment, was conducted by the National Assessment of Educational Progress (NAEP).[67] Researchers tested the performance of English-speaking young adults, twenty-one to twenty-five years old, on three types of material: prose of the sort found at home and at school; such documents as manuals and forms used at work or in civil life; and such quantitative literacy materials as menus and checkbooks, which can require both reading and mathematical skills. Researchers deliberately did not set a literacy cutoff or report an overall illiteracy rate. Using item-response theory, they constructed proficiency scales for each type of material and reported the percentage of young adults at various points along the scale. They found that nearly all young adults, 95 percent or more, were proficient at the simplest tasks, those associated with a rating of 200 or less on each of the three scales. These tasks included locating information in a sports article (prose comprehension), entering personal information on job applications (document literacy), and totaling two entries on a bank deposit slip (quantitative literacy). Literacy proficiency fell off rapidly, however, as one went up the scale. Forty-four percent of young adults failed to reach the 300 proficiency level, one that was associated with locating informa-

64. Norvell W. Northcutt, "Functional Literacy for Adults," in *Reading and Career Education,* ed. Nielsen and Hjelm, 48; APL Project, *Final Report,* 17.
65. Department of Education, *Update on Adult Illiteracy.*
66. Leslie M. Werner, "13% of U.S. Adults Are Illiterate in English, A Federal Study Finds," *New York Times,* April 21, 1986, 1.
67. Kirsch and Jungeblut, *Literacy.*

Directions: Choose the answer that means the same as the word or phrase with a line under it.

Persons may receive benefits if they are eligible.

    a. qualified
    b. complete
    c. single
    d. logical

Directions: Read all of the paragraph first. Draw a line under the best word or phrase to complete each sentence.

To report medical expenses, first indicate how often you pay these expenses. Tell how long _____ will be paying them. Name the persons in

    a. doctors
    b. time
    c. they
    d. you

your household _____ these expenses are paid.

    a. in that
    b. by which
    c. for whom

Figure 3.3. Sample Items from the English Language Proficiency Survey

Source: U.S. Department of Education, *Update on Adult Illiteracy,* 4, 6, 11.

tion in an almanac, map reading, and balancing a checkbook. Eighty percent failed to reach the 350 level, which was associated with paraphrasing an editorial argument, reading a bus schedule, and determining a tip as a percentage of a bill. These findings indicate that although only a small percentage of people are utterly illiterate, literacy problems pervade the society.

The Major Criticisms

The functional-illiteracy rates computed in these studies (see table 3.3) are generally much higher than the self-reported illiteracy rates cited by the U.S. Census and the functional-illiteracy rates based on years of educational attainment. Although at first glance these studies suggest that functional illiteracy is a major educational problem, serious criticisms have been levied against them.

To begin with, several critics questioned whether it was possible to

Table 3.3. Functional Illiteracy Rates

Study	Year	Sample Ages	Tasks	Criteria	Lower Criterion (%)	Higher Criterion (%)
Survival Literacy	1970	16+	Application forms	70%, 90% correct	3.0	13.0
Reading Difficulty Index	1971	16+	Application forms; Telephone; Ads	80%, 90% of weighted items	4.0	15.0
Mini-Assessment	1975	17	Everyday reading	75% correct	12.6	—
Adult Functional Reading	1973	16+	Everyday reading	None set		
Adult Performance Level	1974	18–65	Functional competency	APL 1, APL 1 & 2	19.7	53.6
English Language Proficiency	1982	20+	Multiple choice from applications, official notices	20 of 26 correct	13.0	—
Young Adult Literacy	1985	21–25	Prose comprehension, documents, quantitative, oral language	None set		

Note: All studies were of nationally representative samples.

identify a set of tasks that could measure functional literacy or functional competency for all adults. As Donald Fisher argued, functional literacy is "relative to a given subpopulation. The literacy demands on one subpopulation may include only some of the demands on other subpopulations."[68] Henry Acland made much the same point, arguing that it is impossible to test functional literacy for a national population.[69] William Griffith and Ronald Cervero took this argument one step further, claiming that whatever tasks are included on the test reflect the "value-orientation" of the test designers.[70] They compared the Adult Performance Level Project to previous efforts in life-adjustment education, arguing that it was simply one more attempt to force the individual to adjust to mainstream values. This line of argument overlooks the fact that certain skills are needed by everyone in our society. Acland talked about "rich people's problems" and "poor people's problems," as if reading maps and schedules and writing checks were the province of the well to do, irrelevant to the poor.

With more merit, critics questioned the basis for item selection on the Adult Performance Level test.[71] After creating a large pool of items that measured literacy and problem-solving competencies, APL designers purposely eliminated those that did not favor people with advanced education and job status. But identifying the skills and knowledge associated with success is quite different from identifying the skills necessary for coping. APL's selection method was reminiscent of that of the World War I psychological testing program. The army Alpha tests were field tested on graduate students and officer-training-school candidates, and items that did not favor them were discarded. Later, the psychologists "proved" their test's validity by showing that scores were highly correlated with education and income. Similarly in their final report, APL researchers emphasized that functional incompetence could be linked to education and income, but failed to mention that the test had been designed to produce these very results.

In fact, the correlations between APL scores and socioeconomic indexes were not very high, .31 to .56,[72] so the selection of items by social class were not that systematic. Because the original pool of items generally

68. Fisher, *Functional Literacy and the Schools,* 57.

69. Henry Acland, "If Reading Scores Are Irrelevant, Do We Have Anything Better?" *Educational Technology* (July 1976):25–29.

70. William S. Griffith and Ronald M. Cervero, "The Adult Performance Level Program: A Serious and Deliberate Examination," *Adult Education* 27 (1977):209–24.

71. Ronald M. Cervero, "Does the Texas Adult Performance Level Test Measure Functional Competence?" *Adult Education* 30 (1980):152–65; B. R. Heller et al., cited in J. K. Fischer, W. Haney, and L. David, *APL Revisited: Its Uses and Adaptation in States* (Washington, D.C.: Government Printing Office, 1980), 63; Fisher, *Functional Literacy and the Schools.*

72. Cervero, "Texas Adult Performance Level Test," 158.

measured basic competencies, performance on specific APL items can still illuminate the nature and extent of functional competency. Although some of the Adult Performance Level objectives were culturally and politically loaded, most of the items on the test, as on the other functional-literacy tests, did not reflect any particular bias. For example, individuals were asked to address an envelope, to follow the directions on a medicine bottle, and to determine change from a twenty-dollar bill.[73] It is hard to see what "value-orientation" was being advanced by these tasks.

Using evidence from the Adult Functional Reading Study, Donald Fisher argued persuasively that poor performance on functional-literacy tests resulted from breakdowns at some stage in the test subjects' information processing.[74] We disagree, however, that the typical error was "more or less mechanical," perhaps due to carelessness or inattention rather than to a lack of important literacy skills or vocabulary knowledge.[75] Fisher's model embodied important literacy tasks, requiring the ability to "encode [a] passage," to "identify target and locator propositions," and to "derive search clues." It seems reasonable to say that people who repeatedly make errors in such processing stages have functional reading problems. The researchers who conducted NAEP's Young Adult Literacy Assessment found that the difficulty of an item was related directly to its processing demands, such as the number of features to be matched.[76] After interviewing one hundred students in adult learning centers who had taken the Adult Functional Reading Study test, Richard Murphy found two basic causes of errors: unfamiliarity with everyday words and difficulties with everyday formats.[77] These findings suggest that errors on functional-literacy tests represent serious literacy deficits rather than lapses in routine mechanical processing.

Acland raised an important point when he observed that, in real-life settings, individuals solve many of the problems posed in the tests by relying upon environmental cues and soliciting help from others.[78] He presented several examples from the Adult Performance Level test to illustrate his point. Although 26 percent of the people in the sample could not determine which of the three cereal products was the cheapest per unit weight, Acland noted that some supermarkets now provide unit-pricing labels that make this skill unnecessary. Another 27 percent did

73. APL Project, *Final Report,* 28, 22; Roger Thompson, "Illiteracy in America," *Editorial Research Reports* 1 (June 24, 1983):475–92.

74. Donald L. Fisher, "Functional Literacy Tests: A Model of Question-Answering and an Analysis of Errors," *Reading Research Quarterly* 16 (1981):418–48.

75. Ibid., 443–44.

76. Kirsch and Jungeblut, *Literacy,* chap. 4, 14–16.

77. Murphy, *Adult Functional Reading Study,* 14.

78. Acland, "If Reading Scores Are Irrelevant."

not know the normal human body temperature, but as Acland pointed out, every thermometer clearly marks this point, making such knowledge unnecessary. In determining the right tax from a tax table, 61 percent had trouble, but as Acland discovered from the Internal Revenue Service, only 6 percent of tax filers actually made any kind of arithmetic error in their returns, probably because in real-life situations people get help in completing tasks they may find difficult to accomplish alone.

Although Acland is correct that in real life people frequently receive assistance in literacy tasks, this line of reasoning fails to acknowledge that functional literacy implies self-reliance. No functional task is impossible if you have someone more skilled or educated to do it for you. However, in the real world, many supermarkets do not have unit pricing. Filling out forms incorrectly often causes delays and frustration. When all else fails, getting help may work, but a person should not have to depend upon others to solve the basic tasks of daily living.

Cutoff Scores

To report illiteracy rates, researchers establish a cutoff score—the test score that separates the "functional literates" from the "illiterates." By choosing a higher or lower cutoff score, researchers can arbitrarily control functional-illiteracy rates. Yet, with one exception, designers of the studies described here failed to explain how they chose their cutoffs. The Mini-Assessment of Functional Literacy data can be used to illustrate how sensitive rates are to cutoffs. Researchers chose a 75 percent cutoff and, as a consequence, found that 12.6 percent of the nation's seventeen-year-old students were functional illiterates. Had they chosen instead a 60 percent cutoff, only 2.9 percent would have been found illiterate.[79] Even when a given cutoff seems reasonable, users of functional-literacy test results should bear in mind that cutoffs are arbitrary and that changes in the cutoff score can drastically change the literacy rate.

Cutoffs also impose artificial boundaries. They can create the impression that those who are labeled illiterate are entirely without skills, when, in fact, they may be able to handle many literacy tasks. Ranking individuals on a single scale also can imply that literacy is one dimensional, when it is more appropriately viewed as a rich set of skills that people can use to varying degrees. For such reasons, some researchers choose not to report an overall functional-illiteracy rate.[80]

The most informative method of reporting results is to publish score distributions showing the proportion of the population at various proficiency levels. This reporting method shows that some "functional illiterates" nonetheless possess many functional skills. On the Mini-Assess-

79. Gadway and Wilson, *Functional Literacy*, vii.
80. Murphy, *Adult Functional Reading Study;* Kirsch and Jungeblut, *Literacy.*

Table 3.4. Results of Reading Difficulty Index Study

Task	No. of Items	Percentage of Population		
		All Items Correct	Only One Wrong	None or Only One Right[a]
Telephone rate, directions	4	90	8	1
Housing ads	9	88	7	1
Employment ads	9	92	6	1
Personal ID information	10	93	6	—
Employment information	4	85	9	3
Income information	3	77	16	7
Housing information	8	87	11	—
Automobile information	3	97	1	2
Medical information	3	86	10	4
Citizenship information	6	87	6	—

All tasks	Total no. of Items	Percentage of Population Whose Overall Scores Were				
		100	96–99.9	90–95.9	80–89.9	Less than 80[b]
Weighted test items	59	43	23	19	11	4

Source: Harns and Associates, *National Reading Difficulty Index,* 29–48.
[a]Where — appears, less than 1%.
[b]No further breakdown was given.

ment, for example, most functional illiterates scored above 60 percent. And in some task areas on the Reading Difficulty Index test, more than 90 percent of the subjects answered all items correctly (see the top portion of table 3.4). Researchers in NAEP's Young Adult Literacy Assessment reported proficiency rates on three different literacy scales: prose comprehension, document literacy, and quantitative literacy. This had the advantage of showing that literacy is multidimensional and that performance varies with the type of literacy being considered.

Factors That Might Raise the Estimates
One can argue on several grounds that the reported rates actually underestimate the extent of functional illiteracy in United States society. The samples were not completely representative. The Mini-Assessment, for example, involved only seventeen-year-old *students*. Given that almost 20 percent of high-school students drop out and that their average performance is worse than those who stay in school, we estimate that the Mini-Assessment's 12.6 percent overall functional-illiteracy rate should be raised by about four percentage points (one-fifth of the students are dropouts, which multiplied by a 20 percent estimated illiteracy rate for

dropouts equals 4 percent). Furthermore, because non-English-speaking seventeen-year-olds were excluded from the sample, the rate may in fact be another percentage point higher (1.4 percent of persons aged five to seventeen speak English poorly or not at all).[81] These adjustments would raise the Mini-Assessment rate to about 18 percent. In light of these considerations, results from the Survival Literacy Study and the Reading Difficulty Index test also would have to be raised two to three percentage points.[82]

Second, in some cases the tasks required by the tests were easier than those presented in everyday life. Alex Caughran and John Lindlof, for example, compared the Survival Literacy's Application for Public Assistance with the original government form upon which it was based.[83] The Survival Literacy test form was easier in three important respects. The format had been simplified, it had fewer "difficult" words, and its readability level was grade five to six, compared to the seventh- or eighth-grade level of the original. If the other forms were similarly simplified, functional-illiteracy estimates would need further adjustments; coupled with the corrections for language exclusion, the Survival Literacy results would probably need to be increased from a 3 percent illiteracy rate to about 7 percent. For the Reading Difficulty Index study, researchers simplified the housing and employment ads by removing the abbreviations typically found in newspaper classifieds, thereby ensuring that its results, too, would underestimate illiteracy rates.

Third, because only seventeen-year-olds were tested in the Mini-Assessment and only twenty-one- to twenty-five-year-olds in the Young Adult Literacy study, the results did not reflect the functional-illiteracy rate of the general population. We can extrapolate, however, from the results of the other surveys. In those, the general population's illiteracy rate ranged two to three percentage points higher than that of sixteen- to twenty-four-year-olds. Thus, for Mini-Assessment type items, for example, we would estimate that about 21 percent of the population would be functionally illiterate in English, a figure that includes adjustments for high-school dropouts and non-English speakers. This result is remarkably close to the 21.7 percent Adult Performance Level rate for functional incompetence in reading.

81. Bureau of the Census, *Ancestry and Language in the United States*, 15.

82. Lawrence C. Stedman and Carl F. Kaestle, *An Investigation of Crude Literacy, Reading Performance, and Functional Literacy in the United States, 1880 to 1980* (Madison: Wisconsin Center for Education Research, Program Report 86-2, 1986), 49.

83. Alex Caughran and John Lindlof, "Should the 'Survival Literacy Study' Survive?" *Journal of Reading* 15 (March 1972):429–35.

Understanding the Estimates

A review of the various test groups' performance on individual items provides a better understanding of the nature of functional illiteracy than arguing over summary estimates of how many people are illiterate. Even the item results are necessarily an approximation, however, because the tasks are not identical to their real-world counterparts and the testing populations often underrepresent functional illiterates.

Setting aside for the moment the representativeness of the various samples, and treating the test results as reflective of what most English-speaking adults aged sixteen and over can do, let us look at the functional tasks that the test respondents handled best. On the item from the Adult Functional Reading Study depicted in figure 3.4, only .1 percent had difficulty recognizing the word *milk,* which suggests that most adults can recognize simple words encountered on familiar objects. On the Reading Difficulty Index test, only 2 percent of the subjects made more than one error in telephone-dialing instructions. Among the same test population, 5 percent had similar trouble with housing ads (see figure 3.2 and table 3.4). These results suggest that nearly everyone, 95 to 98 percent of the test subjects, could read simple advertisements and find area-code information in a telephone book. It should be kept in mind, though, that this translates into an estimate of 3 to 7 million people in the population as a whole who had problems with very simple tasks.

The next set of tasks concerned application forms. Performance on the example from the Reading Difficulty Index study depicted in figure 3.5 suggests the depth of the problem. About 7 percent of the participants were unable to mark the spot where the name of their emergency contact should be entered (directions had been given orally). On the driver's

ORAL DIRECTIONS

Item 1   Place a circle around the bottle of liquid that would be safe to drink.

Figure 3.4. Sample Item from the Adult Functional Reading Study

Source: Murphy, *Adult Functional Reading Study: Supplement to Final Report,* 8. Copyright 1973 by Educational Testing Service. Reprinted by permission.

Item 3 **Look at the application for employment. Put an X in the space where you would write the name and address of someone to notify in case of emergency.**

APPLICATION FOR EMPLOYMENT				DATE	

Figure 3.5. Sample Item from the Adult Functional Reading Study

Source: Murphy, *Adult Functional Reading Study: Supplement to Final Report,* 12. Copyright 1973 by Educational Testing Service. Reprinted by permission.

license form of the Survival Literacy Study, 8 percent scored below 90 percent correct. The test asked for such simple information as height, weight, name, and eye color, but included terms that may have confused some readers: conditions that "might impair" driving ability and time "most convenient" to take an exam (see figure 3.1). Such terms, of course, are frequently encountered in bureaucratic forms. Scores on these items suggest that 5 to 8 percent of the population would have trouble filling out job, loan, and license applications.

About one-seventh, or 14 percent, of the test population could not properly read a map, address an envelope (the zip code was not required), or write a check.[84] When asked to follow directions on a medicine bottle that stated, "take two pills twice a day," or to determine how often houses should be inspected for termites when presented with a government brochure that read, "periodic inspections should be made at least every six months if you live where termites are common," 21 percent could not.[85] Extrapolating from the test populations, we may estimate that at least the same percentages in the general American population would have similar difficulties.

About one-third of the subjects were unable to read correctly airline and train schedules, to make change from a purchase, or to determine

84. APL Project, *Final Report.*
85. Ibid., 11; Thompson, "Illiteracy in America," 481.

Look at the description of a group plan for blood donations. Circle whom you should call if you want to become a donor under the group plan.

The Red Cross Blood Program—Our Group Plan

If you are a member of the Red Cross Blood Program, you and members of your family are entitled to receive blood free at any hospital. In order to obtain the blood, you must have the Group Program Chairman, Joan Knapp, sign an authorization form. The form may be signed either before or after the administration of blood.

Who makes this program possible? The Plan requires that at least 20 percent of our employees donate blood during the year.

Can you become a donor? Any staff member between the ages of 18 and 66 is eligible. However, those between 18 and 21 must have the written permission of their parent or guardian.

If you have any questions about the program, or if you are willing to become a blood donor, please call Rex Jackson at 231–0027.

Figure 3.6. Sample Item from the Adult Functional Reading Study

Source: Fisher, "Functional Literacy Tests," 437. Copyright 1973 by Educational Testing Service. Reprinted by permission.

which grades had improved on a report card.[86] In the Adult Functional Reading Study, after reading several short paragraphs describing a blood donation program, 40 percent could not identify the person they should contact if they wished to donate blood (see figure 3.6). Finally, a majority of subjects could not determine when money was due for a parking ticket, locate the tax for a given income on a tax table, determine total purchase price for a mail order, read and fill out a W-4 form, calculate miles per gallon, or put a return address on a business letter.[87]

Based on these studies, we find it reasonable to estimate that about 20 percent of the adult population, or around 35 million people, have serious difficulties with common reading tasks. An additional 10 percent are probably marginal in their functional-literacy skills. What are the consequences of low functional-literacy skills for day-to-day living? Many of those who fall into the lowest fifth in functional-literacy skills are unable to read product labels and must depend upon brand-name logos or pictures for selection of items in a grocery store. Many are unable to

86. Murphy, *Adult Functional Reading Study: Supplement;* APL Project, *Final Report;* Gadway and Wilson, *Functional Literacy.*

87. Gadway and Wilson, *Functional Literacy;* APL Project, *Final Report;* Acland, "If Reading Scores Are Irrelevant"; Northcutt, "Functional Literacy for Adults."

determine whether they are receiving the correct change. Many struggle to read recipes and cannot decipher directions on frozen-food packages. Their physical independence and mobility are hampered by difficulties with traffic signs, street names, and bus and subway schedules. Parents' roles can be seriously undermined by a lack of functional reading skills. Some parents have difficulty reading letters from the school or helping their children with homework. Such literacy problems can be crippling, and the possibility that 20 percent of our population may suffer such problems is alarming. Is functional illiteracy increasing, or have we just rediscovered a long-standing problem?

Historical Trends in Tested Functional Literacy
Nationwide testing of functional literacy did not begin until the 1970s, so it is impossible to establish long-term trends directly. Nevertheless, the 1970s tests provide some hints about short-range trends. Sixty-four of the 1975 Mini-Assessment items were culled from the 1971 National Assessment reading test, and researchers compared scores on those items. They found that the average student's functional-literacy performance rose from 83.7 percent correct in 1971 to 85.9 percent in 1975. We thus know that during the early 1970s, the functional literacy of seventeen-year-old students improved slightly.

Analysts often infer historical trends by comparing the literacy rates of different age groups surveyed at the same time. On the crude literacy and educational attainment measures of the U.S. Census, for example, illiteracy rates decrease with age: each younger age group has a lower illiteracy rate than its older counterparts. The functional-literacy tests, however, do not follow such a consistent pattern. As Copperman pointed out in regard to the 1974 Adult Performance Level test, adults aged thirty to thirty-nine achieved the highest competency rate.[88] That this group was in school during the 1950s suggests that that decade was a heyday for United States schools and for the acquisition of functional-competency skills. Because the performance of the eighteen- to twenty-nine-year-olds approximated that of the forty- to forty-nine-year-olds, who had finished high school by 1952, Copperman concluded that students' performance in the 1970s had deteriorated to the levels of the early 1950s.[89] The Adult Functional Reading Study, administered in 1973, showed a similar pattern.

APL researchers also noticed this pattern, but reached a different conclusion. They argued that the youngest adults scored more poorly because they had had less experience with functional-literacy tasks.[90]

88. Copperman, *Literacy Hoax*, 47.
89. Ibid., 48.
90. APL Project, *Final Report*, 37.

Donald Fisher argued that the youngest groups scored more poorly because they had not yet had as much education.[91] In the Adult Functional Reading Study, for example, sixteen- to nineteen-year-olds had only 11.3 years of schooling compared to 12.6 years for those twenty to twenty-nine. When these differences were considered, the youngest cohorts were actually performing better than would be expected. According to Fisher, then, schools had become better at literacy training. Copperman's argument was also contradicted by the results of the other functional-literacy tests. The Survival Literacy Study and the Reading Difficulty Index showed that the youngest cohort (aged sixteen to twenty-four) was the most literate. These results suggest that the population's functional-literacy skills have improved during the last few decades.

Other evidence about historical trends in functional literacy comes from the portions of standardized tests labeled "work-study" skills. These academic skills are similar to many of those required for the functional-literacy tests: using indexes, alphabetizing, deciphering maps and graphs, and so forth. We have national renorming results for work-study skills covering the last thirty years. The general pattern parallels that for standardized test scores in reading—improvements up to 1970, a minor decline from 1970 to 1977, and recent improvements. As previously discussed, however, using achievement-test renorming results to infer literacy trends is a questionable approach.

The longitudinal evidence, although of dubious quality, thus suggests that from the 1940s to the mid-1970s the population's general functional-literacy skills probably improved to some degree. Whereas students' academic functional skills may have weakened in the 1970s, they seem to have improved over the last decade.

Reading Grade Levels as a Measure of Functional Literacy

Researchers have also measured the extent of functional literacy by comparing the population's reading grade level to that of common reading materials. We describe four major efforts to assess the grade-level reading ability of the population. The Brief Test of Literacy accompanied the Health Examination Survey of the National Center for Health Statistics in 1970.[92] Administered to a representative sample of twelve- to seventeen-year-olds, the test involved seven simple reading passages (see figure 3.7), with a literacy cutoff of early-fourth-grade reading performance. Among this nationally representative age group, 4.8 percent were found to be illiterate.

91. Fisher, *Functional Literacy and the Schools*, 9.
92. Dorothy K. Vogt, *Literacy among Youths 12–17 Years: United States* (Rockville, Md.: National Center for Health Statistics, 1973).

It was a beautiful gift, wrapped with bright red paper and tied with silver string. It was small, but very heavy. No one knew who had brought it, but it had Mr. Jones' name on top. Mr. Jones just smiled and said, "I'll open it when I get home."

01. Whose name was on the top of the gift?

    a) Mr. Jones
    b) Mr. Pike
    c) Willy
    d) The postman
    e) No one knew

02. In what color paper was the gift wrapped?

    a) red
    b) silver
    c) green
    d) orange
    e) yellow

03. Where was the gift going to be opened?

    a) Where it was found
    b) At the police station
    c) In the car
    d) At the office
    e) At home

Figure 3.7. Sample Item from the Brief Test of Literacy

Source: Vogt, *Literacy among Youths 12–17 Years.*

Reginald Corder produced the second set of estimates in 1971.[93] After reviewing data from several standardized-test publishers, he determined the reading levels of students in various grades. Among twelfth graders, for example, 13 percent read below an eighth-grade level. Extrapolating these figures to the general population on the basis of educational attainment, Fisher reported that, of those fourteen years and older, about 7 percent were reading below a fifth-grade reading level and about 30 percent below an eighth-grade level.[94]

The third set of estimates came from the Defense Department's Armed Services Vocational Aptitude Battery, which was administered to

93. Cited in Fisher, *Functional Literacy and the Schools,* 36.
94. Fisher, *Functional Literacy and the Schools,* 36.

a representative sample of eighteen- to twenty-three-year-olds in 1980.[95] The tests were developed to help the military identify qualified recruits and to make assignments to occupations and training programs.[96] The median reading grade level was 9.6, with 18 percent falling below the seventh-grade level.[97]

The Young Adult Literacy Assessment provided the fourth set of estimates.[98] By including items from the 1983–84 NAEP reading test that had been administered to students, researchers were able to express the reading performance of young adults in terms of grade levels. They found that 6 percent of young adults read below the fourth-grade level and 20 percent read below the eighth-grade level.

Reading-level estimates of the population are fraught with problems. The level depends upon the particular reading test used, the types of skills tested, and the difficulty of the items. Additional difficulties are encountered in relating the population's reading level to that of everyday reading materials. Individuals can read and understand much material that is supposedly above their reading grade level. Thomas Sticht and his colleagues found, for example, that the reading level assigned to a job on the basis of its materials was much higher—often three to four grades higher—than the reading level workers needed to perform their jobs satisfactorily.[99] On the major standardized tests, the average sixth grader comprehends about 80 percent of what the average eighth grader does. This suggests that people with sixth-grade reading levels will be able to understand much of the material written at an eighth-grade level.

On the other hand, just because materials are assigned an eighth-grade reading level we must not think that they are fully understood by all persons reading at the eighth-grade level. The reading level of materials has a technical definition—that grade at which the average student can understand 75 percent of what is presented. Thus, even individuals whose grade level matches that of the material will fail to comprehend about one-fourth of it. For certain materials, such as antidote instruc-

95. Irwin Kirsch, *NAEP Profiles of Literacy: An Assessment of Young Adults—Development Plan* (Princeton, N.J.: National Assessment of Educational Progress, 1985), 1; Andrew M. Sum, Paul E. Harrington, and William Goedicke, *Basic Skills of America's Teens and Young Adults: Findings of the 1980 National ASVAB Testing and Their Implications for Education, Employment and Training Policies and Programs* (Boston: Northeastern University, 1986).

96. U.S. Department of Defense, *Counselor's Manual for the Armed Services Vocational Aptitude Battery Form 14* (Washington, D.C.: Office of the Assistant Secretary of Defense, 1984), 3.

97. Kirsch, *Profiles of Literacy*, 1.

98. Kirsch and Jungeblut, *Literacy*, chap. 5, 8.

99. Thomas G. Sticht, ed., *Reading for Working: A Functional Literacy Anthology* (Alexandria, Va.: Human Resources Research Organization, 1975), 85, 86.

tions and warning labels, 100 percent comprehension is essential; for other materials complete understanding is not as crucial.

There are also a variety of technical reasons for caution in using reading-grade-level findings. Researchers used readability formulas to determine a material's difficulty, but different formulas yield different results.[100] Few researchers demonstrated that the passages they tested were representative of the document in question, yet different parts of a document usually differ in complexity.[101] The readability formulas themselves are flawed, and we detail the problems in chapter 7; it may suffice here to note that we do not have great confidence in such measures. However, they pervade the literature on the uses of literacy, so we cannot altogether escape them.

Given the limitations of readability formulas, it makes little sense to explore in great detail the historical patterns. The available evidence is, in any case, scant. Readability formulas were not popularized until the 1940s, and few studies followed the same materials over time. Nonetheless, examples of materials that have been assigned grade levels may be of interest. Sticht, for example, reported that lead articles in such well-known magazines as *Reader's Digest,* the *Saturday Evening Post, Popular Mechanics,* the *Ladies' Home Journal,* and *Harper's* range between the twelfth and thirteenth grades, and have for the last forty years.[102] Mary Monteith reported that the typical magazine article averages eleventh-grade level. Newspaper articles vary between ninth and twelfth grade, and newspaper election coverage tends to be written at the college level. Of popular materials, only best sellers are consistently accessible to readers in the lowest 30 percent of reading ability; ranging from the sixth-grade to the ninth-grade level, these titles have averaged around the seventh-grade level for the past fifty years.[103] Still, as we have noted, 18 percent of those aged eighteen to twenty-three read below the seventh-grade level.

Many job materials also appear to be beyond the reach of those in the bottom 30 percent in reading ability. Sticht evaluated seven U.S. Army occupational manuals and found that more than half were at the eleventh-grade to college level in difficulty. The reading level of materials for cooks, for example, was estimated at ninth grade, those for repairmen and supply clerks at the upper college level.[104]

According to recent reports, many societal tasks involve materials of

100. Ibid., 73.

101. Ibid., 31.

102. Ibid., 184.

103. Mary K. Monteith, "How Well Does the Average American Read? Some Facts, Figures, and Opinions," *Journal of Reading* (February 1980):460–64.

104. Sticht, ed., *Reading for Working,* 51.

great reading difficulty.[105] An apartment lease and food-stamp notices, for example, are at the college level, an insurance policy is at the twelfth-grade level, and an aspirin-bottle label is at the tenth-grade level. Antidote instructions on a bottle of corrosive kitchen lye are at the ninth-grade level, while tax forms and directions on how to prepare a T.V. dinner are at the eighth-grade level. Only a driver's license manual, estimated to be written at a sixth-grade reading level, falls within the grasp of many in the bottom 30 percent.

The reading difficulty of military training manuals has remained roughly the same for the past three decades, but these were not on-the-job materials and researchers did not trace the military's average reading level over the same period.[106] As noted, the reading grade level of magazines and best sellers has remained constant over time, but we have no corresponding data on the population's reading level with which to compare them. Therefore, we can conclude little about functional-literacy trends as measured by reading grade levels. In chapter 7 we report on a detailed attempt to compare the reading grade level of popular reading materials with the education levels of the American population, using 1920 as a case study.

Literacy and Job Performance

Designed to meet the personnel needs of large organizations, job-literacy research was pioneered for the army during World War I.[107] For many decades thereafter, researchers in business tested workers' skills and created occupational ability patterns, which purported to portray the skill levels required for particular jobs.[108] The U.S. Employment Service and the U.S. Department of Defense have continued similar research to the present day.[109] In a newer approach, researchers have interviewed workers and observed them on the job to determine how much they read, for what purposes, and with what strategies.[110] In this section, we dis-

105. S. N. Wellborn, "Ahead: A Nation of Illiterates?" *U.S. News and World Report*, May 17, 1982, 53–57; Kozol, *Illiterate America*, 10, 228.

106. Sticht, ed., *Reading for Working*, 170.

107. Yoakum and Yerkes, *Army Mental Tests*.

108. See the review of early research in Arthur F. Dodge, *Occupational Ability Patterns* (New York: Bureau of Publications, Teachers College, Columbia University, 1935), and also Beatrice J. Dvorak, *Differential Occupational Ability Patterns*, Bulletins of the Employment Stabilization Research Institute, vol. 3, no. 8 (Minneapolis: University of Minnesota Press, 1935).

109. U.S. Department of Labor, *Section II: Occupational Aptitude Pattern Structure: Manual for the USES General Aptitude Test Battery* (Washington, D.C.: Government Printing Office, 1979); Department of Defense, *Counselor's Manual for the Armed Services*.

110. William A. Diehl and Larry Mikulecky, "The Nature of Reading at Work,"

cuss what some argue is a growing discrepancy between the population's literacy level and the skills required to perform most of society's jobs. In doing so, we shall evaluate various efforts to estimate the job-literacy gap.

The history of job-assessment efforts demonstrates the difficulties of determining which level of reading skills is associated with satisfactory job performance. The correlations between test scores and job proficiency have generally been too low to rationalize assigning reading levels. World War I results showed a mixture of high and low correlations. Job-performance rankings of 765 men by infantry company commanders were nearly identical to those from the army skills test. But officer ratings of 374 men in twelve other companies correlated a modest .536 with test scores; army rank, excluding medical officers, was unrelated.[111] The experience of the business world mirrors that of the military. In the 1920s and 1930s, most industries stopped testing employees' entry-level skills, except for clerical positions, because the tests were not good predictors of on-the-job success.[112]

Since World War II, the most comprehensive job-testing program has been conducted by the U.S. Employment Service. Its General Aptitude Test Battery has been validated in more than 550 studies, covering a representative sample from twelve thousand jobs. Depending upon the job, however, the correlations between GATB scores and civilian job performance ranged from only .23 to .58.[113] The Armed Services Vocational Aptitude Battery has produced similar outcomes, with correlations of .36 to .52 for jobs within the communications area, .39 to .77 for data-processing specialists, and .53 to .73 for clerical and supply specialists.[114] Contemporary sociological research has also identified a similarly weak

---

Journal of Reading 24 (1980):221–28; Irwin S. Kirsch and John T. Guthrie, "Adult Reading Practices for Work and Leisure," *Reading Research Quarterly* (1973–74):213–32; Larry Mikulecky, "The Mismatch between School Training and Job Literacy Demands," *Vocational Guidance Quarterly* 30 (1981):174–80; Larry Mikulecky, "Job Literacy: The Relationship between School Preparation and Workplace Activity," *Reading Research Quarterly* 17 (1982):400–19; Larry Mikulecky and Dorothy Winchester, "Job Literacy and Job Performance among Nurses at Varying Employment Levels," *Adult Education Quarterly* 34 (1983):1–15; Mikulecky and Ehlinger, "Influence of Metacognitive Aspects of Literacy," 41–62; John T. Guthrie, Mary Siefert, and Irwin S. Kirsch, "Effects of Education, Occupation, and Setting on Reading Practices," *American Educational Research Journal* 23 (1986):151–60.

111. Yoakum and Yerkes, *Army Mental Tests,* 30, 32, 40.

112. Matthew Hale, "History of Employment Testing," in *Ability Testing: Uses, Consequences, and Controversies,* pt. 2, Documentation Section, ed. Alexandra K. Wigdor and Wendell R. Garner (Washington, D.C.: National Academy Press, 1982), 18–20.

113. Department of Defense, *Counselor's Manual for the Armed Services,* 19.

114. Ibid.

correlation of .3 between test scores and job success.[115] These results suggest that the ability to predict job success from reading skill varies greatly by the type of occupation, and even within a given occupational category. Furthermore, the ability to predict success is often very poor.

These limitations hamper efforts to assess the workplace literacy gap. The military's experience exemplifies the difficulties. In response to training problems during the Vietnam War, military officials embarked on a functional-literacy research program. Concerned that many draftees were insufficiently literate to handle military jobs, they wanted to determine how best to close the gap between personnel and their tasks. Sticht and his colleagues assigned threshold reading levels to different jobs.[116] Depending upon which job-proficiency measure was used, they determined that cooks needed to read at the seventh- through the ninth-grade level, repairmen at the eighth- through the twelfth-grade level, and supply clerks at the ninth- through the thirteenth-grade level. At the time, though, the army personnel's average reading level was only ninth grade. Sticht and his colleagues concluded that "the reading demands of Army jobs, even the less complex ones, far exceed the reading ability of many personnel."

The job-literacy gap may seem serious, but several factors weaken such a conclusion. First, the correlations between the army personnel's reading grade level and the job-proficiency measures were generally low. Depending upon the job, reading grade level correlated from .40 to .57 with the scores on the job-knowledge measures, only .26 to .40 with the scores on the job sample test, and was unrelated to supervisor ratings.[117] The correlation with the job-reading-task measure (.65 to .80) was relatively higher because the measure was a reading test. Subsequent military research also shows relatively low correlations with actual job performance. Workers' basic skills scores have accounted only for 3 percent to at most 26 percent of the variance in hands-on job-performance measures.

Such low correlations mean two things for job assessment. First, a job's reading grade level is particularly sensitive to the criterion used to establish it. For the job-reading performance measure, for example, Sticht and his colleagues chose an 80/70 criterion—that is, jobs were assigned the reading grade level at which 80 percent of the individuals correctly answered 70 percent of the job-reading items. Thus they rated the repairman's job at a ninth- to tenth-grade reading level. The military,

115. Christopher Jencks et al., *Inequality: A Reassessment of the Effect of Family and Schooling in America* (New York: Harper and Row, 1972), 186–87.

116. Sticht, ed., *Reading for Working,* 170–71, 120.

117. Ibid., 67, 43, 59, 17.

however, usually used a 70/70 rule, which would have lowered the reading level of the repairman job by a grade and a half to eighth grade.[118] Given that the test required more reading than the job typically did, an 80/60 criterion might be even more reasonable. With that criterion, the reading level of the repairman job would approach seventh grade—a full two grades less than the level dictated by the 80/70 criterion. For the supply clerk, the results are more dramatic: the reading level drops three grades, from thirteenth to tenth grade, when similar criterion adjustments are made. It should be noted, however, that even with the more liberal criteria, the jobs' reading levels still remained above that of a substantial proportion of military personnel.

Second, and more important, these low correlations suggest that large percentages of workers with minimal basic skills can perform jobs competently, even when the jobs are assigned higher reading grade levels. On the basis of the job sample test, for example, the armor crewman job was assigned an eighth-grade level. Yet 27 percent of those with a ninth- to tenth-grade reading level were placed by their supervisors in the bottom quartile in terms of performance, whereas 35 percent of those at only a fourth- to sixth-grade level were in the top half.[119] In a later review of military research, Sticht concluded that "many of the least competent in the basic skills became above average job performers, while many highly skilled in the basic skills perform job tasks in a below-average manner."[120]

In spite of such difficulties, several researchers have attempted a national assessment of the job-literacy gap. Barbara Lerner, focusing on the bottom of the job pyramid, argued that unskilled people considerably outnumbered unskilled jobs.[121] She based her claim on the Mini-Assessment of Functional Literacy, which showed that in 1970, 12.6 percent of seventeen-year-olds were functional illiterates, twice the Department of Labor estimate that 6.1 percent of jobs were unskilled. But the comparison was misleading. As previously discussed, most of the "illiterates" scored above 60 percent and thus had many functional skills. Furthermore, the Mini-Assessment focused on such general skills as reading maps and using the dictionary, so poor performance did not necessarily mean an individual lacked job-reading skills.

A variety of research suggests that many individuals with limited reading skills can nonetheless acquire and hold jobs. Nearly half the military personnel Sticht and his colleagues tested read below the

118. Ibid., 113, 58.
119. Ibid., 69.
120. Thomas G. Sticht, *Basic Skills in Defense* (Alexandria, Va.: Human Resources Research Organization, 1982), 18.
121. Barbara Lerner, "The Minimum Competence Testing Movement: Social, Scientific, and Legal Implications," *American Psychologist* 36 (1981):1060.

eighth-grade level but performed their skilled jobs satisfactorily.[122] Contrary to the "literacy gap" perspective, low reading-achievement scores (fifth through eighth grade) appeared to present no barrier to job competence among these subjects. Vineberg and Taylor found that one-third of the army personnel with the lowest basic-skills scores were above-average job performers.[123] In a study of workers in diverse occupations, Larry Mikulecky found that some workers (5 percent) were severely limited in their ability to read a ninth-grade passage. Mikulecky commented: "It is possible, it seems, to hold a job if one can barely read."[124] Obviously, severe reading deficiencies would interfere with the ability to acquire and hold jobs, but above a certain threshold, reading level as measured by standardized tests has little to do with job performance.

As noted earlier, 7 percent of the adult population were reading below the fifth-grade level in 1973. This percentage is somewhat larger than the percentage of unskilled jobs (6.1 percent) reported in 1970, but even semiskilled jobs often seem to require little reading. In a study of a black working-class community in the mid-1970s, Heath examined reading demands at home, play, school, and work. She found that workers in semiskilled jobs were not often called upon to read.[125] Their job applications were completed by a personnel officer, and employees received oral instructions about their new jobs. Insurance information and new regulations were posted, but since these were usually explained orally as well, employees "did not find it necessary to read the bulletin board notices."[126] Kirsch and Guthrie, on the other hand, found that reading was a regular part of semiskilled jobs.[127] However, they studied the Analytical Instrumentation Division of a Fortune 500 company, a technical environment in which reading demands are likely to be greater than in the typical semiskilled job. If it is true that many semiskilled jobs require little reading, a great number of jobs would be available to those with minimal literacy skills. If we adopt this premise, the literacy gap at the lowest job levels would vanish.

In a well-known attempt to assess the job-literacy gap in the late 1960s, Ivar Berg and Sherry Gorelick used the Department of Labor's Dictionary of Occupational Titles.[128] Each of the 13,800 job listings includes an index of General Educational Development (GED), a measure of the verbal, reasoning, and mathematical skills necessary to perform

122. Sticht, ed., *Reading for Working,* 63–64.
123. Cited in Sticht, *Basic Skills in Defense,* 17.
124. Mikulecky, "Mismatch between School Training," 179.
125. Heath, "Functions and Uses of Literacy," 129.
126. Ibid., 130.
127. Kirsch and Guthrie, "Adult Reading Practices."
128. Ivar Berg and Sherry Gorelick, *Education and Jobs: The Great Training Robbery* (Boston: Beacon Press, 1971).

the job. Comparing the distribution of these job GEDs to the population's educational levels should enable researchers to estimate the job-literacy gap, but GEDs have several limitations. They are based upon job descriptions rather than actual reading demands, and the scores are often assigned subjectively.[129] There is also no fixed relationship between GED scores and years of schooling. Depending upon which assumptions were made, Berg and Gorelick found that a worker preparation gap emerged or disappeared.[130] They could not determine which assumptions were the most reasonable.

It is important to distinguish between the alleged job-literacy gap and the unemployment problem. Although some individuals may be unable to secure employment because they lack skills,[131] unemployment is caused primarily by economic conditions and a general lack of jobs. The recession of the 1970s, for example, threw millions of people out of work, yet there had been no change in workers' literacy skills. Even if we could make all citizens functionally literate, jobs to employ them all would not suddenly be created.

Given the difficulties researchers have had in assessing the literacy gap in their own times, projections of future workplace literacy gaps are even more shaky. Well-informed scholars have propounded quite different visions. The authors of the educational reform reports of the 1980s, including *A Nation at Risk,* argued that the nation was moving rapidly to a high-technology future that would require far more advanced skills than those currently in demand. Kirsch and Guthrie argued that jobs requiring few or no literacy skills were disappearing and that the changing workplace would require greater literacy among more people.[132] By contrast, Samuel Bowles and Herbert Gintis argued that white-collar work has been proletarianized and that jobs were being "dumbed down."[133] They believed that most work required only limited skills com-

129. See, for example, Thomas G. Sticht and Howard H. McFann, "Reading Requirements for Career Entry," in *Reading and Career Education,* ed. Nielsen and Hjelm (Newark, Del.: International Reading Association, 1975); Sidney A. Fine, "The Use of the *Dictionary of Occupational Titles* as a Source of Estimates of Educational and Training Requirements," *Journal of Human Resources* 3 (1968):367; and Kenneth I. Spenner, "Occupational Characteristics and Classification Systems," *Sociological Methods and Research* 9 (1980):247.

130. Berg and Gorelick, *Education and Jobs,* 58.

131. See, for example, Sum, Harrington, and Goedicke, *Basic Skills of America's Teens and Young Adults.*

132. Kirsch and Guthrie, "Adult Reading Practices."

133. Samuel Bowles and Herbert Gintis, *Schooling in Capitalist America* (New York: Basic Books, 1976); Samuel Bowles, "Second Thoughts on the Capitalism-Enlightenment Connection: Are Americans Over Educated or Are Jobs Dumb?" (Address to Conference on Libraries and Literacy, National Commission on Libraries and Information Services, Washington, D.C., April 1, 1979). See also U.S. Bureau of Labor Statistics, *Economic Projections to 1990,* Bulletin 2121 (Washington, D.C.: Depart-

pared with those that individuals possess, those schools could inculcate, and those that could be learned in restructured jobs. Like Bowles and Gintis, the federal commission that produced *Work in America* in 1983 found that workers were better educated than their jobs demanded, and they recommended a vast expansion in worker control over their jobs and working conditions.[134]

In fact, both trends—dumbing down and rising literacy demands— are occurring simultaneously at different levels in the occupational pyramid and in different sectors. Although reports of the early 1980s often put more emphasis on deskilling, recent reports have argued that low-skill jobs are declining proportionally, not increasing; that better skills are essential to better opportunity for poor and minority workers; and that in order to face an increasingly international, information-oriented economic situation, employers need to build flexible, skilled work teams rather than exploit disposable workers.[135]

The methodological problems inherent in the research on job literacy are formidable, and the limitations of the existing data bases make a valid national assessment of the job-literacy gap unlikely. Policy making cannot await further research that is likely to be as inconclusive as existing research. Whether functional illiteracy is 15 percent or 35 percent, whether the population's reading grade level is seventh or ninth grade, and whether the job-literacy gap is growing smaller or larger are not as crucial as an unqualified recognition that serious literacy problems exist. Workers need both greater autonomy in their jobs and better literacy training if they are to develop their skills fully. In the next section, we discuss the kinds of literacy training that may best achieve those ends.

Job Literacy versus School Literacy

Recent research suggests that schools develop in students a set of literacy skills unlike those typically needed on the job.[136] These findings support

ment of Labor, 1982); Henry M. Levin and R. Rumberger, "Hi-Tech Requires Few Brains," *Washington Post*, January 30, 1983, sec. C, p. 5.

134. J. O'Toole et al., *Work in America: Report of a Special Task Force to the Secretary of Health, Education, and Welfare* (Cambridge: MIT Press, 1973).

135. William B. Johnston and Arnold E. Packer, *Workforce 2000: Work and Workers for the Twenty-first Century* (Indianapolis, Ind.: Hudson Institute, 1987); Gordon Berlin and Andrew Sum, *Toward a More Perfect Union: Basic Skills, Poor Families, and Our Economic Future* (New York: Ford Foundation, 1988); U.S. Department of Labor and U.S. Department of Education, *The Bottom Line: Basic Skills in the Workplace* (Washington, D.C.: Government Printing Office, 1988); U.S. Congress, Office of Technology Assessment, *Technology and the American Economic Transition: Choices for the Future* (Washington, D.C.: Government Printing Office, 1988).

136. Sticht, ed., *Reading for Working*, 183–86; Diehl and Mikulecky, "Nature of Reading at Work," 224–25; Kirsch and Guthrie, "Adult Reading Practices," 231; Rich-

our distinction between a vertical and a horizontal dimension of literacy. Most high-school English classes, for example, focus on the reading and interpretation of literature and on general composition; typically they ignore technical writing and editing and rarely use such job materials as technical manuals, advertising copy, and memoranda. The new research shows that reading in the workplace is more integrated with other tasks and more immediately applied than in school. Workers draw upon a greater variety of reading materials than students do. In fact, workplace literacy has been described as a "social phenomenon" because workers often accomplish job tasks by talking with and observing others.[137] Partly as a consequence, workers are able to perform jobs competently even when they involve reading materials well above their tested reading level.[138] The weak relationship reported earlier between standardized reading scores and job performance also supports the notion that school-reading skills differ from job-literacy skills.

Diehl and Mikulecky distinguished "reading-to-do" from "reading-to-learn" and hypothesized major differences in information processing between the two.[139] Interesting, measures of workers' on-the-job reading strategies, often called "metacognitive" skills, have been shown to be related to job performance. Mikulecky and Winchester found that, although general reading ability did not relate to job performance, "reading to assess while performing a task" did.[140] Mikulecky and Ehlinger also determined that superior-performing workers had better metacognitive skills.[141] Such workers knew how to focus their attention on reading materials and job tasks, had systems for organizing information, could explain how their activities related to their overall purposes, and could monitor their own performance.

Such findings have important implications for job-literacy training. They suggest that job-literacy problems may not be best solved by concentrating on basic academic skills or by raising students' reading grade levels on standardized tests. Indeed, a recent review of military training programs determined that literacy training must involve job-specific

ard L. Venezky, "The Origins of the Present-Day Chasm between Adult Literacy Needs and School Literacy Instruction," *Visible Language* 16 (1982):113–26; and Richard L. Venezky, Carl F. Kaestle, and Andrew M. Sum, *The Subtle Danger: Reflections on the Literacy Abilities of America's Young Adults* (Princeton, N.J.: Educational Testing Service, 1987).

137. Mikulecky and Ehlinger, "Influence of Metacognitive Aspects of Literacy," 43; see also Sticht, ed., *Reading for Working,* 59.

138. Sticht, ed., *Reading for Working,* 85–86.

139. Diehl and Mikulecky, "Nature of Reading at Work," 225.

140. Mikulecky and Winchester, "Job Literacy and Job Performance among Nurses," 225.

141. Mikulecky and Ehlinger, "Influence of Metacognitive Aspects of Literacy."

literacy tasks to be successful.[142] Although traditional basic-skills programs raised workers' academic grade levels, the training had an impact on job performance measures only if it involved direct instruction in job-literacy tasks.

We must be careful, however, in generalizing from the findings about metacognitive skills. The two studies by Mikulecky and associates sampled a limited number of highly literate workers in highly specialized jobs—twenty-seven nurses in the first, twenty-nine electronics technicians in the second. On average, the nurses read at a twelfth-grade level, whereas the technicians ranged between grade twelve and college level.[143] It is uncertain whether these results would be duplicated among workers with lower reading levels or in more typical workplaces with simpler information-processing demands. If future research confirms these conclusions, it would suggest that adult literacy training programs should concentrate on literacy skills related to assessing, organizing, and monitoring workplace information.

Literacy Differences among Groups

Thus far we have looked only at national averages for the entire population, occasionally grouping the data by age to infer trends over time. But literacy is thoroughly enmeshed in the social structure. Its distribution is affected by group relations and differential opportunity structures. In turn, literacy becomes an indicator of status, and reading ability becomes both an instrument and a badge of stratification. The farther back in our history we go, the more abject are the gaps in literacy between groups. As might be expected, women, blacks, other minorities, the poor, southerners, and the foreign born have been less literate on average than their male, white, middle-class, northern, native-born counterparts. Although the gaps in crude literacy have narrowed substantially during this century, gaps in more complex skills are a central concern in our ever-more literate society. To acknowledge these differences and to suggest their magnitude, we survey briefly two of the most important dichotomies: sex and race.

Male-Female Differences

As we noted in chapter 1, women in early America had less access to schooling and high-literacy occupations and displayed lower rates of

142. Sticht, *Basic Skills in Defense*, 53–54.
143. Mikulecky and Winchester, "Job Literacy and Job Performance among Nurses," 7; Mikulecky and Ehlinger, "Influence of Metacognitive Aspects of Literacy," 54.

rudimentary literacy than their male counterparts; women's literacy rates did not catch up with men's until about the middle of the nineteenth century. Indeed, on most measures of rudimentary and middle-level literacy in the past century, women have outperformed men, although the differences typically have not been great. For example, among fourteen- to twenty-four-year-olds in 1910, 5 percent of women and 6.3 percent of men reported themselves to be illiterate. By 1969, the single-percentage-point difference had almost vanished. Similarly, in 1910, 21.6 percent of women had not completed fifth grade, whereas 25.9 percent of men had not. By 1979, the gap had almost closed, but it still favored women, 3.2 to 3.7 percent. For high-school completion, the differences were again small and, until recently, favored women.

Most of the functional-literacy tests display the same gender gap. The Survival Literacy test, for example, indicated that 3 percent of men and 2 percent of women were functionally illiterate. For those in the middle, who were not functionally illiterate but failed to reach functional literacy as depicted by the study, the rates were 14 percent for men and 11 percent for women. On the MAFL, the average seventeen-year-old girl scored 86.5 percent in 1975, whereas the average boy scored 85.2 percent, less than half as large a gap as the 2.9 percent gender difference reported in 1971. In 1975, 89.1 percent of the girls who took the MAFL were functionally literate, compared with 85.4 percent of the boys. Thus, at the entry and middle levels of literacy abilities, recent years have seen a rough parity between men and women, generally tilting slightly toward women.

This is not to suggest, however, that discrimination against women or concepts of differential roles for men and women have vanished. Thus it would be surprising if all literacy skills showed equality. For women, as for other groups, some gaps remain at higher levels. Boys score higher on the mathematics portion of the Scholastic Aptitude Test, and on the Graduate Record Examinations men outscore women in all subject areas except English.[144] Most people attribute these average differences to cultural factors, including differential training, socialization, and aspirations. Over the long course of history, gaps in literacy have tended to narrow; given the intense discussions at present surrounding these gender gaps and the urgent need to recruit women into technical fields, we may expect further equalization in the attainment of literacy skills, test-taking skills, and mathematics skills at the highest levels.

144. Gita Z. Wilder and Kristin Powell, *Sex Differences in Test Performance: A Survey of the Literature,* report no. 89-3 (New York: College Entrance Examination Board, 1989).

Black-White Differences

On all measures of literacy, at all points during the last century, white Americans have been more literate than black Americans. In 1880, the differences were vast, of course, with the American black population emerging from slavery and subject to massive poverty and discrimination. Over the past century, as we noted in chapter 1, differences at the level of rudimentary literacy and primary schooling have almost disappeared. On such higher-level measures as those measured on functional-literacy tests, or as inferred from high-school completion rates, the gaps remain large.

In the 1880 census, only 9.4 percent of whites reported themselves illiterate, compared with 70 percent of nonwhites.[145] By 1979, the white rate was .4 percent, whereas that of blacks was 1.6 percent (for those fourteen years and older). Rudimentary literacy had become nearly universal among the young; differences by race were due almost entirely to the statistical impact of elderly illiterate black people. Among youth aged fourteen to twenty-four, the rates were .18 percent for whites and .23 percent for blacks, well within the range of sampling error.

As for educational attainment, among those aged twenty-five to twenty-nine, 12.9 percent of whites in 1920 had fewer than five years of schooling, compared with 44.6 percent of blacks. By 1985 the rates were identical, .7 percent. For the high-school completion standard, the gap was fifteen percentage points in 1920; 78 percent of whites had not graduated, compared with 93.7 percent of blacks. In 1985 this gap remained large; 13.2 percent of whites reported that they had not completed high school, compared with 19.4 percent of blacks.[146]

The functional-literacy tests of the 1970s also displayed consistently large racial gaps. On the Survival Literacy test, for example, 8 percent of blacks were functionally illiterate, whereas 2 percent of whites were. On the MAFL in 1975, the average seventeen-year-old black scored 74.1 percent correct and the average white scored 87.8 percent. This 13.7 percent gap was down slightly from 1971, when it was 15.6 percent.

145. Data are for persons ten years and older. Although the rate for blacks as a group is not available for 1880, the 1870 and 1890 rates for nonwhite and black Americans are almost identical. See J. P. Lichtenberger, "Negro Illiteracy in the United States," in *The Negro's Progress in Fifty Years,* ed. Emory R. Johnson, Annals of the American Academy of Political and Social Science, 49 (Philadelphia, 1913), 177–85.

146. The 1920 figures are estimates projected backward by cohort from known attainment rates in 1940. John K. Folger and Charles B. Nam, "Educational Trends from Census Data," *Demography* 1 (1964):253. The 1985 data are from Rosalind R. Bruno, *Educational Attainment in the United States, March 1982 to 1985,* Current Population Reports, Population Characteristics, ser. P-20, no. 415 (Washington, D.C.: U.S. Bureau of the Census, 1987), 23, 28.

Functional illiteracy was defined on this test as failure to achieve a score of 75 percent correct. By this standard, 41.6 percent of black seventeen-year-olds were functionally illiterate, compared with 9.2 percent of white seventeen-year-olds. On the APL, fewer than 20 percent of the whites were found to be functionally "incompetent," whereas more than 40 percent of the blacks were.

In terms of general reading performance, on the NAEP reading tests from 1971 to 1988 the average black student at ages nine, thirteen, and seventeen scored below the average white student at the same age levels. Across the decade the gap for nine-year-olds narrowed from 44 points to 29 points; for thirteen-year-olds the gap narrowed from 38 points to 18 points. The gap for seventeen-year-olds narrowed from 55 points to 20 points during those years.[147]

Sensitivity is necessary in interpreting racial gaps in literacy scores. Blacks are disadvantaged in this society in several ways that are known to affect educational performance, such as lower levels of parental education and income. Still, large racial differences persist after controlling for these social factors. After controlling for family income, for example, the Survival Literacy Study rates for blacks were still double those for whites. The Brief Test of Literacy displayed similar gaps after controlling for parental education. These comparisons, however, dealt with only two variables at a time, so the racial correlation could be masking other underlying variables. However, Christopher Jencks and his colleagues conducted a multivariate analysis of racial differences on cognitive tests, and they concluded that less than one-third of the differences could be accounted for by economic background.[148] Irwin Kirsch and Ann Jungeblut applied statistical controls to the considerable gap between white and black scores on the three literacy scales of the Young Adult Literacy Assessment of 1985. They found that controlling for parents' education and occupation, access to literacy materials in the home, age of learning English, educational attainment, and choice of high-school curriculum accounted for about 27 percent of the white-black difference.[149] A large, durable portion of the literacy differences between black and white Americans clearly cannot be explained by measurable economic and family characteristics. In the unexplained portion of the variation lie such elusive but real factors as the effects of prejudice, cultural alienation, discouragement, and differential aspirations, all related to race.

147. Ina V. S. Mullins and Lynn B. Jenkins, *The Reading Report Card, 1971–88: Trends from the Nation's Report Card* (Washington, D.C.: U.S. Department of Education, 1990), 14.
148. Jencks et al., *Inequality*, 82.
149. Kirsch and Jungeblut, *Literacy*, chap. 7.

Literacy Gaps between Other Groups

We will not discuss the literacy gaps that exist between other groups in American society. Those relating to income, language group, recency of immigration, and family income are sometimes discussed and remind us of a persistent point about the history of literacy. In spite of the expansion of education and the proliferation of reading materials, literacy remains inextricably tied to the social structure. It reflects chronic differences among groups as well as the distribution of power in our society.

This chapter traced trends in literacy and reading ability in the United States during the last hundred years. As the patient reader has come to understand, the data are sketchy and the trends are murky. Problems of definition, validity, representativeness, and comparability preclude unambiguous conclusions. Thus we believe that present-day literacy policy should be based on an assessment of our current condition, difficult enough to make, and on the basis of our ideals—not on the basis of alleged declines in literacy skills. The trends are in doubt; the existence of literacy problems in our society is not. We favor strenuous efforts to improve basic literacy skills and to teach all children critical reading and thinking skills.

What can we say about the historical record? First, during the twentieth century, self-reported outright illiteracy almost disappeared when expressed as a percentage of the population. Still, the absolute numbers are substantial. In 1979 nearly a million adults rated themselves as illiterate, and such people clearly have a severe problem in our print-laden technological society.

Second, the big story in twentieth-century literacy is the rise in school attainment. Although some children leave school without sufficient training or skills, a rise in schooling of the magnitude witnessed in the United States indisputably has produced a much more literate population. In 1910 almost one-fourth of the population had not made it to the fifth grade; by 1985 only 2.6 percent had not. In 1910, almost half the adult population had not reached the eighth grade; by 1988, that proportion was 7.1 percent. The median educational level rose four full years between 1940 and 1985, from 8.6 to 12.6 years of schooling.[150]

Third, although it is difficult to make confident statements about trends in students' reading performance before the 1980s, we venture the conclusion that reading achievement for students in school at any given age level has been stable throughout most of the twentieth century.

150. Folger and Nam, "Educational Trends," 253; Bruno, *Educational Attainment,* 53.

Does this mean that things are rosy on the literacy front? Certainly not. The functional-literacy tests showed that a substantial portion of the population, from 20 to 30 percent, has difficulty coping with common reading tasks and materials. The job-literacy measures, for all their limitations, show mismatches between many workers' literacy skills and the reading demands of their jobs. Even if schools today are performing about as well as they have in the past, they have never excelled at educating minorities and the poor or at teaching higher-order skills. And, if the increase in education is the only reason the population has kept up with the increasing literacy demands of our society, there is plenty of reason for concern. It is doubtful that increasing school attainment can continue indefinitely; among some groups, like black males, college attendance is declining, and the ineffectiveness of many inner-city schools makes us doubt the viability of a strategy of more schooling unless significant improvements can be made in the schools.

The solution to rising literacy demands is therefore more difficult now than fifty years ago. Nonetheless, we shall need much better reading skills across the entire population if we are to survive and improve as a democratic society in an increasingly complex age, quite apart from workplace demands for more literacy. Seen in this light, there is much to galvanize renewed efforts at literacy training, at all levels. We need no proof of a great decline to make us concerned. Serving the goals of economic and political participation on the literacy front will require new commitment, more money, and a closer collaboration by educators, employers, community groups, and government agencies.

4 The Great Test-Score Decline: A Closer Look

LAWRENCE C. STEDMAN AND CARL F. KAESTLE

Chapter 3 analyzed trends in reading achievement across the entire twentieth century. This chapter examines in more detail the magnitude and causes of the highly publicized test-score decline that spanned the decade from the late 1960s to the late 1970s. Results from the major standardized tests indicate that this test-score decline ended in the late 1970s, but debates flowing from the decline have shaped policy debates throughout the 1980s. The Iowa Tests of Basic Skills (ITBS), given to third through eighth graders, showed that students' scores rose dramatically between 1977 and 1984.[1] The 1982 Stanford Achievement Test also showed general improvement. Eleventh graders scored four percentiles higher in mathematics and ten percentiles higher in reading than their grade-level counterparts in 1973.[2] Eighth graders' scores were up six percentiles in math and seven in reading. Students showed similar improvements across subjects as different as science and spelling. The National Assessment of Educational Progress (NAEP) results showed that the mathematics scores of thirteen-year-olds rose between 1978 and 1982, whereas seventeen-year-olds' scores remained stable, ending their previous decline.[3]

1. A. N. Hieronymus, E. F. Lindquist, and H. D. Hoover, *Manual for School Administrators: Iowa Tests of Basic Skills* (Chicago: Riverside, 1982); Hieronymus, Lindquist, and Hoover, *The Development of the 1982 Norms for the Iowa Tests of Basic Skills, the Cognitive Abilities Test, and the Tests of Achievement and Proficiency* (Chicago: Riverside, 1983); personal communication with A. N. Hieronymus, University of Iowa, Iowa Testing Program, September 16, 1985.

2. *Some Comments on the Relationship between Scores on the 1973 and 1982 Editions of the Stanford Achievement Test: Stanford Special Report No. 4A* (New York: Harcourt Brace Jovanovich, 1983).

3. Ibid.

The score decline on college entrance tests also ended. Scores on the American College Testing (ACT) Program in English, social studies, and science, for example, have been stable for a decade. ACT mathematics scores dropped until 1983 but rose thereafter. Scholastic Aptitude Test scores stopped declining by 1980, and SAT math scores have even risen a few points in recent years. SAT verbal scores have fluctuated up and down a point or two for most of the past decade.

National scores on the ITBS and NAEP began their upswing in 1977 and 1978. Furthermore, results in Iowa, often used as a national barometer because of that state's long history of comprehensive annual testing, have shown steady increases in most grades since 1978. The National Commission on Excellence in Education, with its dire warnings in 1983 of a nation at risk, was about five years behind the times. Instead of a "rising tide of mediocrity," it should have proclaimed a rising tide of test scores.

One commonly accepted interpretation of the test-score decline goes something like this. A massive decline in academic achievement took place in the late 1960s and early 1970s, especially in verbal skills and especially among high-school students; it was caused by student-centered permissiveness in the schools. Those declines were reversed in the 1980s by tougher standards and training in the basic skills. In spite of its commonsensical simplicity, this interpretation is full of half-truths. Careful review of the evidence points to quite different conclusions. Most test scores did not begin falling until the 1970s; many continued to fall long after "permissive" school reform had been abandoned, which makes it difficult to blame the decline on the social movements of the 1960s. When the decline did occur, it was neither as great nor as alarming as it was portrayed. Furthermore, performance on several tests, including some measures of reading and writing skills, did not decline during the 1970s. In the face of such mixed results, there is reason to be skeptical of claims that there was a severe general decline in academic skills. Finally, the educational changes that were purported to have caused the decline were never as widespread as the critics maintained. Taken together, the evidence suggests that some scapegoating has occurred and that the causes and magnitude of the test-score decline remain in doubt.

How Bad Was the Decline?

As we noted in chapter 3, a substantial body of evidence suggests that test scores remained stable in the 1960s, particularly at the high-school level. The Iowa Tests of Educational Development (ITED), for example, showed steady increases in high-school reading and math scores when they were renormed in 1957, 1962, and 1971.[4] Renormings of the Preliminary Scholastic Aptitude Test (PSAT) showed that high-school juniors maintained their reading and math scores in 1960, 1966, and 1974 comparisons.[5] Metropolitan Achievement Test (MAT) scores for seventh through ninth graders were equal or higher in 1970 than in 1958 on reading, math concepts, science, and social studies.[6] The SAT did show major drops beginning in 1963, but the College Board's Advisory Panel on the SAT Decline found that between two-thirds and three-fourths of the decline during the 1960s was attributable to changes in the population of test takers.[7] Expanded opportunities in the 1960s resulted in more minority, low-ability, and low-income students taking the SAT and enrolling in college. The panel determined that most of the real decline actually occurred in the 1970s, and that even then, some of that can be attributed to the changing characteristics of the test takers—the "compositional effect" mentioned in Chapter 3. The panel's conclusions are supported by renorming studies of most standardized tests, which showed that the major drops occurred between 1970 and 1978.

Critics talked about a "massive decline," "an almost unremitting fall," and "the first major skills decline in American educational history." They presented data in various statistical guises, many of them quite dramatic. Paul Copperman argued in 1979 that the average high-school student of the late 1970s stood at only the thirty-ninth percentile when compared with his or her 1965 counterparts.[8] The drop in SAT verbal scores was almost half a standard deviation. Several tests showed that eleventh and twelfth graders lost a year or more in measured reading ability during the 1970s. Expressed in these ways, the test-score decline appears substantial, but there are several problems with such stark descriptions.

First, many critics of the schools accepted the scores at face value, once again failing to account for changes in the population of test takers. We must distinguish decreases due to a changing test-taker pool from those resulting from a general decline in students' skills. Trends on college entrance exams are especially difficult to interpret because they measure the performance of a self-selected group of students whose com-

4. "The Iowa Tests of Educational Development: A Summary of Changes in the ITED Norms" (University of Iowa, Iowa City, 1971, Mimeographed).
5. Hunter M. Breland, "The SAT Score Decline: A Summary of Related Research," in Advisory Panel, *On Further Examination,* appendix, 25.
6. *Equivalent Scores for Metropolitan Achievement Tests 1970 Edition and Metropolitan Achievement Tests 1958 Edition: Special Report No. 14* (New York: Harcourt Brace Jovanovich, 1971).
7. Advisory Panel, *On Further Examination,* 18.
8. Copperman, "Achievement Decline of the 1970s."

position changes annually. Even in the 1970s, a changing pool of test takers accounted for a substantial portion of the decline. More students from characteristically lower-scoring groups continued to take college entrance tests, including minority students and students intending to pursue nonacademic majors. The College Board's Advisory Panel estimated that between 20 and 30 percent of the decline in SAT scores during the 1970s could be attributed to such changes.[9]

Changes in family size also had an impact on SAT scores, though not as great as some once claimed. Test-score data have shown that first- and second-born children on average score higher than other test takers. A recent study of the period between 1971 and 1977, for example, found that such changes accounted for between 4 and 9.4 percent of the verbal SAT decline.[10] Combined with the other changing characteristics of test takers, this meant that at least 24 to 40 percent of the decline in SAT scores during the 1970s was, in fact, due to factors other than changes in students' performance on the skills measured by the tests.

Trends on standardized achievement tests were similarly affected by changes in the population of test takers, and these effects may have been as substantial for achievement tests during the 1970s as they were for the SAT. During the 1970s a falling dropout rate among black students and increased immigration of Asian and Hispanic students increased the percentage of minority students in our high schools from one-sixth to nearly one-fourth.[11] Such changes probably contributed to lower scores. Finally, evidence suggests that the effects of birth order are, for unknown reasons, greater on standardized achievement tests than on the SAT.

Another contributing factor, albeit a minor one, was the changing age of students. Automatic-promotion policies and earlier school-entering ages combined to make students at any given grade level increasingly younger. Researchers who have studied long-term test-score trends stress the necessity of accounting for the differential maturity of students. This factor, in combination with those already discussed, suggests that demographic changes may account for between 30 percent and 50 percent of the test-score decline on standardized achievement tests during the 1970s.

Critics have assumed, though, that the drop in scores from the mid-1960s to the late 1970s represented a real decline in students' skills.

9. Advisory Panel, *On Further Examination,* 19–20.

10. Robert B. Zajonc and John Bargh, "Birth Order, Family Size, and Decline of SAT Scores," *American Psychologist* 35 (July 1980), 662–68.

11. National Center for Education Statistics, *The Condition of Education* (Washington, D.C.: Department of Education, 1979), 17; U.S. Bureau of the Census, *School Enrollment,* Current Population Reports, ser. P-20, no. 374 (Washington, D.C.: Bureau of the Census, 1981), 35.

Copperman, for example, ignored the huge compositional effect described here when he claimed that students' achievement had fallen to the thirty-ninth percentile. In calculating this decline, Copperman estimated that scores had dropped 2.5 percent of one standard deviation every year from 1965 to 1978. Thirteen years of such a drop yielded an overall decrease of 32 percent of a standard deviation, or eleven percentiles.

But because Copperman did not adjust the scores for compositional changes and because the real skill decline occurred primarily in the 1970s, the overall decline was much smaller than he claimed. Allowing 1.3 to 1.8 percent of a standard deviation per year for seven years (the decline in the 1970s minus the estimated compositional effect) produces a total decline of 9.1 to 12.6 percent of a standard deviation during the 1970s. This amounts to a drop of only four to six percentiles, to the forty-fourth or forty-sixth percentile. Similarly, adjusting grade-level scores for compositional effects reduced apparent declines by up to one-half. Thus on tests that showed as much as a full year's decline, the adjusted decline would be only half that.

How different were the skills of students who scored half a grade level lower than an earlier group? What specific tasks could students no longer perform? Critics assumed that reading tests exclusively measured reading when, in fact, they also measure attitudes, test-taking experience and facility, reasoning skills, the ability to work quickly, and general knowledge. Changes in reading-test scores, therefore, may reflect changes in any or all of these other factors rather than changes in reading ability.[12] Also, standardized tests are constructed so that minor shifts in performance produce major changes in percentile and grade-equivalent rankings. The decline appears large when described in these terms, whereas the actual decrease in performance may be quite small. Oscar Buros, the late editor of the *Mental Measurements Yearbook,* argued that grade equivalents give people a misleading impression of skill levels. He advocated using the percentage of items a student answers correctly as a means of more closely reflecting actual performance.[13] Describing student performance this way provides a very different sense of the magnitude of the skill decline. On many standardized tests, differences between grades amount to only a few percentage points, particularly at the high-school level. On the Science Research Associates (SRA) test, the reading scores of ninth through twelfth graders dropped by a half to a full grade level between 1971 and 1978, but this corresponded to a small

12. For an extended discussion of the tests and their concept of reading, see Stedman and Kaestle, *Investigation of Crude Literacy,* appendix B.

13. Oscar Buros, "Fifty Years in Testing," in *Eighth Mental Measurements Yearbook,* ed. Buros (Highland Park, N.J.: Gryphon Press, 1978), 1976.

drop in the percentage of items answered correctly. Twelfth graders, for example, had dropped an entire grade level in reading, but this represented a drop of only four percentage points, from 72 to 68 percent correct. Mathematics declines were similar.

Several of the NAEP tests showed declines, but these also represented only minor decreases in actual performance. Between 1970 and 1980, the performance of seventeen-year-olds dropped from 64 percent correct to 62 percent correct in inferential reading comprehension; thirteen-year-olds dropped from 56.1 to 55.5 percent. Between 1973 and 1982 the performance of seventeen-year-olds dropped four percentage points in mathematics, and that of thirteen-year-olds dropped two points. Other tests may show larger declines, but the point remains the same: When the declines are expressed in terms of percentages, they are less dramatic than when expressed in terms of grade levels.

Another way to assess the decline would be to ask at what percentage of their former skill levels students are now performing. On the NAEP tests, for example, students were performing at 97 percent of their levels ten years earlier in inferential comprehension and at 92 percent in mathematics. High-school students on the SRA test were reading at about 95 percent of their former levels, a 5 percent decline in the various skills measured by this test. Such an approach provides a more realistic assessment of the decline than the criteria used by the critics.

A third problem in discussions of the test-score decline is that many commentators linked it to national economic problems. The authors of *A Nation at Risk,* for example, argued that the test-score decline threatened our national economic security. But what are the demonstrable educational and economic ramifications of a 5 percent skill decline? The statistical links between academic success at one level and the next are relatively weak, as are those between academic performance and job performance. The correlation between SAT scores and freshman grades, for example, is about .40.[14] The decline of 20 percent of a standard deviation in SAT scores in the 1970s (taking compositional changes into account) would translate into a drop of only 8 percent of a standard deviation in freshman grades. The correlation between achievement-test scores and measures of job proficiency is about .25.[15] Thus the drop of 12.6 percent of a standard deviation in high-school achievement-test scores during the 1970s would translate into a drop in job performance of only 3.1 percent of one standard deviation—or only one percentile point. Furthermore, new workers comprise only a minute proportion of the

14. Advisory Panel, *On Further Examination,* 9.

15. Michael Olneck, "Terman Redux," *Contemporary Education Review* 3 (1984):297–314.

total work force, so recent declines in productivity can hardly be linked to recent changes in test scores. Even if the new workers who entered the labor force each year were underskilled for ten consecutive years, only about one-fourth of the active work force would be affected. Also, labor productivity is only one aspect of total productivity, which also involves capital and management productivity. The combined effect of these weak links is so minimal that the attempt to blame declining economic productivity on declining test scores seems downright silly. It is reasonable and indeed customary for employers to urge the schools to inculcate good work habits and basic skills in their students, and America's long-run economic prospects may depend upon a more highly educated, skillful work force. However, the solutions to such short-run economic problems as our trade balance lie largely outside the classroom.[16]

A fourth problem is that the SATs and standardized achievement tests are not very good indicators of national trends in academic abilities. The SATs appear to provide a national annual barometer of performance changes, but as we noted above, the composition of the test-taking population changes annually, and in any given year, as William Schrader noted, "high school seniors taking the Scholastic Aptitude Test are not representative either of high school seniors generally or of high school seniors planning to enter college."[17]

The credibility of reported downward trends in standardized achievement-test results is questionable as well. As we mentioned in chapter 3, the trends are determined when test publishers introduce redesigned versions of their tests. The new tests are administered to a nationally representative sample of schools, and performance on the new test is linked to the old test results through the use of "equating studies," in which samples of contemporary students are given both the new and the old test. Problems with equating abound. The equating samples are rarely representative of the nation, often involving only a few school districts or a small fraction of the national norming sample. Sometimes only portions of the two versions of the test are administered; occasionally two different groups of students are involved, one given the old version and one the new. Even some test publishers warn against the use of renorming data to infer national trends. Harcourt Brace Jovanovich, the publisher of the Metropolitan and Stanford achievement tests, stated in 1978 that "these data are not appropriate for making generalizations concerning changes over time in the relative achievement of American

16. For a recent article that overestimates the effect of test-score declines on productivity, see John H. Bishop, "Is the Test Score Decline Responsible for the Productivity Growth Decline?" *American Economic Review* 79 (March 1989):178–97.

17. Schrader, *Test Data as Social Indicators*, 5.

students in the basic skill areas."[18] More recently, this same publisher warned of a "popular misconception about changing norms: that a change in the norms from an old test to a new test reflects a change in the ability of the reference groups over time." On the contrary, the publisher continued, "there are simply too many complex and confounding variables to make a sound judgment about performance over time."[19] They cited changes in the national samples of students and the changing relevance of the test content as factors that confound any generalizations. Critics who use renorming evidence to describe national trends typically do not discuss these limitations.[20]

State trends on achievement tests are problematic because data for the 1960s and 1970s were limited to only a handful of states. Iowa is often used as a barometer, but it can hardly be considered representative, since it is largely rural and has few minority students. Although the critics cited data from states whose achievement-test scores declined in the 1960s and early 1970s, other states did not experience such declines. Achievement-test scores for high-school students in Alabama and South Dakota remained stable in the 1960s; junior-high-school students in Mississippi and Michigan registered stable scores in the early 1970s.

The NAEP tests are probably the best indicators of national trends, yet many critics ignored them. Because NAEP reports trends on common items contained in successive tests, renorming studies are unnecessary. Furthermore, it reports results by racial, geographical, and socioeconomic groups, so trends can be analyzed by subgroup. Since test items are made public, schools can independently examine the kinds of skills being measured. Unlike other standardized tests, the NAEP tests are administered to a nationally representative sample of students. Still, NAEP results played little role in critics' discussions, perhaps because they didn't show dramatic declines.

In fact, NAEP results from the 1970s are quite mixed. Thirteen- and seventeen-year-olds maintained their overall reading scores, and nine-year-olds improved theirs in testing carried out in 1970, 1975, and 1980. Seventeen-year-olds slipped in inferential comprehension, but as noted, the drop was minor—from a 1970 level of 64 percent correct to a 1980 level of 62 percent correct. Furthermore, this decline was not universal. The Northwest was the only region experiencing statistically significant

18. Psychological Corporation, *Metropolitan Achievement Tests, 1978 Edition, Equivalent Grade Equivalent Scores for Metro '70 and Metro '78: Special Report No. 20, Revised* (New York: Harcourt Brace Jovanovich, 1978).

19. *Some Comments*, 1.

20. For an extended discussion of the problems with equating and norming, see Stedman and Kaestle, *Investigation of Crude Literacy,* appendix C.

declines in inferential skills, and even there, the scores of boys declined but those of girls did not. The scores of blacks did not fall off significantly. Some commentators argue that the NAEP reading tests are easier than standardized high-school achievement tests. But the percentage of questions missed by seventeen-year-olds on the NAEP tests is comparable to the percentage missed on other achievement tests, and the proportion of the tests devoted to inferential skills is similar as well.[21]

In direct conflict with the gloom-and-doom perspective of many critics, the results on a variety of measures suggest that in many areas, the 1970s was a period of improved, rather than declining, performance. NAEP results, for example, showed that seventeen-year-olds improved their performance on functional-literacy tasks between 1971 and 1975, and that their writing skills remained roughly the same between 1969 and 1979. Rhetorical skill on narrative tasks improved during the period, as did scores on tests of prose cohesion. A 1973/1978 comparison of results on the Metropolitan Achievement Test and the Stanford Achievement Test for grades seven through ten showed a gain of five to six months in reading and six to twelve months in mathematics.[22] Furthermore, those who cite SAT scores as evidence of decline in United States education rarely mention data from the College Board Achievement Tests. Scores in English composition, biology, chemistry, physics, French, and Spanish increased between 1967 and 1976, the years of the worst SAT decline. Although the students who took these tests in 1976 had lower SAT scores than their predecessors, they outscored them on the achievement tests.[23] Also, the PSAT renorming scores were roughly stable from 1960 to 1974, and Project Talent data showed that high-school juniors had "slight gains" in reading comprehension from 1960 to 1970.[24] Finally, James Flynn reviewed sketchy evidence suggesting that I.Q. scores were stable or rising through the period from 1972 to 1978.[25] The picture, then, is much more complex than critics claim, and the contradictory evidence is not easily explained.[26]

21. See ibid., appendix D.

22. Psychological Corporation, *Metropolitan Achievement Tests, 1978 Edition, Equivalent Grade Equivalent Scores between Metro '78 and the 1973 Stanford Achievement Test: Special Report No. 21* (New York: Harcourt Brace Jovanovich, 1978).

23. Advisory Panel, *On Further Examination*, 22.

24. Breland, "SAT Score Decline"; John C. Flanagan, "Changes in School Levels of Achievement: Project Talent Ten and Fifteen Year Retests," *Educational Researcher* 5 (1976):9–12.

25. James R. Flynn, "The Mean I.Q. of Americans: Massive Gains, 1923 to 1978," *Psychological Bulletin* 95 (1984):29–51.

26. For further evidence of mixed test results, see Gilbert R. Austin and Herbert Garber, eds., *The Rise and Fall of National Test Scores* (New York: Academic Press, 1982), chaps. 2, 4, and 5.

What Caused the Decline?

Setting aside for the moment our arguments about the magnitude of the decline, let us look briefly at the explanations critics have offered for decreases in various indicators of academic achievement. Frank Armbruster claimed that in the 1960s "acceptance of improper behavior, and even some types of criminal acts, were becoming commonplace. Adults, even police, could be ignored with impunity."[27] He further claimed that "moderates in our school system lost their prominence and some apparently injudicious activist educators gained influence." These activists allegedly altered curriculum and teaching methods and opened the schools to the values of the slums. Teachers yielded to students the "responsibility of determining when, if, and, within a disturbingly questionable range, even what they would study." When achievement declined, sympathetic media and school boards let educators fix blame anywhere but on the schools. "This sympathetic attitude," Armbruster wrote, "may have been a 'spinoff' from the Kennedy era and later emphasis on the 'War on Poverty.'"

In 1978 Copperman blamed the decline to a great extent on the open-education movement and on a breakdown in authority relations. He criticized the "undisciplined counter-culture approach recommended by Kohl and others of his ilk."[28] He described Charles Silberman's *Crisis in the Classroom,* which advocated more freedom and openness in education, as "one of the most damaging pieces of educational writing to have been published in the past twenty years" and claimed that Silberman's recommendations were widely adopted. Like Armbruster, Copperman claimed that it was "current educational policy to give children a great deal of choice over what, how, and even whether they study." He also argued that free health clinics, runaway centers, and alternative high schools had undermined educational authority by convincing young people that "irresponsibility, hedonism, and laziness comprise an acceptable alternative value system."[29] Echoes of these conservative complaints of the late 1970s could still be heard in the late 1980s.

There are several problems with the explanations offered by these critics. First, they are overstated. If we were to imagine for a moment that the critics' interpretation is correct, then why, in the face of such a major social and educational breakdown, was there a decline only in some types of test scores, whereas others remained stable or improved? The results suggest more resilience and less social deterioration in our system of education than these observers have suggested.

27. Armbruster, *Our Children's Crippled Future,* 8–9.
28. Copperman, *Literacy Hoax,* 64. Copperman's reference is to Herbert Kohl, author of *Thirty-Six Children* (New York: Signet, 1967).
29. Copperman, *Literacy Hoax,* 68, 150, 170.

Second, the timing of the explanations is amiss. Since the decline, such as it was, actually occurred in the 1970s, blaming it on the social movements of the 1960s would require a convoluted lag theory that won't quite work. We do not agree that widespread unrest and disobedience affected most high schools in the nation, but even if we were to allow the critics that point, the greatest student protest took place between 1968 and 1971, whereas the greatest decline in standardized test scores took place between 1971 and 1978. And SAT scores continued to slump until 1980. That may seem like a plausible lag, but it requires transferring the disruptions to the elementary sector of the schools. A student who was in the twelfth grade in 1978 would not have been in high school during the protest years; he or she would have been proceeding from second to fifth grade. His or her high-school years, from 1975 to 1978, were hardly a time of protest or educational experimentation. Blaming the decline on the effects of social unrest in the schools may be fashionable, but the middle to late 1970s were years of educational retrenchment, characterized by a renewed emphasis on the basics, the spread of statewide competency testing, and moves to end social promotion. We can hardly blame the test declines of the 1970s directly on activist educators who, frustrated at their inability to change schools, had effectively abandoned their efforts by the mid-1970s.

An interesting variation on the "problem 1960s" thesis was proposed by Christopher Jencks, who stressed the teachers' loss of nerve, moral uncertainty, and consequent retreat from authority and high standards as an explanation for the test-score decline.[30] We believe that there is truth to the notion that the years of Vietnam and Watergate led to some disillusionment with rationality and tradition, and that this may have had a lingering effect on the public schools, but the pervasiveness of this disillusionment has not been established. Furthermore, we do not look upon such a reaction among young people and educators as unjustified or wholly undesirable. To decide that flexibility, student activism, and even a touch of rebelliousness are harmful because they detract from the pursuit of skills measured on standardized tests would be shortsighted. Among the preoccupations of youth in the 1960s and early 1970s were civil rights, government corruption, the Vietnam War, and other valid concerns. Whatever one's philosophical views, the loss-of-nerve explanation of the test-score decline is but weakly supported by the evidence.

Nor can we accept the explanations of the National Commission on Excellence in Education, which claimed that the high-school curriculum had been "homogenized, diluted, and diffused" and that the resulting "curricular smorgasbord . . . explains a great deal about where we find

30. Christopher Jencks, "Declining Test Scores: An Assessment of Six Alternative Explanations," *Sociological Spectrum* (December 1980):1–15.

ourselves today."[31] The commission's primary evidence for this conclusion was a flawed study of high-school transcripts that compared student
records from twenty-seven high schools in the late 1960s with a national
sample in the late 1970s. The two groups were not comparable, and the
differences in academic courses taken were small and sometimes favored
the later group. A more recent study that involved nationally representative samples showed increases, not decreases, in academic-course enrollments during the 1970s.[32]

Blaming test-score declines on a relaxation of academic standards is
too facile an explanation for the changes of the mid-1970s, when many
contradictory pressures affected the nation's schools. Moreover, some
research indicates that there is no causal connection. Gary Echternacht
studied two groups of high schools—those that maintained their SAT
scores and those in which scores declined more than the national average.[33] He found that the two types of schools did not differ in educational
approach. Truancy, discipline problems, and the permissiveness of teachers had increased similarly in both types of schools. The differences in
the number of academic courses taken by students were minute, sometimes favoring the schools whose scores were declining. English curricu-
la were similar; pass or fail grading and nontraditional course offerings
had expanded to the same extent.

At the elementary-school level, blaming the decline on the open-classroom movement also misses the mark. Although the timing is right, the
movement was never as widespread as its proponents hoped or its critics
feared. In 1970, after several years of visiting schools across the country,
Charles Silberman complained about "what grim, joyless places most
American schools are, how oppressive and petty are the rules by which
they are governed, how intellectually sterile and aesthetically barren the
atmosphere." He found few examples of open schools.[34] By 1973 Silberman had observed a shift toward the open classroom, but he added that

31. National Commission on Excellence in Education, *Nation at Risk,* 18.

32. Jerry West, Louis Diodato, and Nancy Sandberg, *A Trend Study of High School
Offerings and Enrollments: 1972–73 and 1981–82* (Washington, D.C.: Government
Printing Office, 1984, ERIC: ED 153 530). For the 1980s trends, see Margaret E.
Goertz, *Course-Taking Patterns in the 1980s* (New Brunswick, N.J.: Rutgers Univer-
sity, Center for Policy Research in Education, 1989). William Clune (with Janice Pat-
terson and Paula White), *The Implementation and Effects of High School Graduation
Requirements: First Steps toward Curriculum Reform* (New Brunswick, N.J.: Rutgers
University, Center for Policy Research in Education, 1989), analyzes the increases in
academic course-taking and raises some questions about the efficacy of upgraded
course requirements as an educational reform.

33. Gary J. Echternacht, "A Comparative Study of Secondary Schools with Different Score Patterns," in Advisory Panel, *On Further Examination,* appendix.

34. Charles Silberman, *Crisis in the Classroom* (New York: Vintage Books, 1970),
10.

"the classrooms I am talking about constitute a small handful."[35] John Holt, another advocate of the open classroom, observed in 1976 that "many of these innovations were dying or dead soon after [Silberman's] book came out. . . . Most of these lasted only a few years." He concluded that "there never was much 'open education.'" Citing a study of Minnesota schools, Holt suggested that less than 1 percent of the nation's children were in open classrooms.[36]

Whatever its actual extent, the open-classroom movement did not depress national test scores. On the NAEP reading test, for example, nine-year-olds improved their scores between 1970 and 1975, and even the critics of education agree that elementary-school students had stable or rising scores during the 1970s. Furthermore, the American Institutes for Research, reporting on a longitudinal study of thirty thousand elementary and junior-high-school students in thirteen school districts in nine states, found that achievement was unrelated to the level of educational innovation in the classrooms.[37]

Given that the skill decline was less drastic than is typically claimed, a series of nonschool factors could account for a large portion of it, including drugs, television, extracurricular activities, and decreases in motivation. Insufficient attention has been paid to the social and economic disruptions of family life that increased during the 1970s and that might also have hindered educational achievement. Between 1970 and 1978 the divorce rate rose from 3.5 to 5.2 per one thousand people and the number of single-parent families increased accordingly. Households headed by white females increased from 9 to 11.5 percent; households headed by black females increased from 27 to 36 percent. Meanwhile, the unemployment rate in the first half of the 1970s jumped from 4.9 to 8.5 percent, and millions of Americans simply stopped looking for work. We believe that such upheavals in the families and communities of junior and senior high-school students were likely contributors to their lower achievement.

Why Did the Decline End?

An old cliché holds that failure is an orphan, but success has a thousand parents. Writing in 1976, Carol Tavris predicted that when test scores started to rise again, everyone would take credit. "City X will attribute the upswing to their open schools, city Y will praise their unflinching attack on permissiveness. Educator A will pat himself on the

35. Charles Silberman, ed., *The Open Classroom* (New York: Vintage Books, 1973), xvii.
36. John Holt, *Instead of Education* (New York: E. P. Dutton, 1976), 140.
37. Advisory Panel, *On Further Examination,* 41.

back for his summer-school program, and educator B will pass champagne to everyone involved in her 'back-to-the-basics' approach."[38] This indeed happened, although the magnitude of the turnaround was even more modest than the magnitude of the decline. Governors, state legislators, and the sponsors of reform reports suggested that their actions had been important in stemming the tide of mediocrity. President Reagan told the National Association of Secondary School Principals in 1984 that both aptitude and achievement tests "underwent a virtually unbroken decline" from 1963 to 1981, but that "since our Administration put education at the top of the American agenda we've seen a grassroots revolution" to get back to "basic teaching and learning." In 1986 Reagan announced that his Commission on Excellence had "touched off a wave of reforms that swept through nearly every town."[39] Yet achievement-test scores were rising well before President Reagan's election, before the reformers issued their reports, and before the legislatures passed their post-1980 reform bills.

Nonschool factors may have produced part of the reversal. For example, average family size had fallen slightly, so test takers of the 1980s were more often first- or second-born than those of the 1970s and therefore were more likely to score somewhat higher. Changes in the schools, of course, were a factor in the turnaround of test scores. Instruction focused more on the skills that are measured by standardized tests. Many states and school districts adopted competency tests for promotion or graduation. Research on the concept of effective schools emphasized the frequent and systematic testing of pupils. The effective schools formula served widely as the foundation for school-improvement projects. Criterion-referenced testing, which links curricular objectives directly with test items, also assumed a larger role in the schools. With all this increased attention to testing, it is hardly surprising that students' test scores improved somewhat.

But do the improved test scores of the 1980s signal real improvement in the quality of education now provided in our schools? Of course we are gratified to see improved reading scores and a narrowing gap between whites and minority students. But we question whether the current focus on frequent testing and traditional pedagogy addresses two of our schools' most pressing educational problems. First, schools have long struggled to move beyond basic skills to teach higher-order thinking; given this, it is patently illogical to believe that back-to-basics programs

38. Carol Tavris, "The End of the I.Q. Slump," *Psychology Today,* April 1976, 69–74.

39. "Remarks of the President to the National Association of Secondary School Principals, 68th Annual Convention," (White House press release, Washington, D.C., February 7, 1984); Bernard Weinraub, "Reagan Says the Nation's Schools Have Improved," *New York Times,* September 7, 1986.

are the panacea. It may also be counterproductive. Nancy Borkow suggested in the early 1980s that schools were "hitting the basics too hard" and cited evidence that this emphasis hindered the development of higher-order skills.[40] Consultants for the NAEP mathematics program blamed at least part of the decline in problem solving during the 1970s on the back-to-basics movement.[41]

Second, for years the tests have revealed that many students are deficient in the basic literacy and computation skills needed by workers and citizens. Because the pool of students who lacked fundamental skills was large even fifteen years ago, returning to the much-vaunted instructional strategies of the past—strategies that were unsuccessful then—is not a logical solution to this problem either. Results from the NAEP tests illustrate this point. Consider the following two mathematical application items. Given an electric bill with a charge of $9.09 for 606 kilowatt hours of electricity, students were asked to determine the cost per kilowatt hour. The percentage of seventeen-year-olds correctly answering this item declined seven points between 1973 and 1978. More notable is that 88 percent of seventeen-year-olds in 1973 couldn't answer the problem, even though they had gone to elementary and junior high school in the "good old days."[42] The second item reported that a hockey team had won five of its twenty games. Students were asked what percentage of games the team won. On this question, scores fell eight percentage points from 1973 to 1978, but the decline pales when compared to the fact that, even in 1973, only 40 percent of seventeen-year-olds could answer the question correctly. Many items from the 1970 NAEP reading tests show a similar pattern.

Going back farther, to the 1964 international competition in mathematics, thirteen-year-olds in the United States scored quite poorly compared to those in other industrialized nations, even though their schooling had taken place in the 1950s and early 1960s.[43] All the talk about test-score declines and getting back to the basics tends to obscure the long-standing failure of United States schools to teach higher-order skills and to reach the lower third of students. Many of our students need to learn basic skills, but the back-to-basics pedagogy—popularly understood to mean more discipline, tougher grading practices, and traditional

40. Nancy Borkow, *Analysis of Test Score Trends: Implications for Secondary School Policy—A Caution to Secondary School Administrators* (Washington, D.C.: National Institute of Education, 1982).

41. National Assessment of Educational Progress, *Changes in Mathematical Achievement, 1973–78,* Report no. 09-MA-01 (Denver: Education Commission of the States, 1979), 24–25.

42. Ibid., 12.

43. Torsten Husén, ed., *International Study of Achievement in Mathematics: A Comparison between Twelve Countries* (New York: Wiley, 1967).

textbooks—should not be expected to serve the low achievers any better in the late 1980s than it did in the early 1960s.

The 1980s focus on testing has had serious negative consequences. Larry Cuban found that, as a result of the effective-schools movement, many school systems were returning to the pre-1900 notion of a uniform curriculum, using a single set of textbooks for each group. Many teachers were reverting to the old-fashioned method of whole-group instruction, combining lecture, recitation, and seatwork—a strategy that Cuban believed went "far beyond what the research suggests."[44] He criticized the "single-minded quest for higher test scores" for narrowing the schools' agenda to content that is easily measured. As a consequence, less attention is paid to other goals, such as sharing, learning to make decisions, developing self-esteem, and acquiring higher-level thinking skills and aesthetic sensitivities.

Daniel and Lauren Resnick presented evidence from Pittsburgh to show that minimum competency testing encouraged teachers to focus only on the minimum skills to be tested.[45] Deborah Meier, who has taught in inner-city schools for the past two decades, found that the focus on testing was harming the development of good reading skills. The quest for high test scores had particularly harmful effects on children from poor families, she argued. In schools attended largely by children of low-income families, Meier reported "the prevalence of programmed scripts based on behavior-mod techniques, reading 'kits' consisting of hundreds of unrelated paragraphs followed by multiple-choice questions and reams of ditto sheets." Worse, Meier noted, "lower-class schools are often devoid of books (except perhaps workbooks, readers, and *the* textbook); instead of libraries they have remedial reading and audiovisual 'labs.' It's not universal, but it's common."[46] Such acute problems may worsen and spread if the pressure for accountability grows and test-score rehabilitation becomes the central goal of education.

If they are interpreted carefully and thoroughly, standardized tests can reveal national trends, and the learning deficiencies they reflect are of national concern. But the solutions must be largely local. Schools in different settings have different problems. Educators and school boards must identify their students' most pressing needs, ranging from rudimentary skills to critical thinking, and from positive self-image to positive attitudes about academic work. Do students like to read? Can

44. Larry Cuban, "Effective Schools: A Friendly but Cautionary Note," *Phi Delta Kappan* (June 1983):695–96.

45. Daniel Resnick and Lauren Resnick, "Standards, Curriculum, and Performance: Historical and Comparative Perspective," *Educational Researcher* 14 (1985):5–20.

46. Deborah Meier, "Why Reading Tests Don't Test Reading," *Dissent* (Fall 1981):457–66; Meier, "'Getting Tough' in the Schools," *Dissent* (Winter 1984):61–70.

they apply their math skills? Are they achieving in areas not easily tested? Are they learning to appreciate and respect other cultures? Is the curriculum balanced, fair, engaging, inclusive, demanding?

Tests have played an exaggerated role in recent discussions of education reform. No doubt the skills measured by standardized tests did decline somewhat during the 1970s, and some students have always lacked rudimentary skills. We therefore applaud the renewed emphasis on reading and writing and the revived efforts to provide strong academic training in high schools. But we disagree with the perspective that blames a collapse of standards on the turbulent sixties and looks to test scores to measure whether educational problems have been solved.

The challenge is not to get our children back into harness and crack the whip. If that were a viable solution, it would be a simple process. But schools must impart more than basic skills; they must become better places for teachers to work and for children to learn about themselves and their society. This cannot happen with top-down, test-based solutions. The challenge to each community, then, is to find a philosophically appealing and educationally effective balance between common experiences and cultural diversity, between a supportive atmosphere and standards of excellence, between student initiative and the transmission of uplifting knowledge. In this process, tests can play only a limited role.

We suggested in chapter 3 that the test-score decline of the 1970s was relatively insignificant compared with the long-range increases in literacy and schooling over the last century. In this chapter we have shown that the anxieties were only partially justified, that the declines were not as great as some claimed, and that the declines that did occur were not as clearly attributable to the policies and practices of schools in the 1960s and early 1970s as some critics complained. However, we repeat the point we argued at the close of chapter 3. Americans do not need evidence of a decline in reading skills to recognize the urgent need for more effective literacy training. Our literacy needs have escalated beyond our abilities, and the gaps in literacy skills are ominously correlated with racial and ethnic groups. These two factors should be sufficient to motivate a continuing quest for more effective, more sophisticated, and more inclusive literacy training.

III Americans' Reading Activities

5 Literacy as a Consumer Activity

LAWRENCE C. STEDMAN, KATHERINE TINSLEY, AND
CARL F. KAESTLE

We now turn from the detailed analysis of reading abilities to evidence of the actual behavior of readers. This chapter reviews government statistics on the purchase of newspapers, magazines, and books over time. These data speak to two different sorts of questions. First, data collected from retailers establish trends for the entire society over time: How much did Americans spend on reading materials? How did expenditures on reading materials change during the Great Depression? How did they change when television became popular? All of these questions address what Americans did as a whole, on the average. Although we can control for population growth and inflation, this approach is rudimentary. The data are no more than national aggregates, and they report only what people bought, not what they borrowed or what they actually read. Also, these government data distinguish between only three categories of reading material—books, magazines, and newspapers. They do not tell us specifically what reading materials people bought within those categories—who bought the *Atlantic Monthly* and who bought the *Saturday Evening Post,* who bought Sinclair Lewis and who bought Zane Grey. In spite of these shortcomings, the data are systematic over long periods of time, and they do address broad questions of interest.

Another type of consumer-expenditure data—family budgets tabulated by the government—addresses questions about distinct reading publics, defined as those who purchased no reading materials; those who purchased only newspapers; those who purchased newspapers and magazines but no books; and book buyers, who generally also bought newspapers and magazines.[1] Using more detailed longitudinal studies that

1. The generalization that book readers also read newspapers and magazines is supported by various surveys scattered across the years. See, for example, Market

provide data on region, income, occupation, and other family characteristics, we can correlate participation in these reading groups with the social situation of American families.

This chapter says nothing about culture, about the content or meaning of reading. It presents only the cold hard facts about consumers' decisions. At the same time, however, it speaks to issues raised elsewhere in the volume. We discussed the alleged decline of literacy, for example, in chapters 3 and 4, and the data of this chapter are relevant to that question. In this chapter we concentrate on the government's consumer studies; in chapter 6 we analyze social-science surveys of people's self-reported reading habits. Together these chapters detail long-range trends in the reading habits of Americans taken as a whole and the differences among various groups defined by income, race, gender, and education. Thus, the chapter also begins to lay the groundwork for the discussion in chapter 10 about convergence of Americans' reading activities. Has the expansion of literacy drawn Americans into a cohesive reading public with shared practices, or have distinctive groups with distinctive reading practices persisted? This chapter and chapter 6 address those questions at a preliminary level: Have Americans become more similar over time on the level of reading expenditures and in the mix of books, magazines, and newspapers in their reported reading? Chapter 10 will extend the discussion to questions of standardization of content and control of published reading materials.

We begin, then, with the question of decline. The purported decline in literacy in recent decades often has been blamed on the electronic age. Critics have argued that the new mass media, especially television and personal computers, have lured many people, particularly our youth, away from printed text. Some worry that, in spite of the achievement of nearly universal rudimentary literacy by the turn of the century and the widespread popularity of book reading by the 1950s, the nation is now being fragmented. As a result, readers can be divided into an underclass of functional illiterates, poorly educated and uninformed; an aliterate group, who can read but don't, depending instead on the mass media for news and entertainment; and a reading elite, well informed and, when in positions of power, capable of manipulating news and cultural symbols and slogans to their own ends.[2] Democracy itself, so dependent on a well-

Facts, Inc., *1983 Consumer Research Study on Reading and Book Purchasing: Focus on Adults* (New York: Book Industry Study Group, 1984), 22, 26, 27.

2. For an alarmist version, see Townshend Hoopes, "Aliteracy and the Decline of the Language," in *Aliteracy: People Who Can Read but Won't,* ed. Nick Thimmesch (Washington, D.C.: American Enterprise Institute for Public Policy Research, 1984), 38. For a more dispassionate view by a political scientist, see W. Russell Neuman, *The Paradox of Mass Politics: Knowledge and Opinion in the American Electorate* (Cambridge: Harvard University Press, 1986), chaps. 2 and 6.

educated and knowledgeable citizenry, is said to be threatened by these developments. But not all observers have drawn the same conclusions. John R. Bormuth argued in 1978 that, the pervasive influence of the news media notwithstanding, the value and volume of literacy materials have expanded continuously throughout the electronic age.[3]

Has there indeed been a decline in reading activities? Are the trends cyclical or cumulative? Sound policy decisions depend upon solid historical perspective, and the government's consumer-expenditure studies, as well as the social surveys described in chapter 6, add depth to the relatively small body of work on the subject.

The Data

The longitudinal data involve estimates of the aggregated expenditures by all consumers for various items. These data have been collected annually since 1929 by the U.S. Department of Commerce, which publishes them as a part of the national income and product accounts in both absolute and constant dollars. The data are collected from retailers and manufacturers and are adjusted to estimate the amount of money spent by consumers on various products. After eliminating expenditures by businesses and purchases for resale, the Commerce Department provides a total-expenditure figure for all items, a total for recreational expenditures, and the specific amounts spent on two categories of reading materials: (1) books and maps; and (2) magazines, newspapers, and sheet music. From these figures it is possible to calculate how the amount spent on reading materials has varied as a proportion of total and recreational expenditures.

The other type of federally gathered expenditure data is based on family budget surveys conducted by the Bureau of Labor Statistics and the Department of Agriculture. In these studies, selected families were interviewed and asked to provide information on their actual expenditures for a specific period of time, usually one year. The categories of data published from these cost-of-living studies vary from year to year, but all the reports include average expenditures on reading materials by families in different categories, often grouped by occupation, income, and region. Conducted at roughly ten-year intervals, these studies suggest ways in which the average consumer's spending patterns changed over time. They are used to determine the selection of goods and services that make up the Consumer Price Index.[4]

The earliest study of this kind was an 1890 survey of the families of

3. Bormuth, "Value and Volume of Literacy," 118–61.
4. U.S. Bureau of Labor Statistics, *Consumer Expenditure Survey: Diary Survey, 1980–81,* Bulletin 2173 (Washington, D.C.: Department of Labor, 1983), 1.

workers employed in the iron, steel, coal, textile, and glass industries. Reports of this study listed average expenditures per family for books and newspapers, as well as average income and average total expenditures categorized by industry and by state. In 1901, in 1918–19, and in 1934–36, the Bureau of Labor Statistics surveyed wage earners and low- to medium-salaried workers in a variety of cities. The expenditure numbers were reported by region and, in the two more recent surveys, by income. In 1944 and 1950, the bureau expanded its sample to include urban families of all occupations and income levels. These changes also were adopted by the creators of the Consumer Expenditure Survey begun in 1980, which recently produced an updated Consumer Price Index.[5] In addition to the efforts of the Bureau of Labor Statistics, the Department of Agriculture in the 1920s began investigating the expenditure patterns of rural families. The first study with a broad scope, conducted in 1923–24, involved 2,886 white farm families in eleven states. A similar survey was completed in 1955. The two departments have combined their efforts to produce national surveys of family expenditures several times in the last fifty years (see table 5.1, below).

Neither the aggregate-expenditure data provided by industries nor the family-budget data on reading materials are perfect measures of reading activity. As we noted above, people have other sources of reading material beyond what they purchase; conversely, not everything that is purchased is read. The accuracy of the data is also limited in some ways. Until 1972 the family-budget data were based only on heads of households' recollections of their families' previous year's spending, and some errors were thus inevitable. To improve the accuracy of the data, that year the Bureau of Labor Statistics began asking a random sample of families to keep two-week detailed expenditure diaries. Some bias in responses may nonetheless occur as individuals react to the inquiries of government representatives. Daniel Horowitz argued that many people, particularly those with lower incomes, were more likely under such circumstances to inflate their educational expenditures, including those for reading materials.[6] Nevertheless, the federally gathered expenditure data provide a general measure of people's interest in reading and the presence of reading materials in the home.

5. "The Changes behind the CPI's New Look," *Business Week*, March 2, 1987, 24.

6. Daniel Horowitz, *The Morality of Spending: Attitudes toward the Consumer Society in America, 1875–1940* (Baltimore: Johns Hopkins University Press, 1985), 24, and see John Modell, "Patterns of Consumption, Acculturation, and Family Income Strategies in Late Nineteenth-Century America," in *Family and Population in Nineteenth-Century America*, ed. Tamara K. Hareven and Maris A. Vinovskis (Princeton, N.J.: Princeton University Press, 1978).

Trends in Reading Expenditures

The Department of Commerce reports overall reading expenditures and divides them into two categories: newspapers, magazines, and sheet music; and books and maps. Sheet music and maps account for only a tiny portion of the expenditures in their respective categories and have little influence on our findings,[7] so our categories are labeled "newspapers and magazines" and "books."

The Commerce Department's nationally aggregated data show that, except in 1938, personal expenditures on reading materials have risen steadily.[8] Before reaching any conclusions, however, we must account for changes over time in the cost of reading materials. The department recently reported expenditures in constant 1982 dollars, with separate inflation adjustments for each category of items.[9] This allowed price changes for newspapers, magazines, and sheet music to be analyzed separately from those for books and maps (see Appendix).

Reading expenditures, controlled for inflation, fell from 1929 to 1934, rose steadily from 1934 until 1979, and then began a decline (see figure 5.1).[10] But the years of growth in reading expenditures can be attributed

7. In benchmark studies in 1963, 1967, 1972, and 1977, for example, the department found that expenditures on maps made up only .83 percent, .67 percent, .72 percent, and .45 percent, respectively, of the total expenditures on books and maps (personal conversation with Ray Mataloni, analyst for the Bureau of Economic Analysis, February 20, 1987).

8. U.S. Department of Commerce, *The National Income and Product Accounts of the United States, 1929–76, Statistical Tables* (Washington, D.C.: Government Printing Office, 1981), 90–95; U.S. Department of Commerce, *Survey of Current Business,* Vol. 62, no. 7 (Washington, D.C.: Government Printing Office, 1982), 40–41; Department of Commerce, *Survey of Current Business,* Vol. 64, no. 7 (Washington, D.C.: Government Printing Office, 1984), 37–38. The Department of Commerce tries to omit purchases by businesses. We could not determine whether they included purchases of textbooks by school systems, though it would seem consistent with their policy to omit them. The Department of Agriculture and the Bureau of Labor Statistics explicitly exclude such purchases. The purchase of school books by individuals, of course, would be included; as enrollment at high schools and colleges increased, assigned texts formed an increasing portion of book purchases. It is not possible to estimate how large a factor this has been at different periods.

9. U.S. Department of Commerce, *National Income and Product Account Data for 1929–1966.* Supplied by the Bureau of Economic Analysis (Washington, D.C.: Department of Commerce, 1986).

10. In this and subsequent graphs every fifth year of data was plotted. The data points between 1929 and 1939, for example, correspond to 1934. The final data point plotted corresponds to 1986. The Appendix contains the data and calculated figures used to produce these graphs. The expenditure data are from Department of Commerce, *National Income and Product Account Data.* The population data are from Bureau of the Census, *Historical Statistics of the United States,* 10; U.S. Bureau of the Census, *Statistical Abstract of the United States: 1982–83,* 103d ed. (Washington, D.C.: Government Printing Office, 1982), 26, *Statistical Abstract of the United States: 1985,*

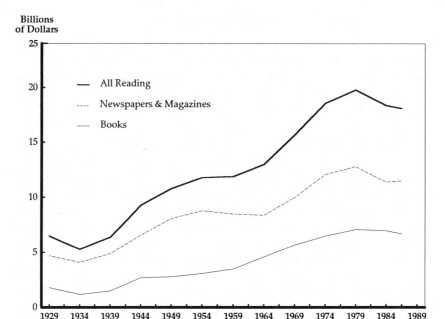

Figure 5.1. Total Reading Expenditures, 1929–1986, in 1982 Dollars

partly to population growth, which we can control for by dividing the expenditures by the number of adults in the population. It should also be remembered that some adults spend nothing at all on reading; as a result, the average expenditure for adults who do spend something is somewhat higher.

When we divide total reading expenditures by the number of people aged eighteen years and older (see figure 5.2), the trends are slightly different. The increases are not as steady or as steep, of course, and spending per person on newspapers and magazines shows a more pronounced downward swing in the 1954–64 period. Still, the general trend in reading expenditures moved downward from 1929 to 1934 and upward from 1934 until 1974, at which point it began to decline. That expenditures continued to increase well into the 1970s suggests that, at least in its earliest decades, the electronic age did not adversely affect the public's purchase of reading materials.

What were the trends in reading expenditures as a percentage of total personal expenditures? Did reading expenditures keep up with expendi-

105th ed. (Washington, D.C.: Government Printing Office, 1984), 26, and *Statistical Abstract of the United States: 1987*, 107th ed. (Washington, D.C.: Government Printing Office, 1986), 8, 14. Graphs by Al Divine, Wisconsin Center for Education Research.

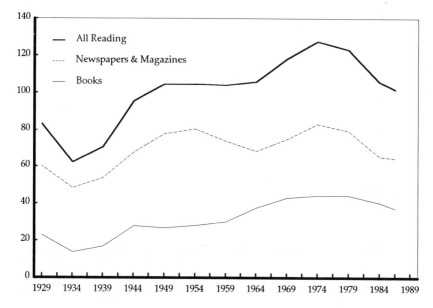

Figure 5.2. Reading Expenditures per Person 18+, 1929–1986, in 1982 Dollars

tures for other recreational activities?[11] Did they parallel expenditures for such mass-media items as radios, televisions, records, and admissions to movies and other recreational events? The proportion of total consumer expenditures devoted to newspapers and magazines apparently has been declining since 1944 (see figure 5.3). In contrast, expenditures on books were stable between 1949 and 1974. Throughout the century, reading expenditures remained a minute portion of total expenditures, peaking at about 1.7 percent.

One can see similar patterns relative to recreation expenditures (see figure 5.4), although the decline in expenditures on books is more precipitous relative to other recreational items than relative to total consumer expenditures (figure 5.3), and it began a decade earlier, in 1964. Reading expenditures at their peak were roughly 32 percent of recreational expenditures; they are currently around 10 percent. Nor have

11. Recreational expenditures are divided into mass-media and non-mass-media expenditures. The mass-media category is divided into reading (expenditures on newspapers and magazines, books and maps) and audiovisual (admissions to movies, theaters, and sports events, and electronic expenditures, which are divided into two categories—one for radios, televisions, records, and musical instruments, and the other for radio and television repairs). Non-mass-media expenditures include those for flowers, seeds, and potted plants, wheel goods, toys, sports equipment, organizational dues, and so forth.

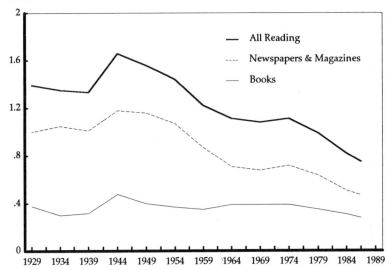

Figure 5.3. Reading Expenditures as a Percentage of Total Expenditures,
1929–1986

Percent

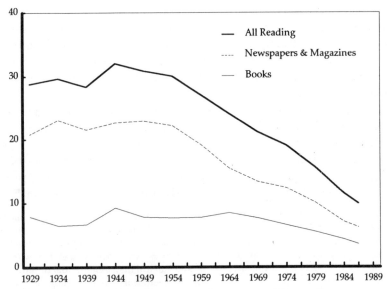

Figure 5.4. Reading Expenditures as a Percentage of Recreation
Expenditures, 1929–1986

reading expenditures kept pace with those for all mass-media items since the 1960s (see figure 5.5). From a peak of over half of all mass-media expenditures, reading expenditures have fallen to about a fourth.

Reviewing these three figures, one sees that reading expenditures as a proportion of total, recreational, and mass-media expenditures currently lag behind 1929 levels (see figure 5.6). Print (reading) expenditures as a percentage of all expenditures for media (including televisions, radios, records, and musical instruments, as well as radio and television repairs) have declined steadily since 1944, falling from more than 90 percent to about 25 percent—again below 1929 levels.

Stated this way, these results might suggest that the public's financial commitment to reading relative to other media commodities has weakened in the face of tremendous growth in available audio and video products. Until recently, however, total reading expenditures in constant dollars had been growing (figure 5.1), suggesting that people continued to value reading even in an expanding audiovisual environment. In recent years, however, it seems that even constant-dollar expenditures on reading have been adversely affected by the current diversity of media choices.

Figure 5.7 demonstrates another trend worth noting: Spending on books has increased relative to expenditures on newspapers and magazines. To the extent that books may be considered more demanding reading, this would suggest that people financially committed to reading are

Percent

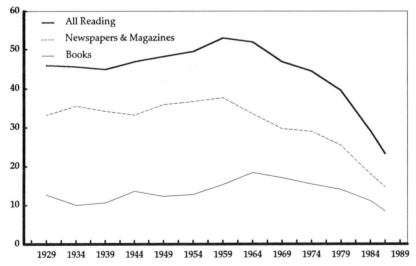

Figure 5.5. Reading Expenditures as a Percentage of Mass-Media Expenditures, 1929–1986

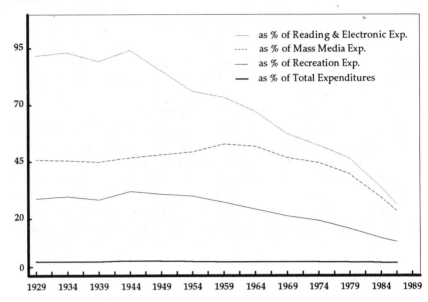

Figure 5.6. Reading Expenditures as a Percentage of Other Expenditures, 1929–1986

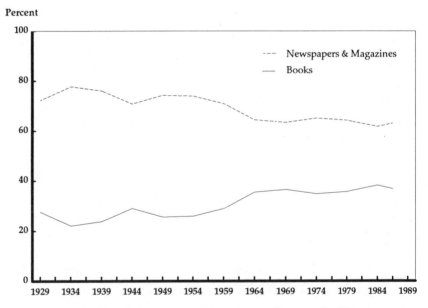

Figure 5.7. Newspapers, Magazines, and Books as a Percentage of Reading Expenditures, 1929–1986

choosing more serious subject matter; on the other hand, the phenomenal growth in formula fiction, such as gothic romances, suggests otherwise. In any case, newspapers and magazines continue to account for a majority of the expenditures for reading materials.

In the final series of figures, we further explore the level of spending on print relative to other media. With the exception of print, all recreation expenditures have risen since the early 1960s as a percentage of total personal expenditures (see figure 5.8). These data call into question a theory developed by Charles Scripps called the Constancy Hypothesis. Scripps held that a relatively constant percentage of available wealth has always been devoted to mass media. Using the Department of Commerce aggregated data, Maxwell McCombs attempted to validate the Constancy Hypothesis.[12] He showed that the proportion of income spent on mass-communication items—including newspapers, magazines, and books, as well as such audiovisual media as radios, televisions, records, and movies—had remained roughly constant between 1929 and 1977. McCombs also showed that expenditures on print media had remained constant relative to other media, but that within the print world, expenditures on newspapers and magazines had declined, whereas the purchase of books and maps had increased.

In fact, expenditures on mass media as a proportion of personal income have not been constant but show a striking downward trend between 1944 and 1964, followed by a steady increase. McCombs tried to validate the Constancy Hypothesis by examining the correlation across his entire time series, 1929–77, a methodology that obscured the intermediate down and up trends. We were able to extend the expenditure record into the 1980s, whereas McCombs stopped at 1977. However, had we duplicated his approach, we too would have concluded that media expenditures were a constant proportion of total expenditures; the overall 1929–86 pattern is roughly stable (see figure 5.8). Furthermore, McCombs found that constant dollars per household expended on mass media actually increased during that period ($r = .228$).[13] The data we have provided in the Appendix show that the 1944–64 decline in media expenditures was due largely to a dramatic decrease in admissions expenditures, particularly for movies. It was not until the 1960s that the electronic age took hold, as evidenced by steady increases in expenditures on audiovisual and electronic items.

12. Maxwell E. McCombs, "Mass Media in the Marketplace," *Journalism Monographs* 24 (August 1972): 1–104; Maxwell E. McCombs and Chaim H. Eyal, "Spending on Mass Media," *Journal of Communication* 30 (Winter 1980): 153–58. For a critique that makes some of the same points we make here, see William C. Wood, "Consumer Spending on the Mass Media: The Principle of Relative Constancy Reconsidered," *Journal of Communication* 36 (Spring 1986): 39–51.

13. McCombs, "Mass Media in the Marketplace," 9, 16.

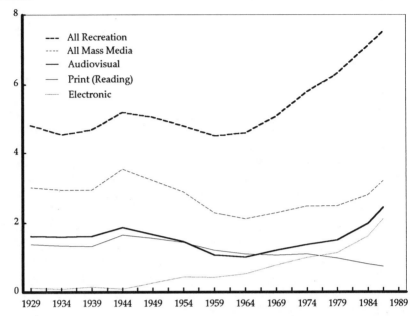

Percent

- - - All Recreation
······ All Mass Media
—— Audiovisual
—— Print (Reading)
·········· Electronic

Figure 5.8. Recreation Expenditures as a Percentage of Total Expenditures, 1929–1986

Figure 5.9 shows trends in media expenditures as a percentage of recreation expenditures. As with other variables, the proportion spent on printed material has decreased whereas those for audiovisual and electronic expenditures have increased. The proportion of recreation expenditures devoted to all mass media is striking, declining steadily between 1944 and 1979; only in the last decade has there been a slight upward trend. The rapid rise in recreation spending in the postwar period was largely for such nonmedia expenditures as toys, sports, boats, flowers, and organization dues. Finally, we compare the declining trend in print expenditures to the rising trend in electronic expenditures as a proportion of total mass-media expenditures (see figure 5.10). The watershed for print expenditures came in 1959, after which they began to decline.

Although the Department of Commerce data are useful, they are nationally aggregated from retail sales records and thus cannot tell us how many people or what percentage of the adult population bought reading materials—information that is crucial to any debate about literacy trends. For example, the trend in constant dollars per capita spent on reading, which was on the rise until 1979, could have been due to an intensification of reading purchases among a small number of people rather than to a widening circle of print buyers.

Percent

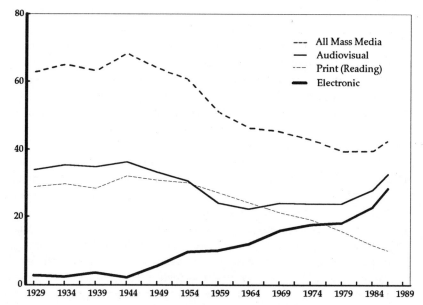

Figure 5.9. Media Expenditures as a Percentage of Recreation Expenditures, 1929–1986

Percent

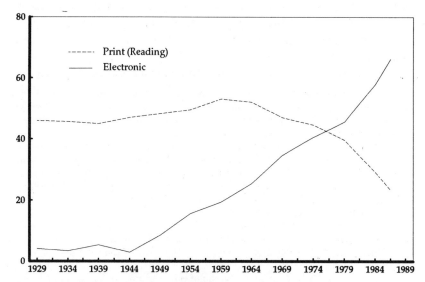

Figure 5.10. Print Expenditures versus Electronic Expenditures, as a Percentage of Mass-Media Expenditures, 1929–1986

We can investigate levels of participation behind these expenditure trends by using cross-sectional studies conducted by the Bureau of Labor Statistics and the Department of Agriculture. The bureau's data showed that 95 percent of the 1950 urban population and 92 percent of the entire 1960 population had purchased reading materials, compared with only 84 percent of the entire 1972 population.[14] We calculated that the average person buying reading materials in 1960 spent about $31, whereas the average buyer in 1972 spent about $44 in constant dollars (see Appendix).[15] Thus a slightly smaller portion of the public spent more money on reading materials in 1972 than a larger portion did in 1960.

The literacy debate also focuses on specific forms of reading materials. It is now widely held that, whatever its effects on reading in general, the electronic age has precipitated the decline of the newspaper as a vehicle of information. Newspaper circulation nationwide has not kept pace with population growth. Surveys have repeatedly shown that the public now gets more news from television or weekly news magazines than from daily newspapers. Yet even this claim is not without its detractors. John Udell argued that the decline in circulation reflected a drop in the numbers of people who read more than one paper per day, but that the number of people who read one newspaper had remained constant.[16] John Bormuth argued that the best measure of actual trends is newspaper pages per household, rather than circulation figures, and he presented data showing a steady increase in this measure throughout the electronic age.[17] And our own data, presented in figure 5.2, show that newspaper expenditures per person in the late 1970s and early 1980s were roughly comparable in constant dollars to those in the late 1940s and early 1950s, in spite of fluctuations during the intervening years.

To resolve this debate, we need data on the percentage of people buy-

14. U.S. Bureau of Labor Statistics, *Study of Consumer Expenditures, Incomes, and Savings: Statistical Tables, Urban U.S., 1950*, vol. 9, *Summary of Family Expenditures for Recreation, Reading, and Education*. Tabulated for the Wharton School of Finance and Commerce, University of Pennsylvania. (Washington, D.C.: U.S. Department of Labor, 1957), 3; U.S. Bureau of Labor Statistics, *Consumer Expenditures and Income, Details of Expenditures and Income: Total United States, Urban and Rural, 1960–61*, Report no. 237–93, supplement 3, pt. A (Washington, D.C.: Government Printing Office, 1966), 2–3, 10–13; and U.S. Bureau of Labor Statistics, *Consumer Expenditure Survey: Interview Survey, 1972–73*, Bulletin 1997 (Washington, D.C.: U.S. Department of Labor, 1978), 54.

15. To derive the average expenditure of those who bought materials, we multiplied the year's population by the percentage of people buying materials, then divided the constant-dollar expenditures on reading by the result of the multiplication.

16. John Udell, *Economic Trends in the Daily Newspaper Business, 1946–1970* (Madison: University of Wisconsin, Bureau of Business Research and Service, 1970), 7–8.

17. Bormuth, "Value and Volume of Literacy," 135–36.

ing newspapers over time. The cross-sectional studies we alluded to earlier, conducted by the Bureau of Labor Statistics and the Department of Agriculture, provided the information. The percentage of people buying newspapers decreased from more than 90 early in the century to fewer than 60 percent by 1972 (see table 5.1).[18] The bulk of this decline apparently occurred in the postwar years. The sharp decline in the 1972 expenditure data could have resulted partly from more thorough interview methodology. We would not want to posit such a large shift entirely on the basis of this study, whose methodology was not comparable to previous surveys and which has not been replicated. Reading surveys discussed in detail in the next chapter suggest more modest declines, but declines nonetheless (see table 6.1, below). For example, 90 percent of the population in 1937 said that they read newspapers regularly; in 1983 that figure had fallen to 70. The percentage who reported that they had read a newspaper "in the past 24 hours" seemed more durable over the years, remaining in the 70 to 80 percent range from 1957 to 1983; but those who said they read a paper "daily" declined from the 70 to 80 percent range to the 50 to 60 percent range. We conclude from this that the spreading influence of the electronic media indeed reduced the public's use of newspapers.

The percentage of the public buying magazines also declined as television use increased, peaking in 1960 at about 62 percent and then reverting to the prewar level of around 45 percent. By contrast, the proportion of book buyers more than tripled, from 15 percent of the white urban population in 1918–19 to more than 54 percent of the entire population by the 1970s (table 5.1). The 1978 and 1983 figures actually underestimate the true percentage of book buyers because they refer to purchases made during the previous six months rather than the previous year.

The evidence about book *reading,* in contrast to book *buying,* does not show a dramatic increase. Indeed, surveys of reading habits indicate that the percentage of active readers—those who reported reading a book at the time of the survey, or regularly, or in the previous month—has remained between 20 and 30 percent since the 1930s (see chapter 6). The percentage who say they have read a book in the past year reveals no clearer trends. Surveys in the early 1960s reported 65 and 70 percent, moving upward in the late 1970s, when surveys reported that between 77 and 84 percent of respondents said they had read a book in the previous year; these findings, however, were contradicted by a Gallup poll in 1983 reporting that only 50 percent had. In sum, although book buying became more common, the percentage who were active readers of books remained

18. Although the earlier studies were not national in scope, they showed that 93.1 to 95.7 percent of low-income and farm individuals bought newspapers. The general population could be expected to have been at least as literate.

Table 5.1. Percentage of People Buying Various Reading Materials in the United States, 1888–1983

Date	Group Surveyed	Newspapers	Magazines	Books
1888–90	Industrial workers	62.4–91.8[a]	—	—
1901	Low-income urban employed	94.7[b]	—	—
1918–19	Low- and medium-income white urban	95.7	46.5	15.4
1923–24	White farm	93.1[c]	—	—
1934–36	Urban emplòyed	71.2 home 39.3 street	45.1	5.0
1941–42	Rural farm	80[c]	—	—
	Rural nonfarm	77[c]	—	—
	Urban	52–100[c,d]	—	—
1950	Urban	91.2	65.7	22.9
1960	Populace	86.0	62.0	42.0
1972–73	Populace	57.6	44.6	60.3[e]
1978	Populace	—	—	54.0[f]
1983	Populace	—	—	46.7[f,g]

Sources: (1888–90) U.S. Commissioner of Labor, *Sixth Annual Report;* U.S. Commissioner of Labor, *Seventh Annual Report.* Sample: 5,000+ families surveyed in 1888–90. Husbands employed in bituminous coal, coke, iron ore, pig iron, bar iron, steel, cotton textile, woolens, and glass industries. Industries chosen because they were the subject of congressional tariff debates.

(1901) U.S. Commissioner of Labor, *Eighteenth Annual Report.* Sample: 25,440 black and white families from principal industrial cities of thirty-three states and Washington, D.C. Families distributed proportionally to industrial employees. Limited to families of wage earners and persons on annual salaries not exceeding $1,200.

(1918–19) Bureau of Labor Statistics, *Cost of Living in the United States.* Sample: 12,096 families of white wage earners and low- or medium-salaried workers, but not self-employed. Survey covered ninety-two cities in forty-two states. Cities varied in size from New York City to towns of a few thousand.

(1923–24) U.S. Department of Agriculture, *Farmer's Standard of Living.* Sample: 2,886 white farm families in eleven states.

(1934–36) Bureau of Labor Statistics, *Money Disbursements of Wage Earners and Clerical Workers.* Sample: 12,903 white and 1,566 black families in forty-two cities with populations aover 50,000. Families had annual incomes over $500, were not on relief, and had at least one earner employed for thirty-six weeks.

(1941–42) U.S. Department of Agriculture, *Rural Family Spending and Saving in Wartime;* Bureau of Labor Statistics, *Family Spending and Saving in Wartime.* Sample: Proportional representation of rural families and single consumers from different regional and racial groups. Sample based on counties, and subsamples of dwellings within the county. 1,300 urban families and single persons form sixty-two cites. Random sample of blocks within the cities and consumer units within blocks.

(1950) Bureau of Labor Statistics, *Study of Consumer Expenditures, Incomes, and Savings,* volumes 9, 13, and 14. Sample: 12,500 families in ninety-one representative cities.

(1960) Bureau of Labor Statistics, *Consumer Expenditures and Income.* Sample: Representative national sample. 13,728 families surveyed.

(continued)

Table 5.1. (continued)

(1972–73) Bureau of Labor Statistics, *Consumer Expenditure Survey: Interview Survey, 1972–73;* Bureau of Labor Statistics, *Consumer Expenditure Survey: Interview Survey, 1980–81.* Sample: Representative national sample. 71,220 families surveyed from the 216 geographical areas used by the Current Population Survey.

(1978) Yankelovich, Skelly, and White, Inc., *The 1978 Consumer Research Study of Reading and Book Purchasing.*

(1983) Market Facts, Inc., *1983 Consumer Research Study on Reading and Book Purchasing,* 21, 165, 213.

Notes: [a]Percentage buying newspapers or books; varies by occupation—coke workers lowest, glass workers highest.

[b]Percentage buying newspapers or books.

[c]percentage buying any of the three types of reading materials.

[d]Variations across income classes.

[e]An overestimate. It includes those purchasing nonsubscription magazines and newspapers.

[f]The percentage buying books in the previous six months.

[g]An underestimate because it leaves out non-book-readers and nonreaders who purchased books for themselves, presumably a small proportion. Calculated by adding percentage of book readers who purchased books for themselves or as gifts and of non-book-readers and nonreaders who purchased books as gifts.

roughly constant at about 25 percent. From the 1950s onward, polls repeatedly reported that more than 50 percent of their respondents had read a book sometime during the previous year, but the data on an upward trend are not consistent.

Why has the percentage of the population buying books increased whereas the percentage of the public reading books has remained relatively constant? The increase in book purchasing may be the result of the rise in disposable income that occurred during the century. Many book readers may have turned to libraries and acquaintances to borrow books in earlier decades, but as people acquired more money to spend on recreation, more people purchased books. However, the circulation of library books per capita was also increasing during the same period, so it was not a question of trading public goods for private goods. Book readers were doing more buying and more borrowing.[19] Contrary to all the dire predictions, the portion of the public that reads books has remained roughly constant during the electronic age and the percentage that buys books has in fact been on the rise.

What about the level of financial commitment to book buying? Using data on the constant dollars spent on books in 1950 and 1970, we estimate

19. Increasing rates of library circulation per capita can be calculated from *Statistics of Public, Society, and School Libraries Bulletin* (published sporadically by the U.S. Office of Education, with varying titles) and from "Public Library Statistics," *American Library Association Bulletin* (also published sporadically).

that book buyers on average spent $43 in constant dollars in 1950 and $31 in 1970.[20] We find, therefore, that although book buying has become more common, the average financial outlay of book buyers is declining. And, as noted previously, book expenditures in constant dollars have been declining since the mid-1960s as a proportion of total, recreation, and media expenditures (see figures 5.3 to 5.5, above). Because the use of constant-dollar expenditures controls for price changes in the goods being purchased, the declines in book expenditures cannot be attributed to a shift from hardbacks to less-expensive paperbacks. The modern electronic age, therefore, has had some adverse impact on book expenditures relative to other expenditures, but not on the percentage of households that read or purchase books.

Different Reading Publics

Our second set of questions concerns whether distinct publics read the different publication forms. Some people did not purchase reading materials at all, some purchased only newspapers, some purchased both newspapers and magazines but no books, and some purchased books as well. We wish to know whether these groups varied by social class and how they changed over time. To answer these questions, we again rely on data from the cross-sectional studies of family budgets. Referring back to table 5.1, we can see that in the early part of the century, the reading public included far more newspaper buyers than magazine buyers and a very limited number of book buyers. Newspaper buying was ubiquitous, yet less than half the public bought magazines, and only 15 percent of white urbanites purchased books. The price of newspapers was so low that income level did not create purchasing patterns discernible in our data to any great degree; this was not the case for magazines and books.

In a previous study using these cross-sectional data David Nord randomly selected three hundred cotton-textile workers' families from the 1888–90 report. Using averages and partial correlations, he analyzed how their expenditures on reading materials varied by income, region, ethnicity, and children's labor status.[21] Reading expenditures as a proportion of discretionary income were lower in the South, among French-Canadian immigrants, and in families with children in the work force. After Nord had completed his work, the entire data set for the 1888–90 study became available on computer tape, so it is now relatively easy to

20. The calculations were as follows: $1.3 billion were spent in 1950 by a population of 151 million; 20 percent, or 30 million, were book buyers (estimated from the urban sample). Dividing $1.3 billion by 30 million people yields $43. Similar calculations were done for 1970, using 50 percent as the percentage of book buyers.

21. David P. Nord, "Working-Class Readers: Family, Community, and Reading in Late Nineteenth-Century America," *Communication Research* 13 (1986): 156–81.

run statistical analyses on the data using the full sample. Multivariate analysis allowed us to examine the association of various family characteristics with expenditures on reading materials (see table 5.2).[22] Stepwise multiple regression sorts out the amount of change in a dependent variable (in the present case, dollars spent on newspapers and books) that is associated with change in an independent variable, while holding constant the effects of the other independent variables. It identifies the most significant variable (in the present case, husband's income); then, holding that variable constant, it identifies the next most significant variable (here, total family income). All our variables combined accounted for about 30 percent of the variance in the dependent variable, a substantial amount for an analysis of this sort. We were interested not only in income but also in region, ethnic identification, and some selected family variables. Our model, then, was one in which the effects of income on the purchase of reading materials were mediated by the relative availability of printed material in different regions, the match between the family's ethnic status and mainstream English culture, and the number and status of children contributing to or making demands on the family economy.

As expected, the two most significant variables were both measures of income. The amount of money spent on lighting, logically enough, predicts to a significant degree the amount of money spent on reading materials. Another measure of disposable income, money spent on amusements and vacations, also correlates significantly. The regional variables were entered as yes-no dichotomies; families who lived in the South or border states, other variables being equal, spent less on newspapers and books, perhaps reflecting less availability as well as lower educational levels. Among the ethnic variables, people from non-English-speaking countries spent less on newspapers and books, as did Canadians and the Irish; less assimilated people, whether or not they spoke English, spent significantly less on reading materials, even after controlling for income and in spite of the relatively thriving foreign-language press in the cities. Larger families were associated with lower reading expenditures, reflecting the strains on their budgets. Other

22. The original study, conducted by the U.S. Department of Labor, was titled *Cost of Living of Industrial Workers in the United States and Europe, 1888–1890*. The data utilized in our analysis were made available by the Inter-University Consortium for Political and Social Research. Neither the collector of the original data nor the consortium bears any responsibility for the analyses and interpretations presented here. The data set and accompanying code book are labeled ICPSR #7711, 3d ed. (Ann Arbor, Mich.: Inter-University Consortium for Political and Social Research, 1986). Both the statistical analysis and much of the interpretation were done at the University of Wisconsin by Marc Goulden, a research assistant for this project, to whom we express our gratitude.

Table 5.2. Stepwise Regression: Expenditures on Books and
Newspapers by U.S. Industrial Workers, 1888–1890
Dependent variable: Dollars spent on books and newspapers
R Square = .30140

Independent Variables	Beta Weight (significant at 5% level)
Husband's income	.141802
Total family income	.290849
Money expended on lighting	.091674
Money expended on amusements and vacations	.119871
Head of household French Canadian (yes/no)	−.103015
Residing in South	−.104367
Residing in border states	−.064111
Head of household French	−.050559
Head of household German	−.050237
Residing in Midwest	.040477
Head of household Irish	−.037991
Number of children at school	.076521
Family size	−.076521
Head of household Canadian	−.025723
Number of children at work	.022904
Head of household Welsh	.021664

Not significant: wife employed out of home (yes/no); number of boarders; owns home
(yes/no); money expended on labor organizations; money expended on other organizations; money expended on religion; money expended on liquor; head of household
Scottish or English; residing in New England or in Middle Atlantic states.

Source: U.S. Department of Labor, *Cost of Living of Industrial Workers in the
United States and Europe.*

things being equal, however, the number of children enrolled in school
was positively correlated with reading expenditures; two explanations
are possible. One, obviously, is that sending children to school is evidence
of the value that a family places on literacy; the second is that school-age
children may be proxies for older families, meaning families with no
children in infancy and with parents farther along in their work careers.
This possibility is reinforced by the positive correlation between the
number of children at work and reading expenditures. Of course, we must
remember that expenditures for reading materials do not necessarily
correlate directly to reading. People who spent less may have borrowed and
shared reading materials more. Nonetheless, the regression analysis suggests that among industrial workers in 1890, apart from the influence of
income per se, those in less-developed regions, those recently arrived in
America, and those with larger families (and fewer children at school or
work) were the least likely to spend money on reading materials.

In order to explore the differences among specific occupations while controlling for income, we selected for a second regression analysis the principal occupational designation in each of seven industries. (The entire study contained 8,544 families; this smaller sample contained 1,640). Out of the hundreds of occupational titles included in the larger study, we chose cotton weavers, wool weavers, coke workers (drawers and levelers), pig-iron fillers, bar-iron puddlers, coal miners, and glass-blowers (see table 5.3). In addition to the occupation of heads of households, the independent variables also included income, ethnicity, and region. The regression analysis accounts for 24.5 percent of the variation in expenditures, with family income again the strongest predictor. Ethnic and regional variables have effects similar to those reported in the larger analysis, but they are not as strong when we introduce occupation. Among occupations, working as a glassblower or a wool weaver significantly correlated with larger expenditures on reading materials. Compared to the other occupations we chose, these two were part of the "labor aristocracy," more autonomous in their work, more politically involved, and logically enough, more likely to purchase reading material, even when such variables as income remained the same.[23]

Regression analysis has allowed us to recognize that although income was a strong predictor of reading expenditures in 1888–90, other variables were independently important. Ethnic and occupational subcultures, as well as regional conditions, influenced people's reading expenditures and their participation in the world of print.[24]

In the late nineteenth and early twentieth centuries most of the expenditures on reading materials probably represented purchases of newspapers rather than books. A 1919 study, for example, showed that about 95 percent of the white urban population bought newspapers, yet less than half bought magazines and only 15 percent bought books (see table 5.1). The select nature of the book-buying group was confirmed during the Great Depression, when only 5 percent of the urban employed continued to buy books. Since then, the size of the groups that purchase

23. Coal miners fit this characterization also, spending more on reading materials than coke workers of similar region and income. However, coal miners tended to work in areas where the supply of reading materials was sparse, so their commitment to reading expenditures was not statistically distinctive enough to be significant in our equation.

24. Nord, "Working-Class Readers," also found southern reading expenditures lower, despite controls for family income and children at work. He, too, argues that although income is an important predictor, ethnic and family culture also played a role, but our results are somewhat different from his (because of our total sample and our use of multiple-regression analysis). His general argument, however—that beyond family income, expenditures on reading materials are associated with indicators of "modern" industrial life (he uses the terminology of "gemeinschaft" and "gesellschaft")—is consistent with our results.

Table 5.3. Stepwise Regression: Expenditures on
Books and Newspapers by Families of Workers in
Selected Industrial Occupations, 1888–1890
Dependent variable: Dollars spent on books and
newspapers R Square = .24461

Independent Variables	Beta Weight (significant at 5% level)
Total family income	.386530
Residing in Midwest (yes/no)	.139613
Residing in Middle Atlantic states	.085802
Husband a wool weaver	.090467
Head of household German	−.066035
Husband a glassblower	.103077
Head of household English	.056423

Not significant: family size; husband's age; husband a cotton
weaver, a coke worker, a pig-iron filler, a bar-iron puddler, a coal
miner; head of household native-born or Irish; residing in New
England or in South.

Source: U.S. Department of Labor, *Cost of Living of Industrial
Workers in the United States and Europe.*

newspapers, magazines, and books has somewhat converged. With newspaper and magazine purchasing decreased and book buying increased,
each of those groups now represents about half of the population (see
table 5.1). Although we cannot tell from these figures whether the same
50 percent is buying all three types of materials, we may presume that
most book buyers also read newspapers and magazines. The data suggest
that a century ago almost every family bought newspapers whereas a
smaller elite bought books; by the 1970s, only about 50 percent of families bought any reading material regularly, but most of them purchased
all three forms: newspapers, magazines, and books.

The purchasing data for recent decades should be compared with the
reading habits reported in the next chapter. About 50 percent of the
population bought books in the 1970s, but only about 25 percent reported
reading one "presently" or in the previous twenty-four hours. These facts
are easily reconciled, since about 40 percent of the respondents reported
reading a book in the previous week and more than 55 percent reported
reading a book in the previous month. The data on magazine purchasing
and use match even more closely. In 1950, 66 percent of families reported
magazine purchases and the 1960 figure was 62 percent; these match
well with findings of surveys of reading habits in the 1960s and 1970s
that 57 to 64 percent of the population read magazines regularly or in the

past week. Whereas the decline in magazine purchasing in 1972 seems an anomaly, the veracity of the decline in newspaper purchasing from 1950 to 1973 is supported by surveys of newspaper reading, which show a gradual decline since the 1950s from an 80 to 90 percent range to a 60 to 70 percent range.

Table 5.4 shows how different print-consuming publics were distributed by income at different points in the century, in four cross-sectional studies. As indicated, income strongly determines the percentage of buyers for each type of reading material. This was not always the case, at least not for newspapers. In 1918–19, for example, income had only a minimal effect on newspaper buying, which remained true even as late as 1950. By 1972, however, the pattern for newspapers reflected the pattern for the other materials.

Although income is certainly an influence on reading expenditures, people with low incomes have nonetheless maintained a substantial commitment to reading (see table 5.4). Newspaper buying dominated their spending early in the century, but a sizable portion purchased magazines and a small but relatively significant percentage purchased books. By 1972, the newspaper and magazine purchases of the lowest-income groups had declined, as had those of the general public, but their book buying had increased more rapidly than the average. This increase occurred primarily during the 1960s. In 1960, for example, between 7 and 22 percent of those in the bottom fourth of the income pyramid purchased books, but by 1972 this group ranged from 31 percent to 43 percent. Indeed, by then, people with low incomes were just as likely to buy books as newspapers. And, although income remained a strong determinant of book buying, 20 to 25 percent of all book buyers came from the bottom third of the income pyramid.[25]

Other evidence suggests that the financial commitment of the lower-income groups has been just as strong as that of higher-income groups. Table 5.5 shows how reading expenditures as a percentage of total and recreational expenditures varied by income group.[26] In each study, the proportion of total expenditures made for reading materials was roughly constant across income classes. This indicates that low-income and high-

25. Calculated from the data in table 5.1. The 1960 and 1972 increase could be due in part to changes in the education and age composition of those with low incomes, chiefly an increase in the number of college students and young college graduates in the low-income category. This would not alter our general conclusion that people with low incomes have spent significant amounts on printed materials throughout the century, but increasing education levels among lower-income families may help account for the spread of book reading across income lines.

26. In each case, the total, recreational, and reading expenditures were averaged, across *all* people in the particular income class. The amounts are in actual dollars for the particular year.

Table 5.4. Percentage of Americans Buying Newspapers, Magazines, and Books by Income Class, 1918–1972

Date	Group Sampled	Income $	% Population	Newspapers	Magazines	Books
1918–19	Low-	All	100.0	95.7	46.5	15.4
	and medium-	under 900	2.7	88.6	22.9	5.4
	income white	900–1,200	20.0	92.8	29.3	8.5
	urban	1,200–1,500	32.7	95.7	43.6	13.9
		1,500–1,800	22.6	97.3	52.4	16.6
		1,800–2,100	13.2	97.2	60.2	21.7
		2,100–2,500	5.8	98.3	65.7	26.4
		2,500+	2.9	98.3	71.1	29.2
1950	Urban	All	100.0	91.2	65.7	22.9
		under 1,000	6.3	61.8	27.7	5.2
		1,000–2,000	12.3	78.7	40.2	9.7
		2,000–3,000	18.7	89.0	56.8	18.1
		3,000–4,000	24.0	95.4	69.7	22.0
		4,000–5,000	16.9	97.6	77.8	27.8
		5,000–6,000	9.5	99.8	83.1	30.8
		6,000–7,500	6.4	98.9	86.0	34.9
		7,500–10,000	3.5	97.6	84.8	56.8
		10,000+	2.4	98.0	86.7	51.9
1960	Populace	All	100.0	86.0	62.0	42.0
		under 1,000	3.7	53.0	24.0	7.0
		1,000–2,000	10.2	65.0	31.0	10.0
		2,000–3,000	11.1	74.0	46.0	22.0
		3,000–4,000	11.8	82.0	54.0	31.0
		4,000–5,000	13.3	88.0	60.0	40.0
		5,000–6,000	12.7	92.0	67.0	45.0
		6,000–7,500	15.1	95.0	74.0	56.0
		7,500–10,000	13.4	97.0	80.0	63.0
		10,000–15,000	6.8	98.0	88.0	71.0
		15,000+	2.0	99.0	90.0	74.0
1972	Populace	All	100.0	57.6	44.6	60.3
		under 3,000	13.4	32.4	17.3	31.2
		3,000–4,000	5.9	41.7	26.1	41.5
		4,000–5,000	5.4	42.7	27.9	42.7
		5,000–6,000	4.9	45.1	34.3	50.2
		6,000–7,000	5.0	45.9	33.5	53.8
		7,000–8,000	4.8	50.8	38.1	56.5
		8,000–10,000	9.8	53.8	41.7	63.2
		10,000–12,000	9.3	61.0	47.9	66.1
		12,000–15,000	12.4	66.2	52.8	70.3
		15,000–20,000	14.8	73.5	60.4	75.6
		20,000–25,000	7.5	76.3	67.1	78.7
		25,000+	6.8	82.7	74.7	83.3

Sources: See table 5.2.

Table 5.5. Household Expenditures, by Income Class, 1918–1982 (in Dollars)

Date	Group	Income $	% Population	Total ($)[a]	Recreational	Reading	Reading % of Total	Reading % of Recreational and Reading
1918–19	Urban	All	100.0	1,434.37	18.90	10.55	.74	35.8
		under 900	2.7	812.89	4.12	6.13	.75	59.8
		900–1,200	20.0	1,075.38	8.33	7.55	.70	47.5
		1,200–1,500	32.7	1,343.80	13.68	9.62	.72	41.3
		1,500–1,800	22.6	1,631.54	20.97	11.47	.70	35.4
		1,800–2,100	13.2	1,924.87	29.23	13.38	.70	31.4
		2,100–2,500	5.8	2,272.18	38.63	15.37	.68	28.5
		2,500+	2.9	2,790.25	61.84	16.46	.59	21.0
1934–36	Urban employed	All	100.0	1,523.88	82.29	15.36	1.01	18.7[b]
		under 200[c]	3.0	[d]				
		200–300	12.2	1,174.44	52.85	11.17	.95	21.1
		300–500	40.2					
		500–600	15.8	1,588.21	88.94	16.49	1.04	18.5
		600–800	18.4					
		800–900	4.6	1,901.64	116.00	19.55	1.03	16.9
		900–1,100	4.0					
		1,100–1,200	.8	2,551.85	137.80	23.18	.91	16.8
		1,200+	1.0					
1935–36	Rural & urban	All	100.0	1,389.00	41.00	13.00	.94	24.1
		under 500	14.2	466.00	6.00	4.00	.86	40.0
		500–750	12.9	704.00	11.00	6.00	.85	35.3

(continued)

Table 5.5. (*continued*) 1918–1982 (in Dollars)

Date	Group	Income $	% Population	Total ($)ᵃ	Recreational	Reading	Reading % of Total	Reading % of Recreational and Reading
		750–1,000	14.6	914.00	17.00	9.00	.98	34.6
		1,000–1,250	13.2	1,127.00	25.00	11.00	.98	30.6
		1,250–1,500	9.8	1,316.00	31.00	14.00	1.06	31.1
		1,500–1,750	8.0	1,512.00	42.00	15.00	.99	26.3
		1,750–2,000	6.4	1,684.00	49.00	16.00	.95	24.6
		2,000–2,500	8.4	1,968.00	62.00	20.00	1.02	24.4
		2,500–3,000	4.3	2,302.00	81.00	22.00	.96	21.4
		3,000–4,000	4.0	2,729.00	105.00	27.00	.99	20.5
		4,000–5,000	1.4	3,276.00	136.00	31.00	.95	18.6
		5,000–10,000	1.7	4,454.00	206.00	41.00	.92	16.6
		10,000–15,000	.4	6,097.00	340.00	57.00	.93	14.4
		15,000–20,000	.2	9,134.00	486.00	69.00	.76	12.4
		20,000+	.3	14,822.00	921.00	126.00	.85	12.0
1941–42	Rural & urban	All	100.0	1,905.00	69.00	16.00	.84	18.8
		under 500	15.4	632.00	12.00	3.00	.47	20.0
		500–1000	18.2	995.00	19.00	7.00	.70	26.9
		1,000–1,500	15.8	1,389.00	33.00	12.00	.86	26.7
		1,500–2,000	14.7	1,768.00	50.00	17.00	.96	25.4
		2,000–3,000	21.1	2,427.00	85.00	22.00	.91	20.6
		3,000–5,000	10.5	3,338.00	144.00	29.00	.87	16.8
		5,000+	4.0					
1944	Urban	All	100.0	2,406.55	67.33	26.27	1.09	28.1
		under 500	4.2	594.00	5.00	8.00	1.35	61.5

500–1000	7.7	939.00	15.00	11.00	1.17	42.3
1,000–1,500	7.1	1,317.00	25.00	15.00	1.14	37.5
1,500–2,000	11.9	1,690.00	45.00	18.00	1.07	28.6
2,000–2,500	13.9	1,946.00	52.00	21.00	1.08	28.8
2,500–3,000	13.2	2,375.00	62.00	27.00	1.14	30.3
3,000–4,000	19.9	2,816.00	82.00	32.00	1.14	28.1
4,000–5,000	9.6	3,428.00	104.00	38.00	1.11	26.8
5,000+	12.5	4,324.00	137.00	43.00	.99	23.9
1950 Urban All	100.0	3,808.00	168.00	35.00	.92	17.2
under 1,000	6.3	1,278.00	26.00	14.00	1.10	35.0
1,000–2,000	12.3	1,768.00	43.00	18.00	1.02	29.5
2,000–3,000	18.7	2,718.00	91.00	27.00	.99	22.9
3,000–4,000	24.0	3,570.00	154.00	34.00	.95	18.1
4,000–5,000	16.9	4,450.00	215.00	40.00	.90	15.7
5,000–6,000	9.5	5,257.00	251.00	45.00	.86	15.2
6,000–7,500	6.4	6,043.00	316.00	53.00	.88	14.4
7,500–10,000	3.5	7,108.00	361.00	59.00	.83	14.0
10,000+	2.4	10,773.00	596.00	84.00	.78	12.4
1960 Populace All	100.0	5,053.62	200.12	44.61	.88	18.2
under 1,000	3.7	1,278.07	27.26	11.28	.88	29.3
1,000–2,000	10.2	1,779.59	37.48	15.69	.88	29.5
2,000–3,000	11.1	2,670.85	72.79	23.28	.87	24.2
3,000–4,000	11.8	3,638.43	120.57	31.28	.86	20.6
4,000–5,000	13.3	4,430.55	161.01	37.49	.85	18.9
5,000–6,000	12.7	5,178.03	189.80	44.86	.87	19.1
6,000–7,500	15.1	6,130.60	254.25	55.27	.90	17.9
7,500–10,000	13.4	7,426.35	326.98	65.19	.88	16.6
10,000–15,000	6.8	9,538.20	471.05	90.34	.95	16.1
15,000+	2.0	14,255.11	664.85	121.40	.85	15.4

(continued)

Table 5.5. (*continued*)

Date	Group	Income $	% Population	Total ($)[a]	Recreational	Reading	Reading % of Total	Reading % of Recreational and Reading
1972–73	Populace	All	100.0	7,996.43	633.88	47.72	.60	7.0
		under 3,000	13.4	3,044.23	133.56	15.85	.52	10.6
		3,000–4,000	5.9	4,011.05	212.90	21.92	.55	9.3
		4,000–5,000	5.4	4,539.14	237.39	23.93	.53	9.2
		5,000–6,000	4.9	5,116.09	304.11	29.62	.58	8.9
		6,000–7,000	5.0	5,750.11	310.72	30.00	.52	8.8
		7,000–8,000	4.8	6,165.00	387.40	36.66	.59	8.6
		8,000–10,000	9.8	6,944.92	459.67	40.83	.59	8.2
		10,000–12,000	9.3	7,926.83	552.43	45.16	.57	7.6
		12,000–15,000	12.4	8,929.86	683.69	53.95	.60	7.3
		15,000–20,000	14.8	10,700.44	895.66	65.08	.61	6.8
		20,000–25,000	7.5	12,665.84	1,247.11	80.62	.64	6.1
		25,000+	6.8	16,713.19	1,856.35	112.49	.67	5.7
1972	Urban	All	100.0	9,421.00	389.00[e]	50.00	.53	11.4
		2,448[f]	20	3,691.00	105.00	18.00	.49	14.6
		6,336	20	6,168.00	209.00	32.00	.52	13.3

176

10,553	20	8,813.00	342.00	47.00	.53	12.1
15,335	20	11,403.00	492.00	61.00	.53	11.0
27,260	20	16,762.00	782.00	93.00	.55	10.6

1982 Urban

All	100.0	18,892.00	870.00e	127.00	.67	12.7
4,097f	20	8,324.00	284.00	59.00	.71	17.2
10,611	20	12,155.00	429.00	86.00	.71	16.7
18,129	20	16,733.00	710.00	116.00	.69	14.0
28,231	20	22,425.00	1,123.00	156.00	.70	12.2
52,267	20	35,171.00	1,851.00	219.00	.62	10.6

Notes: aTotal, recreational, and reading expenditures are in actual dollars for the given year. In some cases, total expenditures fall outside the income range. Income and expenditures were calculated in different ways; their complex definitions are given in the original studies.

bIn 1934–36, the recreation category included reading expenditures, so this column is recreation divided by reading expenditures.

cIn 1934–36 these data were not for income but for total household expenditures per person.

dData not reported for these categories.

eThese figures are entertainment expenditures, which are a subset of recreational ones (trip expenditures, for example, were not included).

fAverage income of people in category.

Sources: For 1918–19, 1934–36, 1941–42, 1950, 1960, and 1972–73, see table 5.2.

(1935–36) U.S. National Resources Committee, *Consumer Expenditures in the United States.* Sample: 60,000 families living in cities, villages, and on farms in thirty states. Data on single individuals drawn from four separate studies.

(1944) Bureau of Labor Statistics, "Expenditures and Savings of City Families in 1944." Sample: Cross-section of city consumers—families and single individuals. 1,700 families in 102 urban communities. Represents all regions of the United States and cities with population over 2,500.

(1982–83) Bureau of Labor Statistics, *Consumer Expenditure Survey: Interview Survey, 1982–83.* Sample: Representative urban sample. 45,089 consumers interviewed.

income groups devoted an equal portion of their total resources to reading. What about reading expenditures as a portion of *all* recreational expenditures? This is perhaps the more illuminating statistic, for it shows the extent to which groups spent their available recreation income on reading materials. Strikingly, the final column shows that low-income groups actually devoted a larger portion of their recreational expenditures to reading materials; in fact, the percentage devoted to reading drops off as income rises. In other words, low-income readers had a stronger commitment to reading relative to recreation than did those in high-income groups.

These data suggest that many people in low-income groups were just as interested in reading as were those in higher-income groups, but lacked the funds necessary to pursue their interest. We conclude, therefore, that the different reading publics were partially determined by economic status but that it would be a mistake to argue that low-income groups were less committed to reading.

Charles Scripps, who originated the Constancy Hypothesis, believed that media purchases were stable across time because they were a necessity rather than a luxury in our society; this thesis, he thought, also explained their spread across different social classes. "Communications have become a staple of consumption in our society," said Scripps, "much like food, clothing, and shelter."[27] Although, as we have shown, the Constancy Hypothesis is incorrect, some communication media (newspapers earlier and television later) seem to have become essential rather than discretionary for most Americans. Even books may be more necessary than discretionary for many people in a society that has become very print-oriented, offering readers everything from tax-preparation guides to home-repair manuals. The big question for the future is to what extent that necessary communication will be accomplished by the substitution of electronic media for print media.

The electronic age has emerged during the past few decades. But it is only one aspect of the postwar growth of a leisure society, in which increasing portions of total income have been committed to recreation. Reading, as an important element of recreation, shared in that growth. In particular, book buying spread to a majority of the population and low-income groups increased their book buying during this period. But reading expenditures grew more slowly than other expenditures, and consequently, over the past several decades, they have decreased drastically as a percentage of total, recreational, mass-media, and electronic-item

27. Charles E. Scripps, *Economic Support of Mass Communication Media in the United States, 1929–1963* (Cincinnati, Ohio: Scripps-Howard Research, 1965), cited in McCombs, "Mass Media in the Marketplace," 5.

spending. As a percentage of these budgets, they now lag behind 1929 levels.

The data also suggest in several ways that the electronic age checked the expansion of the market for newspapers and magazines. First, constant-dollar expenditures on these print items, controlled for population growth, were roughly comparable in the late 1940s and early 1980s. By contrast, book expenditures continued to rise until 1979. Second, expenditures on newspapers and magazines fell as a percentage of reading and recreation expenditures. Third, the percentage of the public buying newspapers and magazines seems to have fallen over the course of the century, though the data are not conclusive. Finally, in recent years there has even been a downturn in the total amount of constant dollars spent on reading.

No doubt there are distinct reading publics in America today, in terms of the types and amounts of reading people do. But in terms of the print forms—newspapers, magazines, and books—Americans are a more homogeneous group of print buyers today than they were in 1890, when the working classes bought mostly newspapers and book buying was predominantly an activity of highly educated, higher-income groups. Today a majority of the public buys some books. Nevertheless, the average expenditure by book buyers and the average portion of disposable income devoted to books have declined, and the proportion of the population purchasing newspapers has declined as well.

One of the possible policy implications of these findings is that if we are concerned about the literacy skills of our nation's students, we must also be concerned about the reading habits of its adults. If parents wish to place a value on reading, they must demonstrate it. If policy makers value adult reading, they need to find appropriate ways for government to support the world of print literacy in a democracy—not only through increased funds for adult literacy training but also through the support of libraries, writing projects, and regulatory policies that encourage a thriving press. Only with such efforts, coupled with excellent literacy training in our schools, can we ensure effective reading training of our students and foster widespread, active reading among adults.

6 Surveying American Readers

HELEN DAMON-MOORE AND CARL F. KAESTLE

Historians interested in the reading habits of Americans from the 1880s to the 1920s have little systematic, nationwide data other than the government expenditure reports discussed in the previous chapter. Starting in the 1930s, however, educators, librarians, pollsters, and publishers have periodically asked Americans what types of publications they read and how often. This chapter moves from expenditure data to the actual reading activities reported in surveys. The determination of trends in reading habits is hampered by several difficulties, especially the lack of comparability from one survey to the next. Local studies vary in quality and are limited by their necessarily small and diverse samples. National studies are difficult to compare because the questions they pose about reading change continually. Finally, surveys of reading habits sometimes suffer from the conscious or unconscious biases of the groups conducting the research.

We hope to overcome these problems in this chapter. First, as an introduction to the data, we discuss the various schools of thought that have prompted and shaped reader studies. Next, we sort through national studies to find comparable questions and establish trends for the reading public as a whole. Third, we explore divergent reading publics by examining data that are broken down by age, sex, race, education, and income. Finally, we look at three local studies; research based in single communities can capture more details about the uses of literacy. Although they are scattered geographically and chronologically, these old one-shot studies can provide the raw materials for a more humanized history of reading.

Schools of Thought among Researchers

The earliest studies of reading habits, which appeared in the first quarter of this century, were largely conducted by librarians. As Stephen Karetzky details in *Reading Research and Librarianship,* early studies were designed to determine what attracted readers to libraries and how library use could be increased.[1] The first reader studies also were spurred by the general development of the social sciences and by a sense that the reading public was expanding rapidly. Early studies generally took the form of library-book-circulation analyses. These studies were helpful to the extent that they defined the broad contours of book popularity, but they did not reveal anything about the characteristics of the readers, and they involved a circularity to which librarians unintentionally contributed: novels were the most popular genre, so librarians put more novels on their shelves, and thus people read more novels. Some librarians began to conduct community surveys with more diverse questions, but they too served largely to promote increased use of the library. Most of these studies were isolated and subjective, and produced information of little value to later researchers.

A small group of theses written between 1900 and 1925 have more to offer to historians of reading. In 1929 William S. Gray and Ruth Munroe summarized the major results of reader studies between 1900 and 1925, relying heavily on two such theses for their general findings.[2] These were Rhey Boyd Parsons's "A Study of Adult Reading," a University of Chicago doctoral dissertation, and Burton K. Farnsworth's "A Study of the Reading Habits of Adults," a Utah Agricultural College master's thesis.[3] These two studies were among the earliest to survey larger, if still local, samples; to ask general questions like "Did you read a book in the past six months?" and "Do you regularly read magazines or newspapers?" They also reported results for various subpopulations delineated by age, sex, occupation, education, and marital status. On the basis of these studies, Gray and Munroe concluded that by the end of the first quarter of the twentieth century, 50 percent of Americans read books, 75 percent read magazines, and 95 percent read newspapers.[4] Parsons and Farnsworth found that reading varied by education, age, gender, occupa-

1. Karetzky, *Reading Research and Librarianship,* 3–23.
2. William S. Gray and Ruth Munroe, *The Reading Interests and Habits of Adults: A Preliminary Report* (New York: Macmillan, 1929).
3. Rhey Boyd Parsons, "A Study of Adult Reading" (Ph.D. diss., University of Chicago, 1923); Burton K. Farnsworth, "A Study of the Reading Habits of Adults" (M.A. thesis, Utah Agricultural College, 1925).
4. Gray and Munroe, *Reading Interests and Habits of Adults,* 262. They seem to have relied chiefly on Parsons for these rates. Parsons's subjects, drawn from Chicago and its environs, were probably more active readers than the nation as a whole.

tion, residence, and accessibility of materials, relationships that were confirmed by later studies.[5] These studies were the first to identify what Gray and Munroe called a "communications elite," that is, a group of people who regularly read books and tended also to read more magazines and newspapers and to see more movies.[6]

The 1930s brought a movement to study reading scientifically, pioneered and led in large part by Douglas Waples of the Graduate Library School at the University of Chicago. Waples held a low opinion of earlier reader studies, believing that surveys should feature larger samples, determine motives for reading, and make some effort to determine readability and accessibility. Waples's earliest book, *What People Want to Read About,* written with Ralph Tyler, suggested that people liked to read what was most familiar to them.[7] This early work made its most interesting observations about gender. Waples and Tyler's study revealed that men avoided reading about art and culture, whereas women were less likely to read about politics, economics, and science. "Without attempting to discriminate between the social values" of these sets of interests, the authors suggested that American society would be improved more by women taking a greater interest in the latter topics than by men taking a greater interest in art.[8] *What People Want to Read About* examined people's stated reading preferences, but in subsequent research Waples and Leon Carnovsky concluded that what people actually read is the result not only of their interests but also of the accessibility and readability of reading materials.[9] Thus, studies of reading interests cannot be taken as evidence of actual reading. Nonetheless, hundreds of studies of readers' interests have been produced since the 1930s. Although many suffer from problems of reliability and validity, some are better than others and too tempting for the historian of reading to ignore.[10] Even more interesting among the burgeoning reading research activities of the 1930s are a few in-depth studies of reading activities in individual communities, which we discuss below.

5. Karetzky, *Reading Research and Librarianship,* 18.

6. Gray and Munroe, *Reading Interests and Habits of Adults,* 262–63.

7. Douglas Waples and Ralph W. Tyler, *What People Want to Read About* (Chicago: University of Chicago Press, 1931).

8. See Karetzky, *Reading Research and Librarianship,* 97.

9. Douglas Waples, "Relation of Subject Interests to Actual Reading," *Library Quarterly* 2 (January 1932):42–70; Waples, *Research Memorandum on Social Aspects of Reading in the Depression* (New York: Social Science Research Council, 1937); Leon Carnovsky, "A Study of the Relationship between Reading Interests and Actual Reading," *Library Quarterly* 4 (1934):76–110.

10. The literature and the methodologies are scrutinized in Alan C. Purves and Richard Beach, *Literature and the Reader: Research in Response to Literature, Reading Interests, and the Teaching of Literature* (Urbana, Ill.: National Council of Teachers of English, 1972), 61–144.

The late 1930s also saw an interest in reading on the part of the early pollster George Gallup. Though Gallup's questions were narrow and his surveys sporadic, the data he gathered are crucial to the historian of reading trends in the twentieth century. In 1937 Gallup first asked, "Are you reading a book at the present time?" and his polling organization has made periodical inquiries into levels of book and newspaper reading ever since. (The Gallup Organization has measured magazine reading for the most part only by popularity of selected titles.) The data, although limited, have three positive features: They are national, they are based on scientific sampling procedures, and their questions are, to some degree, comparable over time.[11]

The 1940s saw the addition of industry studies to the field of reading surveys. Some had appeared in the thirties, but those conducted in the 1940s took an interest in readers' characteristics as well as book sales and distribution. Industry studies conducted in the 1940s for the most part concluded that Americans did not read enough, but they argued primarily that book producers and distributors like themselves were responsible. Researchers believed that if distribution were improved and the quality of available books raised, readers would read more and better books.[12]

One of the most prominent of these studies was Henry Link and Harry Hopf's *People and Books: A Study of Reading and Book-Buying Habits,* conducted for the Book Manufacturers Institute in 1946.[13] This national study of four thousand adults concluded that 71 percent had read from a book and 40 percent from a magazine "yesterday." These rates are higher than those reported in other contemporary national polls. In the same year Wilbur Schramm found that 20 percent had read a book "yesterday" and 38 percent had read a magazine "yesterday".[14] Of Link and Hopf's 106 towns, 103 were the site of a college or university; their sample is much better educated than the national average.[15] Yet some of the tables control for education, and the book as a whole provides some interesting information about reading among a rather well-educated, middle-class sample.

11. The Gallup polls are compiled in George H. Gallup, ed., *The Gallup Poll: Public Opinion, 1935–1971,* 3 vols. (New York: Random House, 1972), and George H. Gallup, ed., *The Gallup Poll: Public Opinion, 1972–1977,* 2 vols. (Wilmington, Del.: Scholarly Resources, 1978).

12. Karetzky, *Reading Research and Librarianship,* 327–28.

13. Henry C. Link and Harry A. Hopf, *People and Books: A Study of Reading and Book-Buying Habits* (New York: Book Industry Committee, 1946).

14. Schramm data cited in John Robinson, "The Changing Reading Habits of the American Public," *Journal of Communication* 30 (Winter 1980):147.

15. Bernard Berelson, "Review of Link and Hopf, *People and Books,*" *Library Quarterly* 17 (January 1947):71–73.

The years between 1950 and the present have seen the continuation of reader studies by the same interested parties: educators, librarians, pollsters, and industry groups. In addition, social scientists and communications theorists joined the field. Many university-based researchers of the 1950s continued in the didactic advocacy stance long held by librarians and reading experts. For example, in a 1956 article entitled "What Do Adults Read?" Lester Asheim summarized earlier reader studies from the 1930s and 1940s and deplored the number of Americans who were nonreaders.[16] By the 1970s some researchers took a more detached tone. In a 1979 review Larry Mikulecky did not seem as alarmed as Asheim had been by figures showing declining readership; nonetheless, he said that the United States could be considered an "aliterate" nation.[17] But in "The Changing Reading Habits of the American Public" (1980), John Robinson countered such warnings.[18] Robinson used time-use studies to demonstrate that the reported reading declines were largely nonexistent. He also looked at reading-frequency figures, concluding that overall reading declines, to the extent that they existed at all, were due in large part to a decline in newspaper reading among young people. The past two decades, then, have witnessed an increase in descriptive surveys of reading habits, a continuation of the didactic tradition that warns about the "death of print," and the development of arguments by other commentators who believe that reading is alive and well in America.

National Trends over Time

Our compilation of national comparable data about reading over the past fifty years is necessarily limited to a rather narrow group of questions, all of which measure the frequency of book, magazine, and newspaper reading. Time-use studies occasionally inquired about reading, but these are very difficult to compare over time because the questions vary across studies. Hence the most useful national data are drawn from questions like "Are you reading a book presently?" and "Did you read a newspaper yesterday?" Table 6.1 represents a composite picture drawn from dozens of sources.

The most popular print form is the newspaper, and the most regular and continuous data pertain to the reading of newspapers. Gallup first

16. Lester Asheim, "What Do Adults Read?" in *Adult Reading: The Fifty-fifth Yearbook of the National Society for the Study of Education,* ed. Nelson B. Henry (Chicago: University of Chicago Press, 1956), 5–28.

17. Larry J. Mikulecky, Nancy Leavitt Shanklin, and David C. Caverly, *Adult Reading Habits, Attitudes and Motivations: A Cross-Sectional Study* (Bloomington: Indiana University, School of Education, Monographs in Language and Reading Studies, 1979), 3.

18. Robinson, "Changing Reading Habits," 141–51.

Table 6.1. Frequency of Reading Newspapers, Magazines, and Books, 1937–1985

Year	Read a Newspaper — Daily, Every Day	Read a Newspaper — Past 24 Hours	Read a Newspaper — Regularly, Usually	Read a Magazine — Past 24 Hours	Read a Magazine — Regularly, Usually	Read a Magazine — Past Week	Read a Book — Past 24 Hours	Read a Book — Regularly, Usually	Read a Book — Presently	Read a Book — Past Week	Read a Book — Past Month	Read a Book — Past Year	Read a Book — Completed in Past Year
1937			90[a]					28[a]/31[a]	29[b]				
1938			88[b]										
1939			80[a]										
1940			80[a]										
1941			81[b]										
1942			74[a]/79[b]										
1943	76[c]		78[d]										
1944			78[a]/79[b]										
1945			88[e]	38[f]									
1946							20[f]						
1947													
1948			90[e]						26[a]/21[h]		25[g]/29[g]	50[g]	
1949													
1950									21[h]				
1951													
1952									18[h]				
1953			85[a]						19[a]/17[h]				
1954							21[a]/20[i]		22[a]		43[h]	82[h]	
1955													
1956			81[a]										
1957	77[f]	70[a]	77[a]/79[a]	27[f]			18[f]		23[a]/17[h]		21[j]		
1958			82[a]										
1959													

(continued)

185

Table 6.1. (continued)

Year	Read a Newspaper			Read a Magazine			Read a Book						
	Daily, Every Day	Past 24 Hours	Regularly, Usually	Past 24 Hours	Regularly, Usually	Past Week	Past 24 Hours	Regularly, Usually	Presently	Past Week	Past Month	Past Year	Completed in Past Year
1960													
1961			80[k]		65[k]							70[l]	
1962					61[l]							65[l]	46[l]
1963					57[l]								
1964													
1965							17[l]						
1966	73[f]			25[f]			17[f]						
1967													
1968													
1969											26[m]		
1970													
1971	69[o]	73[n]		39[n]		66[o]	33[n]			50[d]	26[h]		
1972													
1973													
1974													
1975	66[p]	76[q]	66[f]	38[q]		62[q]				44[q]	56[r]		84[r]
1976	66[r]	68[f]/80[q]		28[q]/39[q]		57[q]/64[q]	22[f]			44[q]/42[q]			
1977	62[e]	64[a]/78[q]		39[q]		64[q]				42[q]			
1978	57[e]	81[q]/75[q]		42[q]		59[q]				38[q]	59[s]	55[t]	77[s]
1979		75[q]											
1980				40[q]/38[q]									
1981	55[u]	75[q]/79[q]		38[q]									
1982	54[e]	76[q]/78[q]		40[q]									
1983	55[e]	73[q]/78[q]	70[m]	37[q]/41[q]	57[v]		25[i]	46[m]				50[w]	
1984													
1985	53[e]												

Sources: The Roper Center for Public Opinion Research in Storrs, Connecticut, has computerized more than 10,000 public-opinion polls conducted since 1936. We contracted with them to search for questions on Americans' reading habits. The results of this search were transmitted on paper copies reporting individual survey items. Notes a, d, e, and g of this table refer to materials provided by the Roper Center, followed by the name of the original polling organization. Thus, "Roper Center: Gallup" refers to a Gallup poll for the year indicated in the table.

a Roper Center: Gallup.

b American Institute of Public Opinion data, reported in Strunk, comp., *Public Opinion*, 48, 515.

c NORC data, reported in Strunk, comp., *Public Opinion*, 515.

d Roper Center: Office of Public Opinion Research.

e Roper Center: National Opinion Research Center.

f Robinson, "Changing Reading Habits of the American Public," 143, 147.

g Berelson, *Library's Public*, 7.

h Gallup, *Gallup Poll, 1935–1971*.

i Wood, "Book Reading," 39.

j *Bowker Annual of Library and Book Trade Information*.

k Newsprint Information Committee, *National Study of Newspaper Reading*.

l Ennis, *Adult Book Reading in the United States*.

m *Gallup Poll Index*, 1970.

n Sharon, "What Do Adults Read?" 159.

o Sharon, *Reading Activities of American Adults*, appendix, 26.

p Robinson and Jeffres, *Changing Role of Newspapers in the Age of Television*, 3, reporting NORC data.

q Roper Center: Roper.

r Mikulecky, Shanklin, and Caverly, *Adult Reading Habits, Attitudes, and Motivations*, 9, citing Gallup book data from 1976.

s Gallup Organization, *Book Reading and Library Usage*.

t Yankelovich, Skelly, and White, *Consumer Research Study on Reading and Book Purchasing*.

u Roper Center: Los Angeles Times.

v Gilbert, *Compendium of American Public Opinion*, citing United Media Enterprises Report on Leisure in America data for 1983. (70 percent read newspapers "every day or almost"; 57 percent read magazines once, twice, or more per week; 46 percent read books for pleasure once, twice, or more per week.)

w Market Facts, *1983 Consumer Reaserch Study on Reading and Book Purchasing*, 64. The data are for those who read a book in the past six months, not the past year.

asked readers about newspaper reading in 1937, and as table 6.1 suggests, the questions posed in subsequent polls have focused on three basic types of information: (1) Do you read a newspaper daily or every day? (2) Did you read a newspaper yesterday? (3) Do you read a newspaper regularly? The earliest national figure, from 1937, indicated that 90 percent of respondents characterized themselves as regular newspaper readers. The figures for regular newspaper readership ranged from 74 to 90 percent from the late 1930s through the 1950s. No consistent trend is evident in newspaper reading in these years, but the values from 85 to 90 percent all occur before 1955, whereas the values for the late 1950s cluster around 80 percent. Data for the sixties and early seventies are more sporadic, and the dominant question form switched from "regularly" to "daily." The years from 1967 to 1985 featured a steady decline in daily newspaper reading, from 73 percent of Americans reporting such activity in 1967 to 53 percent in 1985.

Some surveys have gathered data on newspaper reading among particular groups. Parsons's 1923 study of the Chicago area suggested that 91 percent of even those with less than an eighth-grade education read the newspaper regularly, and virtually all of the study's occupational groups reported high levels of daily newspaper reading as well.[19] In fact, barbers reported reading the newspaper more often than teachers did.[20] Newspaper reading has cut across class lines, occupations, educational levels, and gender, but there are some indications that regular reading of newspapers may differ by age group. John Robinson's time-use data offer an important age-cohort perspective on the recent decline in newspaper reading. Studies conducted during the 1970s suggested that adults under the age of thirty read newspapers less frequently than had previous generations, a trend that seems to be continuing. Robinson speculates that increased mobility led to a reduced reliance on local newspapers and suggests that young Americans have in recent decades turned increasingly to television for their news.

Data about magazine reading are sparser but suggest a more consistent level of readership than are represented by the data on newspaper reading. Some polls have asked if magazine reading was "weekly" or if the subject had read a magazine "yesterday." More commonly, pollsters asked if people read magazines "regularly." The figure for magazine reading held fairly steady at percentages in the high 60s from 1947 to 1960 and then declined slightly, to the high 50s from 1963 to 1983.

Pollsters and the book industry have been interested for years in how much the American public reads books; they have collected abundant data on book reading from the 1930s to the present. Because this cate-

19. Parsons, "Study of Adult Reading," 65, 74.
20. Gray and Munroe, *Reading Interests and Habits of Adults,* 34–35.

gory has seen a significant amount of variation in question phrasing, however, comparability is limited. As seen in table 6.1, questions have ranged from "Have you read a book daily?" to "yesterday," "regularly," "presently," "in the past month," "completed in the past month," "past 6 months," "past year," and "completed in the past year." "Are you reading a book presently?" was the question asked most often between 1937 and 1957; positive responses ranged from 17 percent to 31 percent, hovering around 20 percent for most of the period. "Did you read in a book yesterday?" yielded similar results during these years. The same question about reading "yesterday" was asked four times between 1964 and 1984, with the percentage constant at about 25 percent.

The question designed to measure book reading in the past month exemplifies the ways that inconsistent phrasing and the influence of industry interests can distort the reading picture. When Yankelovich, Skelly, and White conducted a study for the Book Industry Study Group in 1978, they asked respondents whether they had read *in* a book in the past month.[21] Because researchers had traditionally asked whether readers had *completed* a book in the past month, the 1978 figure naturally was higher, and the researchers improperly concluded that book reading was on the rise among Americans. In point of fact, although it seems to be the case that book reading is holding its own, the available data do not support the conclusion that an increasing percentage of people are regular book readers.

In terms of the American population as a whole, the major reading trends of the past fifty years can be summarized as follows: daily newspaper reading has declined from the 80–90 percent range to the 50–60 percent range. The percentage of people who report that they read magazines regularly seems level (usually about 38 to 42 percent when people are asked whether they read a magazine in the past twenty-four hours, or bunched around 57 to 65 percent when people are asked whether they read magazines "regularly" or have read one in the past week). The proportion of respondents who say they read books regularly has remained constant at about 20–25 percent of the population; the number of positive responses increased substantially when the question was rephrased to inquire whether they had read (or completed) a book during the previous year. This question was asked frequently during the 1960s and 1970s, and although the results vary quite widely, the trend was generally upward—from a range of 46 to 75 percent in the 1960s to a range of 56 to 84 percent in the 1970s. Also, as we noted in chapter 5, the percentage of households purchasing a book in the previous year in-

21. Yankelovich, Skelly, and White, Inc., *The 1978 Consumer Research Study of Reading and Book Purchases* (Darien, Conn.: Book Industry Study Group, 1978).

creased to 60 percent by 1972 and has remained in the 50 percent range in more recent surveys (1978 to 1983).

Within the parameters of these national averages, of course, reading patterns exhibit great diversity. Some of this variation is associated with differences in age, education, sex, race, and income.

Reading Publics

Age

As early as 1923, Parsons's Chicago sample demonstrated variations in reading by age group. Book and magazine reading for the most part declined steadily as the age of readers rose (see table 6.2). Newspaper reading, on the other hand, remained virtually constant at all age levels. As we shall see, however, the relationship between age and reading can change from one historical period to another.

The decline in book reading as people aged, observed by Parsons in 1923, is supported to some degree by later national samples. The first two columns of table 6.3 present data on book reading for the nation in 1949 and 1966. They also show a regular decline in book reading as people get older, a tendency reported in a variety of surveys. Gallup characterized young people as heavier readers and older people as lighter readers in a study of library use in 1978.[22] Link and Hopf's 1946 study suggested that respondents under the age of twenty-nine were more active readers.[23] Although the Gallup figures for 1955 and 1984 do not support this generalization (table 6.3), other surveys have noted the connection between youth and book reading, and have generally attributed it to steadily increasing education levels of successive cohorts, not to changes in reading habits during the life course of individuals.[24]

In exploring the relationship between age and reading, several complications arise. First, as we have noted, age can be a proxy for education. At any given historical moment, younger people will have higher levels of education than older people. Thus, one must attempt to control for education when looking at age. Second, the relationship between age and reading may differ for books, newspapers, and magazines, and the relationship between age and the reading of any single form may change over time. Although Parsons found a regular, negative relationship between

22. Gallup Organization for the American Library Association, *Book Reading and Library Usage: A Study of Habits and Perceptions* (Princeton, N.J.: Gallup Organization, 1978).

23. Link and Hopf, *People and Books,* 62–63.

24. The Johnstone Adult Education/NORC survey of 1962, Jan Hajda's 1964 dissertation on reading in Baltimore, and a Gallup poll of 1971 all note the connection and are summarized in John Y. Cole and Carol S. Gold, eds., *Reading in America, 1978* (Washington, D.C.: Library of Congress, 1979), 41–42.

Table 6.2. Percentage of Readership by Age: Chicago, 1923

Age Group	N	Books	Magazines	Newspapers
Under 30	104	66.4	85.6	96.0
31–39	90	53.4	78.9	97.8
40–49	52	42.3	67.3	96.0
50–59	35	42.9	71.4	97.0
60 and older	33	39.4	60.6	100.0

Source: Parsons, "Study of Adult Reading," 40.

age and book reading in 1923, he found no relationship between age and newspaper reading. But by the 1950s a relationship began to develop, and by 1977, Robinson noted, age was correlated strongly and positively with newspaper reading. Still, the correlation does not demonstrate that as people get older, they read newspapers more. We must distinguish between a maturation effect (when people age, their reading habits change) and a cohort effect (as a given cohort ages, it brings its constant reading habits with it into a new age bracket). Robinson demonstrated that the association of newspaper reading with older readers was due more to cohort effects than to maturation effects; if one follows a cohort across table 6.4 from 1946 to 1977, for example, the rate of newspaper reading declines only slightly. In 1946, 84 percent of those born between 1908 and 1917 read newspapers; by 1977, 80 percent of that cohort still read them. The table also shows, however, that each succeeding generation reads less frequently. The percentage of newspaper readers in the youngest cohort—those aged twenty to thirty years—dropped in each succeeding survey, from 85 percent to 75 percent, to 64 percent, and then to 42 percent. The effect of adding new cohorts with lower newspaper reading

Table 6.3. Book Readership by Age, 1949–1984

	Positive Responses to the Gallup Poll Question: "Are You Reading a Book Presently?"					
Age Group	1949 (%)	1966 (%)	Age Group	1955 (%)	1984 (%)
21–29	26	34	18–34	20	23
30–49	21	24	35–49	17	27
50 and older		18	50 and older	24	25
50–65	18				
65 and older	16				

Sources: For 1949 and 1966, Gallup, Gallup Poll . . . 1935–1971, 795, 1996; for 1955 and 1984, Wood, "Book Reading," 39.

Table 6.4. Percentages of Estimated Daily Newspaper Reading,
by Respondent Cohorts, 1946–1977

Cohort Born In	1946[a] (N = 4,000)	1957[b] (N = 1,919)	1967[c] (N = 3,095)	1977[c] (N = 1,520)
1948–57				42
1938–47			64	57
1928–37		75	77	69
1918–27	85	78	78	76
1908–17	84	79	78	80
1898–07	87	78	77	72
1888–97	86	76	75	
Before 1888	83	78		
Average period difference	−7	−1	−4	

Source: Robinson, "Changing Reading Habits," 144.

[a]Proportion of the sample who used a newspaper "yesterday" (exact question not described).

[b]"What kind of newspaper do you read? About how often do you read (name of paper)—daily, several times a week, weekly, less often than once a week."

[c]"How often do you read a newspaper: every day, a few times a week, once a week, less often than once a week, never."

habits thus creates the strong negative correlation between youth and newspapers.

What are the possible ramifications of these processes for present policy? One cannot trust that new cohorts who don't read newspapers as youths will automatically start to read them as they mature; the cohort analysis suggests otherwise. Yet the relationships between age and reading appear to fluctuate across time, so reform and restructuring are possible.

Education

We have seen that the correlation of book reading with age has been attributed largely to education. Not only does education largely explain differences in reading associated with age, but also it is a major determinant of reading at any given age. All surveys—indeed, the entire history of the reading public—support this simple truth.

Parsons measured the relationship between education and reading in his 1923 Chicago study (see table 6.5). Newspaper reading was high for all groups, book reading declined steadily and steeply as educational level declined, and magazine reading showed a less consistent and less dramatic decline as educational attainment decreased. This might have resulted from magazines being more often designed for mass appeal than

Table 6.5 Percentage Who Read Books, Magazines, and Newspapers, by Education: Chicago, 1923

Amount of Education	N	Books	Magazines	Newspapers
Graduate training	18	100.0	100.0	100.0
College graduate	44	93.2	97.3	100.0
Some college	25	76.0	100.0	100.0
High-school graduate	65	50.8	83.1	98.5
Some high school	41	58.5	90.2	100.0
Eighth grade completion	45	35.6	60.0	93.3
Less than eighth grade	56	21.5	57.1	91.0
Foreign/no schooling in America	20	20.0	20.0	100.0

Source: Parsons, "Study of Adult Reading," 74.

books were at this time. Hazel Ormsbee's study *The Young Employed Girl* (1926) found that less-educated girls were more likely to read "trashy" magazines than books of any kind.[25]

Change over time regarding education and reading is represented in table 6.6. Although the questions asked in the surveys represented were not strictly comparable, it is clear that the relationship between educational groups has remained roughly constant over the years. Those who attended college reported more reading than high-school attendees, and they in turn reported more than those who never went past grade school. (One exception: in 1955, the grade-school reading percentage was higher than that for high school, an anomaly for which we have no explanation). The patterns of change over time are less clear. Starting at a high of 52 percent in 1949, the proportion of college-educated respondents who reported that they were reading a book declined to 43 percent in 1952 and to a low of 30 percent in 1955. Because further education is generally associated with increased book reading, this sharp decline is worthy of note, especially since it persisted after the introduction of paperback books. Perhaps it was caused by the expansion of higher education to people whose parents had lower incomes and less education and thus were less book oriented. In any case, as the number of college students continued to increase, the proportion of book readers among college graduates began to rise, to 41 percent in 1966 and 50 percent in 1971. In 1984, the book-reading rate for college-educated people was back down to 37 percent. Reading among high-school attendees also bottomed out around 1955, at 17 percent, down from 23 percent in 1949. Reading in that group rose to 25 percent in 1966 and then declined slightly to 20 percent in 1984. The grade-school figures are low and erratic, zigzagging between 6 and 20

25. Hazel G. Ormsbee, *The Young Employed Girl* (New York: Woman's Press, 1927), 75.

Table 6.6. Percentage of American Adults Who Read Books, by Education, 1949–1984

Education attained	1949	1952	1955	1966	1971	1984
College	52	43	30	41	50	37
High school	23	19	17	25	22	20
Grade school	10	6	20	9	18	10

Sources: Gallup, *Gallup Poll,* II, 795, 1109; Wood, "Book Reading," 39; Gallup, *Gallup Poll,* III, 1996, 2285.

percent. All studies have shown positive correlations between higher educational levels and higher levels of reading. The percentage of regular book readers in the whole population has remained roughly level or even increased somewhat since the 1940s (see table 6.1) because more people have reached higher levels of education, not because of an increase in the rate of book reading at a particular education level.

Sex

In 1923 Parsons identified a relationship between gender and frequency of reading. Women were more likely to read books and magazines, whereas men were more likely to read newspapers (see table 6.7). In 1947 the Magazine Advertising Bureau concluded that 64 percent of men and 74 percent of women were magazine readers, and in 1983 the Book Industry Study Group showed that 60 percent of its sampled "book readers" (one book read per month) were women.[26] Gallup data showing change over time by sex support Parsons's generalization that more women than men read books. Women's book reading has been consistently higher than men's by 3 to 7 percent and has held steady at about 25 percent since 1949 (see table 6.8). Men's active book reading, at 18 percent in 1949, increased to 23 percent by 1984. The data are consistent with the following speculation. In the 1940s and 1950s a considerable share of magazines and books were targeted at women, the majority of whom did not work outside the home. As increasing numbers of women sought employment in the marketplace, however, their reading activity leveled off at about 26 percent. Concurrently, as men became better educated, their reading levels increased, thereby narrowing the gender gap and leaving women readers only slightly more active than their male counterparts.

26. Magazine Advertising Bureau, *Magazine Reader Count for County, State, and Nation* (New York: Magazine Advertising Bureau, 1949); Market Facts, *1983 Consumer Research Study,* 74.

Table 6.7. Readership by Sex: Chicago, 1923

	N	Books	Magazines	Newspapers
Men	204	51.0%	74.1%	98.0%
Women	110	57.2%	80.9%	93.0%

Source: Parsons, "Study of Adult Reading," 45.

Race

Some studies have noted differences in reading rates between white and black Americans. Caution is necessary in interpreting such conclusions because the cross-cutting variables in black-white reading differences are even more confounding than those that characterize male-female reading differences. Like the male-female contrast, the black-white contrast is associated with differences in educational levels, occupational distribution, and income. Unlike males and females, blacks and whites have different geographical distributions, thus confusing the identification of racial differences in reading habits with yet another important intervening variable. For example, a study of daily newspaper readership in 1961 asked people in households that regularly subscribed to or purchased papers whether they had read a paper the previous day. Nationally, among such subscriber or purchaser households, 82 percent of white respondents had read a paper the day before, whereas 69 percent of black respondents had. However, the results were partly attributable to regional differences: 73 percent of southern whites had read a paper, compared with 77 percent of northern blacks.[27]

A case study of Lansing, Michigan, illustrates another highly correlated variable in reading differences by race: the influence of income.[28] In mass-communication behavior, the low-income white group was more similar to the low-income black group than to the general population. In other words, the use of television, newspapers, and magazines differed little by race when controlled for income. Nonetheless, whatever the causes of racial differences in reading behaviors, they have persisted. The Book Industry Study Group reported recently that whereas nonwhites made up 15 percent of their general sample, they composed 35 percent of their nonreading respondents and only 10 percent of their

27. Newsprint Information Committee, *A National Study of Newspaper Reading: Size and Characteristics of the Newspaper Reading Public* (New York: Audits and Surveys, 1961), 1:3.
28. Bradley Greenberg and Brenda Dervin, "Mass Communication among the Urban Poor," *Public Opinion Quarterly* 34 (1970):224–35.

Table 6.8. Active Book Readership by Sex, 1949–1984

	1949 Reading a Book at Present	1955 Read in a book Yesterday	1966 Finished a Book in Past Month	1984 Read in a Book Yesterday
Men	18%	16%	20%	23%
Women	24%	23%	25%	26%

Sources: Gallup, *Gallup Poll,* II, 795, III, 1996; Wood, "Book Reading," 39.

book-reading respondents.[29] Again, these studies are not systematic or comparable enough to plot trends; one can say only that racial differences in reading patterns continue to occur for a variety of reasons. A considerable share of racial differences can be explained by income, education, and region. In some studies, an additional share remains after controlling for these variables, unexplained but statistically correlated with racial identity.

Income

Many studies have examined differences in reading patterns by income. Link and Hopf discovered that 64 percent of their upper-income respondents had read a book within the past month (those were called "active readers"), compared with 48 percent of middle-income respondents and 36 percent of lower-income respondents.[30] Of course, income is also highly correlated with educational levels, a correlation that Link and Hopf tried to explore. Among upper-income respondents, the proportion who were active readers varied greatly by education level: 73 percent of college graduates, 59 percent of high-school graduates, and 37 percent of elementary-school graduates had read a book in the past month. The same data for middle- and lower-income respondents in this sample show that education dominates income as a predictor of reading (see table 6.9).

The Advertising Research Foundation found similar income-related differences in newspaper reading in 1961. Among households that subscribed to or regularly purchased newspapers, 85 percent of adults in higher-income households (over $10,000 per year) had read a newspaper the day before, whereas only 52 percent of adult respondents from the lowest income group had.[31] More than two decades later, in 1983, the Book Industry Study Group found similar relationships.[32] In the lowest

29. Market Facts, *1983 Consumer Research Study,* 74.

30. Link and Hopf, *People and Books,* 59.

31. Newsprint Information Committee, *National Study of Newspaper Reading,* 1:18.

32. Market Facts, *1983 Consumer Research Study,* 78.

Table 6.9. Respondents Who Read a Book Last Month,
by Income and Education, 1945

	College	High School	Elementary School
Upper income	73%	59%	37%
Middle income	69%	50%	23%
Lower income	69%	46%	23%

Source: Link and Hopf, *People and Books*, 60–61.

income bracket (below $15,000 per year), 35 percent of the respondents were book readers, 54 percent read other materials, and 11 percent were nonreaders. In the top income bracket (over $40,000 per year), 70 percent were book readers, 29 percent read other materials, and about 1 percent were nonreaders. The correlation of income and education identified by Link and Hopf in the 1940s persisted in the surveys of the 1960s and 1980s, especially among older adults. The resulting picture is not surprising: across the decades the most active readers are higher in income and education; conversely, nonreaders tend to be disproportionately poorer and less educated. These are averages, of course; there are exceptions in both directions. Still, the association of income and education with high levels of reading activity is pervasive and enduring.

Community Studies

Thus far we have presented trends across time for the American reading public as a whole, and we have considered national studies that reported differences by age, education, sex, race, and income. In both of these efforts we have simply reported frequencies: how many people said that they had read a book or a newspaper or a magazine in a certain period. Some local readership studies go much farther, exploring attitudes about reading, different types of reading material, and different functions of reading. Three examples will illustrate how these local, detailed studies can pose more interesting questions than national studies can. Unfortunately, because researchers have different purposes and because the samples and methods vary from one study to another, such detailed studies generally are not comparable with one another. Nonetheless, they offer more details about what people read and why.

Rural Girls in the City

In 1927 the Southern Woman's Educational Alliance conducted a study of 255 rural adolescent women who migrated to Durham, North

Carolina, or Richmond, Virginia, to work.[33] The researchers wanted to examine the cultural environment from which the women came, to determine what impact the city had had on their activities outside the workplace, and to recommend steps that could be taken to foster self-improvement and wholesome leisure activities. In spite of its bias toward high culture and its mixture of research with moral reform, the study is valuable in that it used case studies to put behavior into the context of actual individual lives. Julia Franklin, for example, was chronicled in a five-page sketch. Julia lived on the meager cotton farm of her uneducated father, attended school irregularly until the age of twelve, and then dropped out to work on the farm. When she was fifteen, her father died, and she took her mother and retarded brother to the city so that she could work in the mills. Despite these difficult circumstances, Julia took advantage of the activities of the YWCA and a church in the city. She used all of her salary to maintain her family in a small house. Saved from discouragement by the Bryn Mawr Summer School for Industrial Workers, Julia became a success story. Looking forward enthusiastically to her second summer of learning, she was coping with the stresses of city life. "She has schooled herself to be as contented as possible. Meanwhile, she lives an intense inner life but throws herself into whatever opportunities are offered."[34]

With only a slightly moralistic tone, the interviewers described the less-inspiring story of Elsie Kinney, who left school in her country town after seventh grade because she had fallen behind her age group. At age eighteen she came to work as a department-store clerk in Durham, liked the city, liked the girls at the store, and was, according to the interviewer, "mainly interested in having a good time." Her favorite magazines were *True Stories* and *Romance*. Reading had different uses for different respondents, whether the interviewers liked it or not. Because Elsie "had a very limited intelligence," they decided that her "mentality, work and social instincts" were well matched.[35]

Some of these young women read escapist fiction for entertainment, some read for self-improvement, some for both. But on average, city life offered these women more romance magazines, more movies, more socializing, and less churchgoing than they had experienced in the countryside. The investigators advocated better guidance in rural schools and better housing, clubs, and cultural opportunities in the city.

Although the authors tabulated various data on the education, living arrangements, and leisure activities of the women, the real richness of

33. O. Latham Hatcher, *Rural Girls in the City for Work: A Study Made for the Southern Women's Educational Alliance* (Richmond, Va.: Garrett and Massie, 1930).
34. Ibid., 14.
35. Ibid., 19.

this type of study comes through the individual vignettes. Though they are filled with subjective judgments, these case studies illustrate how reading activities complemented different goals and different situations. The reading habits of these urban migrants seem to have been influenced both by their education and by the cultural milieu into which they drifted in the city.

Woodside Does Read!

Some community studies have relied more upon statistics and less upon subjective information about the lives of individual respondents. However, in cases in which participation was voluntary and participants were self-selected, the results cannot be generalized to the whole population. Grace Kelley distributed 4,100 questionnaires in the Woodside area of Queens, New York, in the fall of 1933 to learn about the use of public libraries; 1,000 questionnaires were returned.[36] One must assume that, on the average, the people who responded to a mail questionnaire about their reading habits were more active readers than the population as a whole. But the Woodside researchers were not interested in a random sample; they wanted to determine the tastes and purposes of the active readers who used public libraries. Also, unlike the Southern Alliance researchers, the Woodside researchers announced that they had an "open mind," that they wished merely to determine what purposes were served by the public library and then to build a collection of books to serve those purposes. Although they seemed periodically to forget that their 1,000 respondents were not representative of the entire population, they nonetheless provided much interesting detail, fleshing out our picture of the active reading public in one urban area. Of course, we also do not know whether people are truthful on such questionnaires, but that problem is endemic to all studies of the reading public.

When respondents were asked to indicate whether various activities were "among my main leisure activities," reading came out ahead of radio listening for all groups, but especially among older readers and more educated readers.[37] More highly educated readers read the *New York Times* or the *Herald Tribune,* whereas less-educated readers read the *News* or the *American.* Of *New York Times* readers, 80 percent said they enjoyed reading; 57 percent of *News* readers said they did.[38] When asked to consider a list of popular adventure and romance magazines like *True Story, Ranch Romances, Argosy,* and *Dream World,* few respondents

36. Grace O. Kelley, *Woodside Does Read: A Survey of the Reading Interests and Habits of a Local Community* (Jamaica, N.Y.: Queens Borough Public Library, 1935).
37. Ibid., 129–30.
38. Ibid., 156.

said they read them, but many wrote comments in the margins, such as, "This trash has no place in the public library," "God forbid," and "None, thank Heaven."[39] Gender differences emerged in the acquisition of books. More men bought books, whereas more women joined book clubs and used the libraries. In their advice to the library, many respondents requested more modern authors and fewer classics. Most nonusers of libraries who nonetheless chose to respond said they were too busy to read anything more than a daily newspaper or a favorite magazine or lived too far from a library to take the trouble.[40] Nonuse also varied by education level. Some of this stratification within the reading public is familiar from the national reader studies, but the community studies draw more connections and yield more colorful anecdotal evidence.

People and Books in a Metropolis

The strengths and weaknesses of community studies are evident in another well-known study of reading habits, conducted in Baltimore in 1961. Jan Hajda, a doctoral student in the sociology department of the University of Chicago, attempted to discover what personal and family characteristics were associated with active book reading.[41] To attain a large enough sample to make results statistically significant, Hajda had to rely on phone interviews; as in national polls, his data are self-reported. On the positive side, the interviews were long and covered much more detail than did national polls, both in terms of the respondents' reading behavior and their other characteristics.

Hajda's respondents included too few men to permit confident generalization; the study thus focuses on women readers. Of the 1,913 female respondents, 41 percent had read a book in the previous year. Among the book readers, about 30 percent said they read more than ten books a year, frequently read book reviews, and didn't care about best-seller popularity (Hajda labeled this group "quality" readers). Another 27 percent of the book readers, who also said they read more than ten books a year, depended less on reviews and more on popularity (Hajda called these women "heavy" readers). The remaining 43 percent of the book readers read fewer than ten books a year (Hajda called them "light" readers).

Exemplifying the quirky judgments often made in community studies, Hajda did not count the Bible, prayer books, cookbooks, encyclopedias, or dictionaries as books. Even with these omissions, 76 percent of his respondents' households contained books (compared with 96

39. Ibid., 158–59.
40. Ibid., 123, 177, 191.
41. Jan Hajda, "An American Paradox: People and Books in a Metropolis" (Ph.D. diss., University of Chicago, 1963).

percent that contained a television set). Hajda spent considerable effort exploring the social characteristics of nonreaders, light readers, and frequent (that is, heavy and quality) readers. The intensity of reading followed predictable lines of income, occupation, and race, but the impact of these factors was much reduced when the data were controlled for education level. Education even explained most of the lower reading frequencies associated with his older respondents. Although Hajda emphasized the salience of the respondents' education level, he also pointed out that the reading habits of parents and spouses influenced those of the respondents. A lifelong reading habit could be predicted by the types of books an adolescent reported reading; biography, history, and poetry were most positively associated with frequent reading among adults.

Hajda argued that any interest in abstract ideas or remote places encouraged book reading; conversely, if a person focused mainly on proximate concerns, book reading was reduced. Strong kinship ties among women correlated with lower reading time; indeed, marriage itself, holding employment status constant, was associated with lower levels of reading. Hajda also explored the relationship among different print forms. In most cases, the reading of magazines, newspapers, and books was mutually reinforcing; however, there was a clear hierarchy among these print forms, with almost all of the women reading a newspaper. Education affected the mix very strongly (see table 6.10). Among Hajda's high-education group, only 8 percent read nothing except a regular newspaper, whereas 32 percent read newspapers, magazines, and books regularly. Among less-educated women, 30 percent read only newspapers regularly, whereas 6 percent read all three forms of material. In spite of its limitations, the Hajda study is a useful reminder that reading habits were not simply a function of such formal attributes as educational attainment, age, sex, and race but also were shaped by human relationships—family responsibilities and the interests and reading habits of family members.

In this chapter we have looked at three kinds of studies: national frequency trends for the population as a whole, national frequency trends for subgroups of the population, and community studies that looked at the reading activities of a limited population in a particular place at one point in time. The national frequency trends provide a skeletal framework for picturing the development of the American reading public, and the community studies provide some flesh for the skeleton. What do the trends look like?

The American reading public has expanded greatly in the past century, but research does not go back to the earliest decades, when much of the expansion took place. We infer that newspaper, magazine, and book

Table 6.10. Frequency of Reading Three Print Forms, by Education: Baltimore Women, 1961

Print Form	High Education (High School or More)		Low Education (Some High School or Less)	
	N	%	N	%
All regular book readers	333	38.5	101	9.9
Regular book readers who also regularly read:				
Magazines and newspapers	273	31.6	65	6.4
Newspapers but not magazines	36	4.2	25	2.4
Magazines but not newspapers	19	2.2	6	0.6
Neither magazines nor newspapers	5	0.6	5	0.5
All occasional book readers	236	27.3	137	13.4
Occasional book readers who also regularly read:				
Magazines and newspapers	183	21.2	83	8.1
Newspapers but not magazines	28	3.2	41	4.0
Magazines but not newspapers	19	2.2	10	1.0
Neither magazines nor newspapers	6	0.7	3	0.3
All non-book-readers	296	34.2	783	76.7
Non-book-readers who regularly read:				
Magazines and newspapers	202	23.4	355	34.8
Newspapers but not magazines	66	7.6	297	29.1
Magazines but not newspapers	17	2.0	34	3.3
Neither magazines nor newspapers	11	1.3	97	9.5
Totals	865	100	1,021	100

Source: Hajda, "American Paradox," 387. The data are recalculated from his table 6.7.

Note: Regular book reader = read in a book in the past two weeks; occasional book reader = read in a book in the past year, but not in the past two weeks; non-book-reader = none in more than a year; regular magazine reader = weekly; regular newspaper reader = daily.

reading expanded between the 1880s and the 1920s because we can observe decreasing prices, escalating circulation figures, and rising education levels. But our studies of the reading public do not allow us to chart that expansion. From the 1940s, when survey research on this topic became more common, most trends are level or downward. Although, as we noted in chapter 6, the percentage of households that purchase books is increasing, the regular book-reading public has remained about constant, in the 20 to 25 percent range. The regular magazine-reading public has also remained roughly at the same level, around 60 percent; regular newspaper reading has declined from the 80 to 90 percent range to the 50 to 60 percent range, largely as a result of television news. These figures, however, leave much unsaid and unexplored. They do not tell us much about the reading activities of infrequent readers or of those with low literacy skills—such individuals only dart in and out of the picture. The national surveys tell us little about the reading experiences of disadvantaged and foreign-language groups; even the community studies tend to explore mainstream reading material and mainstream cultural institutions. What does emerge, however, is a picture of a developing reading public with three major components. First, there is a group of infrequent readers and nonreaders on the periphery of these surveys. At the other end of the spectrum is a reading elite of highly educated and very active readers, whose reading fare has become progressively more diverse and more available in the past four decades. Finally, there is a very large middle group of less active but still regular readers who spend their reading time on newspapers and magazines more than on books. These popular readers share with the elite group much common cultural content through syndicated newspaper services and shared magazines like the *Saturday Evening Post* and *Ladies' Home Journal*. However, this largest body of American readers also displays immense variety and many divergent reading interests, some associated with class, race, gender, and education, others merely with the profusion of diverse content available in an affluent, consumer-oriented economy.

In the next chapter we focus on a single point in time—1920—and compare data about the public's education levels and reading habits with an assessment of the readability levels of some major publications. In the course of this experiment, we develop further the picture of an elite reading public and a popular reading public.

7 Highbrow and Middlebrow Magazines in 1920

WILLIAM VANCE TROLLINGER, JR., AND
CARL F. KAESTLE

This chapter sketches the outlines of the reading public in 1920 and then analyzes some of the popular reading materials available to those readers. We aim to find out how difficult various publications were to read, and how they matched readers' abilities. The bridge we build between readers and texts is very crude, but it is a bridge nonetheless. We chose 1920 because it is the earliest date for which we have not only circulation figures and best-seller lists but some rough idea of school-attainment rates among adults and a survey of reading habits in a large metropolitan area.

We imagined that some of the influential newspapers, books, and magazines of the time were written at a level of difficulty that made them inaccessible to many readers. If true, this would have implications for the stratification of the reading public on the basis of literacy ability. If the less-accessible reading materials also functioned as badges of status and channels of influence, that would say something about the role of literacy in the distribution of power; but that goes beyond what we can demonstrate here. We hope to show simply that there are methods by which one can match data on the readability of prose with data on the education levels of readers in the past and speculate about the differences between highbrow and middlebrow reading. Our experiment along these lines suggests that the difficulty of prose probably helped stratify the reading public, in addition to whatever other factors influenced people's choices of reading material.

The Reading Publics of 1920

Americans in 1920 reported low levels of outright illiteracy. Among whites the self-reported illiteracy rate was 4 percent; 23 percent of American blacks reported that they could not read, down from 30 percent a decade earlier. Education levels had risen steadily in the late nineteenth and early twentieth centuries. Thus, among those in their late fifties in 1920, about 2.5 percent had graduated from high school, whereas among those in their late thirties, 6 percent had. About 16 percent of seventeen-year-olds in 1920 had graduated from high school. College graduation was rarer still; 2.6 percent of twenty-three-year-olds had received a bachelor's degree. Although the higher reaches of education were restricted, school enrollment up through the junior-high years was very common.[1] A large national sample of those between thirteen and twenty-two years old in 1920 later reported an average of 9.4 total years of schooling, ranging from an average of 7.5 years among those whose fathers were in the lowest occupational status to an average of 13 years among the children of the highest-status fathers.[2] The years of schooling attained by the whole population, of course, would have been considerably lower than 9.4 years. Although we have no exact data on the older cohorts, school-enrollment rates were increasing, and thus the rate of school attainment would be lower for older Americans. Folger and Nam, projecting back from known data for cohort groups in 1940, estimated the median school years completed for those aged twenty-five and older in 1920 to be 8.2 years.[3] The United States, like many other industrial countries sixty-five years ago, had widespread basic literacy training in elementary schools and a much more exclusive group trained in higher literacy skills in high schools and colleges. The difficulty of a printed text could therefore have had a dramatic effect on the range and character of its potential audience.

Book readers—in 1920 as today—tended to be people with at least a high school education. Urban residence and parents with higher educational attainment also fostered reading; in other words, the more print-laden and literate one's surroundings, the more likely one was to become a book reader (see chapter 6 above). The Parsons study of reading habits in 1923 confirmed that the audience for books was much more limited than that for magazines and newspapers. Parsons surveyed 314 adults in the Chicago area, an urban area with greater access to books and higher levels of education than the national average. Among Parsons's subjects 48 percent were high-school graduates and fully 76 percent had eight or more years of schooling. Whereas only 3 percent of his respondents said that they did not read a newspaper, 23 percent did not read magazines,

1. U.S. Bureau of the Census, *Fourteenth Census of the United States* (Washington, D.C.: Government Printing Office, 1920).

2. Unpublished analysis by Michael R. Olneck and Dae D. Hahn of two data sets: the 1962 Occupational Changes in a Generation Survey, and the 1973 Occupational Changes in a Generation Replication Study.

3. Folger and Nam, "Educational Trends from Census Data," 253.

and 47 percent reported not having read any books in the previous six months. Considering our speculation that the average years of schooling across the whole population was about eight years, we find it interesting to focus on those in Parsons's study who had finished only eight years of schooling. Their rates of reading participation were well below the average of his sample as a whole: 7 percent did not read newspapers, 40 percent did not read magazines, and 64 percent had read no books in the previous six months.[4]

Popular Reading Materials in 1920

Given this range of education levels and reading habits, we wished to assess the readability of popular print material in different categories. Were books in general more difficult to read than magazines and newspapers? Were highbrow publications like the *New York Times* and the *Atlantic Monthly* written at a greater level of difficulty than local newspapers and the immensely popular *Saturday Evening Post?*

Of newspapers, we examined the *New York Times* (circulation: 368,000); its less-stuffy rival, the *New York World* (330,000); a midwestern urban newspaper, the *Milwaukee Journal* (102,000); and a midwestern small-town newspaper, the *Beaver Dam (Wisconsin) Daily Citizen* (2,000). We looked at one story that was carried in all four newspapers, a report on the expulsion of socialists from the New York State Assembly in April 1920.

Our choices among magazines were the highbrow *Atlantic Monthly* (95,000), the middlebrow *Saturday Evening Post* (2,021,000), and the lowbrow *Argosy* (449,000).[5] In keeping with the dates of our newspaper articles, we analyzed a fiction article from an April 1920 issue of each of these magazines. We also analyzed nonfiction articles from the *Atlantic* and the *Post* on the same topic: profiteering in post-World War I America. The *Argosy* did not carry any nonfiction pieces.

Finally, we selected the nonfiction and fiction best sellers of 1920. In fact, it wasn't simple to ascertain which books were the most popular. Publishers and booksellers traditionally have not divulged the precise number of copies of a particular book that have been sold. Best-seller lists typically have been constructed from calls to selected bookstores across the country, sometimes no more than fifteen to twenty-five stores in all. The lists' derivation from a limited and perhaps unrepresentative sample is not the only problem. If, for example, twenty small stores reported that Book A was first in sales, and five large stores reported that

4. Parsons, "Study of Adult Reading," 34, 40, 74.
5. Circulation figures are from N. W. Ayer & Son, *American Newspaper Annual and Directory* (Philadelphia: N. W. Ayer & Son, 1920).

Book B was first, A will rate higher on the best-seller list even though more copies of B may have been sold. Annual best-seller lists represent little more than simple averages of these potentially inaccurate weekly or monthly lists.[6] In spite of these problems, a historian of popular print material in twentieth-century America must depend on these lists. In choosing the most popular nonfiction book for 1920 we opted for Alice Payne Hackett's roster, the monarch of best-seller lists.[7] Hackett developed her 1920 list from the monthly lists published in *Publishers' Weekly* and *Books of the Month.* Her top two in 1920 were Philip Gibbs's *Now It Can Be Told,* which was an account of World War I, and John Maynard Keynes's *The Economic Consequences of the Peace.* But Hackett's list presents yet another problem not mentioned above. A best-seller list for a particular year fails to reflect the fact that a book's total sales as a best seller will often be distributed over a two- or even three-year period. Fortunately, we had an alternative source to Hackett when it came to fiction books: Irving Harlow Hart's "Best Sellers in Fiction during the First Quarter of the Twentieth Century."[8] In constructing his twenty-five-year list, Hart noted *all* of the months a book was on the standard best-seller lists. Using Hart's compilations, we chose to examine the top four fiction books that included 1920 as one of their primary sales years: Sinclair Lewis, *Main Street;* Vicente Blasco Ibañez, *The Four Horsemen of the Apocalypse;* Harold Bell Wright, *The Re-Creation of Brian Kent;* and Zane Grey, *Man of the Forest.* We decided to look at four novels because we wanted to compare an acclaimed classic, *Main Street,* with the Wright and Grey pulp novels.

The Readability of Popular Prose

Publishers, journalists, and teachers have long used readability formulas to determine the reading ease or difficulty of prose passages. Most involve a combination of three variables: sentence length, word length, and word familiarity.[9] Rudolf Flesch is the most important individual in the development of readability formulas. Flesch viewed himself as the missionary of clear, direct prose, a crusader who sought to instruct people to write less like John Dewey and more like Erle Stanley Gardner.

6. Robert W. Frase, "Economic Trends in Trade Book Publishing," in *Books and the Mass Market,* ed. Harold K. Guinzberg, Robert W. Frase, and Theodore Waller (Urbana: University of Illinois Press, 1953), 21–42.

7. Hackett, *Fifty Years of Best Sellers.*

8. Harlow Irving Hart, "Best Sellers in Fiction during the First Quarter of the Twentieth Century," *Publishers' Weekly,* February 14, 1925, 525–27.

9. George R. Klare, "Assessing Readability," *Reading Research Quarterly* 10 (1974–75):62–102; George R. Klare, "Readability," in *Handbook of Reading Research,* ed. P. David Pearson et al. (New York: Longman, 1984), 681–744.

George Klare observed that Flesch's 1948 Reading Ease formula has "become the most widely used of all readability formulas."[10] The formula's popularity has stemmed in great part from its simplicity:

Reading Ease = 206.835
    Minus: .845 times the number of syllables per 100 words
    Minus: 1.015 times the average number of words per sentence

In translating the resulting scores, a low score means difficult reading and a high score means easy reading, on a scale from 0 to 100 (see table 7.1).[11]

Flesch's Reading Ease formula would seem to be a godsend to historians of literacy. Not only is it easily understood and implemented, but it does not include the variable of vocabulary familiarity. Hence, the historian using Flesch escapes the problem that a word familiar in 1980 might not have been familiar in 1920. Using the Reading Ease formula, a scholar can quickly compute the reading difficulty of printed material in the past and with a few computations, can chart changes over time. However, over the past fifteen years, reading researchers have mounted an increasingly heavy attack on the Flesch measuring device and other readability formulas. One basic criticism is directed at the procedures used to verify that any particular formula does indeed reflect the reading difficulty or ease of a written passage, that is, the validation procedures.[12] Moreover, the readability scales are text based; they cannot account for a reader's previous knowledge, fatigue, and the like. Finally, creators of all formulas make the unwarranted assumption that their formulas, derived from particular passages, are applicable to other unrelated passages.

These problems should be enough to make historians hesitate before using traditional readability formulas. But an even more prominent recent criticism is that readability formulas are atheoretical. That is to say, the standard variables used to measure readability, such as word length, are only tangentially related to what makes a text more or less understandable.[13] Still, the purpose of readability formulas is to predict reading difficulty, not to explain what makes a text readable. Traditional readability formulas do correlate quite positively with scores on comprehension tests; for this reason, and because of their simplicity, readability formulas are used widely in education. Thus it seems plausible

10. Klare, "Readability," 686.
11. Rudolf Flesch, "Why So Much Illiteracy?" *New York Times,* June 3, 1985, 21.
12. Klare, "Assessing Readability"; Klare, "Readability"; Ramsay Selden, "On the Validation of the Original Readability Formulas," in *Text Readability: Proceedings of the March 1980 Conference,* ed. Alice Davison, Robert Lutz, and Ann Roalef (Urbana: University of Illinois, Center for the Study of Reading, 1981), 10–30.
13. See Kintsch and Vipond, "Reading Comprehension and Readability," 337.

Table 7.1. Flesch Readability Ratings of 1920 Reading Materials

Interpretation of the Scale:

Score	Difficulty	Approximate Grade Level
0–30	Very difficult	15+
30–50	Difficult	11–14
50–60	Fairly difficult	9–10
60–70	Standard	7–8
70–80	Fairly easy	6
80–90	Easy	5
90–100	Very easy	4

A. Newspapers (story on the expulsion of socialists from the New York State Assembly, April 1, 1920):

	Reading Ease of Story	Approximate Grade Level
New York World	23.1	15+
New York Times	39.8	12–13
Milwaukee Journal	43.2	11–12
Beaver Dam Daily Citizen	49.5	10–11

B. Periodicals (nonfiction article on profiteering):

	Reading Ease of Article	Approximate Grade Level
Atlantic Monthly, April 1920	52.0	10
Saturday Evening Post, April 3, 1920	64.7	7–8

C. Periodicals (fiction):

	Reading Ease of Story	Approximate Grade Level
Atlantic Monthly, April 1920 ("The Third Window")	80.4	5–6
Saturday Evening Post, April 3, 1920 ("A Prince There Wasn't")	45.7	11
Argosy, April 10, 1920 ("Anything Once")	60.5	8–9

D. Best sellers (nonfiction):

	Reading Ease of Book	Approximate Grade Level
Philip Gibbs, *Now It Can Be Told*	64.6	7–8
John Maynard Keynes, *The Economic Consequences of the Peace*	39.6	12–13

(*continued*)

Table 7.1. (*continued*)

E. Best sellers (fiction):

	Reading Ease of Book	Approximate Grade Level
Sinclair Lewis, *Main Street*	74.2	6
Vicente Blasco Ibañez, *The Four Horsemen of the Apocalypse*	64.3	7–8
Zane Grey, *Man of the Forest*	83.1	5
Harold Bell Wright, *The Re-Creation of Brian Kent*	64.1	7–8

that historians could use traditional readability formulas to gain a rough idea of how difficult or easy readers would have found a particular text in the past.[14]

We can also use the more sophisticated readability measurements that have resulted from recent research. In the past decade readability research has moved far beyond surface features of the text. Like reader-response critics in literary studies, who think hard about the process of text interpretation for an "implied" reader, some text-based models of comprehension consider carefully the different mental processes involved in understanding a text. Drawing on linguistics and computer science as well as cognitive psychology, reading researchers have constructed models of how the content and organization of texts affect the hypothetical average reader. Some have emphasized syntactic structure, others cohesive connections in the prose, others the importance of textual signals.[15] We have chosen two models derived from this recent work: one, embodied in a computer program by Sheryl Young, assesses both the density of propositions in a text and the number of inferences required to

14. For studies that have traced readability over time, see James C. Craig, "The Vocabulary Load of the Nation's Best-Sellers from 1662 to 1945: A Study in Readability" (Ph.D. diss., University of Pittsburgh, 1954); Lydia D. Schulze, "Best-Sellers Evaluated for Readability and Portrayal of Female Characters" (M.A. thesis, Rutgers University, 1976); Jean C. Barganz and Kenneth L. Dulin, "Readability Levels of Selected Mass Magazines, 1925–1965," in *Reading: Process and Pedagogy, Nineteenth Yearbook of the National Reading Conference,* ed. George B. Schick and Merrill M. May, 2 vols. (Milwaukee, Wis.: National Reading Conference, 1971), 2:26–30.

15. John Dawkins, *Syntax and Readability* (Newark, Del.: International Reading Association, 1975); Margaret A. Richek, "Effect of Sentence Complexity on the Reading Comprehension of Syntactic Structures," *Journal of Educational Psychology* 68 (1976):800–806; Judith W. Irwin, "The Effect of Linguistic Cohesion on Prose Comprehension," *Journal of Reading Behavior* 12 (Winter 1980):325–32; Bruce Britton et al., "Effects of Text Structure on Use of Cognitive Capacity during Reading," *Journal of Educational Psychology* 74 (1982):56; Tom Trabasso, Tom Secco, and Paul Van Den Broek, "Coherence in Narrative Text," in *Learning and Comprehension of Text,* ed. H. Mandell, Nancy Stein, and Tom Trabasso (Hillsdale, N.J.: Lawrence Erlbaum, 1983).

understand it.[16] The second, an "inference load formula" by Susan Kemper, emphasizes the causal structure of a text and, like Young's, the number of inferences required.[17]

These formulas measure readability for the average reader; they have nothing to do with individual readers' varied motivations and interests, all of which play a crucial role in the reading process. Nonetheless, like the Flesch formula, the Young and Kemper models yield ratings that predict with high accuracy the difficulty real readers will encounter with texts, on average. Moreover, they are theoretically superior because they tell us something about why prose passages are difficult or easy.

The Readability of 1920 Prose Selections

To begin our analysis of these selected books and articles, we applied the Flesch Reading Ease test to all of them. In keeping with Flesch's instructions, we randomly selected three 100-word passages from each article, and twenty-five 100-word passages from each book. We applied the formula to each passage and then computed an average Reading Ease score (see table 7.1).[18]

The analysis of newspaper articles yielded no real surprises. The New York newspaper articles were more difficult than the Wisconsin newspaper articles. As might be expected, the *Milwaukee Journal* and the *Beaver Dam Daily Citizen* did not send their own reporters to cover the expulsion of socialists from the New York Assembly; we assume that both newspapers used wire-service stories. But their easier readability ratings lead us to speculate that perhaps newspaper editors in "the hinterland" rewrote wire-service stories with an eye toward simplifying the prose.

We translated these Reading Ease scores into rough grade equivalents. The reader should recall how inexact such grade-level estimates are when applied to text. They do not predict how well a given person can read a given piece, even when we know the grade-level rating of the piece and the school attainment of the reader. Also, we do not know that eight

16. Sheryl Young, "A Theory and Simulation of Macrostructure" (Ph.D. diss., University of Colorado, 1984). Young's work draws on James R. Miller and Walter Kintsch, "Readability and Recall of Short Prose Passages: A Theoretical Analysis," *Journal of Experimental Psychology* 6 (1980):348, and van Dijk and Kintsch, *Strategies of Discourse Comprehension*.

17. Susan Kemper, "Measuring the Inference Load of a Text," *Journal of Educational Psychology* 75 (1983):391–401.

18. A full identification of the passages and the procedures for applying Flesch are included in William Vance Trollinger, Jr., and Carl F. Kaestle, *Difficulty of Text as a Factor in the History of Reading* (Madison: Wisconsin Center for Education Research, Program Report 86–13, 1986, ERIC Document Reproduction Service no. ED 312 625).

years of schooling resulted on the average in an ability to read at an eighth-grade level, though the stability of achievement scores analyzed in chapter 3 suggests that it is a reasonable guess. Acknowledging the roughness of the tools, we can nonetheless say that the Wisconsin papers' stories on the New York socialists appear to have been written at the tenth- or eleventh-grade reading level, slightly above the national average school-attainment rate. The New York papers, especially the *World* in the case of this particular story, were at higher levels, well above the national average.

In contrast to the newspaper analyses, applying the Flesch Reading Ease test to books did produce some surprises. Certainly it was no revelation that *The Economic Consequences of the Peace* by John Maynard Keynes was rated much more difficult to read (around the twelfth-grade level) than the five other best sellers. But one may be startled to discover that Sinclair Lewis's *Main Street* had a higher Reading Ease score than Harold Bell Wright's *The Re-Creation of Brian Kent* and the translation of Vicente Blasco Ibañez's *The Four Horsemen of the Apocalypse*. The technical reason for this is simple: Lewis's sentences are much shorter, particularly in comparison with Wright's elongated sentences. This result illustrates one of the problems with the Flesch test. No theoretically sound reason exists for assuming that short sentences are necessarily easier to read than long sentences. Still, it might be true that short sentences generally make a text more readable. If so, perhaps the heightened readability of *Main Street* contributed to its best-seller status.

A major surprise emerged from our evaluation of periodical fiction. We expected that the highbrow *Atlantic* would contain the most difficult prose, followed in order by the *Post* and the *Argosy*. But according to the Flesch formula, the *Post* story was difficult to read, the *Argosy* story was rated in the range of Flesch's "standard" category (around seventh to eighth grade), and the *Atlantic* story ranked between "fairly easy" and "easy" to read. Could it be that, at least in some cases, low- and middlebrow fiction in the 1920s was much more difficult to read than its highbrow counterparts? To test these anomalous results, we applied the more sophisticated Young and Kemper models to the *Atlantic* and *Post* stories.

Middlebrow and Highbrow Fiction: A Technical Analysis

We examined the *Atlantic* passage rated by the Flesch formula to be the easiest and the *Post* passage assessed to be the most difficult. Because the Kemper and Young models perform better with longer selections, we extended each of the original passages by more than a hundred words. The story from the *Saturday Evening Post,* which describes a successful play, uses flowery language and long sentences. Its reading-ease score is 36.7 (difficult). The plot of the *Atlantic* story centers on a man who is afraid of a ghost named Malcolm. Its vocabulary is relatively simple, and its sentences are relatively short. Its Flesch reading-ease score is 82.0 (easy). These seemed good examples to test with a more sophisticated analysis. We wanted to determine whether a more thorough analysis of the prose would confirm the Flesch readability estimate or would reveal some different characteristics. The text of each story excerpt follows.

The Play. From "A Prince There Wasn't," by John Peter Toohey, *Saturday Evening Post*, April 3, 1920, 16–17, 124, 127, 130.

The Ganges Princess was the dramatic sensation of a decade. It had been running for a solid year at the huge Hendrik Hudson Theater in New York, having weathered a hot summer with hardly a noticeable falling off of receipts. It was Chester Bartlett's first venture into what is technically known as the legitimate field, and he had staged it with that lavish disregard for expense and with that keen sense of the artistic which had given him preeminence as a producer of light musical entertainment.

Written by one of America's most flamboyant playwrights, it told a turgid story of Oriental passion and treachery set against a spectacular background depicting scenes in ancient India. As sheer spectacle it quite transcended anything hitherto attempted in the United States. It presented a series of settings which were so flaming in their color, so permeated with the mystery of the East and so splendid in their suggestion of great size and vast distances that each new revelation was invariably greeted with gasps of amazement from the audience. A cast bristling with distinguished names gave verisimilitude to the somewhat bombastic dialogue, and purely incidental members of the company included a troupe of fifty real nautch girls, six elephants, five camels and a flock of sheep.

The Ghost. From "The Third Window," by Anne Douglas Sedgwick, *Atlantic Monthly*, April 1920, 496–513.

He heard, as he waked next morning, that it was heavily raining. When he looked out, the trees stood still in gray sheets of straightly falling rain. There was no wind.

The mournful, obliterated scene did not oppress him. The weather was all to the good, he thought. He had always liked a rainy day in the country; and ghosts don't walk in the rain. If Malcolm hadn't come in the moonlight, he wouldn't come now. He felt sunken, exhausted, and rather sick; yet his spirits were not bad. He was fit for the encounter with Antonia.

When he went down to the dark dining-room, darker than ever today, he found only one place laid. The maid told him that both the ladies were breakfasting in their rooms. This was unexpected and disconcerting. But he made the best of it, and drank his coffee and ate kedgeree and toast with not too bad an appetite. A little coal-fire had been lighted in the library, and he went in there after breakfast and read the papers and wrote some letters, and the morning passed not too heavily.

But at luncheon-time his heart sank, almost to the qualm of the night before, when he found still only one place laid. After half an hour of indecision over his cigarette, he wrote a note and sent it up to Antonia.

The program developed by Sheryl Young attempts to simulate the reading process, or, at least some important aspects of it.[19] The first step in this analysis is to "propositionalize" the text, which involves dissecting the sentences into their simplest discrete propositions. The sentence "He heard, as he waked next morning, that it was heavily raining" thus becomes six "micropropositions": he heard rain; he waked; he heard it when he waked; the time was morning; it was raining heavily.[20]

If an inference is required for the computer to relate one microproposition to the previous text, the human researcher provides the inference as a new, special microproposition. The computer is programmed to mimic the reading process in the following way. It reads each microproposition, storing it in short-term memory, until short-term memory is full, when it moves earlier micropropositions to long-term memory. The computer relates each microproposition to the preceding text by linking identical words, by relating nouns to their modifiers, and by calling up the other relationships it is programmed to recognize. If it cannot relate a microproposition to the material in short-term memory, it searches long-term memory, which takes more time (that is, it slows down comprehension). This is called a "reinstatement." Inferences are also noted, for they also slow comprehension in human readers. The product of this analysis is twofold: a tree diagram showing the relationships between all of the micropropositions in the text, and an analysis of the macrostructure, the main ideas, and which key micropropositions belong to each macrostructure.

The difficulty in comprehending a given text is assessed by determining how many reinstatements are necessary, how many inferences are necessary, and how deep the tree structure of micropropositions becomes.

19. Young, "Theory and Simulation of Macrostructure."

20. All of the micro- and macropropositions are given in Trollinger and Kaestle, *Difficulty of Text*, appendix C. Sheryl Young propositionalized our texts. We thank her for this technical assistance.

One can also measure the density of micropropositions and the number of macropropositions for a text of a certain length. All of these would affect speed of comprehension. The emphasis, however, is on inferences, reinstatements, and depth of subtrees: Does the reader have to do a lot of searching around and figuring things out? Texts that are difficult to comprehend may simply be poorly organized and incoherently written, or they may be subtle, aesthetically challenging, and composed of complex ideas. In our two stories, the Young analysis clearly reverses the comprehensibility predictions of the Flesch readability test. The *Atlantic* article about the ghost proves to be more difficult, partly because the ideas are more difficult and partly, perhaps, because it is not written as clearly as it might be. The *Saturday Evening Post* article, in spite of its fancy words and longer sentences, is very simple to comprehend.

In terms of the Young program, the story about the play had five macropropositions, no reinstatements, no inferences, and eleven levels of microstructure. It had 89 micropropositions in its 211 words (or 42.2 per 100). The ghost story had six macropropositions, required one reinstatement and two inferences, and had twelve levels of microstructure. It had 101 micropropositions in its 227 words (or 44.5 per 100 words). One of the necessary inferences (that Malcolm was a ghost) proved to be particularly difficult for human readers. In an informal experiment, we gave the two excerpts to four office workers and asked them to write down the main ideas of each of the two passages. None had any difficulty with the passage about the play; all had some difficulty writing an accurate summary of the ghost story.

Figures 7.1 and 7.2 present the tree structures for the micropropositions of the two stories. The dotted lines outline the macropropositions for each story. The macropropositions for the story about the play, from the *Saturday Evening Post,* are easy to draw; the key proposition is related in a hierarchical way to the other main micropropositions. For the *Atlantic Monthly*'s ghost story, it is almost impossible to draw circles around the macropropositions: some of the key micropropositions are on other subtrees altogether. This is a graphic representation of the kind of messiness the human reader had to sort out in comprehending the story about Malcolm, the ghost who didn't show up on rainy days.

We do not claim, of course, that all seemingly simple prose in the *Atlantic Monthly* was incredibly difficult to read, or that everything in the *Saturday Evening Post* was at a homogeneously simple level in terms of its logical structure, its rhetoric, and the complexity of its ideas. What this exercise suggests is that we can learn more about the difficulty of text from the techniques recently developed by cognitive psychologists than we can from old-fashioned readability formulas. It just happened in this case that the analysis of macrostructure confirmed the common-

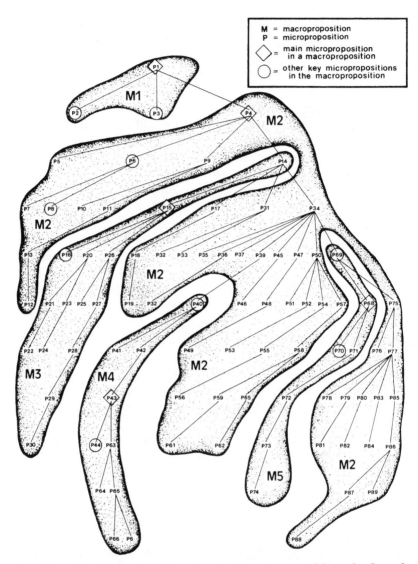

Figure 7.1. "The Play": Tree Structure of a Story Excerpted from the *Saturday Evening Post,* April 3, 1920 (Young-Miller Analysis). Figures 7.1–7.4 designed and produced by Al Divine, Wisconsin Center for Education Research.

sense prediction that one usually finds more sophisticated (or at least more difficult) prose in the *Atlantic* than in the *Post.*

Using the Young program proved to be expensive and time-consuming, as we had expected. The program is complex; it is a research device, not a pragmatic replacement for a readability formula. Susan Kemper's work on inference load appeared to be a different and more feasible way to

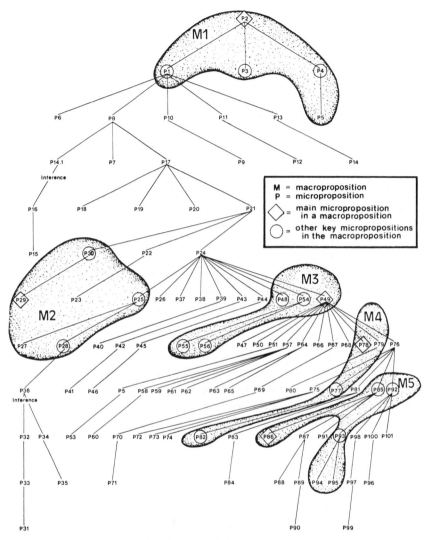

Figure 7.2. "The Ghost": Tree Structure of a Story Excerpted from the *Atlantic Monthly,* April 1920 (Young-Miller Analysis)

explore the macrostructure of a text, so we applied it to these same stories. Kemper's model is predicated on the notion that texts consist of chains of causally connected events, actions, and states. According to Kemper, the ease or difficulty of the text is dependent on the degree to which the events, actions, and states are explicitly connected. The more inferences a reader is required to make, the harder the selection will be to read.

In order to use Kemper's model we had to "decompose" our two stories into event chains. We began by parsing the text into clauses, classifying each clause as an action (A), a physical state (PS), or a mental state (MS). Thus classified, the clauses were ready to be organized into an event chain that we created in accordance with Kemper's rules concerning causal connections. According to Kemper:

1. ACTIONS—result in—PHYSICAL STATES
2. ACTIONS—initiate—MENTAL STATES
3. PHYSICAL STATES—initiate—MENTAL STATES
4. PHYSICAL STATES—(dis)enable—ACTIONS
5. MENTAL STATES—provide reasons for—ACTIONS

These are the only types of causation in this system. An event chain cannot move directly from action to action, from a physical state to a physical state, from a mental state to a mental state, or from a mental state to a physical state. All such sequences require inferred actions or states to fill the gaps in causal connection. Following these guidelines, and under Professor Kemper's watchful eye, we created an event chain for each story. These event chains are displayed in figures 7.3 and 7.4, with the inferences circled. The chains completed, we were ready to apply Kemper's inference load formula to our two stories.[21] We obtained scores of 2.30 for the *Post* passage and 10.48 for the *Atlantic* passage; according to the Kemper formula, the *Post* prose was written at a second-grade level, whereas the *Atlantic* prose was appropriate only for readers with at least a tenth-grade education. In keeping with the Young formula, these results contradict the Flesch Reading Ease scores and confirm the notion that the highbrow magazine story was more difficult to read than the middlebrow magazine story.

Our foray into the world of readability theory on behalf of historical studies suggests two points, one methodological and one substantive. The methodological point is this: There are ways to study the readability of published reading materials from the past, ways to relate to the mental skills required of readers, not just to the mechanical features of word length and sentence length. Certainly these more complex new formulas are not perfect instruments, and they cannot account for the prior knowledge of the reader. No text-based readability model can explore a reader's interaction with the subtleties and larger meaning of style and structure. How does a reader react, for example, to Ernest Hemingway's simple sentences? The comprehension of these may depend upon the reader's prior understanding of Hemingway's views about Spain, manhood, and war. His simple style is itself a cultural statement, a reaction against

21. Susan Kemper supervised our construction of the event chain. We appreciate her technical assistance.

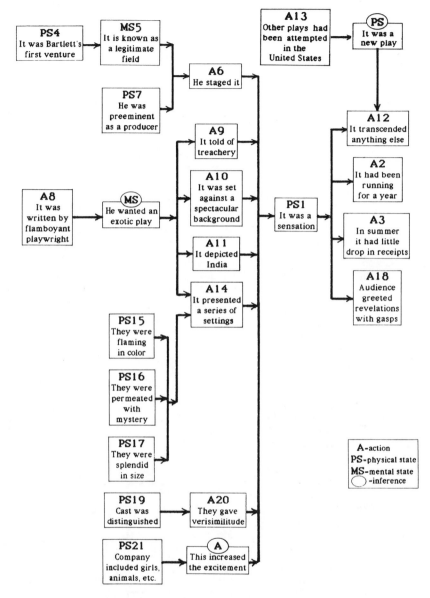

Figure 7.3. "The Play": Event Chain of a Story Excerpted from the *Saturday Evening Post,* April 3, 1920 (Kemper Analysis)

more flowery prose, which for some readers will become part of the larger meaning, beyond the meaning of the individual sentences. Nonetheless, although the new readability formulas are flawed and destined to be superseded, the basic point seems uncontroversial: For those who wish to take the time, there are now ways to analyze the readability features of a

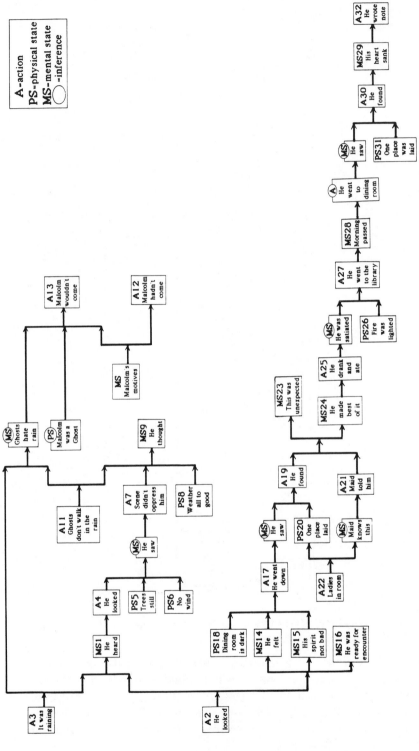

Figure 7.4. "The Ghost": Event Chain of a Story Excerpted from the *Atlantic Monthly*, April 1920 (Kemper Analysis)

text that are more theoretically relevant and more interesting than traditional readability formulas.

The substantive point is more speculative. Our evidence about the reading public and the available reading materials suggest that a rather small proportion of the population were advanced readers who enjoyed access to a broad range of materials, whereas other readers were limited to more popular publications. The prose read by the advanced readers differed not only in vocabulary and sentence length but also in the difficulty of the mental processes required. The notion that the audience for the *Atlantic* and the *New York Times* was limited in 1920 by the difficulty levels of the publications seems even more plausible in light of recent reading-achievement assessments. For example, the National Assessment of Educational Progress's 1985 literacy assessment, which we discussed in chapter 3, showed that even today few Americans read well at a level requiring critical and interpretive skills.[22]

All this smacks of the old 1950s distinction between high culture and popular culture. However, our reaction to such a split is quite different from that of the high-culture priests who feared its erosion by popular forms in the 1950s. We believe that high literacy has shown great staying power. We are more impressed than ever with its complexity, its influence, and its apparent inaccessibility to the average reader. In saying this we are not making a value judgment regarding average readers. There is no question that many readers of the popular press succeeded in their jobs and led virtuous, intelligent lives, and perhaps it does not matter that most people could not read the *Atlantic Monthly*. But the fact remains that the educational system equipped only a limited number of people with sophisticated reading skills, reading skills that also acted as an entry qualification and a necessary prerequisite to participation in many commanding institutions of society. In this regard, educational stratification contributed to the stratification of American society and was reflected in the varying complexity of publications read by adults. In spite of expanded educational opportunity and vastly increased school attainment, recent functional-reading assessments suggest that literacy is similarly stratified today.

22. Kirsch and Jungeblut, *Literacy: Final Report.*

IV Literacy and Diversity in American History

8 Autobiographies and the History of Reading: The Meaning of Literacy in Individual Lives

KATHERINE TINSLEY AND CARL F. KAESTLE

Even the frequent book readers of the elite reading public display an endless diversity of reading practices and purposes. To get closer to this diversity, we studied autobiographies, searching for testimony about the acquisition and uses of literacy. Frequent book readers tend to be highly educated, and people who write autobiographies fit the category; they tend to be either highly schooled or intensely self-taught. Nonetheless, they come from very diverse economic and cultural circumstances, and they demonstrate how individuals created their identities and what role reading played in the process.

In chapter 2 of this volume Carl Kaestle suggested a model of agency within constraints. People use literacy not only for information and entertainment but also in shaping their cultural and political beliefs. They do so within constraints of cultural inheritance and class relationships, but individual responses to those constraints are unpredictable. In general, published reading materials are heavily weighted toward assimilation and loyalty to mainstream institutions, but family and friends may shape the reading opportunities of an individual and provide diverse perspectives on American society.

To explore the function of literacy in the lives of young people in America around the turn of the century, we chose about thirty autobiographies of women who grew up between the 1870s and the 1920s. In some respects, we are treating this period as static; for a few aspects of literacy, however, we shall point out apparent trends across the period. The analysis of autobiographies is not a science; it is used here to humanize and deepen the analysis that we have derived from other sources. Also, except for a few examples drawn from a larger, ongoing study of autobiographies, we limit the discussion here to women. Women's autobiographies in general are more revealing about daily activities than men's autobiographies, which tend to focus on public events. Furthermore, we believed we would gain coherence in this case study by holding gender and race constant while we investigated a variety of family settings, reading practices, and career outcomes.[1]

Autobiographers write for the public, often with a commercial market or a political cause in mind. They describe their lives as viewed from a single point in time. Looking back on events, they are in a position to evaluate turning points and to invest particular events with a significance that may not have been apparent to them at the time they occurred. Faulty memory, selective rendering of the facts, exaggeration, modesty, and hypocrisy all can come between an autobiography and the life actually lived. Nonetheless, reading is a commonplace activity; except for a possible tendency to exaggerate the amount of reading they did or to over-emphasize their appreciation for high culture, there is little reason to suspect distortion in autobiographers' descriptions of reading activities.

One must also consider biases in the social status of people who write autobiographies. Certain groups within the population are disproportionately represented. Authors usually represent the wealthier and more educated levels of society, although a careful search in specialized bibliographies will uncover a number of books written by working-class authors or authors with little formal education. Still, the very act of writing a book implies a certain familiarity with the literary world, so the author's reading habits may not be typical of other individuals of his or her social and educational background. In spite of these limitations, one can learn about a reasonably wide cross-section of the population of readers through autobiographies.[2]

The special virtue of autobiographies in the history of reading is that they allow us to move our focus from the content of reading materials to

1. All of our autobiographers in this chapter are white; Carl Kaestle expects to explore literacy's role for black autobiographers in future essays. On the special meaning of autobiography for women writers, see Susan Stanford Friedman, "Women's Autobiographical Selves: Theory and Practice," in *The Private Self: Theory and Practice of Women's Autobiographical Writings,* ed. Shari Benstock (Chapel Hill: University of North Carolina Press, 1988), 34–62.

2. Two excellent general bibliographies of American autobiography exist, as well as numerous specialized guides that provide the researcher ready access to literally thousands of published autobiographies. Louis Kaplan, *A Bibliography of American Autobiography* (Madison: University of Wisconsin Press, 1961); Mary Louise Briscoe, *American Autobiography, 1945–1980: A Bibliography* (Madison: University of Wisconsin Press, 1982); Patricia K. Addis, *Through a Woman's I: An Annotated Bibliography of American Women's Autobiographical Writings, 1946–1976* (Metuchen, N.J.: Scarecrow Press, 1983); Russell C. Brignano, *Black Americans in Autobiography: An Annotated Bibliography of Autobiographies and Autobiographical Books Written since the Civil War,* rev. ed. (Durham, N.C.: Duke University Press, 1984).

the purposes of reading. Some reading activities were ubiquitous, had no dramatic consequences, and were widely shared across classes: the pleasure of a tale read aloud to children, the consolation of Bible reading, the ritual of reading the baseball scores in the daily newspaper, and so on. Other reading experiences played an important role as individuals' careers moved toward certain values, goals, and social locations: it is these aspects of literacy—the adoption of an ideological perspective, a cultural heritage, and skills for a social role—that give literacy its weighty importance as social history and social policy. A typology that includes both the casual and the momentous uses of literacy will be helpful in surveying our autobiographies. We can group the purposes of reading under five headings: pleasure or escape; day-to-day information; economic or spiritual self-improvement; cultural promotion of dominant or minority cultures; and critical understanding and dissent.[3]

A single text can serve several purposes for any specific reader, or different purposes for different readers, and most readers read for all five of these purposes at different times. The same text, obviously, can be variously informative, entertaining, culturally assimilationist, and self-improving. Nonetheless, the typology of purposes can serve as a tool for considering such factors as family, class, and gender in an individual's reading career. For the more consequential, social purposes of reading, we can ask: What was at stake? What was to be gained from the reading? Who controlled the reading materials? Who was urging the reader to read them? For example, a child who grew up in a middle-class family and whose parents had many educational advantages faced different future prospects than a working-class child whose parents had relatively little education. When these two children went to school (usually not the same school) and encountered the school version of appropriate high culture—Shakespeare, Thomas Jefferson, and a proper business letter—their situations were different and so were the stakes. For the middle-class child from the highly educated family, the cultures of the school and the family were consonant; the school was an extension of the culture that surrounded the child at home. Furthermore, the payoff from high culture was clearer; one could assume that whether one liked Shakespeare or not, successful, cultured people needed to know about his work. For the working-class child from the less-educated family, or from a non-English tradition, the school's version of high culture was more dissonant from the culture of the family, and the payoff was less clear. The cultural

3. For other typologies of reading purposes, see Heath, "Functions and Uses of Literacy"; John R. Bormuth, "Reading Literacy: Its Definition and Assessment," *Reading Research Quarterly* 1 (1973–74):7–66; Kirsch and Guthrie, "Adult Reading Practices"; and William S. Gray, *Reading: A Research Retrospective, 1881–1941,* ed. John T. Guthrie (Newark, Del.: International Reading Association, 1984), 9.

capital to be gained from the acquisition of knowledge about Shakespeare was less certain. Nonetheless, many working-class families strove to promote such learning in their children, and many working-class children adopted these ambitions and worked hard to achieve them. Some gained the cultural capital needed to succeed by mainstream standards, and some gained the critical literacy skills that would allow them to learn and express alternative perspectives.[4]

The Purposes of Literacy

Our autobiographies abound in examples of reading for the five purposes listed in our typology. We shall give brief examples of the first three—entertainment, information, and self-improvement—to convey a sense of the range of descriptions of reading activities included in autobiographies and to identify a few trends. Then we shall focus on the other two—cultural promotion and dissent—for more in-depth analysis.

Reading for Entertainment

When people read for entertainment, some scholars label it "escapist" reading, but this somewhat derogatory term is usually applied to popular literature, not to elite literature. Popular literature, some have suggested, transports the reader to an unreal, more pleasant world, in contrast to great literature, which helps readers to understand important lessons about real life.[5] Although we reject such a crude dichotomy, there is something to be said for the notion of reading as escape, across all classes and across all types of imaginative literature.

As Janice Radway has pointed out, the concept of escape can mean two different things: one may imagine oneself in a different world through

4. On the concept of cultural capital, see Pierre Bourdieu, *Distinction: A Social Critique of the Judgment of Taste,* trans. Richard Nice (Cambridge: Harvard University Press, 1984), chap. 1; on its application to empirical research, see Paul DiMaggio, "Cultural Capital and School Success: The Impact of Status Culture Participation on the Grades of U.S. High School Students," *American Sociological Review* 47 (1982):189–201, and Paul DiMaggio and John Mohr, "Cultural Capital, Educational Attainment, and Marital Selection," *American Journal of Sociology* 90 (1985):1231–61.

5. Q. D. Leavis, *Fiction and the Reading Public* (London: Chatto and Windus, 1932), pt. 3. Other writers on the "escapism" of popular reading materials include the following. Gareth Stedman Jones endorses the concept in *Languages of Class: Studies in English Working Class History, 1832–1982* (Cambridge: Cambridge University Press, 1983), 88; Richard Hoggart took a similar view of popular novels of the 1950s in *Uses of Literacy,* 196. Citing Gramsci, Michael Denning attacks the notion in *Mechanic Accents,* 65–69.

reading, but also, the activity of reading can itself be an escape from other unpleasant activities. The romance readers whom Radway studied used reading as escape in both of these senses. They were transported to exotic places and identified with heroines whom they admired. But they also valued reading as a suspension of other activities, such as being pressured to watch their husbands' favorite television programs.[6]

Our autobiographers from the Progressive era also expressed these two related but distinct functions of reading for escape. Anne Ellis, a working mother and a widow in the 1910s, escaped exhaustion and loneliness. In the evenings, she said, "[I was] so tired that I never read for instruction—only for amusement and to relax. . . . Many times I have read all of Mark Twain's books—he's a great relaxer. Today, as much as I should like to, I cannot recall a single passage."[7] Hope Summerell Chamberlain, growing up in the 1880s in a well-to-do Chapel Hill family, escaped to a tree with a book for a delicious, sensuous experience: The children's periodical *Saint Elmo,* she said, "devoured of a summer's afternoon, along with many soft peaches, in a convenient crotch of a tree, was indeed a glorious feast."[8] Rose Cohen read stories to escape the Jewish ghetto of New York in the 1890s. She discovered that one could rent books from soda-water dealers for a few pennies, and she started reading one each week. "I now lived in a wonderful world. One time I was a beautiful countess living unhappily in a palace, another time I was a beggar's daughter singing in the street."[9] Farther south, in Tennessee, Lillian Spurrier escaped her kitchen duties, to her ultimate betterment. She lived with her two daughters in her mother's house. One day in 1904 she became so absorbed in *The Prisoner of Zenda* that she forgot to take a cake from the oven. When her mother scolded her about the wasted provisions, Lillian decided to move out, take up photography, and make enough money so she would never again feel chagrined over something so simple as a burnt cake. Her daughter wrote in her autobiography, "For years afterward, whenever we had a specially good dinner or got new dresses, Mother would say, 'We have the Prisoner of Zenda to thank for that.'"[10]

Not all autobiographers couched their descriptions of reading in the language of escape, but it was obviously an important source of entertainment in a pre-electronic culture, especially for those on tight bud-

6. Janice A. Radway, *Reading the Romance: Women, Patriarchy, and Popular Literature* (Chapel Hill: University of North Carolina Press, 1984), 90–93.

7. Anne Ellis, *"Plain Anne Ellis": More about the Life of an Ordinary Woman* (Boston: Houghton Mifflin, 1931), 24–25.

8. Hope Summerell Chamberlain, *This Was Home* (Chapel Hill: University of North Carolina Press, 1938), 196.

9. Rose Cohen, *Out of the Shadow* (New York: George Doran, 1918), 189.

10. Mildred Spurrier Topp, *Smile Please* (Boston: Houghton Mifflin, 1948), 1–2.

gets. Elizabeth Gurley Flynn, born in 1890, grew up in the Bronx in a poor Irish family. "There were no amusements for children, or for adults either. There were no movies—the nickelodeon started later—no radios, no television, not even the old-fashioned phonograph, which also came later. . . . Reading was our sole indoor pastime, especially in the long winter nights."[11]

Although some of these individuals describe being silently absorbed in their books, much reading for entertainment in the late nineteenth and early twentieth centuries involved reading aloud. References to family reading traditions abound in the autobiographies. Rose Cohen shared her rented books by reading aloud. Remembering the time when she rented *David Copperfield,* she wrote: "What a happy two weeks we spent! . . . With what joy I looked forward to the evening when after supper we would all gather around the lamp on the table and sister or I would read aloud while mother sewed and the little ones sat with their chins very near the table. . . . For just to read became a necessity and a joy. There were so few joys."[12]

Growing up in the 1890s in Wisconsin, Elizabeth Corbett remembered that "when Grandma came for a visit, she always read aloud by the hour to the assembled family. She read beautifully, and neither her patience nor her throat ever seemed to tire." On winter evenings, the reading would continue upstairs after supper, and "if the reading aloud went on until midnight or even later, the little girl in the next room always lay wide-eyed and enchanted."[13] In the 1880s Marietta Minnigerode's mother read mournful Tennyson poems to her and her sister, and Marietta remembered sitting at her knee with "the horribly agreeable sensation of woe that crept over me and the lumps that rose in my throat; I would be compelled to cough frequently . . . then my little sister would suddenly burst into a loud boo-hoo, and I would follow suit." Later, Marietta read Dickens's *Pickwick Papers* to her ailing father, and confessed that "personally, Dickens bores me—I blush to say it—but in reading aloud with the male of the species, it will be recorded that women usually read what the listener enjoys rather than matter of their own choosing. What difference does it make? To see a man settle down contentedly in an easy chair before a fire, and listen to a tale he loves, as he smokes a cigar and toasts his toes, is a pleasant thing."[14]

Reading aloud was not confined to the home. Eleanor Roosevelt went

11. Elizabeth Gurley Flynn, *The Rebel Girl: An Autobiography; My First Life (1906–1926),* rev. ed. (New York: International Publishers, 1973), 40.

12. Cohen, *Out of the Shadow,* 190–91.

13. Elizabeth Corbett, *Out at the Soldiers' Home: A Memory Book* (New York: Appleton-Century, 1941), 122–23.

14. Marietta Minnigerode Andrews, *Memoirs of a Poor Relation* (New York: E. P. Dutton, 1927), 179, 269.

once a week in the 1920s to read to women at the New York Women's Trade Union League. As Rose Schneiderman described it, "The girls delighted in her and the books she read. The clubroom looked so warm and cozy with them scattered around on the sofa and chairs, listening intently to what she was reading—sometimes poetry, sometimes a novel."[15] Occasionally one finds references to readers in factory situations. One factory owner described such an arrangement and its purposes: "The cigar makers, both men and women, sat at long tables facing each other. The work was monotonous, the workers were temperamental and, to keep them from getting into acrimonious disputes, I had an entertainer for them—a girl. She would read to them for an hour and then for another hour she would play records for them on the old-fashioned phonograph with the big horn."[16] In some work settings, workers gained a measure of control over the reading material allowed. Elizabeth Gurley Flynn described a 1913 visit to a cigar factory in Tampa. "There was a platform, like a pulpit, five or six feet above the ground, up over the heads of the workers. A man called a 'reader' sat up there, employed by the workers with the employer's consent and cooperation because it was conducive to quiet and concentration. He read papers, pamphlets and books in Spanish and Italian. The workers decided what he should read. The contents were usually extremely radical. The day we were there he was reading a pamphlet on birth control."[17]

A few of the early autobiographies indicate that reading aloud was a valuable skill that could be cultivated. Ella Reeve Bloor's father brought English classics home, often asking her to read aloud and encouraging her to cultivate a pleasing style. He stressed the importance of clear enunciation and insisted that she read with expression.[18] Thomas Lamont, an autobiographer whose father was a minister, recalled that a minister's wife who had "a gift for reading aloud [was] always in great demand at every kind of social function, church or other."[19]

Reading aloud was much more a part of American culture in the early 1900s than in the last few decades. We found fewer references to reading aloud in the later autobiographies, and in a survey of adult reading habits conducted in 1971, not a single one of the 1,067 respondents reported reading aloud at home.[20] In contrast, turn-of-the-century memoirs often have sentimental reminiscences of family bonds

15. Rose Schneiderman, *All for One* (New York: Paul S. Eriksson, 1967), 153.

16. David E. Albert, *Dear Grandson* (Philadelphia: Olivier, Maney, 1950), 131.

17. Flynn, *Rebel Girl*, 185.

18. Ella Reeve Bloor, *We Are Many* (New York: International Publishers, 1940), 21.

19. Thomas W. Lamont, *My Boyhood in a Parsonage: Some Brief Sketches of American Life toward the Close of the Last Century* (New York: Harper and Brothers, 1946), 36–37.

20. Amiel T. Sharon, *Reading Activities of American Adults* (Princeton, N.J.: Edu-

strengthened through reading aloud, reminders of a function of reading that is waning today.

Reading for Information

Reading for information is so mundane, so continuous, and so ubiquitous that autobiographers say little about it. Without doubt, reading for information increased over the decades, as the functions of print multiplied, knowledge expanded, and the proportion of people working in information-laden jobs increased. Harriette Simpson Arnow, who grew up in Kentucky in the 1910s and 1920s, mentions information gained from reading in sources as diverse as catalogs (for seeds), newspapers (for news of river traffic), and magazines (for political background on national elections). She tells of heightened interest in the evening reading and discussions as World War I approached. "The talk of my parents after reading the daily paper was filled with strange words: *Serbia, Austria-Hungary,* and *Germany* and the *Kaiser* repeated over and over, but not so often as the one word *war.*" Other threatening events, like a rumored influenza epidemic, could heighten interest in the newspapers.[21] These late-nineteenth- and early-twentieth-century autobiographies illustrate the use of print for information in diverse areas of life—raising children, pruning trees, making love, and being a good social worker.[22] No doubt some people had been reading about such matters of everyday conduct earlier, but until the twentieth century religion, politics, and fiction comprised the foundation of family reading. The diversification of subject matter and the explosion of print led to a changing balance between "intensive" and "extensive" reading.

Some scholars have argued that there was a watershed in the late eighteenth and early nineteenth centuries, a shift from intensive reading—the repeated reading of a familiar text—to extensive reading, characterized by quicker reading, once only, of diverse texts on many different subjects (see chapter 2). A shifting balance is a better metaphor than a watershed; intensive reading continued (especially Bible reading) but was joined by more extensive reading, much of it falling into the category of reading for information. When reading material was scarce and expensive, single texts were read repeatedly. Books on religion, law, and

cational Testing Service, 1972), appendix, 251. A few of the respondents (1.2 percent) reported reading aloud, but at work or at school, not at home.

21. Harriette Simpson Arnow, *Old Burnside* (Lexington: University of Kentucky, 1977), 60, 63, 76, 108, 117.

22. Ellis, *"Plain Anne Ellis,"* 24; Betty MacDonald, *The Egg and I* (Philadelphia: J. B. Lippincott, 1945), 55; April Oursler Armstrong, *Home with a Hundred Gates* (New York: McGraw-Hill, 1965), 35; Bertha Caper Reynolds, *An Uncharted Journey: Fifty Years Growth in Social Work* (New York: Citadel Press, 1972), 157–58.

politics were treated as reference books, consulted over the years. Literature, too, was read over and over, until stories became old friends. Some of these traditions persisted into the twentieth century. We did not find them in the female autobiographies that we chose for this study, but we found some examples in male autobiographies from the early decades of the century. One young southern gentleman read *Ivanhoe* "once a year all his life long."[23] In the North, a young YMCA secretary, Ward Adair, said that he "made a practice of poring over the best available literature, by the hour, and . . . I could get as much benefit from the fiftieth reading of one of Tennyson's Idylls or one of Shakespeare's Tragedies, as I could from the first time over." Throughout his life, he said, he indulged the "vice of reading certain bits of fiction from seven to fifty times." But when he wrote this in the 1930s he seemed to believe that his audience would find the practice unusual, and he referred to it as "a strange sort of habit."[24] Reading for information may have reduced intensive reading, but people's devotion to the Bible and some readers' insatiable love for favorite texts ensured that intensive reading would remain among the uses of literacy.

Reading for Self-improvement

The Bible served several purposes. It was a storybook, a devotional work, and a guide to conduct. In this last regard it joins other works of self-improvement, which included works of advice and inspiration for conduct in spiritual, moral, psychological, and economic affairs. If the Bible may be characterized as a book for spiritual and moral self-improvement, it is certainly the most popular item in the category and appears most frequently in the autobiographies as the prime source to which literate people have turned for consolation and advice. Around the turn of the century Annie Vaughan Clary's grandmother read to her from the Bible and taught her to believe in God.[25] In 1981, 45 percent of the respondents to a Gallup poll said that they read the Bible at least monthly. Bible reading, for whatever purpose, remained a prominent activity in America.

Of course, reading for self-improvement involved much more than religious reading. Literacy itself was a badge of status as well as a means of further self-improvement. Elizabeth Gurley Flynn's mother im-

23. William Alexander Percy, *Lanterns on the Levee: Recollections of a Planter's Son* (Baton Rouge: Louisiana State University Press, 1941), 56.

24. Ward Adair, *The Road to New York* (New York: Association Press, 1936), 53–54, 203.

25. Annie Vaughan Clary, *The Pioneer Life* (Dallas, Tex.: American Guild Press, 1956), 50.

pressed this upon her children growing up in poverty in the South Bronx at the turn of the century. "She read widely—newspapers, magazines and books. After we came to New York City in 1900, she went to night school to improve her penmanship and spelling and to hear lectures on Shakespeare. All during our childhood she read aloud to us—from Irish history, poetry, and fairy stories. The family library was always referred to as 'Momma's Books'."[26]

As the century progressed, commercial publishers produced more and more reading material aimed explicitly at self-improvement. The development of paperback book publishing and marketing fostered an endless array of advice and self-help books, both religious and secular, offering guidance on personality, success, child rearing, and the family.[27]

Reading for Cultural Maintenance and Critical Perspectives

Our first two categories of reading purposes—entertainment and information—consist largely of casual, habitual accompaniments to the reader's daily routine. The third category, reading for self-improvement, can be casual and habitual, but also transforming. Conversions occur; relationships are altered. The consequences of reading become more serious as we move through our taxonomy of purposes; categories four and five are the most consequential, because they deal with reading for the acquisition of values, critical thinking skills, and cultural capital. The fourth, reading for cultural assimilation and maintenance, is often dramatic because it embodies the contest between subcultures and the mainstream culture in our pluralistic society. This tug-of-war takes place in families, schools, churches, and the print media and may include two different processes. One grows up in the culture of one's parents and their allied institutions, but one may also convert to a culture distinct from one's family culture, as in the case of immigrants' children who strive to adopt Anglo-American speech, dress, customs, and values. The fifth category also pertains to the acquisition of values: the use of literacy to gain critical perspective, often in contrast to received family tradition, but always involving a set of principles about justice and social relations that allow one to step back and evaluate custom and the status quo. This is not to suggest that these reading purposes are mutually exclusive. Most literate people encountered and accepted elements of various subcultures—beyond whatever ethnic subculture they inherited—ele-

26. Flynn, *Rebel Girl*, 30, 40.
27. Sharp critiques of popular writing about the family and about personality development are found in Christopher Lasch's *Haven in a Heartless World: The Family Besieged* (New York: Basic Books, 1977), and *The Culture of Narcissism: American Life in an Age of Diminishing Expectations* (New York: W. W. Norton, 1979).

ments, for example, of Anglo-American high culture, mainstream popular culture, and some critical perspectives. But lives can change dramatically, depending upon the mix. Because publishers are often pervasively influenced by the dominant economic and political structures, reading materials generally lean heavily toward assimilation. Literacy doesn't operate in neutral territory. The amount of critical reading material is constrained by many forces. Because assimilative and critical reading combine to shape individuals' social values, cultural identity, and political understanding, we discuss these last two categories together.

We begin with a memoir by a woman from a highly educated family. Hope Summerell Chamberlain was born in 1870 in Salisbury, North Carolina. Her father was a physician, and her mother was extremely well-read. Mrs. Summerell's library included Shakespeare, Dickens, Thackeray, Emerson, Irving, Austen, and other standard-bearers of high culture. She subscribed to *Harper's Magazine* and *Godey's Lady's Book,* which she shared with her neighbors.[28] Hope's mother impressed upon her that too much learning would be considered "a monstrous excrescence upon a womanly personality," yet she provided a rich and varied reading environment. Hope accepted Shakespeare "as a story book," along with Scott and Dickens, but she "desired something more sensational." She read novels by Augusta Evans Wilson and John Esten Cooke and "generally preferred them to such housekeeping stories as Miss Alcott wrote." Regarding the magazine *Saint Elmo,* Summerell said that "a reasonable amount of trash is very good for the growing imagination." Dime novels, a highly desirable form of trash, "were by no means easy for a girl to come by, unless she had a brother from whom to purloin them."[29] This home environment, plus a private-academy education, provided a comfortable and wide-ranging introduction to print culture, both high and popular. Reading for pleasure blended easily with the proper upbringing for a young lady destined to be the wife of a professor and a member of polite society in Raleigh.

The autobiography of Josephine Baker describes a different kind of middle-class female career. Hers began in the same type of rich, supportive reading environment, with the same assumptions about the probable destiny of a female, but concluded with a twist: Baker became a physician and a public figure. Born in 1873 in Poughkeepsie, New York, to a lawyer father and a Vassar-trained mother, Baker said she "was reared in a thoroughly conventional tradition and took to it happily. I understood that after I left school I would go to Vassar, and then, I supposed, I

28. Chamberlain, *This Was Home,* 86–87.
29. Ibid., 196.

would get married and raise a family."[30] Josephine's parents were well-connected; she met William Dean Howells and Louisa May Alcott in her youth. She read Alcott, Horatio Alger, and *Harper's Magazine* and remembered fondly the long afternoons "when Cornelia Kinkead and I used to visit each other and sit for long hours, each immersed in a book and rarely speaking to the other." Baker was "thoroughly trained in the business of being a woman," she said, and although she later became a pioneer in a male-dominated field, she reflected that it was "a good world that I lived in." She attended a private school founded on very progressive principles. Baker was inclined to be a tomboy, "trying to make it up to Father for being a girl." When her only brother died, followed soon after by her father, she decided not to attend Vassar and instead went to New York City, where she enrolled in medical school. Baker became a physician, popular lecturer, and head of the Bureau of Child Hygiene in New York City.[31]

Summerell and Baker exemplify women from affluent Anglo-American families with highly educated parents. The culture of their families matched the culture of the institutions around them. Their reading emphasized high-literacy culture; literacy functioned to prepare them for privileged roles rather than to question them. For some children born into affluent families, however, aesthetic pleasure and easily accumulated cultural capital were not the most important results of their acquisition of sophisticated literacy skills. Something in their youthful experiences led them to reject privilege and the structures that supported it; something (or someone) led them to read in the literature of dissenting traditions.

Ella Reeve Bloor, daughter of a druggist, was raised in Bridgeton, New Jersey, in the 1870s and 1880s. Her father introduced her to books by Scott, Eliot, and Dickens, who became a special favorite. She and her father would discuss the various characters "as though they were members of the family." As noted earlier, she often read aloud for her father, and he helped her to cultivate a pleasing style.[32] But significant people in her life encouraged her in more iconoclastic directions. Her great-uncle Daniel Ware, a Greenbacker and a former abolitionist, challenged her accepted notions of life and supplied books that led her beyond traditional thinking. Together they read the sermons of Unitarian Robert Ingersoll and the works of Darwin.[33] Bloor later became interested in socialism and union activities. Time and again women who pursued careers in radical movements credited written material with either the

30. Josephine S. Baker, *Fighting for Life* (New York: Macmillan, 1939), 2.
31. Ibid., 9, 12–13, 16–17.
32. Bloor, *We Are Many,* 21.
33. Ibid., 29–30.

initial inspiration or the clinching argument that precipitated their com- mitment. Like other autobiographers who pursued radical ideas and ac- tivities, Bloor's reading interacted with and reinforced her contact with radicals. She dated her initial commitment to socialism to the mid-1890s. A close friend, Dr. M. V. Ball, had introduced her to socialist ideas and given her books by Marx and Engels. She had read them faithfully but "was not yet able to apply the socialist theories . . . to actual conditions of the time." The breakthrough came when she heard a socialist speaker discuss the free-silver question. He argued that collective ownership, not cheap money, would solve the workers' problems. "He put it so simply and directly that all I had been hearing and reading about Marx's teaching suddenly clicked." That evening she decided to become a socialist. Later she worked with the New York Labor News Company to help produce and distribute English translations of French and German socialist classics.[34]

The written word could be of momentous importance to working-class families. The four decades that surrounded the turn of the century were decades of turbulent immigration and labor organization. Important cul- tural and political battles were waged, both face-to-face and through the printed word—in schools, in newspapers, in leaflets, and on bulletin boards. Of course, like those raised in affluent families, working-class youths adopted different strategies and experienced different outcomes. Reading could encourage exuberant enthusiasm for assimilation, it could reinforce and inform resistance to the structure of American soci- ety, or it could soothe and entertain the weary worker. Although strat- egies and outcomes differed, working-class families, and particularly immigrant working-class families, shared some characteristics that had a bearing on the acquisition and uses of literacy. Their educational re- sources were generally scarce, and the payoff for acquiring the cultural capital of mainstream traditions was not automatic. The easy entrée to the world of learning thus was often missing, as was the high degree of overlap between family culture and school culture.

Mary Antin, daughter of Russian immigrants in Boston, provides a well-known case of successful Americanization through public schooling and personal drive. At age thirty, announcing that she had "been made over," Antin told her life story in *The Promised Land,* which depicts the use of literacy to master mainstream culture and itself became a classic in the literature of assimilation. Acknowledging that the assimilation of immigrant children caused a "sad process of disintegration of home life," Antin argued nonetheless that, like childbirth, it was worth the pain for the parents to see their child remade into "an American." "From my little

34. Ibid., 45–46, 54.

room on Dover Street," she said, "I reached out for the world, and the world came to me."[35] Through school, through libraries, through conversations with teachers and fellow students, she became self-consciously American. "To be alive in America," she said, "is to ride the central current on the river of modern life. . . . It would have been amazing if I had stuck in the mire of the slum. By every law of my nature I was bound to soar above it, to attain the fairer places that wait for every emancipated immigrant." Antin accepted American society as it was, and she celebrated its institutions. In free schools, free libraries, and free lectures, she was welcomed "at a hundred open doors of instruction." Through her schoolbooks she came to worship George Washington and to feel a thrill at the phrase "my country." But she also read at home, including "every kind of printed rubbish that came into the house," like the weekly story papers "that circulated widely in our neighborhood because subscribers were rewarded with a premium of a diamond ring." And she read her father's Yiddish newspapers, which she said were excellent. But on balance, Mary Antin's reading was in English, so even her leisure reading helped assimilate her to Anglo-American culture: she mentions Louisa May Alcott, Horatio Alger stories, and the Rollo books.[36] At the end of *The Promised Land* Antin tells how she sat on the stone steps of the Boston Public Library one afternoon and had a vision of herself, "emerging from the dim places where the torch of history has never been, creeping slowly into the light of civilized existence, pushing more steadily forward to the broad plateau of modern life."[37]

Like Mary Antin, Emma Goldman was born to a Russian immigrant family of modest means, and she, too, experienced conflict over her educational aspirations. In Russia her father had tried to marry her off at age fifteen. When she protested, he threw her French grammar into the fire, saying, "'Girls do not have to learn much! All a Jewish daughter needs to know is how to prepare *gefilte* fish, cut noodles fine, and give the man plenty of children.'" "I would not listen to his schemes," wrote Goldman in her autobiography. "I wanted to study, to know life, to travel."[38] There the similarity with Mary Antin ceases. As a youth, both in Russia and America, Goldman made her own way as a factory worker. Emigrating to Rochester, New York, in 1880, she found the labor scene turbulent and the press conservative. The accounts of the Haymarket affair in the Rochester newspapers were so vituperative that she sought to discover what really happened by attending meetings of the local German so-

35. Mary Antin, *The Promised Land* (Boston: Houghton Mifflin, 1911), xi, 271, 355.

36. Ibid., 222–28, 257–59.

37. Ibid., 356, 359, 364.

38. Emma Goldman, *Living My Life,* 2 vols. (New York: Da Capo Press, 1970), 1:12.

cialists. Through them she was introduced to the socialist newspaper *Der Freiheit.* "I began to read *Der Freiheit* regularly. I sent for the literature advertised in the paper and I devoured every line on anarchism I could get, every word about the men, their lives, their work. I read about their heroic stand while on trial and their marvelous defense. I saw an opening before me."[39] After Goldman moved to New York City in 1889, she continued to study the works of various radical thinkers, and in her subsequent career she was intimately involved in the writing and dissemination of anarchist views in pamphlets, magazine articles, and books.

Rose Schneiderman, born in 1882 in the Russian section of Poland, shared Goldman's youthful experience in some regards: she emigrated as a young girl to New York and became a factory worker. Her subsequent career in union organizing depended to as great an extent on printed material as did Goldman's crusade in support of anarchist ideas. Schneiderman called the handbills she distributed to factory workers "the arms of the union."[40] Employers were determined to keep such materials out of the hands of their employees. In union fights, the mere possession of a piece of union literature could be grounds for dismissal. Autobiographical sketches written by workers in the 1930s recount such experiences. One woman remembered a man who was fired for hanging up union leaflets in a washroom. Other accounts describe how organizers gathered addresses so they could mail information about the union directly to the workers' homes.[41]

The autobiography of Elizabeth Gurley Flynn illustrates another variation in the literacy environment of working-class families. Her mother, Flynn said, was "lace-curtain" Irish, whereas her father was "shanty" Irish. Her mother loved and knew books, admired accomplished women, and favored equal rights for women.[42] The influence of her suffragist mother and her anti-imperialist father, combined with strong training in the Bill of Rights and debating in public high school and a childhood of working-class poverty, moved Flynn toward a radical critique. "We were conditioned in our family to accept socialist thinking long before we came in contact with socialism as an organized movement," Flynn wrote.[43] Her father had voted for socialist Eugene Debs in 1900, and grinding poverty inclined Elizabeth and her parents to conclude that there was "something wrong" with the society. "It is not strange, therefore, that in such a household our minds were fertile fields for socialism, when the seeds finally came." The "seeds" were door-to-

39. Ibid., 1:9.
40. Schneiderman, *All for One,* 107.
41. Andria Taylor Hourwich and Gladys L. Palmer, eds., *I Am a Woman Worker* (New York: Arno Press, 1974), 67, 84–87, 144.
42. Flynn, *Rebel Girl,* 32.
43. Ibid., 44.

door leaflets announcing a Sunday evening socialist forum, which they began attending, and from which they brought home the weekly socialist paper the *Worker*. "We were surprised to learn how many Socialists had been elected to city offices around the country and how strong the movement was internationally. Our horizons broadened, beyond the South Bronx and the struggle for Irish freedom. Socialism was a great discovery—a hope, a purpose, a flame within me."[44] This flame was soon fed by utopian books by Edward Bellamy and William Morris, a pamphlet by Kropotkin recommended by a young anarchist friend, and Upton Sinclair's *The Jungle*.[45] By the time she was sixteen, Flynn was speaking at socialist rallies in Harlem.

Whereas Flynn was virtually born into socialism, Vera Weisbrod didn't encounter it seriously until her stay in a tuberculosis sanitorium after her graduation from college. Weisbrod grew up in New York City around the turn of the century. Her father, a woodcarver, was frequently unemployed; the family's reading fare was sparse. On Sundays it was limited to the Bible, until later in her youth, when "Sunday discipline was relaxed to include the newspaper with its funnies."[46] Vera discovered a public library within a few blocks of her home while she was in grade school, but the imposing building awed her and she was afraid to enter. She overcame her fears a few years later with the help of a friend: "At last I found myself in that Mecca of books, shelves full of many I had wanted to read and many never yet heard of—all mine now! . . . all of these treasures and more I could possess at last."[47] She first heard of socialism from a friend in the sanitorium and subsequently attended a Socialist party meeting. Thereafter she began reading Marx and Engels, and gradually her reading shifted from poetry and novels to socialist newspapers and pamphlets. In 1925, while helping to organize workers in the Passaic textile strike, she met her future husband. He was a devoted member of the Communist party, and she learned that he had been drawn to it as a result of "his intensive reading and pondering of the works of Lenin that were available then, especially *State and Revolution*."[48]

Of course, many young immigrant women facing a new culture and a new language became neither radical critics like Vera Weisbrod nor zealous converts like Mary Antin. For most, the initial issue with reading was not cultural capital so much as coping with a new society and trying

44. Ibid., 46–47.
45. Ibid., 48–49.
46. Vera Buch Weisbrod, *A Radical Life* (Bloomington: Indiana University Press, 1977), 7.
47. Weisbrod, *Radical Life,* 19, 39.
48. Ibid., 65, 74–76, 104.

to eke out some enjoyment and understanding from the printed word. But even in the context of such reading purposes, cultures could clash. Rose Cohen, who rented books from soda-water vendors in New York in the 1890s to read them nightly in her family circle, described the scene when she brought the first book home. All the younger children gathered round, but her mother looked on disapprovingly. "I began to read aloud . . . I could see that she was listening but the sad look had not left her eyes. When again she looked up . . . on her face there was a healthy look of interest and curiosity. . . . From that time many happy evenings were ours."[49] Rose's father, however, recognized the transforming potential of English books and the possible threat to tradition and religion.

> Father did not take kindly to my reading. How could he! He saw that I took less and less interest in the home, that I was more dreamy, that I kept more to myself. Evidently reading and running about and listening to "speeches," as he called it, was not doing me any good. But what father feared most was that now I was mingling so much with Gentiles and reading Gentile books, I would wander away from the Jewish faith. This fear caused great trouble and misunderstanding between us.[50]

Rose's father was not the only one who understood the potential for conflict. When Rose asked to borrow a copy of the New Testament from some nurses who had befriended her at Presbyterian Hospital, they refused: "I am afraid, Ruth dear, we can not give it to you. You see your father would think, 'True, the nurses have been kind to my daughter but they have led her away from our faith.'" Even without the New Testament, however, some of the damage had already been done. When Nurse Brewster led her up to the library to substitute a romance for the desired New Testament, Rose mused: "She put me into a deep chair and then she knelt before the bookcase. She hummed cheerfully as she looked from shelf to shelf, and I sat and watched her. Her every motion to me was new and interesting and charming. She represented the people I wanted to know, the new life I desired."[51] Reading enriched Rose Cohen's life. It helped her escape the confines of the Lower East Side ghetto, to imagine different worlds and to ponder social issues. It also imperiled her acceptance of family traditions, thus alarming her father; her autobiography ends in her youth, so we leave Rose Cohen at this transitional point, poised to enter adulthood, still sorting out her cultural identity.

Another interesting immigrant autobiography was written by Bella

49. Cohen, *Out of the Shadow,* 187–91.
50. Ibid., 254.
51. Ibid., 249.

Visono Dodd, born in Italy in 1904. Her parents preceded her to New York; she followed them when she was six and spent a few years in East Harlem, where she first learned English. Teased by her siblings about her dress, she "turned with zeal to the task of becoming an American Child."[52] Within a year the Visono family moved to Westchester, where Bella's father became a successful grocer. Although they lived in a Catholic neighborhood, they stopped going to church. Bella grew up as an Italian immigrant in the suburbs—secular, relatively affluent, and determined to become Americanized. She was an enthusiastic reader, and she followed politics at a young age. World War I began when she was in grade school. "I became an avid reader of newspapers. I read the gruesome propaganda charging the Germans with atrocities. My imagination was stirred to fever pitch. I never lost the newspaper habit after that."[53] When Bella was twelve, her foot was run over as she got off a trolley and had to be amputated. Housebound for most of a year, she read books from the library, as well as some left in her house by previous owners. Among this miscellany were sermons by John Wesley, which she found "sturdy," and Charles Sheldon's *In His Steps,* which "made a profound impression on me."[54] But the most influential reading event of her life came a few years later, after she had been fitted with an artificial foot and began high school. One day a girl brought her an issue of *The Call.* "I felt my heart beat with excitement as I read the articles on social justice. . . . Unconsciously I enlisted, even if only emotionally, in the army of those who said they would fight social injustice, and I began to find the language of defiance intoxicating."[55]

Dodd attended Hunter College and learned more from a college teacher who distributed books on Communism to those who were interested. After graduation, she became a teacher and an active member of the Communist wing of the teachers' union. Eventually she undertook full-time Communist party work. In 1949, Dodd had a change of heart and was expelled from the party. In time she moved to embrace the Catholic faith to which she was born; the decision was again guided by influential friends and materials she had read.[56]

Bella Visono Dodd eschewed the comfortable assimilation that her family situation would have allowed. Neither poverty nor religion nor parental resistance stood between her and the attractions of Anglo-American culture and the benefits of mainstream institutions. But she

52. Bella V. Dodd, *School of Darkness* (New York: P. J. Kenedy and Sons, 1954), 11.
53. Ibid., 18.
54. Ibid., 20.
55. Ibid., 22.
56. Ibid., 26.

was not destined to follow the path of Mary Antin. No theories or patterns will entirely tidy up the wonderful diversity presented in autobiographical accounts. But thinking about families' situations can nonetheless help us think about the functions of literacy. Some of our autobiographers grew up surrounded by high culture and educational advantages. For them, literacy and schooling were natural developments. Others lacked resources for literacy and education, or had parents from different traditions; for them, the content and style of literacy offered by American institutions were foreign, requiring contemplation and struggle. Just as radicals can develop from any ethnic group or class situation, so highly sophisticated establishment success stories can begin anywhere. Still, the uses of literacy were shaped by the family environment, and the stakes were different for children in different social situations.

People acquire culture, values, ambitions, and political leanings from a wide range of sources, both personal and literary. The particular importance of reading in this process is that printed text can vary tremendously from the formative local influences of family, church, and school. In earlier times, a stranger from an exotic place could come into a town and testify that the earth was round, that miracles had occurred, or that somewhere peasants were revolting against landowners. In a literate society, books perform this function; they are more plentiful and more transportable than living informants, but they can be just as exotic, wondrous, and disruptive. Thus our autobiographies portray immigrant parents who grew nervous when their children began reading English books, and novice radicals whose critique of society crystallized after reading an inspiring socialist tract.

We do not mean to imply that most books were dissonant or exotic. Many books encountered by young people supported their family or ethnic culture; indeed, parents strove to ensure that outcome. Most books introduced in schools supported the mainstream culture and capitalist institutions. The politics of literacy is precisely the struggle to manage the potential opportunities and disruptions presented by reading. Again, no predictive generalizations can be made about the impact of class and family upon the uses of literacy, especially when literacy skills were good and a great diversity of books was available, as was the case for most of our autobiographers. But the rich range of alternatives that paraded in front of our autobiographers was absent for many Americans over the last century, due to a lack of either literacy skills or diverse reading materials. In chapters 3 and 4 we showed that a substantial portion of our population has failed to achieve high-level literacy. In chapters 9 and 10 we consider the extent to which our society has provided access to diverse texts, and we discuss various constraints imposed on the production of reading materials. Finally, we move from the microlevel of individual readers to the macrolevel of publishing, the market for reading materials, and the surrounding culture that shapes them.

9 Gender, Advertising, and Mass-Circulation Magazines

HELEN DAMON-MOORE AND CARL F. KAESTLE

In the autobiographies described in chapter 8 literacy is often portrayed as a tool of assimilation to mainstream culture, sometimes welcomed, sometimes resisted. Assimilation to mainstream culture can be seen as part of a larger process of cultural consolidation. In American history this process has proceeded at the level of both high culture and popular culture. The public schools, with some help from public libraries and print media, have long endorsed and dispensed a diluted version of Anglo-American high culture. Commercial popular culture has added to the consolidation process by producing a steady stream of news stories, advertisements, comics, and fiction that are increasingly standardized.

To some degree, then, the institutions of literacy—schools, libraries, and publishing companies—are instruments of cultural consolidation. In other regards, however, literacy is used to reinforce the distinctive traditions, cultures, and interests of subgroups within the population, as well as to maintain stereotypes and divisions between groups. Here and in chapter 10 we explore the extent to which literacy has been used both to consolidate culture and to maintain differences. We are interested in the motives and the mechanisms for these contrasting processes and in whether the balance between them has shifted over time. Sometimes these seemingly antagonistic functions of literacy—consolidating and differentiating readers—go hand in hand. In this chapter, for example, we shall see that efforts to expand the consumer economy and to create strongly differentiated roles for women and men were complementary. For this inquiry, we turn from the study of readers to the producers of print—to the economics of publishing and the cultural values of publishers. Specifically, we explore the role of gender in the production of popular magazines.

It must first be noted that the world of American mass-circulation magazines has long been organized on gender lines. Both explicitly and implicitly, top-selling magazines for adults in this country have sorted themselves out by gender; although some magazines have crossed gender lines successfully, most magazines are either for women or for men. This gender differentiation among magazines deserves closer scrutiny not only because it is germane to the inquiry concerning consolidation versus distinct reading publics, but also because recent decades have seen great concern and policy discussion about the injustices of gender discrimination and the role of popular culture in perpetuating differential, traditional roles for women and men. When did gender differentiation in magazines originate, and why? Why has it been so persistent and pervasive? What effect has it had on the cultural ideas presented in popular American magazines?

This chapter focuses on the rise of gender-targeted magazines and on their subsequent character over the last hundred years. After a brief examination of gender and reading prior to the 1890s, we examine the founding of two of the earliest and most successful gender-targeted magazines in America: the *Ladies' Home Journal* and the *Saturday Evening Post*. Tracing the evolution of these magazines allows us to analyze the factors that made them successful, such as their resonance with popular views of women and men and their skill at exploiting new national markets for consumer products and gender-targeted advertising. The *Journal* and the *Post* are apt examples of the interaction of gender and magazine production, and both served as prototypes for other magazines in their genres. Above all, the story of these magazines illuminates the influence that advertising had on the character of early mass-circulation American magazines, and the extent to which advertising and the character of such magazines became inextricably entwined.

Finally, we turn to the nature of the mass-circulation magazine during the twentieth century, focusing on the ten best-selling magazines at twenty-year intervals from 1900 to 1980. The general contours of the industry and specific cases within it support the notion of a special relationship between advertising and mass-circulation magazines, a relationship that has differed for male- and female-targeted publications but that has been equally important to both.

The complexity of the topic has led us to restrict this inquiry to best-selling magazines. Attempting to trace gender patterns over a century precluded the possibility of examining the myriad of smaller publications available to Americans over the years. We also focus on the variable of gender, while excluding those of class and race, in seeking to establish the contours of the gender-differentiated, middle-class, mass-circulation magazine market. We hope that future studies will tell the equally important story of magazines differentiated by class and race, some of which also have gender definitions.

Gender and Reading before 1880

Of course, gender and reading were intertwined long before the emergence of the mass-circulation women's magazine. In their study of Puritan childhood education, Maris Vinovskis and Gerald Moran suggested that by the late seventeenth and early eighteenth centuries Puritan women were responsible for catechizing their children and hence for reading the Bible in the home.[1] Women's increasing responsibility for the spiritual and academic nurturing of their children was a compelling reason to expand their educational opportunities; by the early nineteenth century, this association of women with religion and with the teaching of young children in the family helped to initiate the feminization of schoolteaching. In *Women of the Republic* Linda Kerber suggested that reading among elite groups was already differentiated by gender to some degree in the eighteenth century. "The literary culture of republican America was bifurcated. Men were said to read newspapers and history; women were thought to exercise their weaker intellects on the less demanding fare of fiction and devotional literature."[2] Thus from at least the eighteenth century there seems to have been some differentiation between what men read and what women read.

But many American women did not read at all in the eighteenth century, and it was not until the first half of the nineteenth century that factors combined to create a new, larger reading public. Literacy and schooling were expanding, especially for women. By midcentury, 90 percent of American whites said they were literate, and as we saw in chapter 1, the women's rates had caught up with the men's. Technological advances in printing and paper making made literature accessible to more readers than ever before. *Harper's Magazine,* one of the new organs of middle-class culture, proclaimed in the 1850s, "literature has gone in pursuit of the million, penetrated highways and hedges, pressed its way into cottages, factories, omnibuses, and railroad cars, and become the most cosmopolitan thing of the century."[3] In her study of nineteenth-century domestic novels Helen Papashvily asserted that the "newly literate in both sexes" were demanding the same thing: to be amused.[4] That women were an important part of the new reading public is suggested by the female-oriented materials that began to proliferate in the early nine-

1. Moran and Vinovskis, "Great Care of Godly Parents," 24–37.
2. Linda K. Kerber, *Women of the Republic: Intellect and Ideology in Revolutionary America* (Chapel Hill: University of North Carolina Press, 1980), 235.
3. Hart, *Popular Book,* 86.
4. Papashvily, *All the Happy Endings,* 38–39.

teenth century. As we saw in chapter 2, a distinctly female novel-reading public emerged in the first half of the century, and according to Cathy Davidson, many novels spoke to women's concerns in dissident voices. Reading had become an important activity for women, at least among the middle and upper classes.

The functions of reading for women broadened in the nineteenth century as well. By the 1830s affluent women were reading not only novels but also such up-scale publications as *Godey's Lady's Book*. With its fashion plates, sentimental fiction, and piano sheet music, to say nothing of its two-dollar annual subscription price, *Godey's* was geared to an elite audience. The magazine's circulation reached 150,000 by 1860, making it the first major American women's magazine. But by the 1880s *Godey's* and other magazines like it had been eclipsed by a different kind of publication: the practical helpful-hints magazine.

Although some women may have experienced increased leisure time in the early days of industrialization, Ruth Schwartz Cowan has suggested that for most women, traditional chores simply gave way to new ones. As stoves replaced open fireplaces and such foodstuffs as flour were commercially produced, diets became more varied and cooking more complicated; as fabrics were produced outside the home and paper patterns were made available for home use, wardrobes became more elaborate.[5] New tasks created larger gaps between the experiences of one generation of women and the next, a problem exacerbated in some cases by physical separation due to migration.[6] New technologies were adding new activities to women's role, and women often were separated from traditional sources of information and advice; in such a culture, helpful-hints literature became increasingly relevant to many women's everyday concerns. In sum, the nineteenth-century reading public expanded to include a greater number of women. In addition, the scope of women's reading broadened to encompass practical information that enhanced daily living as well as material for entertainment and cultural edification.

Daniel Horowitz's *The Morality of Spending* and Alfred Chandler's *The Visible Hand* both date the major take-off of America's consumer culture to the 1880s, when it was stimulated by the rapid business expansion and the development of national markets occurring in those years.[7]

5. Ruth Schwartz Cowan, *More Work for Mother: The Ironies of Household Technology from the Open Hearth to the Microwave* (New York: Basic Books, 1983), 47–65.

6. Robert V. Wells, *Revolutions in Americans' Lives: A Demographic Perspective on the History of Americans, Their Families, and Their Society* (Westport, Conn.: Greenwood Press, 1980), 107–9, 121–24.

7. See Horowitz, *Morality of Spending,* xxv-xxvii, and Alfred D. Chandler, *The Visible Hand: The Managerial Revolution in American Business* (Cambridge: Harvard University Press, 1977), 289–91.

As continuous-processing machinery became capable of producing much greater numbers of goods than had ever been possible before, national markets became not only attractive but also necessary. The decade of the 1880s saw the nearly simultaneous invention of continuous-process machinery for making flour, breakfast cereals, soup and other canned products, matches, photographic film, and cigarettes.[8] With the dramatic improvement of the nation's transportation and communications infrastructure, the stage was set for the rise of mass markets.

Women had traditionally been responsible for making and using a number of the products that were increasingly produced by continuous-process machinery—a crucial factor in the history of consumption and advertising. Since these earliest mass-produced items were assumed to be of interest to women, and since producers needed to "move" them and used advertising to do it, a substantial amount of early advertising was targeted especially to women. By the late 1880s women were perceived to be the major consumers of household goods and perhaps to be the key decision makers in the purchase of clothing, entertainment, and other items.[9]

Many women's magazines founded in this period had explicit ties to women's new functions in the consumer economy. *McCall's, Pictorial Review,* and the *Delineator* all grew out of flyers featuring dress patterns, and the *Woman's Home Companion* and *Good Housekeeping* both originated as mail-order journals.[10] The recognition of women's power to consume thus led to the creation of magazines for women that were highly identified with consumption, a pattern that would only be strengthened throughout the twentieth century.

To some degree, Cyrus Curtis and Louisa Knapp Curtis were responding to these trends when they established the *Ladies' Home Journal.* They spoke to the women's concerns discussed above, and they soon found an enthusiastic readership and group of advertisers. But large social processes like the creation of gender roles under corporate capitalism are mediated by real individuals making decisions about day-to-day goals, conditioned as these may be by the cultural and economic environment.

8. Chandler, *Visible Hand,* 289.

9. For the best analysis of views of women as consumers, see Michael Schudson, *Advertising, the Uneasy Persuasion: Its Dubious Impact on American Society* (New York: Basic Books, 1984), especially chap. 5. See also William R. Leach, "Transformations in the Culture of Consumption: Women and Department Stores, 1890–1925," *Journal of American History* 71 (September 1984), 319–42; Susan Porter Benson, *Counter Cultures: Saleswomen, Managers, and Customers in American Department Stores, 1890–1940* (Urbana: University of Illinois Press, 1986); and Cowan, *More Work for Mother.*

10. Theodore Peterson, *Magazines in the Twentieth Century,* 2d ed. (Urbana: University of Illinois Press, 1975), 201–6, 140–42, 215–17.

Indeed, when we look closely at the establishment of the *Ladies' Home Journal* it seems that the magazine was created virtually by accident.

The *Ladies' Home Journal*

Late in the summer of 1883, Cyrus Curtis, publisher of a weekly Philadelphia newspaper called the *Tribune and the Farmer,* found his paper three columns short. In search of material that could be gathered quickly and easily from other sources, Curtis proposed a "woman's department" to fill the space.[11] The column ran regularly thereafter, featuring odds and ends from various sources. This "selected matter" was culled from what Curtis thought were reliable "exchanges," or newspapers and advice pamphlets, but his wife, Louisa, criticized his choices, saying, "I don't want to make fun of you, but if you really knew how funny this material sounds to a woman, you would laugh, too."[12] Louisa soon moved from the *Tribune's* business department to the editorial department, filling the women's department with material of her choosing, and the column grew to fill a page. The section began to stimulate a great deal of correspondence, and the Curtises decided to publish a monthly supplement to the weekly *Tribune.* The first issue of that supplement, published by Cyrus Curtis, edited by Louisa under her maiden name of Knapp, and called the *Ladies' Home Journal,* appeared in December 1883.[13]

The *Ladies' Home Journal* therefore evolved from a newspaper column to a department to a supplement, which soon outstripped the original paper in popularity. Although the practical details of this evolution are unremarkable, its cultural ramifications are quite striking. The creation of the "woman and home" column and its evolution into the *Ladies' Home Journal* illustrate the importance of women as readers in the new consumer economy of the late nineteenth century. Gender and reading were being welded together in pervasive and profoundly consequential ways.

Cyrus Curtis and Louisa Knapp were remarkably successful with their young magazine. The *Journal's* circulation was 25,000 at the end of its first year, double that in six more months, and by 1886 had reached the impressive figure of 400,000. In a few short years the magazine had evolved from a collection of helpful hints in a newspaper to a phenomenon in the publishing industry. The time was ripe for practical magazines geared to a new broad group of women readers. Advertisers were seeking a forum for their messages that would create a national

11. Edward Bok, editorial, *Ladies' Home Journal,* November 1893, 13.
12. Edward Bok, *A Man from Maine* (New York: Charles Scribner's Sons, 1923), 92.
13. Ibid., 95.

market for goods, and Cyrus and Louisa both were adept at sensing needs and creating a product to meet them.

But there was a certain incongruity about a commercial magazine for women, which Cyrus and Louisa struggled with, and this underscores the character of the times in which the *Journal* was born. In a striking way the *Journal* bridged the gap between the private and the public world, in part due to the special character of the Curtises' partnership and in part because of a general trend toward the commercialization of culture. Louisa edited the *Journal* out of her home, eschewing contact with the public world of business—a world restricted to men. From her home she fashioned a magazine with a sincere, sisterly tone, a magazine intended to serve as a "helpmate" to the woman of the 1880s. Given Cyrus's concomitant intense drive for advertising, the early *Journal* featured both an intimate tone and a highly commercial face. If its readers saw this as incongruous, they certainly seemed prepared to live with it.

In fact, as the magazine became more commercial and pervaded by advertising, the two approaches began to blend and to inform one another. Louisa's editorial features increasingly urged women to consume, and Cyrus's advertising increasingly employed an intimate tone in addressing potential buyers. The *Ladies' Home Journal* was the first major commercial magazine for women in America, establishing the formula that has characterized American middle-class women's magazines for more than a century, a formula combining household-hint departments, fiction, biographical sketches (today's celebrity profiles), and reflections on gender roles. But most important, the magazine focused on these issues in a highly commercial context, with editorial content reinforcing advertising, and vice versa. This reciprocal relationship between gender-based advertising and women's magazines has given both phenomena a long-lived and central place in American consumer culture. Manufacturers believed, correctly, that almost all products were gender specific in their markets, and that women made the great majority of purchasing decisions; manufacturers thus increasingly targeted advertising at women.[14] If consumer purchases had not been so gender segregated, perhaps magazines in general would not have been so gender targeted, but of course the two forms of segregation were mutually reinforcing. Magazines taught the public the very roles that advertising campaigns advocated.

In five short years the *Ladies' Home Journal* had become a big business, and this evolution was signaled by changes in management as well as in its commercial face. In 1889 Louisa Knapp relinquished her post as editor, reportedly after her daughter complained, "Oh, Mamma, when-

14. Schudson, *Advertising,* 173–77.

ever I want you, you have a pen in your hand."[15] The development of magazine publishing as a big business quite possibly shut many women out of editorial and managerial positions; twentieth-century mass-circulation magazines in general were not edited by women until the second women's movement beginning in the 1960s. Men were thought to have the superior management skills needed to run a magazine like the *Journal,* with its circulation of more than half a million. To replace Louisa, the Curtises hired Edward Bok, a highly educated and experienced businessman.

The *Saturday Evening Post*

With Bok handling more of the business details of the *Journal,* Curtis turned his attention to realizing his dream of a magazine for men. Analysts differ as to just how specific Curtis's vision of the second magazine was, but it seems safe to say that he wanted it, like the *Ladies' Home Journal,* to serve primarily as a vehicle for advertising. It also seems safe to say that Curtis's vision for the new magazine featured some notion of a male audience, since the *Journal* was already doing so well in reaching women.

Curtis kept his eye open for the appropriate vehicle, and in 1897 an opportunity presented itself. A friend of his, Albert Smythe, owned a dying Philadelphia magazine called the *Saturday Evening Post.* As the magazine's masthead later proudly announced, it had been founded in 1729 as the *Pennsylvania Gazette.* Its lineage was distinguished. Loosely associated with Benjamin Franklin (an association Curtis and his editor would later exaggerate), the paper in one incarnation published Edgar Allen Poe's "The Black Cat." Nathaniel Hawthorne, James Fenimore Cooper, and Harriet Beecher Stowe were among its other famous contributors.[16] The nineteenth-century *Post* was devoted to "Morality, Pure Literature, Foreign and Domestic News, Agriculture, Science, Art and Amusement" and at various times and under different owners was touted as "A Mammoth Paper," "The Very Pearl of Literary Weeklies," and "The Great Family Paper of America."[17]

By 1897, the *Post,* in spite of its illustrious heritage, was faltering badly. Curtis stepped in and struck a bargain, paying only a thousand dollars for the full rights to the *Saturday Evening Post.* He put William George Jordan, formerly an assistant editor of the *Journal,* in charge of the new weekly, and the first Curtis-owned issue appeared on October 10,

15. Mary Louise Curtis Bok, "Louisa Knapp Curtis," in *Notable Women of Pennsylvania* (Philadelphia: Pennsylvania Publishing, 1952), 256.
16. James Wood, *The Curtis Magazines* (New York: Ronald Press, 1971), 33–34.
17. Ibid., 33.

1897. Working under the relatively ineffectual Jordan was a young man named George Horace Lorimer. Lorimer had been a reporter in 1897 for the Boston *Herald* when the announcement came in over the press wire that Cyrus Curtis had bought the *Post* and was looking for an editor. Lorimer was hired to serve in a secondary capacity, but within a few months he had proven his capabilities and became editor of Curtis's *Post.*

Given the *Journal's* rapid success, some analysts have assumed that the same was true of the *Post.*[18] This was decidedly not the case. By the end of 1900, three and a half years after Curtis had acquired the *Post* and nearly two years after Lorimer had become its editor, the *Post* was costing the Curtis Publishing Company thousands of dollars a month. Its advertising increased from 2 percent of its columns in 1898, to 5 percent in 1899, to 15 percent in 1900, but even 15 percent was only half the advertising that the *Journal* had featured in its very first issue in 1883. In addition, the *Post's* circulation in 1899 was less than 300,000, a level the *Journal* had surpassed fifteen years before. Curtis had given full rein to his new editor, Lorimer, who from the start seemed to be capable and efficient: Why, then, the long struggle for success?

The reasons are numerous and interrelated, some obvious and some more subtle. In the first place, Lorimer inherited a mess. Knapp had started the *Journal* with a clean slate, and Bok had inherited an established periodical with a strong formula and a solid circulation. The *Post,* in contrast, had already been struggling for years before Curtis bought it—and he promptly hired William George Jordan, a weak editor, to run it. Moreover, Curtis and Lorimer had to launch their new enterprise under the watchful eye of a maturing publishing establishment. Curtis and Knapp had been able to start the *Ladies' Home Journal* largely without professional notice, allowing them time to test public reaction without much interference. But from the day that Curtis purchased the *Post,* he and Lorimer faced skepticism from much of the publishing community. *Printers' Ink,* the primary journal of the publishing industry, was especially derisive about the new magazine's chances for success. Writers for *Printers' Ink* in the late 1890s suggested that a weekly format was outdated, that no publisher could produce a decent magazine and sell it for only five cents a copy, and that men had plenty of magazines and newspapers to read anyway.[19]

The last issue is the most important, particularly for purposes of gender analysis. On this point a comparison of the *Ladies' Home Journal*

18. See, for example, Salme Harju Steinberg, *Reformer in the Marketplace: Edward W. Bok and the* Ladies' Home Journal (Baton Rouge: Louisiana State University Press, 1979), 8.

19. John Tebbel, *George Horace Lorimer and the* Saturday Evening Post (Garden City, N.Y.: Doubleday, 1948), 20.

and the *Post* is instructive. As we have seen, the *Journal* began almost accidentally, but three conditions nurtured its early success: (1) an easily identified range of interests known as "women's interests" could be gathered quickly and packaged neatly, first in a column, then on a page, finally in a magazine; (2) advertisers were ready, even anxious, to sell their products to women; and (3) women responded immediately and positively to the Curtises' column, page, and supplement, indicating a clear demand for the new women's publication.

The *Post* was targeted at men, but its formula was less specific than that of the *Journal*. Defining the range of content for the *Post* proved to be a challenging task for its editor. Perhaps even more important was that when the *Post* became a Curtis publication and defined men as businessmen, there was no phalanx of advertisers eager to reach businessmen. The concept of a men's publication was a much more difficult idea to sell to advertisers, partly because they had been convinced by Curtis that they should be reaching women, and partly because the availability of business-related products lagged behind household products in the 1890s. Finally, as noted above, readers did not respond to the *Post* with anything like the enthusiasm that women had shown for the *Journal* fifteen years before.

These contrasts suggest that a major problem for the early *Post* was market identity and acceptance. The *Journal* had a clear formula from the beginning, one that remains striking in its breadth and simplicity: the magazine sought to speak to every major interest in a middle-class woman's life. The formula that Lorimer proposed for the *Post* was narrower but equally striking and simple: to inspire and entertain middle-class men with discussions of and stories about their chief interest in life—work. In trying to execute this formula, Lorimer had to weigh his editorial aspirations against the demands of commercialism and publishing success.

Articles and stories about business were hard to come by in 1897, and the *Post* was forced to broaden its scope beyond the business formula. In response, Lorimer widened the magazine's focus to include more biography, political articles, and romance and adventure stories, at least in part because he wanted to appeal to as many men as he could. He wrote to his friend Senator Albert Beveridge in 1899: "I'm beginning to see that the man of the day wants a variety, and we're trying to meet that demand by broadening our scope. I'd like an article from you about the everyday goings-on in Washington, one that will get young men interested in the way real government works."[20] The desire on Lorimer's part to reach as broad a male audience as possible was entirely compatible with Curtis's

20. George Horace Lorimer, to Albert Beveridge, June 5, 1989, Lorimer File, Historical Society of Pennsylvania, Philadelphia.

own impulses, which helps to explain why Curtis did not protest as the *Post* took on a significantly different cast than he had originally intended. For although Curtis wanted a business magazine, he wanted even more a magazine that would appeal to many middle-class men, a mass-circulation magazine that the husbands of *Journal* readers would buy. And, of course, not all of those husbands were businessmen: They were doctors, lawyers, teachers, farmers, and shop foremen. Curtis and Lorimer wanted a mass magazine, and if a magazine targeted at businessmen would mean an exclusive magazine, Curtis preferred broadening the magazine's formula.

The *Post*'s evolution highlights a crucial fact about the male role, today as in the early twentieth century. Although work may have been the central source of identity for almost all men, the specialized nature of work as a source of identification meant that it did not automatically create a shared culture among all men. In other words, men may have shared their focus on work, but the very nature of work had as much potential to separate as it did to connect them. The moment an editor in Lorimer's day tried to speak to one type of worker he effectively excluded others. Even business, with its rapid growth in the late nineteenth century, seemed too narrow a category to be the backbone of a mass-circulation magazine for men. Lorimer therefore tried to reach as many men as possible by addressing a constellation of interests instead of just one.

But even this broadening would not be the last market adjustment for the *Saturday Evening Post*. In spite of Lorimer's many editorial successes, by the turn of the century the *Post* was still struggling financially. Circulation in 1900 remained under 400,000, far below what Curtis and Lorimer had hoped for, and by the end of 1901 the *Post* had lost more than $1.25 million because advertisers were reluctant to purchase space. Even when the *Post* was at its most masculine in tone and content, a full 25 percent of its advertising offered female-targeted household products. (Presumably the Curtis business department was able to convince advertisers that some women had from the start been reading their husbands' copies.) Unable to attract enough male-targeted advertising to succeed as a big-time commercial venture, the *Post* willingly underwent a major identity change to attract the national advertising that it needed to thrive and grow.

Three developments in 1902 support the notion of a fundamental relationship between advertising and the gender orientation of the magazine and its audience, developments that informed and reinforced one another: The *Post* broadened its content as well as its image to focus more on women's interests; household advertising grew markedly, contributing to a significant overall increase in advertising sold by the magazine in 1902; and the *Post*'s circulation rose substantially during that year.

Lorimer believed initially that some women would read a quality magazine for men, and letters to the editor suggest that some women had indeed read the *Post* from its earliest days as a Curtis publication. But the *Post* also became somewhat more feminine in content over the first decade of the twentieth century. From the outset, the regular inclusion of love stories had complicated the *Post*'s masculine image, but beginning in late 1901 and early 1902 the magazine increasingly included political commentary on women's role and featured nonfiction by women. Still largely masculine in tone and style, with robust and satirical editorials and business and political nonfiction articles, by about 1905 the *Post* had broadened its range enough to become what the culture recognized as a family magazine.

By 1908 Lorimer was boasting about the gender mix of the *Post*'s audience: "Who says that *The Saturday Evening Post* is a magazine for men only? We number women readers not by tens but hundreds of thousands."[21] Although it is impossible to determine the precise gender makeup of the *Post*'s audience, the magazine's circulation leapt as it broadened its content and continued a promotional campaign aimed at women. Late in 1902 and early in 1903, 55,000 readers were added to the magazine's circulation list, by far the fastest rise in *Post* circulation figures to that point.[22]

Advertisers soon jumped on the bandwagon. As Edward Bok later put it, "Advertisers were chary . . . but they thought they would 'try it for an issue or two.'"[23] Household advertisements helped to fuel this significant increase, growing from 25 to 30 percent of the *Post*'s total advertising and representing its more elaborate and expensive ads. Other categories grew significantly in these years as well. Entertainment- and work-related products would vie over the course of the decade for second place in percentage of overall advertising, and education and self-improvement advertisements provided another major source of revenue for the *Post*. But household advertisements carried the magazine during its lean years and contributed to its efforts around 1902 and 1903 to become a commercial magazine. These ads, geared almost exclusively to women, constituted the magazine's largest single category of advertising and formed the commercial backbone of the *Post* during its crucial early years of growth.

Hence the *Post* needed to count a substantial number of women—who had become the culture's primary consumers—among its regular read-

21. *Saturday Evening Post,* June 20, 1908, 1.

22. This adjustment of the *Post*'s target audience is also discussed in Jan Cohn, *Creating America: George Horace Lorimer and the Saturday Evening Post* (Pittsburgh: University of Pittsburgh Press, 1989), chap. 2.

23. Bok, *Man from Maine,* 161.

ers. The campaign for those readers seems to have been somewhat successful by about 1905, as evidenced by circulation increases and a broader family image for the *Post,* and it was much more successful by 1909. It is clear, then, that women were reading the *Post,* but that does not answer the important question: why were they drawn to a magazine that had been touted for several years as a men's publication, one that had historically paid scant attention to women's concerns? Some speculative answers to this question emerge from a comparison of the evolution of the *Post*'s content and audience with the character of the *Journal*'s content and audience during the same period.

Gender, the *Post* and the *Journal*

The *Ladies' Home Journal* by this time was a mature, stable enterprise. Edward Bok continued as the *Journal*'s editor (and would until 1919), and the magazine featured much the same format and tone as it had since Bok's taking over the editorship in 1889. There was one subtle change, however, which bears directly on the issue of gender configuration of the magazine's audience: The first decade of the twentieth century saw a proliferation of articles addressed to men, articles considering such issues as success versus failure, the nature of twentieth-century fatherhood, and the advantages of the "strenuous life."

The fact is that Bok hoped for the same kind of broadening for the *Journal* that Lorimer seemed to be achieving for the *Post.* Bok's interest was prompted by the desire to make the *Journal* as big a seller as it could be and by his assessment of the future of women's magazines. Writing in 1919, Bok made explicit an assumption that seems to have guided the *Journal*'s editorial content as early as 1900.

It is a question, however, whether the day of the woman's magazine, as we have known it, is not passing. . . . The interests of women and of men are being brought closer with the years, and it will not be long before they will entirely merge. This means a constantly diminishing necessity for the distinctly feminine magazine. Naturally, there will always be a field in the essentially feminine pursuits which have no place in the life of a man, but these are rapidly being cared for by books, gratuitously distributed and issued by the manufacturers of distinctly feminine domestic wares; for such publications the best talent is being employed, and the results are placed within easy access of women, by means of newspaper advertisements, the store-counter, or the mails. These will sooner or later—and much sooner than later—supplant the practical portions of the woman's magazine, leaving only the general contents, which are equally interesting to men and to women.[24]

Given his undisputed status as an editorial wizard, Bok was an extremely bad predictor of future gender trends in magazines. Nonetheless, acting on this judgment, Bok began purposefully to direct the *Journal*'s general material to men as well as to women, in an attempt to hasten the "merging of interests" that he perceived.

As with the *Post*, it is impossible to describe with any certainty the gender constituency of the *Journal*'s audience, but the evidence suggests a different gender mix than that of the *Post*'s readership. Most compelling is that the *Journal* never achieved the broader family image that the *Post* was enjoying by 1905. The *Ladies' Home Journal*, in spite of Bok's desires and predictions, remained a magazine for "ladies" through 1910, and to this day it is, of course, a "woman's magazine."

The contrasting tones of the two magazines may explain this difference to some extent. Bok's *Journal* (as distinguished from Knapp's earlier version) employed a preachy, moralistic style that may have been less inviting to men than Lorimer's more open, less judgmental style would have been to women. But why would women tolerate Bok's preaching when men were not willing to? Historians need to examine this matter more closely, but traditionally Americans seem to have prescribed women's behavior more explicitly than men's, and women seem to have listened to those prescriptions even if they have not always abided by them.[25] Women may therefore simply have been more accustomed to being addressed in a moralizing tone and willing to take what they could from it. This does not preclude the possibility, however, that women found the *Post*'s less-judgmental style appealing. The *Post*'s crossover in target audience may have succeeded in part because of the magazine's more open tone.

A second possible explanation for the different readerships of the *Post* and the *Journal* relates to the stigma that may have been attached to a man interested in a "women's" magazine. As noted earlier, the *Journal* itself had contributed to a certain differentiation of reading matter by gender in the nineteenth century, a differentiation that had further increased by the first decade of the twentieth. The genre of mass-circulation middle-class women's magazines had matured, with *McCall's, Good Housekeeping,* and *Woman's Home Companion* joining the *Journal* as major forces in the publishing industry. Magazines other than the *Post*

24. Ibid.

25. For an important discussion of the gap between prescribed and actual behavior, see Jay E. Mechling, "Advice to Historians on Advice to Mothers," *Journal of Social History* 9 (Fall 1975):44–63.

were geared for American men of the times, including *Field and Stream* and the *American Magazine.*

Added to this more salient gender differentiation of magazines was the culture's increasing concern regarding the development of masculinity.[26] By the turn of the century effeminate or "sissified" boys and men were frequently commented on, worried about, and ridiculed, which might well have discouraged males from reading a magazine called the *Ladies' Home Journal.* On the other hand, women's lives and interests were expanding in scope at the turn of the century, and women probably had more flexibility to "cross over" in their reading choices. Although the circumscribed nature of women's role received more attention in discussions of gender, in this regard women may have had more freedom than men to transcend traditional boundaries in reading interests.

A final cultural reason for the gender crossover in the case of the *Post* and not in the case of the *Journal* is that women seemed to be more interested in learning about men than men were in learning about women. The content of both the *Journal* and the pre-1902 *Post* supports this notion. The *Journal* regularly considered the nature of men's personal lives, at least from a woman's standpoint, whereas the *Post,* as a men's magazine, considered women's issues only if they extended to matters of public policy. Exploring the personal lives of both men and women did become important to the *Post* as it became a magazine explicitly intended for women as well as for men, but even then the *Post* never featured the *Journal's* level of consideration. The *Journal* believed that its female readers were interested in issues related to the quality of both men's and women's personal lives; given the enormous success of the magazine among women, there is no reason to think otherwise. But extending this discussion to address men as well did not broaden the audience the way Bok hoped it might, suggesting that men were not as interested in examining their own, or women's, personal lives.

Whatever the reasons, by 1903 the *Post* enjoyed a mixed readership by gender whereas the *Journal* remained a magazine read primarily by women, and this contrast eventually allowed the *Post* to outstrip its sister publication in both circulation and advertising revenues. The *Journal* remained ahead of the *Post* in the earliest years of the twentieth century, becoming the first American magazine to reach a circulation of one million in February of 1903, and running upward of $1 million advertising per year. The *Post* did not begin to catch up to the *Journal* until the end of the first decade of the century, when its circulation broke one million. Its advertising revenues went over the $1.5 million mark in 1908. The *Post* boomed during the World War I years, reaching the unheard-of circula-

26. See Peter N. Stearns, *Be a Man! Males in Modern Society* (New York: Holmes and Meier, 1979).

tion figure of two million by the war's end. In the period between the wars, the *Post* outsold all other American magazines in advertising (over $30 million in revenues in 1922) and stayed at the top of the Ayer's circulation list for many years.[27] The *Journal's* offspring therefore eventually overtook its parent to become the most popular and the most commercially successful magazine in the United States.

Both magazines revealed their commercial foundations in ways other than the advertising they carried, most notably in promoting middle-class consumption and discussing couples' money management. Both the *Journal* and the *Post* suggested that women be responsible for money management in the family, lauding women's economic savvy and thrifty tendencies. But at the same time the *Post* was a business-oriented magazine designed to appeal to sellers, and it regularly featured tips on precisely how sellers might "tease and tantalize" female shoppers. Between 1900 and 1910 the *Post* ran a number of articles on selling to women, all of them promoting the best ways to manipulate women into buying. For example, an article by Joseph Smith in 1907 discussed "Getting On in the World. Steps and Missteps on the Road to Fortune—The Feminine Mind." Smith, a drygoods salesman, noted that three-quarters of American retail purchases were made by women; hence smart businessmen "must appeal to them." Smith addressed in particular the issue of pricing as it related to women, asserting the need for careful comparison pricing and clear statements on what women would save, since "the feminine mind is weak on abstractions and arithmetic." The answer, Smith proposed, was to give that mind "concrete facts and definite prices."[28]

Isaac Marcosson in 1910 echoed the importance of catering to women shoppers, and he noted some other perceived attributes of female consumers. In a piece called "The Woman Shopper—How to Make Her Buy," Marcosson observed that the wife shops for the whole family and is therefore an essential target for advertising and in-store promotional campaigns. Such campaigns, he argued, must be guided by the notion that a woman does not know exactly what she wants but needs to "have the leisure to pick and choose." Marcosson's advice on attracting women and enticing them to buy covered a wide range: Put stores in proximity to theaters, provide free bus rides to the store, place appealing items on the main floor, and offer fashionable merchandise. Marcosson even suggested providing free child care to shoppers. The manager of a department store could never rest easy, Marcosson concluded; the need for constant effort was the "price you must pay for a woman's trade."[29]

27. Peterson, *Magazines in the Twentieth Century,* 2d ed., 13.
28. *Saturday Evening Post,* March 2, 1907, 16.
29. Ibid., August 20, 1910, 12.

The *Post* thus respected women's ability to handle family finances but at the same time encouraged businessmen to do anything to convince women to buy. Both the *Post* and the *Journal* were dominated by this theme of women as consumers, but the *Post* broadened the idea to include men. Between 1900 and 1910 the *Post* increased advertising products intended for men. This was an important new development in advertising and magazine history, precipitated by the national production of commodities thought to be of importance to men, like automobiles, and encouraged by the presence of a forum like the *Post* and, as of 1915, the *American*. General magazines like the *Atlantic* and *Scribner's*, with their relatively inexpensive advertisements for books and other periodicals, had preceded the development of national markets for male-oriented products; more-focused periodicals for men, like *Field and Stream*, tended to carry a narrow range of advertising closely related to their content.

The *Post* of the early twentieth century boasted increasing numbers of ads for business-related machines and books, clothing, and opportunities for education and self-improvement. Perhaps most significant, in terms of visual impact and long-term relationship to the magazine, were the advertisements for automobiles that began to appear in the *Post* in 1903. Fords and Oldsmobiles were regularly advertised in the decade between 1900 and 1910, with lavish illustrations designed to entice first-time car buyers.

Most of the car advertisements were geared to men, and *Post* ads in general were targeted either to men or to women, not both. But the mix of the *Post*'s audience allowed some limited but interesting crossover in advertisement targeting. For example, an ad in 1905 pictured a smiling woman in the driver's seat of a new Oldsmobile, with the caption: "Makes everyone your neighbor—the Oldsmobile has endeared itself to the feminine heart just as it has established itself in the business world."[30] Similarly, crossover in the *Post* is illustrated by a 1908 ad for Pompeiian Face Cream, that urged men to convince their wives of the benefits of the cream; a later ad suggested that the cream was also beneficial for men.

Such crossover was limited but regular and was possible only because the early-twentieth-century *Post* had become known as a family magazine. Even so, gender-targeted advertising of one kind or another was what propelled both the *Post* and the *Journal* to commercial success, and both magazines were highly profitable enterprises by the end of 1910. The two magazines both reflected and shaped their times; they represented and discussed various images of men and women, they urged consumption, and they provided a forum for commercial messages. A

30. Ibid., February 25, 1905, 27.

significant legacy of Cyrus Curtis's magazines, therefore, was their reinforcement of and support for a gender-segmented consumer culture.

The Curtis magazines also contributed substantially to the parallel gender differentiation in the content of mass-circulation American magazines, a general development that has affected a significant portion of the twentieth-century magazine market. Patterns noted in the *Journal* and the *Post* reappeared frequently in the top-selling mass-circulation magazines over the course of the twentieth century. This was in part because the *Journal* and the *Post* were influential models and in part because the factors that shaped the *Journal* and the *Post* shaped later magazines as well.

Indeed, many magazines repeated the *Journal*'s success. American mass-circulation women's magazines have been relatively easy to establish and relatively long-lived. The Ayer's magazine-circulation lists tell the story of the twentieth century vis-à-vis women's magazines (see table 9.1), which have consistently been among the nation's top-selling magazines, with a few titles appearing repeatedly: *Ladies' Home Journal, Woman's Home Companion, McCall's,* and *Good Housekeeping.* In any given year, titles targeted for women have represented from four to six of the top ten circulation magazines in the country. Most of these top sellers followed the *Journal* formula until the 1950s, when the women's market expanded to include the supermarket magazines, specifically *Woman's Day* and *Family Circle,* both of which were in the top ten in 1980. Commercial magazines targeted for women have had huge circulations for much of the twentieth century, with advertising revenues commensurate with their large circulations.

The pool from which advertisements could be drawn was not unlimited, however, because of the rather rigid gender targeting of the genre. During the middle decades of the twentieth century, other women's magazines followed the *Journal*'s early lead to try to broaden their images, out of a similar combination of pecuniary motive and sense that the future of women's magazines was questionable. For example, in 1945 *McCall's Magazine,* under the editorship of Otis Wiese, was broadened to appeal to middle-class men and children as well as women. According to Theodore Peterson, "the new editorial pitch was based on what Wiese called 'togetherness'—a family's living not as isolated members but as a unit sharing experiences."[31] The policy failed not only as a device to attract readers; more importantly, it failed also to attract any new, male-oriented advertising. For the reasons noted in discussing the *Journal*'s attempt to create crossover—the problems of tone, format, lack of interest from men, and the stigma of men reading women's publications—

31. Peterson, *Magazines in the Twentieth Century,* 2d ed., 204.

Table 9.1. Top Ten Paid-Circulation Magazines, 1900–1980

Rank in 1900	Type	Circulation (thousands)	Established
1. *Ladies' Home Journal*	W	846	1883
2. *Munsey's Magazine*	G	650	1889
3. *Hearthstone*	W	610	1891
4. *Boyce's Monthly*	W	604	1897
5. *Metropolitan and Rural Home*	G	500	1871
6. *Delineator*	W	500	1873
7. *Household Guest*	W	500	1891
8. *Ladies' World*	W	434	1879
9. *Farm Journal*	F	382	1877
10. *McClure's Magazine*	G	369	1893

Rank in 1920	Type	Circulation (thousands)	Established
1. *Saturday Evening Post*	G	2,021	1897
2. *Ladies' Home Journal*	W	1,823	1883
3. *Pictorial Review*	W	1,605	1899
4. *Gentlewoman*	W	1,500	1871
5. *McCall's Magazine*	W	1,201	1870
6. *Comfort*	W	1,197	1888
7. *Woman's Home Companion*	W	1,085	1873
8. *Collier's*	G	1,064	1888
9. *American Magazine*	M	1,038	1876
10. *Cosmopolitan*	G	1,021	1886

Rank in 1940	Type	Circulation (thousands)	Established
1. *Woman's Home Companion*	W	3,131	1873
2. *Saturday Evening Post*	G	3,104	1897
3. *Ladies' Home Journal*	W	3,084	1883
4. *McCall's Magazine*	W	2,941	1870
5. *Collier's*	G	2,745	1888
6. *Farm Journal & Farmer's Wife*	G	2,442	1877
7. *Life*	G	2,382	1936
8. *Good Housekeeping*	W	2,276	1885
9. *Liberty*	G	2,359	1924
10. *American Magazine*	G	2,189	1876

(*continued*)

Table 9.1. (*continued*)

| | | Circulation | |
Rank in 1960	Type	(thousands)	Established
1. *Reader's Digest*	G	12,134	1922
2. *TV Guide*	G	7,028	1953
3. *Life*	G	6,108	1930
4. *Saturday Evening Post*	G	6,005	1897
5. *Ladies' Home Journal*	W	5,755	1883
6. *Look*	G	5,701	1937
7. *McCall's Magazine*	W	5,492	1870
8. *Everywoman's Family Circle*	W	5,121	1932
9. *Better Homes & Gardens*	W	4,799	1922
10. *Good Housekeeping*	W	4,438	1885

| | | Circulation | |
Rank in 1980	Type	(thousands)	Established
1. *TV Guide*	G	21,548	1953
2. *Reader's Digest*	G	18,094	1922
3. *National Geographic*	G	10,250	1888
4. *Better Homes & Gardens*	W	8,033	1922
5. *Family Circle*	W	7,612	1932
6. *Woman's Day*	W	7,536	1937
7. *Modern Maturity*	S.I.	7,000	1957
8. *McCall's Magazine*	W	6,503	1876
9. *College Game*	S.I.	6,053	1968
10. *Ladies' Home Journal*	W	5,633	1883

Source: Ayer's Annual Directory of Newspapers and Magazines.

Note: W = Women's; M = Men's; G = General or Family; F = Farm; S.I. = Special Interest.

there has never been a significant crossover or broadening in audience by gender for a women's magazine in America.

The Dilemmas of Men's Magazines

Producers of men's magazines faced a different limitation: the small number of nationally marketed male-targeted goods, significantly smaller than the number targeted for women. This restriction, combined with assumptions about the male sex role, has led to two approaches in the twentieth-century world of commercial magazines for men: special-interest magazines created specifically to draw large numbers of specialized advertisements, and general magazines like the *Post,* which broadened its focus to speak to women as well. Because of their very nature most of the magazines in the first category have not been among the top sellers in America, but a brief glance at *Playboy*—a remarkably successful special-interest magazine—is in order.

Since the founding of *Field and Stream* in 1895 commercial magazines for men have frequently focused on a special interest: sports, woodworking, or financial matters, for example. In 1952 a young man named Hugh Hefner decided that there was a place on the men's market for a new magazine:

> The most popular men's magazines of the time were the outdoor-adventure books—*True, Argosy* and the like. They had a hairy-chested editorial emphasis with articles on hunting, fishing, chasing the Abominable Snowman over Tibetan mountaintops. . . . *Esquire* had changed its editorial emphasis after the War, eliminating most of the lighter material—the girls, cartoons, and humor. So the field was wide open for the sort of magazine I had in mind.[32]

Playboy's special interest—sex—was different, but it was its advertising that most distinguished it from earlier men's magazines. From the start, Hefner recognized the importance of up-scale, quality advertising to his magazine; in fact, he borrowed money to run it until 1954, carrying no advertising until his circulation was high enough to attract the kind of advertising he wanted. *Playboy*'s advertisements set it apart from earlier "girlie" magazines. Instead of muscle creams and cheap sex aids, *Playboy* featured a multitude of advertisements for liquor, cigarettes, clothing, cars, stereos, soaps and colognes, and other men's products. Able to attract a wide-ranging and stable group of advertisements over the years, *Playboy* worked its way up the circulation chart to the number eleven spot in 1980.

32. Hugh Hefner, quoted in Thomas Weyr, *Reaching for Paradise: The Playboy Vision of America* (New York: Times Books, 1978), 3.

Other magazine producers have overcome the limitation of the men's market by broadening their publications to appeal to women, as demonstrated by the *Saturday Evening Post*. Several major twentieth-century magazines followed the *Post*'s example, including *Collier's, Cosmopolitan,* the *American Magazine,* and the *Farm Journal and Farmer's Wife.* Each of these magazines began in the late nineteenth or early twentieth century as a men's magazine, and after broadening to include women, each appeared in Ayer's top ten in either 1920, 1940, or both (see table 9.1). Of course, many factors and circumstances combined to make these magazines commercially successful; gender crossover is but one. But the fact that through 1960 all of the top ten circulating magazines were either family or women's magazines does support the notion that advertising to women was crucial to the biggest mass-circulating magazines. Crossover therefore contributed in a significant way to the commercial success of some of the most important twentieth-century American magazines.

Not all successful "family" magazines started as publications for men. Perhaps the most popular family magazine of all, *Life,* was targeted to both men and women from its founding in 1936. The original idea for *Life* came from Clare Boothe Luce, who conceived of the idea for an American picture magazine to parallel the popular French magazine *Vu*. Henry Luce gave substance to the idea, considering it early on as a family magazine, but only after toying with the idea of establishing a women's magazine. "In the end," Luce said later, "we decided that the plain fact was as a group of general news journalists, we were not really very deeply interested in the matter of a woman's magazine. And so, however attractive the possibilities might have been from a publishing standpoint, we decided to forget it."[33]

Although Luce may have decided not to cater exclusively to women, he remained highly conscious of the women's market. In the summer before *Life*'s first issue appeared, Luce was sent a thirty-four-page list of advertisers committed to buying space. Loudon Wainwright reports: "Some of the accounts were Zenith Radio, Seagram's Crown Whiskey, Maxwell House Coffee, United Air Lines, Four Roses Whiskey, General Motors. Luce replied that he thought the list was 'fine except for perhaps a little too much liquor. I like Wrigley's and Maxwell,' he said, 'and would like to see a few more female advertisements.'"[34] Attracting female-targeted advertising and women readers, Luce knew, was good business.

Although not all family-oriented magazines broadened from men's

33. Loudon Wainwright, *The Great American Magazine: An Inside History of Life* (New York: Alfred A. Knopf, 1986), 6.
34. Ibid., 42.

magazines, all of the biggest ones from quite early in the century sold huge numbers of gender-targeted advertisements. Cyrus Curtis was one of the pioneers who demonstrated what came to be a basic principle of publishing: A publisher could lose millions of dollars on circulation by selling a magazine at less than production cost and still reap millions of dollars in profit from advertising. The *Post* issue dated December 7, 1929, was a monument to this policy; Theodore Peterson described it as follows: "Weighing nearly two pounds, the 272-page magazine contained enough reading matter to keep the average reader occupied for twenty hours and twenty minutes. From the 214 national advertisers appearing in it, Curtis took in revenues estimated at $1,512,000."[35] Similarly, a single issue of *Life* in October 1960 carried $5 million worth of advertising. Such huge advertising revenues were common among the big magazines of the 1950s and 1960s, magazines like *Life,* the *Post,* and *Look,* which all appeared among the top ten circulators on Ayer's list for 1960.

But the days of such huge circulations and huge revenues for these magazines were numbered by a single invention: television. Analysts agree that the dependence of general family-oriented magazines on very large audiences and on very large profits from advertising made them extremely vulnerable to the threat presented by the rise of television as an entertainment and commercial medium.[36] Other factors, such as the political mood of the 1960s and various managerial mistakes, played some role in the demise of the "giants," but the overwhelming factor seems to have been the competition from television for the attention of former readers and, even more, for the advertising dollar. The *Post* died in 1969, and *Look* and *Life* in 1972. Even where there was still audience interest, the magazines became too expensive to produce when advertising was increasingly difficult to attract.[37]

Women's Magazines: Recent Developments

Family magazines were not the only magazines vulnerable to television's inroads on advertising. Since the founding of the *Journal* in 1883, women's magazines had been heavily dependent on advertising

35. Peterson, *Magazines in the Twentieth Century,* 2d ed., 23.

36. See esp. A. J. van Zuilen's *The Life Cycle of Magazines: A Historical Study of the Decline and Fall of the General Interest Mass Audience Magazine in the United States during the Period 1946–1972* (Vithoorn, Netherlands: Graduate Press, 1977).

37. The only major general-interest magazine left among the top ten in 1980 was *Reader's Digest.* Founded in 1922, the *Digest* has always been something of an anomaly. The reprinting function of the magazine has given it an extremely low production overhead, allowing it to remain above the fray of competition with television.

revenues, and that dependence only increased as the century wore on. For instance, the October 1946 issue of the *Ladies' Home Journal* was 246 pages long and brought in over $2 million from 334 advertisers.[38] Women's magazines to the present have enjoyed circulation figures and advertising revenues as high as any. Why then did mass-circulation women's magazines not succumb to the financial difficulties presented by shifts from magazine to television advertising?

The answer is complicated. Some women's magazines did succumb, most notably the Crowell Company's *Woman's Home Companion*. But others have thrived and lived to be more than one hundred years old: The *Journal, McCall's,* and *Good Housekeeping* have all recently published their centennial issues. One major reason for the success of these and other women's magazines is that the genre could play as both "general interest" and "special interest." When advertisers chose television over general magazines because television could reach "everyone," there was no basis on which general magazines could compete; television could reach a broad audience more efficiently and effectively. But the breadth of television advertising worked in favor of the women's magazines, at least to the extent that those magazines were able to scale back their expectations for share of revenue. For there was still a place in the culture for a national forum that would guarantee a more targeted audience, in this case, women.

And women's magazines as a genre adapted to the smaller amounts of advertising that they were able to attract, avoiding going out of business completely. Magazine sizes were cut back and circulations reduced, and the top sellers sharpened their images somewhat to give clearer audience definitions to advertisers. Hence *Good Housekeeping* and the *Journal* began to cater to the older woman, whereas *Redbook* and *McCall's* catered to the younger. Middle-class women's magazines have had to lower their sights in terms of audience share and advertising revenue in order to stay in business, but stay in business they have.

The relationship between gender-targeted advertising and middle-class women's magazines thus appears to be more mutually reinforcing than ever. An example of a very different kind of women's magazine will illustrate just how symbiotic this relationship between advertising and the women's magazine formula has become.

Ms. magazine was founded in 1972 as a magazine for women with an explicitly feminist stance and an implicitly disapproving view of traditional women's magazines. At the beginning *Ms.* was very selective about the advertising it ran and, in fact, served as something of a watchdog in the print-media advertising world, running a column called "No Com-

38. Peterson, *Magazines in the Twentieth Century,* 2d ed., 23.

ment," which displayed the sexist advertising run in other magazines and newspapers. But the founders of *Ms.* were as interested in surviving as a mainstream periodical as they were in making political statements about advertisements, and that interest led to a striking evolution in the *Ms.* handling of advertising.

The first stage in that evolution was to move from attacking advertisements they didn't like to luring advertisements they wanted. In the late 1970s *Ms.* worked to attract advertisers who had not before targeted women, advertisers of products like cars and such traditionally male services as investment counseling. *Ms.* was successful in attracting some of that advertising, but not successful enough to avoid a second shift of strategy. That second change, prompted by the desire to remain a viable middle-class commercial magazine, focused on attracting traditional companies who advertised in mainstream middle-class women's magazines, including advertisers of food, cosmetics, and fashion. In its desire to remain alive as an advertisement-sponsored periodical, *Ms.* was forced to cater to some of the very advertisers it had once ridiculed.

And the irony did not stop there: *Ms.* staffers found themselves in the odd position of working to get advertisements that bore little or no resemblance to the content of the rest of the magazine. In 1986 "The Phil Donahue Show" featured editors from nine major women's magazines, including the oldest periodicals and more recent comers like *Ms.* and *Working Woman.* Suzanne Levin, managing editor of *Ms.*, described the struggle *Ms.* was then experiencing to broaden beyond automotive and financial advertising "to get the rest of the advertising that women also need to look at and need to know about. . . . You have to remember that we are the only magazine here that does not have editorial support [relevant articles, columns in the magazine itself] for cosmetics, for fashion, for food."[39]

The dilemma for *Ms.*, then, was as follows: The magazine implicitly and sometimes explicitly eschewed the traditional women's magazine formula, but at the same time, to remain a vital mainstream magazine for women, it needed the advertising that had become so bound up with that formula as to be indistinguishable from it. *Ms.* strayed farther and farther from its original tone and purposes in an attempt to become commercially viable, but it never became profitable. In 1990 its editors announced a last-ditch effort to save the magazine by raising the price, reducing the frequency of publication, and eschewing advertising altogether.[40]

39. "Donahue" transcript #01287, Multimedia Entertainment, Inc., Cincinnati, Ohio, January, 1986. Because shows are syndicated, transcripts are not precisely dated.

40. *New York Times,* March 3, 1990, p. C10.

From the 1880s, when Cyrus Curtis and Louisa Knapp fashioned a mass magazine for women, to the 1980s, when *Ms.* struggled to remain a mainstream periodical, advertising has played a crucial role in shaping gender-targeted magazines' identities and success. The relationship between advertising and women's magazines has been clear and powerful from the beginning: Women were viewed as the culture's primary consumers; magazines were conceived as forums for national advertisements to women; and traditional woman-targeted advertising and magazines alike have flourished ever since. The relationship of advertising to men's magazines has been less simple but equally potent: The narrower range of goods marketed for men has supported the proliferation of special-interest magazines for men and forced men's magazines to speak to women's interests as well. These patterns have held for over one hundred years and show no signs of shifting in the near future.

Feminists suggest that mass-circulation magazines perform a disservice to society by reinforcing stereotypes about men and women. Since Betty Friedan's *The Feminine Mystique* appeared in 1963, popular magazines, especially those for middle-class women, have come under attack for encouraging traditional images of women and men and for promoting consumption through images and claims that have little to do with products' characteristics or consumers' actual needs. The example of *Playboy* cited earlier, along with much other advertising for men, suggests that men are as vulnerable to commercial exploitation as women.

In spite of the critics, the relationship between advertising and magazines is unlikely to change. It is durable, it is circular, and it is subject to minimal regulation. For both sexes, but especially for women, magazines provide a forum for gender-targeted advertising; in turn, gender-targeted advertising supports those magazines that best showcase their messages, to wit, magazines with the strongest emphasis on consumption and on sex roles that most resemble those in the advertisements. This symbiotic relationship makes the profitable production of alternative magazines extremely difficult.

Gender segregation is pervasive in magazines and advertising, as is the promotion of consumption through images and anxieties related to traditional sex roles. Furthermore, we generally refrain from legally regulating the content of publications, including advertisements, except in cases of fraud or health hazards. Critics are thus left only the strategies of raising consciousness, rousing support for alternatives, and education. Public opinion about women's roles is shifting, and public policies in related areas, such as affirmative-action hiring of women and sex-role socialization in classrooms and textbooks, may eventually contribute to reducing sexist content in magazines and advertisements.

In the meantime, pervasive differences in reading material aimed at women and at men continue. This is one dimension on which popular reading material has not drawn American readers together to promote common aspirations, interests, and expectations. In short, popular magazines reflect and reinforce a culture divided by gender. The divisions are stubbornly persistent because they are so intimately involved in the social strategies of capitalism and consumption.

10 Standardization and Diversity in American Print Culture, 1880 to the Present

CARL F. KAESTLE

Chapter 9 explored the commercial production of reading materials by examining the role of gender in the magazine industry. This chapter enlarges the canvas to include all sorts of diversity in books, magazines, and newspapers. It looks at the interplay of culture, marketing, education, and politics in fostering or reducing the diversity of printed materials in America.

At any given time, literacy can serve both cultural diversity and cultural consolidation, but the mix between those functions shifts over time. The content of newspapers, magazines, and books does not predetermine how readers will use them, but the level of standardization in these print forms does set some limits. Access to a great diversity of printed materials is not possible if diverse printed materials are not produced; conversely, cultural consolidation through exposure to shared information, heroes, and symbols can occur only if the common messages are widely produced and distributed.

Diversity is a difficult concept to define and measure. The immigrant press, for example, was diverse in language but often assimilationist in content; a paper in Lithuanian that advertised national brand-name products thus performed both functions. Furthermore, there is a big difference between ideological and topical diversity. Defining diversity as "the range of themes, styles, and messages available at a given time," Paul DiMaggio drew a contrast between mass culture, which tends to standardize, and two types of diverse production systems. Materials of "class culture" are produced for tightly segmented markets based on class or status groupings; those of "pluralistic culture" are based more on differences of taste and interest. Writing in 1977, DiMaggio judged pluralistic cultural production to be thriving whereas class-culture production had waned somewhat. In addition to this shift of balance in diverse production systems, further consolidation of mass culture has occurred since 1977, particularly in book publishing.[1]

Reading materials whose audience is defined by such important social-status groupings as race, gender, and class (DiMaggio's class culture) generally have stronger ideological implications than those based on differences in topical interests and leisure pursuits (DiMaggio's pluralistic culture). I have therefore termed the two types "ideological" and "topical." Herbert Gans, arguing against the "decline-and-fall school of social analysis," made a similar point in 1961: "Once upon a time, the story goes, America was diverse in peoples and cultures, but today it is a society of middle-class conformists." Gans agreed that although ethnic and regional subcultures had declined, new forms of diversity had replaced the old. "Much of the declining diversity was based on traditions and on constraint; much of the present diversity is a result of the enlargement of choice."[2] In spite of the emphasis Gans and DiMaggio have placed on the expansion of diversity based on preferences rather than on primary social identities, this chapter will argue that some areas of publishing that expanded in the 1960s and 1970s represent genuine ideological diversity—the feminist press, the fundamentalist press, gay periodicals, and black-owned book publishing, for example.

Although we should keep in mind the distinction between ideological and topical diversity, both are woven in and out of this chapter's analysis. Diversity is defined here in terms of the number of publications, their independence from one another in terms of control, their topical variety, and their ideological variety. Standardization, conversely, is illustrated in this essay by evidence that more people were reading the same publications, by the consolidation of control, and by a reduction in the diversity of language, topics, and ideology. Thus, for example, wire services boosted standardization, whereas paperback books encouraged diversity.

Diversity in print has been created by many forces in American history: regionalism, immigration, freedom of expression, racism, creativity, class stratification, and the sheer geographic immensity of the country. Some of these forces are positive features of American life, whereas others clearly are not. The literature of the oppressed may have power and beauty, but we do not therefore celebrate oppression. On the

1. Paul DiMaggio, "Market Structure, the Creative Process, and Popular Culture: Toward an Organizational Reinterpretation of Mass-Culture Theory," *Journal of Popular Culture* 11 (1977):436–52.

2. Herbert Gans, "Diversity and Homogeneity in American Culture," chap. 11 in his *People and Plans* (New York: Basic Books, 1968), 141, 149, based on his "Diversity Is Not Dead," *New Republic*, April 3, 1961, 11–15. Gans pursues a similar point again in "Symbolic Ethnicity: The Future of Ethnic Groups and Cultures in America," *Ethnic and Racial Studies* 2 (January 1979):1–18.

other side of this polarity, both positive and negative forces encourage cultural consolidation. Standardization of reading material has been furthered by the rise of education rates, the hegemonic impulses of mainstream leaders, the effects of large-scale capitalism on the publishing industries, and the impact of technology in shrinking distances.

Consolidation has long been a theme in discussions about the uses of literacy in the twentieth century. Some commentators have portrayed it in an optimistic light. John Dewey believed that the hope of democracy lay in our becoming one people through a popular press.[3] More than Dewey would have wished, our sense of common identity has been forged as much by Dick Tracy and Dear Abby as by the Federalist papers or our knowledge of foreign trade. Still, to the extent that we have become "one nation," it has been partly through our shared exposure to the images, heroes, and values of popular print forms and, more recently, of the electronic media. At the same time, printed matter has been crucial in maintaining subcultures and asserting alternatives. Political and religious activists have recognized this; they place great emphasis on their publications. Defenders of the dominant culture have always known it, too; they have often tried to suppress or control dangerous diversity in print. Along with the kinds of diversity that pluralists admire, our definition also encompasses diversity caused by prejudice. One cost of a free press in a diverse society is that print can be enlisted in the service of intolerance and insularity. As we saw in the discussion of gender and magazines in chapter 9, distinct reading publics can be based on stereotypes and fostered for exploitation. Cultural distinctiveness is not always defined by the group that is affected.

Many analysts, however, emphasize the positive virtues of diversity in print and see consolidation as a threat to both quality of literature and freedom of thought. They see the tension between diversity and standardization as a war between democracy and capitalism. As we saw in chapter 2, Raymond Williams argued that the expansion of democracy led to the expansion of popular reading materials, whereas capitalism caused cultural products to be mediocre and exploitative. Short of a fundamental shift to socialism, he was not very optimistic. He called the expansion of culture the "long revolution," and for Williams it was not only incomplete but also headed to no good end. Harold Innis, also discussed in chapter 2, was more of a technological determinist. He saw history as a long one-directional process of consolidation. The problem for him lay not so much with capitalism as with the mass media and their association with standardization, nationalism, and amorality. For both Innis and

3. See John Dewey, *The Public and Its Problems* (New York: Henry Holt, 1927), chap. 5, and Dewey, review of *Public Opinion*, by Walter Lippmann, *New Republic*, May 3, 1922, 286–88.

Williams, mass commercial culture warred against diversity, localism, and participation. Writing in the 1950s, both saw the previous century as a dreary march toward the national, the corporate, the superficial, and the technical. The problem for both was how to revive and support local communities that could participate in the creation of print culture.

Whereas Innis and Williams contrasted mass commercial culture with indigenous participatory culture, an assortment of American critics in the 1950s contrasted mass culture with high culture. These critics were concerned not only with standardization but also with the quality of mass culture; though they came from a variety of political perspectives, they agreed that "massification" produced trash and threatened to destroy the traditions of high culture, whose texts they considered elegant, thoughtful, and unpatterned.[4] Since the 1950s there have been many critiques of the standardization of popular media and of capitalism's role in that standardization. Some argue that the two are inseparable, that capitalism has fostered the homogenization of print matter because cultural production in a capitalist system aims for a safe, standardized product. According to this argument, cultural production, like all other capitalist production, seeks large-scale operations and ideological stability. It thus shuns ethnic and political diversity, aiming instead to exploit as many readers as possible on behalf of commercial values.[5] These analyses set forth three major criticisms—homogenization, the deterioration of quality, and exploitation. Although these processes cannot be wholly disentangled, this chapter focuses largely on the notion of homogenization, or cultural consolidation.

The terms in this inquiry are loaded. "Diversity" and "pluralism" sound good, but "fragmentation" and "dissension" do not. "Cohesion" and "unity" sound desirable, "conformity" and "standardization" do not.

4. Many relevant essays are collected in Bernard Rosenberg and David M. White, eds., *Mass Culture: The Popular Arts in America* (Glencoe, Ill.: Free Press, 1957), and Jacobs, ed., *Culture for the Millions?* A smattering of the extensive literature on the 1950s critique of mass culture follows. Edward Shils, "Daydreams and Nightmares: Reflections on the Criticism of Mass Culture," *Sewanee Review* 65 (1957):587–608, is a review of the Rosenberg and White book by one of the participants in the debate; Raymond A. Bauer and Alice H. Bauer, "American Mass Society and Mass Media," *Journal of Social Issues* 16 (1960):3–66, attempts an empirical refutation of the thesis of decline; Herbert Gans, *Popular Culture and High Culture* (New York: Basic Books, 1974), turns the cultural judgment upside down; and Brantlinger, *Bread and Circuses,* places it in a larger theoretical and historical context.

5. Bagdikian, *Media Monopoly;* Joseph Turow, *Media Industries: The Production of News and Entertainment* (New York: Longman, 1984); Whiteside, *Blockbuster Complex;* Michael Parenti, *Inventing Reality: The Politics of the Mass Media* (New York: St. Martin's Press, 1986). Interesting precursors to this literature are Morris Ernst, *The First Freedom* (New York: Macmillan, 1946), and Bryce W. Rucker, *The First Freedom* (Carbondale: Southern Illinois University Press, 1968). For a rosier view, see Compaine, ed., *Who Owns the Media?*

One can try to balance consolidation and diversity by subscribing to a cultural ideal of healthy diversity within a set of shared values and knowledge. However, actual trends in cultural production are governed not by ideals, but by technology, the profit motive, legal and political constraints, education levels, and other factors.

It often seems that standardization and assimilation are aligned on one side, with diversity and dissent on the other. Standardized reading material leans toward maintaining the status quo and assimilating people to a mainstream culture. Conversely, cultural diversity in print is aligned with choice, challenge, and individual self-growth. But America's history is, in reality, a tangle of subcultures and myriad patterns of cultural self-definition. For Mary Antin, the enthusiastic assimilationist discussed in chapter 8, self-growth led her away from her family's culture to conform ardently to mainstream values. Conversely, immigrant and religious subcultures, in the very process of conserving their own values and traditions and urging their children to do the same, have contributed to diversity and dissent within the larger society. The polarities don't line up because the cultures of family, ethnic group, school, and workplace often don't; each individual's cultural identity is acquired by reconciling or choosing among these cultures, as we discussed at length in chapter 8. Literacy can expand the thoughtfulness of such choices, not only on the side of dissent but also on the side of tradition. Much assimilation, of course, takes place not through thought and choice but through habituation and conformity. Literacy can serve these functions too.

Cultural consolidation is often associated with popular literature, such as formula fiction and mass-circulation magazines, in part because critics, whether besieged defenders of high culture or proponents of the capitalist system, worry about the threat from commercial mass culture. However, their critiques overlook a second front of cultural consolidation in the history of American literacy, the curriculum of the schools. The schools' version of the consolidation process has involved high culture, not popular culture. Schools have long taught and supported a watered-down or introductory version of high culture. As larger numbers of students spent more years in school, larger numbers of people were exposed to the canon of great writers, to landmark political documents, and to other aspects of Anglo-American high culture. Libraries contributed to this effort, and they too expanded rapidly in the late nineteenth and early twentieth centuries. One of the most persistent and pervasive arguments among librarians has been whether this high-culture function should be paramount, or whether libraries should provide more of the popular literature people seem to want. In schools, the priority of high culture is more secure, although critics have complained that the traditional content has eroded in recent decades and that basal readers should contain more good literature and less pabulum concocted to appeal to children. Still, a far greater percentage of our population was exposed to a smattering of high culture in 1980 than in 1880, because a far greater percentage reached high school.

The schools' role as purveyors of sketchy high culture serves at least three functions. First, educators believe that literature and the arts provide students with substantive benefits: enlightenment, critical thinking, aesthetic uplift, and good character. In the late nineteenth century, for example, the literary focus of the language-arts programs of public schools was justified by its capacity to impart morality.[6] Second, knowledge of high culture can act as cultural capital with real mobility value. Some students absorb enough knowledge of high culture in school classes and in related extracurricular activities to have an impact on their careers. Paul DiMaggio has demonstrated that cultural capital (measured by self-reported involvement in literature and the fine arts) correlates with school grades and with the selection of highly educated marital partners, even when controlling for the family background and measured academic ability of the student.[7] Third, the schools serve to legitimate high culture as a badge of superiority without destroying the exclusiveness of the group that possesses it, because the schools advocate the superiority of high culture without teaching most people very much about it. This is a necessary condition of high culture as cultural capital: it must be both restricted and recognized. Like professionals, who must maintain the difficult balance between monopolizing their expertise and informing the public about their skills enough to engender its respect, possessors of high culture would derive no status benefit if no one knew about it.[8] As DiMaggio has noted, "particularly in the case of a dominant status group, it is important that their culture be recognized as legitimate by, yet be only partially available to, groups that are subordinate to them."[9]

There are, then, two aspects of the consolidation process, both of which are complicated. On the high-culture side, the very value of the exclusiveness of an elite culture depends upon a wide recognition of its

6. See Arthur N. Appleby, *Tradition and Reform in the Teaching of English: A History* (Urbana, Ill.: National Council of Teachers of English, 1974), chap. 2; Venezky, "Origins of the Present-Day Chasm; and G. Stanley Hall, "The High School as the People's College," *Journal of the Proceedings of the Forty-first Annual Meeting of the National Education Association* (1902):265.

7. DiMaggio, "Cultural Capital and School Success," DiMaggio and Mohr, "Cultural Capital."

8. On this function of professional expertise, see Magali Sarfatti Larson, *The Rise of Professionalism: A Sociological Analysis* (Berkeley: University of California Press, 1977), chaps. 4 and 11.

9. DiMaggio, "Cultural Entrepreneurship in Nineteenth-Century Boston, Part II," 303.

legitimacy. Widespread dissemination of a standard high culture at a superficial level thus goes hand in hand with the restriction of sophisticated education in high culture. In the realm of popular culture, capitalism clearly fosters standardization through conglomeration, syndication, centralization, and formulas, but it also promotes, serves, and exploits a dizzying array of diverse interests in our affluent society, some of which are based on topical and incidental identities like hobbies, whereas others are based on ideological and fundamental identities like race and gender. The historical task is to sort out these processes over time and to connect trends in publishing with trends in the broader society.

Readers in 1880

We return again to our starting point of 1880, when the country was broadly, if not highly, literate. School attendance levels were high. Among whites ages five to nineteen, 62 percent reported attending school for some time in the previous year. Local studies suggest that school enrollment clustered in the age range from eight to twelve; school enrollment among this age group was very high among all social classes. School leaving by older children was heavily correlated with ethnicity and parental occupation. One result of this system of widespread but brief education among whites was that 90 percent of them said they were literate. Self-reported literacy rates were somewhat lower for the foreign born (about 88 percent) and much lower for black Americans (less than 40 percent). Schooling was less prevalent in the South for both blacks and whites, but elsewhere white Americans had achieved high rates of rudimentary literacy, and the literacy rate for black Americans was climbing rapidly.[10] The implications of these statistics for adult reading are hard to determine. Only a small portion of people (fewer than 5 percent) graduated from high school, and the book-reading public was probably drawn largely from this small pool. Although newspapers had become less expensive during the nineteenth century, cheap popular magazines and the popular tabloid newspapers were still in the future, the stuff of a second "reading revolution" to come in the 1890s.

Still, print matter was more important in some ways in 1880 than it is today, because travel was less common and there were no electronic media. America was a nation of strangers, characterized by deeply embedded ethnic communities. North and South were divided; the races lived

10. Sanford Winston, *Illiteracy in the United States, from 1870 to 1920* (Chapel Hill: University of North Carolina Press, 1930); Ken A. Simon and W. V. Grant, *Digest of Education Statistics* (Washington, D.C.: Government Printing Office, 1970); Carl F. Kaestle and Maris A. Vinovskis, *Education and Social Change in Nineteenth-Century Massachusetts* (New York: Cambridge University Press, 1980), chap. 4.

apart; labor and management seemed on the verge of a new kind of civil war. Into these diverse communities, knowledge about faraway events and ideas was introduced through newspapers and magazines. If you were a German factory worker in Chicago, and if you developed a critical perspective on work and politics—from your own experience and analysis, from friends, from family or group political traditions—you might decide to read the daily socialist newspaper, *Arbeiter Zeitung*. This would in turn help shape your view of capitalism and of news more generally. If you worked with people who were not readers of *Arbeiter Zeitung,* you might become a transmitter of the information and values that impressed you in that paper. Similarly, if you were a struggling, disgruntled farmer in Ohio, and your view of world events came from the weekly *Grange Bulletin* published in Cincinnati, this might have a central influence on how you interpreted forces beyond your neighborhood that mattered to you. If you were an affluent and highly educated banker, you might choose the *North American Review,* which would reinforce many of your views and inform you of world affairs. Although there was not as much printed matter in the 1880s as later, and not as much topical variety, there were nonetheless distinctly different printed sources of news and opinion, and they played a central role in the transmission of ideas.

Reading helped to create various communities that stretched beyond geographic locale. People of the same religion, the same trade, or the same ethnic group reinforced shared identities by reading specialized newspapers and journals. Various subcultures had emerged within the reading public. There were highly educated people who chose the genteel culture in *Harper's Weekly* and *Scribner's Monthly,* there were enough rural readers to keep four farm journals among the ten best-selling magazines, and dime novels found plenty of readers, many of them working class, as we saw in chapter 2.

During the century between the 1880s and the 1980s, some forces led toward greater diversity of publications, whereas others fostered greater homogenization. The analytical task here is to explore how the mix of these simultaneous processes changed over the decades and whether, on balance, the history of popular print matter in America is well described as an inexorable march toward consolidation. This chapter asserts the following generalizations about the past century's developments in American publishing: First, from the 1880s to the 1920s, contrary trends operated, leaning toward diversity in the 1880s and 1890s, and tipping toward standardization increasingly after 1900. Second, from the 1920s to the 1950s, the forces for standardization predominated, leading to the zenith in the print media's portrayal of a bland, homogeneous American culture. Third, in the 1960s and 1970s, various factors produced a new blend of diversity within a widely shared media culture. In spite of the simplifying terminology of standardization and diversification, however, what happened in the 1960s and 1970s was not a return to a pre-1920 diversity. It was a new blend of centrifugal and centripetal forces, a new version of diversification within some irreversible interdependence and widely shared communication. It is an intriguing puzzle, this recent history, which raises important questions about one-directional accounts of the history of print culture.

The 1880s to the 1920s

After 1880, publications became cheaper and more diverse. Some also became more shrill in their political views, for it was a time of economic depression, heavy immigration, and labor-management warfare. Cultural elites worried about all this diversity. Was American society coming apart? Historians like to say that the period from the 1880s to the 1920s was characterized by a "search for order."[11] The increase in immigration, largely from southern and eastern Europe, prompted cries for immigration restriction and Americanization. The newcomers arrived just in time for the explosion of new print matter. Newspapers were using rotary presses, appealing to broader audiences, and garnering bigger advertising revenues. This drove down the price and provided more range—from the staid old *New York Times,* to new sensationalist urban papers like Joseph Pulitzer's *New York World,* to country papers like the Peoria *Gazette.*

A "magazine revolution" began in the mid-1890s, and by the turn of the century, ten-cent magazines accounted for more than 80 percent of all magazines purchased. Men in leather chairs in clubs worried about the quality of the new, cheap magazines. One defender of *Harper's* and *Scribner's* wrote that the older magazines had "the only audience worth addressing, for it contains the thinking people." But S. S. McClure, one of the most successful of the new editors, told Lincoln Steffens, "My mind and my taste are so common that I'm the best editor."[12] Among the leading magazines were two emerging types: pictorials and, as we saw in chapter 9, women's magazines. The *Ladies' Home Journal* cracked the million-circulation barrier in 1903. By 1920 it was joined by fourteen other magazines with over a million in paid circulation. Religious peri-

11. Robert H. Wiebe, *The Search for Order, 1877–1920* (New York: Hill and Wang, 1967). See also William Graebner, *The Engineering of Consent: Democracy and Authority in Twentieth-Century America* (Madison: University of Wisconsin Press, 1987), and Ellis W. Hawley, *The Great War and the Search for a Modern Order: A History of the American People and Their Institutions, 1917–1933* (New York: St. Martin's Press, 1979).

12. John Tebbel, *The American Magazine: A Compact History* (New York: Hawthorne Books, 1969), 166, 177.

odicals and Sunday-school papers rivaled the big-selling secular magazines.[13]

The number of foreign-language newspapers increased every year from 1885 (when there were 822 foreign-language papers) until 1913 (when there were 1,323).[14] The immigrant press was simultaneously a force for diversity and a force for cultural consolidation. The profusion of foreign languages and foreign news dramatized American ethnic diversity, and its appeal to the working class made the immigrant press a potential forum for prolabor ideas and politically radical perspectives. In other ways, however, the immigrant press was a conservative and homogenizing force. Most papers promoted citizenship, evolved toward English-language publication, instructed their readers about American institutions, and encouraged American consumerism through paid advertising.[15] If the period from 1880 to 1900 was the golden age of the foreign-language press, the period from 1900 to 1920 was the period of its rapid domestication.

Not all papers were assimilated into the mainstream, however. The radical press thrived until World War I. In 1912, there were more than three hundred socialist periodicals, including thirteen daily socialist papers.[16] The labor press also expanded. From broadsides urging job actions to monthly craft journals like the *Locomotive Fireman's Magazine,* labor activists depended on the printed word to express their point of view at a time of increasing class tensions and hard economic times.

Book production was much more limited than that of magazines and newspapers, but even there we can see tendencies toward consolidation and expansion of the reading public as well as renewed diversity. In the 1880s cheap paper editions of English works of fiction, both traditional and new, were becoming very popular. They spread the classics much farther than had been the case earlier in the nineteenth century. One commentator claimed that "Goethe, Dante and Shakespeare [are] read in the backwoods of Arkansas and in the mining camps of Colorado, in the popular 16 and 20 cent editions, by people who could never have afforded

13. Ayer, *American Newspaper Annual.*

14. Park, *Immigrant Press,* 318. See also Joshua A. Fishman, Robert G. Hayden, and Mary E. Warshauer, "The Non-English and the Ethnic Group Press, 1910–1960," in Fishman et al., *Language Loyalty in the United States,* 51–74.

15. Park, *Immigrant Press;* John Briggs, *An Italian Passage: Immigration to Three American Cities, 1890–1930* (New Haven and London: Yale University Press, 1978), chaps. 6 and 8; Marion Tuttle Marzolf, *The Danish-Language Press in America* (New York: Arno Press, 1979); Mordecai Soltes, *The Yiddish Press: An Americanizing Agency* (Philadelphia: Jewish Publication Society, 1925); Carl Wittke, *The German-Language Press in America* (Lexington: University of Kentucky Press, 1957).

16. Joseph R. Conlin, ed., *The American Radical Press, 1880–1960,* 2 vols. (Westport, Conn.: Greenwood Press, 1974), 6.

the books" in hardbound editions.[17] The expansion of the cheap book series into contemporary fiction was encouraged by the lack of an international copyright law. Indeed, publishers of the inexpensive series became leading opponents of a proposed copyright law. The classics would not be affected, but the economic fate of these publishers depended on pirated editions of new works. In addition to Scott, Dickens, and Eliot, countless English mystery writers were sold in paper editions by Riverside, Appleton, and other venturesome publishers. In 1886 twenty-six such series issued 1,551 titles.[18]

In spite of opposition, the copyright law passed in 1891, supported by the more prestigious publishers, who opposed the cheap paper editions, by America authors, whose works were too expensive compared with pirated English fiction, and by American typesetters, after Congress included a clause requiring protected foreign works to be set and produced in the United States. The copyright law led to a new emphasis on American authors and to a new diversity in the book market as a whole. In this burst of activity, some writers expressed critical attitudes about society, foreshadowing Theodore Dreiser, Hart Crane, American realism, and muckraking journalism.[19]

Meanwhile, some conservatives feared not just political dissent in print but the fragmentation of knowledge among educated people. Could the very best writings in American culture unify an expanding body of readers? There was a threefold increase in the number of books published between 1880 and 1900, and there were more high-school and college graduates to read them. But these new readers had to choose among a confusing array of publications, and consensus about what was "best" was eroding with the onset of literary modernism. An insistent demand for information and expertise accompanied the expansion of the press in the early decades of the twentieth century, and it threatened the hegemony of liberal culture.[20]

In spite of these worries about splintering in the reading public, there were some underlying forces of standardization. Affecting not only the publishing industries but also the entire society was the modern national-level corporation, which became the dominant business organization in America by World War I. Competition in the mass market created a new culture of advertising and consumerism. The brand names, the products, and the advertisements all became part of American culture. Big national corporations gave us Campbell soups and Diamond

17. Shove, *Cheap Book Production,* 40.
18. Ibid., 24–28.
19. Hart, *Popular Book,* 179; Lehmann-Haupt, Wroth, and Silver, *Book in America,* 318.
20. Rubin, "Self, Culture, and Self-Culture in Modern America."

matches, but big-scale enterprise also affected the way the publishing industry itself operated.[21]

Newspaper content became more standard with the arrival of the national wire services and syndicated features; notions of an "objective" stance and a standard style gained ground as reporters found themselves producing stories that would run simultaneously in newspapers across the country. By the 1890s the Associated Press was joined by the United Press and other news services. Comics began in 1896 with the "Yellow Kid," followed by "The Katzenjammer Kids" the next year. In the 1890s the Hearst news service was distributing travel columns, Sunday magazine articles, and columns like Mr. Dooley. People around the country thus increasingly were reading the same materials.[22]

The period from the 1880s to the 1920s, then, witnessed both diversification and standardization of published reading material, with diversity predominating before 1900, and standardization gaining. Between the 1920s and the 1950s the forces for consolidation went into high gear.

The 1920s to the 1950s

As the period opened, heightened concern about political radicals and foreign influences was dramatized in the Red Scare. The wartime drive for unity and the fear of subversion had spawned massive government propaganda and the suppression of dissenting publications. It did not simply dissipate after the war, but created harsher pressures for conformity and assimilation.[23] In addition, Congress restricted immigration; with fewer and fewer first-generation immigrants in the population, immigrant newspapers tended to fold or Americanize. Education levels rose; as increasing numbers of people attended and completed high school, the potential book-reading public expanded. Whereas only 32 percent of fourteen- to seventeen-year-olds were in school in 1920, by 1950 more than 77 percent were.[24] Newspapers exposed an increasing

21. Chandler, *Visible Hand;* Richard W. Fox and T. J. Jackson Lears, eds., *The Culture of Consumption: Critical Essays in American History, 1880–1980* (New York: Pantheon Books, 1983); Stephen Fox, *The Mirror Makers: A History of American Advertising and Its Creators* (New York: William Morrow, 1984). For contrasting views on the manipulative power of advertising, see Stuart Ewen, *Captains of Consciousness: Advertising and the Social Roots of the Consumer Culture* (New York: McGraw-Hill, 1976), and Schudson, *Advertising.*

22. Watson, *History of Newspaper Syndicates;* Bill Blackbeard and Martin Williams, eds., *The Smithsonian Collection of Newspaper Comics* (Washington, D.C.: Smithsonian Institution Press, 1977).

23. See David M. Kennedy, *Over Here: The First World War and American Society* (New York: Oxford University Press, 1980), chap. 1; Harry N. Scheiber, *The Wilson Administration and Civil Liberties, 1917–1921* (Ithaca: Cornell University Press, 1960).

24. Simon and Grant, *Digest of Education Statistics.*

number of readers to comics, sports, and national events, while radio and the movies created other popular heroes.

The number of cities with competing daily newspapers dropped dramatically. The total number of newspapers thus was declining at the same time that circulation was increasing. Chains controlled more and more papers—in 1910, 10 percent, and by 1935, 40 percent. All papers carried less local news and more syndicated features. After traveling around the country in 1930, Oswald Villard, editor of the *Nation,* observed that "one finds the same comics, the same Sunday magazines, the same special features in almost all of [the papers], and, of course, in most of them precisely the same Associated Press news."[25] Publishers had to consolidate so they could afford expensive typesetting machines and presses. Although more and more people were reading newspapers, the newspapers they were reading were more and more alike.

Magazines experienced a similar evolution. They were driven by the need for advertising revenue, and they reflected the cultural pressures for conformity that characterized American life. The number of periodicals declined slightly between 1930 and 1958, even though the population and the reading public increased.[26] The big leaders got the big circulations and the big advertising accounts. By 1920, Curtis, publisher of the *Ladies' Home Journal,* the *Saturday Evening Post,* and *Country Gentleman,* already had 40 percent of all advertising dollars, and Crowell, with *Collier's* and the *Woman's Home Companion,* had another 12 percent.[27] Some critics emphasize that the dependence on advertising inhibited the publication of views critical of the capitalist system.[28] Whatever the effect of such self-censorship, advertising had two additional impacts: it increased the number of readers who read the same best-selling magazines, and it provided some of America's popular culture through the advertising copy itself. From Maine to New Mexico, readers of popular magazines knew that "L.S.M.F.T." was the abbreviation for "Lucky Strike Means Fine Tobacco."

By 1920 annual growth in magazine circulation was greatly outstripping population growth. Back in 1880, no magazine circulation had equaled 1 percent of the United States population. By 1920, eight magazines had circulations bigger than 1 percent of the population; by 1950, twenty-four did.[29] By then the leading magazines in America were mostly like each other, and they were found in most middle-class homes.

25. Emery, *The Press and America,* 461, 465.
26. Peterson, *Magazines in the Twentieth Century,* 2d ed., 68.
27. Ibid., 84–85.
28. Bagdikian, *Media Monopoly,* 235.
29. Calculations from Ayer's *American Newspaper Annual.*

Life, Look, Collier's, and the *Saturday Evening Post* helped to set the agenda of public issues and social reform.[30] The *Ladies' Home Journal, Woman's Home Companion, McCall's,* and *Woman's Day* catered to middle-class women's interests. *Reader's Digest* and *Time* presented busy people with a ready selection of news and views.[31]

Books did not follow this pattern as closely, but there were efforts at standardization; examples include the creation of the Literary Guild and the Book-of-the-Month Club in the 1920s, which resulted in the large-scale distribution of standardized book lists. A different form of standardization of book reading took place through the schools. As more people went to high school and as the canon of literary works taught became standardized, more American teenagers were introduced to the same books at the same time.[32]

Meanwhile, the range of content in printed publications narrowed somewhat, even as the total amount of publication increased. The foreign-language press declined after 1920. The press of the populists, socialists, anarchists, and other radicals fragmented, failed, or moved underground. The Hispanic press was waning by the 1950s, and in 1954 a sociologist predicted, "it is probable that in 15 years the Spanish-language press will virtually have died out."[33] He was incorrect, but his projection reflected the trends of his day.

Censorship or subtle self-censorship probably was no worse in 1950 than in 1880, but it should be mentioned as a constraint on diversity, preventing books from straying along paths deemed immoral or politically dangerous. In *Purity in Print,* Paul Boyer emphasized that our society has generally resisted blatant censorship crusades like those of the antivice societies of the 1920s; nonetheless, censorship efforts combined with marketing factors to produce some chilling effect. In the 1930s, "manuscripts were nervously evaluated in the light of Depression tastes," wrote Boyer. "In a time of financial stringency, the mass distribution of broadly popular books became the goal. . . . The mass-market standards of the book clubs continued subtly to influence the editorial judgments of publishers with an eye on this lucrative source of sales."[34] The movie industry concurrently and voluntarily supported efforts to revive confidence in and loyalty to traditional American values, and in

30. Van Zuilen, *Life Cycle of Magazines.*
31. Ibid.
32. On the literary canon in American high schools, see Appleby, *Tradition and Reform in the Teaching of English,* chap. 3.
33. John Burma, quoted in Felix Guttierez, "Spanish-Language Media in America: Background, Resources, History," *Journalism History* 4 (Summer 1977):34.
34. Paul S. Boyer, *Purity in Print: The Vice-Society Movement and Book Censorship in America* (New York: Scribner's, 1968), 262.

the postwar anti-Communist days rooted out dissenters and dissent with a vengeance.[35]

By the early 1950s the artifacts of American popular culture had achieved cultural homogenization. Radios reached everybody, newspapers were heavily consolidated, and the leading magazines were similar in content and appearance and devoted to selling the same products. War and McCarthyism had dampened political dissent, movies followed safe formulas, and the foreign-language press was a mere shadow of what it had been. The organization man was a central cultural image; homemaking for women was a value promoted throughout the world of print. Big labor had become respectable and unions were organized; they bargained by agreed-upon rules.

Of course, dissent and diversity still existed. Many Americans remained excluded from power and privilege, and many expressed their dissent. But one wouldn't find it in the reading materials that faced most readers each day. Technology, capitalism, politics, and education had combined to homogenize the world of print as never before. The society was not really homogeneous, but print culture was, to an unprecedented degree.

The 1950s to the 1980s

Who was waiting in the wings? Herbert Marcuse, C. Wright Mills, Norman Mailer, Martin Luther King, and Gloria Steinem. Said Mills: "Let the old women complain wisely about 'the end of ideology.' We are beginning to move again."[36] By the end of the decade, the nervous, conformist mainstream culture of the 1950s was under assault. From the mid-1960s to the mid-1970s American public life bristled with diversity—a youth rebellion, an exploding civil rights movement, a white ethnic revival, the women's movement, increased immigration among Hispanic and Asian groups, and a revival of fundamentalist Protestantism. All of these divergent forces had an impact on reading in America.

Technological and marketing factors reinforced these divergent tendencies. The paperback revolution provided drugstores and newsstands with titles on all sorts of topics, both wide-ranging and controversial. The general-interest magazine gave way to magazines targeted at more

35. Robert Sklar, *Movie-Made America: A Cultural History of American Movies* (New York: Random House, 1975), chaps. 11 and 15. Gerald Mast, ed., *The Movies in Our Midst* (Chicago: University of Chicago Press, 1982), contains several relevant essays on the motion-picture code of 1930 and on the House Un-American Activities Committee hearings of 1947 and their aftermath.

36. C. Wright Mills, "The New Left," in *Power, Politics and People,* ed. Irving Horowitz (New York: Ballantine Books, 1963), 259.

focused groups because television had garnered the advertising revenues for general audiences. Into this market situation marched all the audiences of the 1960s and 1970s, producing both topical and ideological diversity.

There was a revival of the foreign-language press in general, and of the Hispanic press in particular. Non-English newspapers and periodicals increased from 704 in 1962 to 1,031 in 1982, whereas the number of English-language publications remained stable, prompting Joshua Fishman to conclude that "contrary to 'popular wisdom,' the ethnic mother-tongue press in the U.S.A. constitutes a vigorous institutional field of activity."[37] The rise of the Spanish-language press was spectacular, from 49 publications in 1960 (with a circulation of about 500,000) to 165 publications in 1980 (with a circulation of more than 2.5 million).[38]

The religious press also thrived in this period, particularly among fundamentalist and evangelical Protestants. Although rooted in the 1920s and 1930s, the fundamentalist press grew slowly, even after the founding of the Christian Booksellers Association in 1950. In the 1970s, however, fundamentalist and evangelical publishing mushroomed; the number of bookstores affiliated with the Christian Booksellers Association increased from 1,000 to 2,400 between 1971 and 1978. The publishing activities of this religious subculture were immense and largely invisible to the mainstream press. In 1982 Francis Schaeffer's *Christian Manifesto* was outselling *Jane Fonda's Workout Book* by a two-to-one margin, yet the *Workout Book* was the *New York Times* number one best seller, and Schaeffer's book wasn't even on the list.[39]

The radical press also revived and expanded in the late 1960s, solidifying dissent and reinforcing doubts about American mainstream institutions. Although many countercultural publications had failed or been commercialized by the late 1970s, in its heyday the "underground press" counted perhaps two million readers, and there was a sense of tremendous diversity, questioning, and innovation in these publica-

37. Joshua A. Fishman et al., "Ethnicity in Action: The Community Resources of Ethnic Languages in the United States," in *The Rise and Fall of the Ethnic Revival: Perspectives on Language and Ethnicity,* ed. Fishman et al. (New York: Mouton, 1985), 214.

38. Ofelia Garcia et al., "The Hispanic Press in the United States: Content and Prospects," in *Rise and Fall of the Ethnic Revival,* ed. Fishman et al., 344.

39. Carol Flake, *Redemptorama: Culture, Politics and the New Evangelicalism* (Garden City, N.Y.: Anchor Press, 1984), 151, 165; see also J. Alan Youngren, "Christian Booksellers Find Happiness in Slow Growth," *Christianity Today,* September 4, 1981, 64, which discussed the "tremendous and tumultuous growth" of the early and mid-1970s.

tions.[40] A new feminist press subsequently emerged, and it has endured. *Ms.* magazine and the academic journal *Signs* were only two examples of a widespread movement that created hundreds of books, journals, publishing units, and bookstores.[41] The gay press, tiny and insecure before the 1950s, also expanded. *One,* the *Mattachine Review,* and the *Ladder* began in the 1950s. In 1958 *One* was protected from obscenity charges by the Supreme Court, and in the 1960s and 1970s gay publications increased exponentially, contributing to gay liberation activities in the 1970s and to the development of a strong gay subculture.[42]

Black-owned book publishing experienced a dramatic rise after 1960. Increased economic status, rising racial pride, and expanded civil rights activity combined to encourage "the most rapid proliferation of new black book publishers in the century."[43] The output of titles by black-owned publishers soared from fewer than 15 between 1950 and 1954 to more than 165 between 1970 and 1974.[44] The relationship of the black press to cultural consolidation and cultural diversity is complicated. In some ways the development of the black press fits the patterns outlined above: starting from the limited-circulation special-interest publications of the 1880 to 1920 period, black publishing shared the trend toward consolidation, with the advent of national advertising, newspaper chains like the Scott World papers, and general-interest magazines like *Ebony.* Furthermore, many black magazines of the 1950s acquiesced in a homogenized middle-class consumer stereotype. But in the 1960s and 1970s black publishing took off, due to the same interaction of technology and marketing with political and cultural activism that fueled the publications of other groups. In spite of these similarities, the black press remained consistently diverse; some publications were more radically separatist, some more assimilationist, and—as with the immigrant press—a single publication could serve both purposes simultaneously.

Small-press publishing in general soared in the 1960s and 1970s. Offset printing and entrepreneurship created such publishing sensations as *The Whole Earth Catalog.* In 1958, 1,000 publishers issued 13,500 titles; by 1985, 15,000 publishers, most of them issuing fewer than 5 titles each, issued 50,000 new titles.[45] Offset printing is less

40. Everette E. Dennis and William L. Rivers, *Other Voices: The New Journalism in America* (San Francisco: Canfield Press, 1974); Donna Lloyd Ellis, "The Underground Press in America: 1955–1970," *Journal of Popular Culture* 5 (Summer 1971):102–24.

41. Fox-Genovese, "New Female Literary Culture."

42. Alan D. Winter, *The Gay Press: A History of the Gay Community and Its Publications* (published by the author, 1976).

43. Joyce, *Gatekeepers of Black Culture,* 101.

44. Ibid., 147.

45. Michael Gabriel, "The Growth of the Small Publisher in the United States, 1960–1985," unpublished research paper, University of Wisconsin, January 1986.

capital intensive as a technological innovation; people can (and do) produce commercially viable books in their basements. The small-press phenomenon is an interesting counterpoint to the consolidating trends of bookstore franchising and formula-romance production, and it tells us something about the relationship of technology to the diversity of print culture. Rotary letterpress printing may have led initially to diversity of newspaper style and content, as the reading public expanded and editors like Pulitzer and Hearst shaped new popular dailies; but in the long run, letterpress technology required large-scale organization and capital and thus contributed to the drift toward consolidated control. Offset printing, in contrast, does not carry with it the necessary connection to large-scale control. Like microcomputers, offset presses are amenable to small-scale individualization of output. Thus the argument against technological determinism is not simply that any technology can be used to any purpose (which is false), but that different technologies can lead in different directions and that their impact depends not only upon their own inherent qualities but also upon cultural factors. And in the late 1960s and early 1970s cultural factors favored the expression of diversity.

Schools also reflected the newly diverse world of print culture in the 1970s. Aided by the availability of paperbacks and individualized curriculum materials, some schools presented wider cultural views, more racially and ethnically diverse and more flexible on moral issues. When they did so, public schools alienated some of their oldest allies—middle-class Protestants with traditional values.[46] Alienation and broken consensus about public schools conformed to a general mistrust of institutions in the 1970s. Watergate was simply the last straw; Americans had been on a slide toward political alienation since 1960.[47]

Was everything coming apart? Of course not. Some features of American reading materials were very sturdy. Consumerism, patriotism, the comic strips, professional athletics, advertisements that appealed to sexual stereotypes, newspapers that focused on sensational crime—all of these characterized our reading material from the 1950s through the 1980s, with little change. Many publications survived almost unchanged in appearance and outlook—among them *Playboy,* the *New York Times Book Review, Newsweek,* the *Ladies' Home Journal,* the *National Review,* and *National Geographic.* It must be acknowledged that the diverse new publications of the 1960s and 1970s thus joined a considerable roster of publications that had survived for decades with little change. And be-

46. Carl F. Kaestle, "Moral Education and Common Schools in America: A Historian's View," *Journal of Moral Education* 13 (May 1984):101–11; Robert M. O'Neil, *Classrooms in the Crossfire* (Bloomington: Indiana University Press, 1981), chap. 2.

47. James D. Wright, *The Dissent of the Governed* (New York: Academic Press, 1976), chap. 7.

yond the publishing industries many processes of consolidation in American life continued. Education levels continued in a convergent direction in the 1960s and early 1970s. Inexpensive travel and the ubiquitous presence of the electronic media continued, as did the concentration of newspaper ownership. The paperback industry moved from diversity toward an emphasis on the blockbuster best seller, and a large share of other paperback sales were in formula romances. Most Americans of the 1980s were plugged into the same electronic news, the same big-network entertainment, and the same fast-food franchises.

Still, the print world was more diverse in 1985 than in 1955. One needed only to compare *Ms.* with *Penthouse* to appreciate how diverse some of our leading publications had become. The experiences of the 1960s and 1970s suggest that capitalism and the technology of modern publishing do not always increase standardization of the printed word. Although the powerful forces of consolidation properly give rise to concern about the quality and diversity of print publication in the future, there has thus far always been an interplay between diversity and standardization, and that diversity has been both topical and ideological. This interpretation is less deterministic than that of Harold Innis or Raymond Williams. Despite the numbing mediocrity and homogenization of much popular culture, and despite the general trend toward cultural consolidation, there has always been the possibility of rejuvenation and diversification, sometimes as a general trend, always as a minor counterpoint to the dominant culture in print.

Will the future bring further homogenization, along with a deepening of the passivity and exploitation characteristic of the worst of popular culture, or can American culture as reflected in print be continually renewed through the initiative of creative and committed people? We can easily imagine a drab future twenty years from now. Almost all the bookstores will belong to two national bookstore chains, and 75 percent of their business will come from formula romances; 90 percent of the newspaper-reading population will read a single four-color national newspaper that assiduously supports government policies. Rupert Murdoch will own the most prestigious literary publishing houses and determine the selection of novelists to be published. Although such glum predictions are plausible, the important point is that we can affect the outcome. We must not sit helplessly by and wonder what technology and capitalism will do to us, and we must not think that a political revolution is the only way to modify the effects of technology and capitalism on the production of culture. We must convince educators, legislators, and readers in general that the future of print is important to democracy and to healthy diversity. Policies as far-flung as antitrust legislation, postal rates, taxes on publishers' inventories, procedures for school textbook selection, and budgets for the state humanities endowments relate to the future of diversity in print. Beyond formal policies, influential people who believe in diversity need to muster public opinion in support of pluralistic education, in support of independent bookstores, and against censorship. If we could convince everyone to think more comprehensively, more pluralistically, and more urgently about the future of print, we could be more optimistic. In the publishing industries, as in other important areas of collective life, we are not well advised to let free-market forces entirely govern outcomes. And we must not treat the production of culture as we would the production of widgets.

The ideal, of course, is a culture that offers many easy opportunities for expression, orally and in print, a culture with lots of debate, but still a culture with shared knowledge and values, promoted by schools, families, the electronic media, and the print media, a culture in which the heroes of the civil rights movement become important along with the heroes of the American Revolution, feminist classics along with the traditional standard works, black and Hispanic poets along with Anglo poets. Although the ideal can never be fully realized, it is an ideal worth having as a guide when fighting the blandness of basal readers and situation comedies, when contending with frustrated advocates of Anglo conformity and back-to-the-fifties curriculum, or when pondering the delicate issues of government support and regulation of cultural production.

Epilogue

Even if this ideal of healthy diversity and a shared pluralistic culture were to be accepted by all Americans, an optimistic vision of the future is impossible if higher levels of literacy do not become more widespread. A common culture cannot be shared if the literacy abilities needed to understand and enjoy it are not shared. The history of American literacy is a story of narrowing literacy gaps, but recent literacy assessments have made us painfully aware that literacy abilities still vary dramatically across racial, ethnic, and income groups. We must not tolerate this kind of diversity. The fundamental threat posed by America's literacy problems today is not that the Japanese will beat us at math tests and computer chips, but that democracy will wane in the twenty-first century.

As we saw in chapter 3, alarming gaps exist between the basic literacy skills of different groups defined on the basis of ethnicity or income. At higher levels of literacy, the problems become pervasive across all social groups. We are at a historic moment in the 1990s, analogous to the 1920s in some ways but at a higher literacy level. In the 1920s, just when

Americans thought they had achieved some control over rudimentary literacy rates by limiting immigration and improving the reach of public schooling, testing experts began to warn that among the nominally literate were far too many who could not use their literacy. The army's entrance tests displayed shocking gaps between the races, gaps that were heavily discussed during the 1920s. And when the 1930 census reported low outright-illiteracy figures, the reading expert William Gray reminded educators that there were millions "who have learned to engage in the very simplest reading and writing activities but have not attained functioning literacy."[48]

Today it appears again that the viability of democratic politics and the productivity of our economic system depend on a further escalation of our literacy expectations. Reports that deskilled jobs are increasing must not distract us from the abundant evidence that overall literacy requirements are increasing in the workplace. Reports that most people get their news from television must not overshadow the fact that if people are to be empowered, they require critical reading and writing skills.

Higher-level critical literacy abilities for all children must become a central goal of schools. Other public policies must complement the literacy work of the schools, for they cannot do it alone. History tells us that oppressed groups in America have focused on literacy as a critical tool and as an entrée into the mainstream. They have acquired literacy skills through a combination of formal public institutions, such mediating institutions as clubs and churches, and the family. The recent study of literacy by the National Assessment of Educational Progress reinforced the notion that schools cannot do the job alone. In that assessment the reading abilities of young adults correlated with a wide variety of family factors—not just race, family income, and their parents' educational level, but also the number of publications that entered the home and how often the youths read them.[49]

The implications of this finding for public policy are problematic. It is easier to affect formal institutions through public policy than it is to influence the family. There are, nonetheless, both direct and indirect ways in which government can affect the literacy potential of families. We can spend more money on adult literacy agencies, and we can focus it in different ways, for example, toward parents whose own literacy abilities are inadequate and who want to help their children read better. Other direct policies include high-quality day-care centers and income support for the mothers of young children. While implementing these policies, governments can bolster mediating institutions and push liter-

48. William S. Gray, "Catching Up with Literacy," National Education Association, 71st Annual Meeting, *Proceedings* (Washington, D.C., 1933), 280.
49. Kirsch and Jungeblut, *Literacy: Final Report,* chap. 7.

acy to a higher place on their agendas. Adult literacy training can be done in collaboration with day care, or in libraries, or by "storefront" neighborhood organizations. Policies indirectly related to literacy are equally necessary and even more difficult. Because motivation for learning is as important as a family's resources, we must try to remove motivational obstacles to learning. We must fight discrimination, drugs, unemployment, and low wages. We must work toward a fair society, in which there will be ample opportunity for all to use their literacy abilities in meaningful ways.

The ideal of a diverse but inclusive literacy requires effort on both sides of the equation—we need both a lively diversity of accessible reading materials and a highly literate population. The first condition seems to ebb and flow, but it is in tension with the long-run trend toward consolidation in the publishing industries and has not been the focus of much public policy or debate. Considering the free-speech guarantees of our Constitution and the capacity of various technologies to serve diversity as well as standardization, it might seem that the capacity for diverse printed expression will always be with us and is not in need of further guarantees. But considering the powerful effect of the profit motive, of marketing, and of organizational structure in the publishing industries, such a laissez-faire attitude is dangerous. In the absence of imaginative policies that will protect and foster diverse access to print, corporate policies, corporate priorities, and corporate organization threaten important avenues of expression in our society. Because the erosion is generally gradual and inoffensive to most citizens, most policy makers do not become aroused. We hope that historical awareness will lead readers to think about the need to protect diversity in print.

To achieve the second requisite—the general diffusion of high-level literacy skills—we must mobilize schools, families, and other institutions in a new escalation of literacy abilities. If we can do this while preserving the diversity and the broad participation that are essential to democratic life, we will have preserved and deepened the essential connection between literacy and the Republic.

Appendix

Personal Expenditures in Billions of Constant 1982 Dollars
(constant dollars are determined separately for each category)

	1929	1934	1939	1944	1949	1954	1959	1964	1969	1974	1979	1984	1986*
Total consumption	471.4	390.5	480.5	557.1	695.4	822.7	979.4	1,170.6	1,456.7	1,674.0	2,004.4	2,246.3	2,419.1
Total recreation	22.7	17.7	22.5	28.9	35.1	39.4	44.1	53.7	74.0	97.1	126.7	159.9	182.2
Mass media	14.2	11.5	14.2	19.8	22.5	23.9	22.5	24.9	33.5	41.7	50.1	63.0	77.7
Reading	6.5	5.3	6.4	9.3	10.8	11.8	11.9	13.0	15.7	18.6	19.8	18.4	18.1
Magazines and newspapers	4.7	4.1	4.9	6.6	8.1	8.8	8.5	8.4	10.0	12.1	12.8	11.4	11.5
Books and maps	1.8	1.2	1.5	2.7	2.8	3.1	3.5	4.6	5.7	6.5	7.1	7.0	6.7
Audiovisual	7.7	6.3	7.8	10.5	11.6	12.1	10.6	12.0	17.8	23.1	30.3	44.6	59.6
Electronic	.6	.4	.8	.6	1.9	3.7	4.4	6.3	11.6	16.9	22.8	36.4	51.4
Radios, TVs, and records	.6	.3	.7	.4	1.4	2.7	3.1	4.8	9.6	13.9	19.7	33.8	48.7
Radio and TV repair	.0	.1	.1	.2	.5	1.0	1.2	1.5	2.0	3.0	3.1	2.6	2.7
Admissions	7.1	5.9	7.0	9.9	9.7	8.3	6.2	5.7	6.2	6.2	7.4	8.2	8.1
Motion picture	5.9	5.3	6.2	8.8	8.1	6.7	4.2	3.2	3.2	3.2	3.4	3.4	3.2
Legitimate theaters	1.0	.4	.6	.9	.9	1.0	1.2	1.1	1.0	1.1	1.8	2.3	2.6
Spectator sports	.2	.2	.3	.2	.7	.6	.8	1.3	2.0	2.0	2.2	2.4	2.4
Non-mass-media	8.5	6.2	8.3	9.2	12.7	15.5	21.6	28.8	40.6	55.4	76.6	96.9	104.5
Nondurable toys and sports supplies	1.3	.9	1.2	1.3	2.8	3.7	5.0	6.4	8.9	11.7	15.6	19.9	21.1
Durable toys and sports equipment	.6	.4	.8	.9	1.9	2.6	4.4	5.1	9.7	14.3	21.0	22.4	27.3
Flowers, seeds, and plants	1.0	.7	1.3	1.1	1.2	1.5	1.7	2.6	3.7	4.4	4.9	5.1	5.8
Clubs and fraternal organizations	2.2	1.7	1.6	1.6	2.1	2.1	3.0	3.2	3.5	3.1	3.4	4.2	4.5
Commercial amusement	2.0	1.4	1.8	1.8	2.1	2.1	2.7	4.1	4.7	7.1	10.0	13.2	13.4
Parimutuel net receipts	.1	.2	.3	.8	.8	1.1	1.3	1.8	1.9	2.1	2.2	2.1	2.1
Other	1.3	1.0	1.3	1.8	1.9	2.4	3.6	5.5	8.1	12.7	19.5	29.9	30.3
Print (reading) + electronic	7.1	5.7	7.1	9.8	12.7	15.5	16.3	19.3	27.3	35.4	42.6	54.8	69.6
Population (millions)	121.8	126.4	130.9	138.4	149.2	162.4	177.8	191.9	202.7	213.3	225.1	237.0	241.5
Population 18 years and older (millions)	78.6	84.6	90.3	97.2	103.4	108.7	114.8	122.2	132.9	145.4	161.0	174.2	178.0

Calculated data (calculated from the above data before rounding):	1929	1934	1939	1944	1949	1954	1959	1964	1969	1974	1979	1984	1986
Reading Expenditures per person	53.70	41.64	48.67	66.97	72.58	72.82	67.18	67.51	77.49	87.02	88.13	77.80	75.06
Magazines and newspapers	38.86	32.44	37.09	47.49	54.02	53.96	47.75	43.58	49.19	56.77	56.78	48.09	47.49
Books and maps	14.84	9.20	11.58	19.48	18.56	18.86	19.43	23.93	28.30	30.25	31.34	29.70	27.57
Reading Expenditures per person (18 & over)	83.17	62.24	70.52	95.41	104.67	108.76	104.08	106.00	118.17	127.71	123.22	105.84	101.83
Magazines and newspapers	60.19	48.49	53.75	67.66	77.91	80.59	73.98	68.43	75.01	83.32	79.40	65.43	64.43
Books and maps	22.98	13.75	16.78	27.75	26.77	28.17	30.10	37.58	43.16	44.39	43.83	40.41	37.40
Reading as % total	1.39	1.35	1.33	1.66	1.56	1.44	1.22	1.11	1.08	1.11	.99	.82	.75
Magazines and newspapers	1.00	1.05	1.01	1.18	1.16	1.07	.87	.71	.68	.72	.64	.51	.47
Books and maps	.38	.30	.32	.48	.40	.37	.35	.39	.39	.39	.35	.31	.28
Magazines and newspapers as % reading	72.37	77.90	76.21	70.91	74.43	74.10	71.08	64.55	63.48	65.24	64.43	61.82	63.27
Books and maps as % reading	27.63	22.10	23.79	29.09	25.57	25.90	28.92	35.45	36.52	34.76	35.57	38.18	36.73
Reading as % recreation	28.81	29.67	28.33	32.03	30.84	30.03	27.08	24.11	21.21	19.12	15.65	11.53	9.95
Magazines and newspapers	20.85	23.12	21.59	22.71	22.95	22.25	19.24	15.57	13.47	12.47	10.09	7.13	6.29
Books and maps	7.96	6.56	6.74	9.32	7.89	7.78	7.83	8.55	7.75	6.64	5.57	4.40	3.65
Reading as % mass media	45.95	45.63	44.92	46.92	48.21	49.51	53.03	51.99	46.93	44.54	39.60	29.25	23.33
Magazines and newspapers	33.25	35.55	34.23	33.27	35.88	36.69	37.70	33.56	29.79	29.06	25.51	18.09	14.76
Books and maps	12.70	10.08	10.68	13.65	12.33	12.82	15.34	18.43	17.14	15.48	14.08	11.17	8.57
Electronic as % mass media	4.17	3.39	5.38	2.93	8.45	15.55	19.32	25.31	34.60	40.50	45.54	57.69	66.21
Mass media as % total	3.02	2.95	2.95	3.55	3.23	2.90	2.30	2.13	2.30	2.49	2.50	2.81	3.21
Audiovisual	1.63	1.61	1.63	1.88	1.67	1.47	1.08	1.02	1.22	1.38	1.51	1.99	2.46
Electronic	.13	.10	.16	.10	.27	.45	.44	.54	.79	1.01	1.14	1.62	2.13
Recreation as % total	4.81	4.54	4.68	5.19	5.05	4.79	4.51	4.59	5.08	5.80	6.32	7.12	7.53
Print as % (print + electronic)	91.67	93.08	89.30	94.12	85.09	76.10	73.30	67.26	57.56	52.38	46.51	33.65	26.05
Mass media as % recreation	62.71	65.02	63.08	68.27	63.97	60.65	51.05	46.46	45.21	42.92	39.53	39.42	42.64
Audiovisual	33.89	35.35	34.75	36.24	33.13	30.62	23.98	22.27	23.99	23.80	23.88	27.89	32.69
Electronic	2.62	2.20	3.39	2.00	5.40	9.43	9.86	11.74	15.64	17.38	18.00	22.74	28.23
Print	28.81	29.67	28.33	32.03	30.84	30.03	27.08	24.11	21.21	19.12	15.65	11.53	9.95

*1986 figures are estimates.

Sources:

Expenditure Data: U.S. Department of Commerce, *National Income and Product Account Data for 1929–1986*.

Population Data: U.S. Bureau of the Census, *Historical Statistics of the United States*; U.S. Bureau of the Census, *Statistical Abstract of the United States: 1982–83*, 103d ed.; *Statistical Abstract of the United States: 1985*, 105th ed.; and U.S. Bureau of the Census, *Statistical Abstract of the United States: 1987*, 107th ed.

Bibliography

BOOKS, REPORTS, AND DISSERTATIONS

Adair, Ward. *The Road to New York*. New York: Association Press, 1936.

Addis, Patricia K. *Through a Woman's I: An Annotated Bibliography of American Women's Autobiographical Writings, 1946–1976*. Metuchen, N.J.: Scarecrow Press, 1983.

Adult Performance Level Project. *Final Report: The Adult Performance Level Study*. Washington, D.C.: U.S. Office of Education, 1977.

Advisory Panel on the Scholastic Aptitude Test Score Decline. *On Further Examination*. New York: College Entrance Examination Board, 1977.

Albert, David E. *Dear Grandson*. Philadelphia: Olivier, Maney, 1950.

Aldiss, Brian W., with Wingrove, David. *Trillion Year Spree: The History of Science Fiction*. New York: Atheneum, 1986.

Anderson, Richard C., et al. *Becoming a Nation of Readers: The Report of the Commission on Reading*. Washington, D.C.: National Institute of Education, 1985.

Andrews, Marietta Minnigerode. *Memoirs of a Poor Relation*. New York: E. P. Dutton, 1927.

Antin, Mary. *The Promised Land*. Boston: Houghton Mifflin, 1911.

Appleby, Arthur N. *Tradition and Reform in the Teaching of English: A History*. Urbana, Ill.: National Council of Teachers of English, 1974.

Armbruster, Frank E. *Our Children's Crippled Future: How American Education Has Failed*. New York: Quadrangle, 1977.

Armstrong, April Oursler. *Home with a Hundred Gates*. New York: McGraw-Hill, 1965.

Arnow, Harriette Simpson. *Old Burnside*. Lexington: University of Kentucky Press, 1977.

Austin, Gilbert R., and Garber, Herbert, eds. *The Rise and Fall of National Test Scores*. New York: Academic Press, 1982.

Ayer, N. W. & Son. *American Newspaper Annual and Directory*. Philadelphia: N. W. Ayer & Son, 1880ff. (Title varies.)

Bagdikian, Ben H. *The Media Monopoly*. 3d ed. Boston: Beacon Press, 1990.

Bailyn, Bernard. *Education in the Forming of American Society*. Chapel Hill: University of North Carolina Press, 1960.

Baker, Josephine S. *Fighting for Life*. New York: Macmillan, 1939.

Baughman, James L. *Henry R. Luce and the Rise of the American News Media*. Boston: Twayne, 1987.

Baym, Nina. *Novels, Readers, and Reviewers: Responses to Fiction in Antebellum America*. Ithaca: Cornell University Press, 1984.

———. *Women's Fiction: A Guide to Novels by and about Women in America, 1820–1870*. Ithaca: Cornell University Press, 1978.

Benson, Susan Porter. *Counter Cultures: Saleswomen, Managers, and Customers in American Department Stores, 1890–1940*. Urbana: University of Illinois Press, 1986.

Berelson, Bernard. *The Library's Public: A Report of the Public Library Inquiry*. New York: Columbia University Press, 1949.

Berg, Ivar, and Gorelick, Sherry. *Education and Jobs: The Great Training Robbery*. Boston: Beacon Press, 1971.

Berger, Peter, and Luckmann, Thomas. *The Social Construction of Reality*. Garden City, N.Y.: Doubleday, 1966.

Berlin, Gordon, and Sum, Andrew. *Toward a More Perfect Union: Basic Skills, Poor Families, and Our Economic Future*. New York: Ford Foundation, 1988.

Blackbeard, Bill, and Williams, Martin, eds. *The Smithsonian Collection of Newspaper Comics*. Washington, D.C.: Smithsonian Institution Press, 1977.

Bloor, Ella Reeve. *We Are Many*. New York: International Publishers, 1940.

Blumler, Jay G., and Katz, Elihu, eds. *The Uses of Mass Communications: Current Perspectives on Gratifications Research*. Beverly Hills, Calif.: Sage, 1974.

Bobinski, George S. *Carnegie Libraries: Their History and Impact on American Public Library Development*. Chicago: American Library Association, 1969.

Bok, Edward. *A Man from Maine*. New York: Charles Scribner's Sons, 1923.

Bold, Christine. *Selling the Wild West: Popular Western Fiction, 1860–1960*. Bloomington: Indiana University Press, 1987.

Bonn, Thomas L. *Heavy Traffic and High Culture: New American Library as Literary Gatekeeper in the Paperback Revolution.* Carbondale: Southern Illinois University Press, 1989.

Borkow, Nancy. *Analysis of Test Score Trends: Implications for Secondary School Policy—A Caution to Secondary School Administrators.* Washington, D.C.: National Institute of Education, 1982.

Bourdieu, Pierre. *Distinction: A Social Critique of the Judgment of Taste.* Trans. Richard Nice. Cambridge: Harvard University Press, 1984.

The Bowker Annual of Library and Book Trade Information. New York: R. R. Bowker, 1964.

Bowles, Samuel, and Gintis, Herbert. *Schooling in Capitalist America.* New York: Basic Books, 1976.

Boyer, Paul S. *Purity in Print: The Vice-Society Movement and Book Censorship in America.* New York: Charles Scribner's Sons, 1968.

Brantlinger, Patrick. *Bread and Circuses: Theories of Mass Culture as Social Decay.* Ithaca: Cornell University Press, 1983.

Briggs, John. *An Italian Passage: Immigration to Three American Cities, 1890–1930.* New Haven and London: Yale University Press, 1978.

Brignano, Russell C. *Black Americans in Autobiography: An Annotated Bibliography of Autobiographies and Autobiographical Books Written since the Civil War.* Rev. ed. Durham, N.C.: Duke University Press, 1984.

Briscoe, Mary Louise. *American Autobiography, 1945–1980: A Bibliography.* Madison: University of Wisconsin Press, 1982.

Brown, Richard D. *Knowledge Is Power: The Diffusion of Information in Early America, 1700–1865.* New York: Oxford University Press, 1989.

Bryson, Lyman, ed. *The Communication of Ideas.* New York: Institute for Religious and Social Studies, 1948.

Buswell, Guy T. *How Adults Read.* Chicago: University of Chicago, Department of Education, Monographs, no. 45, 1937.

Campbell, Angus, and Metzner, Charles. *Public Use of the Library and Other Sources of Information.* Ann Arbor: University of Michigan, Institute for Social Research, 1950.

Carroll, John B., and Chall, Jeanne S. *Toward a Literate Society.* New York: McGraw-Hill, 1975.

Cawelti, John G. *Adventure, Mystery, and Romance.* Chicago: University of Chicago Press, 1976.

———. *The Six-Gun Mystique.* Bowling Green, Ohio: Bowling Green University Popular Press, 1971.

Chadwick, John. *The Mycenaean World.* Cambridge: Cambridge University Press, 1976.

Chamberlain, Hope Summerell. *This Was Home*. Chapel Hill: University of North Carolina Press, 1938.

Chandler, Alfred D. *The Visible Hand: The Managerial Revolution in American Business*. Cambridge: Harvard University Press, 1977.

Charvat, William. *The Profession of Authorship in America, 1800–1970*. Columbus: Ohio State University Press, 1968.

Cipolla, Carlo. *Literacy and Development in the West*. Harmondsworth, England: Penguin Books, 1969.

Clanchy, Michael. *From Memory to Written Record: England, 1066–1307*. Cambridge: Harvard University Press, 1979.

Clary, Annie Vaughan. *The Pioneer Life*. Dallas: American Guild Press, 1956.

Clune, William; Patterson, Janice; and White, Paula. *The Implementation and Effects of High School Graduation Requirements: First Steps toward Curriculum Reform*. New Brunswick, N.J.: Rutgers University, Center for Policy Research in Education, 1989.

Cohen, Rose. *Out of the Shadow*. New York: George Doran, 1918.

Cohn, Jan. *Creating America: George Horace Lorimer and the Saturday Evening Post*. Pittsburgh: University of Pittsburgh Press, 1989.

Cole, John Y., and Gold, Carol S., eds. *Reading in America, 1978*. Washington, D.C.: Library of Congress, 1979.

Compaine, Benjamin, M., ed. *Who Owns the Media? Concentration of Ownership in the Mass Communications Industry*. New York: Harmony Books, 1979.

Conlin, Joseph R., ed. *The American Radical Press, 1880–1960*. 2 vols. Westport, Conn.: Greenwood Press, 1974.

Copperman, Paul. *The Literacy Hoax: The Decline of Reading, Writing, and Learning in the Public Schools and What We Can Do about It*. New York: William Morrow, 1978.

Corbett, Elizabeth. *Out at the Soldiers' Home: A Memory Book*. New York: Appleton-Century, 1941.

Coser, Lewis, A.; Kadushin, Charles; and Powell, Witter W. *Books: The Culture and Commerce of Publishing*. New York: Basic Books, 1982.

Cowan, Ruth Schwartz. *More Work for Mother: The Ironies of Household Technology from the Open Hearth to the Microwave*. New York: Basic Books, 1983.

Craig, James C. "The Vocabulary Load of the Nation's Best-Sellers from 1662 to 1945: A Study in Readability." Ph.D. diss., University of Pittsburgh, 1954.

Cremin, Lawrence A. *American Education: The Colonial Experience, 1607–1786*. New York: Harper and Row, 1970.

———. *American Education: The Metropolitan Experience, 1876–1980*. New York: Harper and Row, 1988.

————. *American Education: The National Experience, 1783–1876.* New York: Harper and Row, 1980.

————. *Traditions of American Education.* New York: Basic Books, 1977.

Cressy, David. *Literacy and the Social Order: Reading and Writing in Tudor and Stuart England.* London: Cambridge University Press, 1980.

Culler, Jonathan. *On Deconstruction: Theory and Criticism after Structuralism.* Ithaca: Cornell University Press, 1980.

Daniel, H. *Public Libraries for Everyone: Growth and Development of Library Services in the United States, Especially since the Passage of the Library Services Act.* Garden City, N.Y.: Doubleday, 1961.

Daniel, Walter C. *Black Journals of the United States.* Westport, Conn.: Greenwood Press, 1982.

Darnton, Robert. *The Business of Enlightenment.* Cambridge: Harvard University Press, 1979.

————. *The Kiss of Lamourette: Reflections in Cultural History.* New York: W. W. Norton, 1990.

Davidson, Cathy. *Revolution and the World: The Rise of the Novel in America.* New York: Oxford University Press, 1986.

Davis, Kenneth C. *Two-Bit Culture: The Paperbacking of America.* Boston: Houghton Mifflin, 1984.

Dawkins, John. *Syntax and Readability.* Newark, Del.: International Reading Association, 1975.

de Camp, L. Sprague. *Literary Swordsmen and Sorcerers: The Makers of Heroic Fantasy.* Sauk City, Wis.: Arkham House, 1976.

del Rey, Lester. *The World of Science Fiction, 1926–1976: The History of a Subculture.* New York: Garland, 1980.

Denning, Michael. *Mechanic Accents: Dime Novels and Working-Class Culture in America.* London: Verso, 1987.

Dennis, Everette E., and Rivers, William L. *Other Voices: The New Journalism in America.* San Francisco: Canfield Press, 1974.

Dewey, John. *The Public and Its Problems.* New York: Henry Holt, 1927.

Diringer, David. *The Alphabet: A Key to the History of Mankind.* 3d ed. New York: Funk and Wagnalls, 1968.

Dodd, Bella V. *School of Darkness.* New York: P. J. Kenedy and Sons, 1954.

Dodge, Arthur F. *Occupational Ability Patterns.* New York: Bureau of Publications, Teachers College, Columbia University, 1935.

Douglas, Ann. *The Feminization of American Culture.* New York: Alfred A. Knopf, 1977.

Dublin, Thomas. *Women at Work: The Transformation of Work and Community in Lowell, Massachusetts, 1826–1860.* New York: Columbia University Press, 1979.

Dvorak, Beatrice Jeanne. *Differential Occupational Ability Patterns*. Bulletins of the Employment Stabilization Research Institute, vol. 3, no. 8. Minneapolis: University of Minnesota Press, 1935.

Eisenstein, Elizabeth. *The Printing Press as an Agent of Change: Communications and Cultural Transformations in Early-Modern Europe*. Cambridge: Cambridge University Press, 1980.

Ellis, Anne. *"Plain Anne Ellis": More about the Life of an Ordinary Woman*. Boston: Houghton Mifflin, 1931.

Emery, Edwin. *The Press and America: An Interpretive History*. 3d ed. Englewood Cliffs, N.J.: Prentice-Hall, 1972.

Engelsing, Rolf. *Der Burger als Leser: Lesergeschichte in Deutschland, 1500–1800*. Stuttgart: Metzlersche, 1973.

Ennis, Philip H. *Adult Book Reading in the United States*. Chicago: National Opinion Research Center, 1965.

Equivalent Scores for Metropolitan Achievement Tests 1970 Edition and Metropolitan Achievement Tests 1958 Edition: Special Report No. 14. New York: Harcourt Brace Jovanovich, 1971.

Erenberg, Lewis A. *Steppin' Out: New York Nightlife and the Transformation of American Culture, 1890–1930*. Westport, Conn.: Greenwood Press, 1981.

Ernst, Morris. *The First Freedom*. New York: Macmillan, 1946.

Escarpit, Robert. *The Book Revolution*. London: George Harrap, 1966. Originally published as *La Révolution du livre*. Paris: UNESCO, 1965.

———. *The Sociology of Literature*. Trans. Ernest Pick. Painesville, Ohio: Lake Erie College Press, 1965. Originally published as *Sociologie de la littérature*. Paris: Presses Universitaires de France, 1958.

Ewen, Stuart. *Captains of Consciousness: Advertising and the Social Roots of the Consumer Culture*. New York: McGraw-Hill, 1976.

Farnsworth, Burton K. "A Study of the Reading Habits of Adults." M.A. thesis, Utah Agricultural College, 1925.

Farr, Roger; Fay, Leo; and Negley, Harold. *Then and Now: Reading Achievement in Indiana (1944–45 and 1976)*. Bloomington: Indiana University, School of Education, 1978.

Farr, Roger; Tuinman, Jaap; and Rowls, Michael. *Reading Achievement in the United States: Then and Now*. Bloomington: Indiana University, Final Report to the Educational Testing Service, 1974.

Fiedler, Leslie. *Love and Death in the American Novel*. New York: Criterion Books, 1960.

Fischer, J. K.; Haney, W.; and David, L. *APL Revisited: Its Uses and Adaptation in States*. Washington, D.C.: Government Printing Office, 1980.

Fish, Stanley. *Doing What Comes Naturally: Change, Rhetoric, and the*

Practice of Theory in Literary and Legal Studies. Durham, N.C.: Duke University Press, 1980.

————. *Is There a Text in the Class? The Authority of Interpretive Communities.* Cambridge: Harvard University Press, 1980.

Fisher, Donald L. *Functional Literacy and the Schools.* Washington, D.C.: National Institute of Education, 1978.

Fishman, Joshua, et al. *Language Loyalty in the United States: The Maintenance and Perpetuation of Non-English Mother Tongues by American Ethnic and Religious Groups.* The Hague: Mouton, 1966.

Flake, Carol. *Redemptorama: Culture, Politics and the New Evangelicalism.* Garden City, N.Y.: Anchor Press, 1984.

Flynn, Elizabeth Gurley. *The Rebel Girl: An Autobiography; My First Life (1906–1926).* Rev. ed. New York: International Publishers, 1973.

Folger, John K., and Nam, Charles B. *Education of the American Population.* Washington, D.C.: Government Printing Office, 1967.

Fox, Richard W., and Lears, T. J. Jackson, eds. *The Culture of Consumption: Critical Essays in American History, 1880–1980.* New York: Pantheon Books, 1983.

Fox, Stephen. *The Mirror Makers: A History of American Advertising and Its Creators.* New York: William Morrow, 1984.

Freund, Elizabeth. *The Return of the Reader: Reader-Response Criticism.* London: Routledge, Chapman and Hall, 1987.

Furet, François, and Ozouf, Jacques. *Reading and Writing: Literacy in France from Calvin to Jules Ferry.* Cambridge: Cambridge University Press, 1982. Originally published as *Lire et écrire: L'alphabétisation des français de Calvin à Jules Ferry.* Paris: Editions de Minuit, 1977.

Gadway, Charles J., and Wilson, H. A. *Functional Literacy: Basic Reading Performance.* Denver: Education Commission of the States, 1976.

Gallup, George H., ed. *The Gallup Poll: Public Opinion, 1935–1971.* 3 vols. New York: Random House, 1972.

————. *The Gallup Poll: Public Opinion, 1972–1977.* 2 vols. Wilmington, Del.: Scholarly Resources, 1978.

Gallup Organization for the American Library Association. *Book Reading and Library Usage: A Study of Habits and Perceptions.* Princeton, N.J.: Gallup Organization, 1978.

Gans, Herbert. *People and Plans.* New York: Basic Books, 1968.

————. *Popular Culture and High Culture.* New York: Basic Books, 1974.

Gates, Arthur I. *Reading Attainment in Elementary Schools: 1957 and 1937.* New York: Bureau of Publications, Teachers College, Columbia University, 1961.

Geherin, David. *The American Private Eye: The Image in Fiction.* New York: Frederick Ungar, 1985.

Gelb, Ignace J. *A Study of Writing.* Rev. ed. Chicago: University of Chicago Press, 1963.

Gilbert, Dennis A. *Compendium of American Public Opinion.* New York: Facts on File Publications, 1988.

Gilmore, William. *Reading Becomes a Necessity of Life: Material and Cultural Life in Rural New England, 1780–1835.* Knoxville: University of Tennessee Press, 1989.

Ginzberg, Eli, and Bray, Douglas W. *The Uneducated.* New York: Columbia University Press, 1953.

Ginzburg, Carlo. *The Cheese and the Worms: The Cosmos of a Sixteenth-Century Miller.* Trans. John and Anne Tedeschi. New York: Penguin Books, 1982.

Goertz, Margaret E. *Course-Taking Patterns in the 1980s.* New Brunswick, N.J.: Rutgers University, Center for Policy Research in Education, 1989.

Goldman, Emma. *Living My Life.* 2 vols. New York: Da Capo Press, 1970.

Goody, Jack. *The Domestication of the Savage Mind.* Cambridge: Cambridge University Press, 1971.

Goody, Jack, ed. *Literacy in Traditional Societies.* Cambridge: Cambridge University Press, 1968.

Goulart, Ron. *The Dime Detectives.* New York: Mysterious Press, 1988.

Gould, Stephen J. *The Mismeasure of Man.* New York: W. W. Norton, 1981.

Graebner, William. *The Engineering of Consent: Democracy and Authority in Twentieth-Century America.* Madison: University of Wisconsin Press, 1987.

Graff, Harvey. *The Legacies of Literacy: Continuities and Contradictions in Western Culture and Society.* Bloomington: Indiana University Press, 1987.

———. *The Literacy Myth: Literacy and Social Structure in the Nineteenth-Century City.* New York: Academic Press, 1979.

Grant, W. S. *Comparative Study of Achievement in Reading in 1916 and 1948.* Grand Rapids School Survey. Grand Rapids, Mich.: Board of Education, 1949.

Grant, W. V., and Eiden, L. J. *Digest of Educational Statistics.* Washington, D.C.: Government Printing Office, 1982.

Gray, William S. *Reading: A Research Retrospective, 1881–1941.* Ed. John T. Guthrie. Newark, Del.: International Reading Association, 1984.

Gray, William S., and Monroe, Ruth. *The Reading Interests and Habits of Adults: A Preliminary Report.* New York: Macmillan, 1929.

Griffith, Sally Foreman. *Home Town News: William Allen White and the Emporia Gazette.* New York: Oxford University Press, 1989.

Hackett, Alice Payne. *Eighty Years of Best Sellers, 1895–1975*. New York: R. R. Bowker, 1977.

Hajda, Jan. "An American Paradox: People and Books in Metropolis." Ph.D. diss., University of Chicago, 1963.

Hamerow, Theodore. *The Birth of a New Europe*. Chapel Hill: University of North Carolina Press, 1983.

Harnischfeger, Annegret, and Wiley, David. *Achievement Test Score Decline: Do We Need to Worry?* St. Louis: Central Midwestern Regional Educational Laboratory, 1975.

Harris, Louis, and Associates, Inc. *The 1971 National Reading Difficulty Index: A Study of Functional Reading Ability in the United States, for the National Reading Center*. Washington, D.C.: National Reading Center, 1971.

————. *Survival Literacy Study*. Washington, D.C.: National Reading Council, 1970.

Harris, Michael H., and Davis, Donald G., Jr. *American Library History: A Bibliography*. Austin: University of Texas Press, 1978.

Harris, William V. *Ancient Literacy*. Cambridge: Harvard University Press, 1989.

Hart, James D. *The Popular Book: A History of America's Literary Taste*. New York: Oxford University Press, 1950.

Hatcher, O. Latham. *Rural Girls in the City for Work: A Study Made for the Southern Women's Educational Alliance*. Richmond, Va.: Garrett and Massie, 1930.

Havelock, Eric. *Origins of Western Literacy*. Toronto: Ontario Institute for Studies in Education, 1976.

————. *Preface to Plato*. Oxford: Basil Blackwell, 1963.

Hawley, Ellis W. *The Great War and the Search for a Modern Order: A History of the American People and Their Institutions, 1917–1933*. New York: St. Martin's Press, 1979.

Hieronymus, A. N.; Lindquist, E. F.; and Hoover, H. D. *The Development of the 1982 Norms for the Iowa Tests of Basic Skills, the Cognitive Abilities Test, and the Tests of Achievement and Proficiency*. Chicago: Riverside, 1983.

————. *Manual for School Administrators: Iowa Tests of Basic Skills*. Chicago: Riverside, 1982.

Hoggart, Richard. *The Uses of Literacy*. London: Chatto and Windus, 1957.

Holland, Norman. *Five Readers Reading*. New Haven and London: Yale University Press, 1975.

Holt, John. *Instead of Education*. New York: E. P. Dutton, 1976.

Holub, Robert C. *Reception Theory: A Critical Introduction*. London: Methuen, 1984.

Horowitz, Daniel. *The Morality of Spending: Attitudes toward the Consumer Society in America, 1875–1940*. Baltimore: Johns Hopkins University Press, 1985.

Hourwich, Andria Taylor, and Palmer, Gladys L., eds. *I Am a Woman Worker*. New York: Arno Press, 1974.

Houston, Rab A. *Literacy in Early Modern Europe: Culture and Education, 1500–1800*. New York: Longman, 1988.

———. *Scottish Literacy and the Scottish Identity: Illiteracy and Society in Scotland and Northern England, 1600–1800*. Cambridge: Cambridge University Press, 1985.

Hunter, Carmen S. F., and Harman, David. *Adult Illiteracy in the United States: A Report to the Ford Foundation*. New York: McGraw-Hill, 1979.

Husén, Torsten, ed. *International Study of Achievement in Mathematics: A Comparison between Twelve Countries*. New York: Wiley, 1967.

Inkeles, Alex, and Smith, David. *Becoming Modern: Individual Change in Six Developing Countries*. Cambridge: Harvard University Press, 1974.

Innis, Harold A. *The Bias of Communication*. Toronto: University of Toronto Press, 1951.

Iser, Wolfgang. *The Act of Reading: A Theory of Aesthetic Response*. Baltimore: Johns Hopkins University Press, 1978.

———. *Prospecting: From Reader Response to Literary Anthropology*. Baltimore: Johns Hopkins University Press, 1989.

Jacobs, Norman, ed. *Culture for the Millions? Mass Media in Modern Society*. Princeton, N.J.: D. Van Nostrand, 1961.

Jencks, Christopher, et al. *Inequality: A Reassessment of the Effect of Family and Schooling in America*. New York: Harper and Row, 1972.

Johnston, William B., and Packer, Arnold E. *Workforce 2000: Work and Workers for the Twenty-first Century*. Indianapolis, Ind.: Hudson Institute, 1987.

Jones, Gareth Stedman. *Languages of Class: Studies in English Working Class History, 1832–1982*. Cambridge: Cambridge University Press, 1983.

Joyce, Donald F. *Gatekeepers of Black Culture: Black-Owned Book Publishing in the United States, 1817–1981*. Westport, Conn.: Greenwood Press, 1983.

Kaestle, Carl F. *Pillars of the Republic: Common Schools and American Society, 1780–1860*. New York: Hill and Wang, 1983.

Kaestle, Carl F., and Vinovskis, Maris A. *Education and Social Change in Nineteenth-Century Massachusetts*. New York: Cambridge University Press, 1980.

Kaplan, Louis. *A Bibliography of American Autobiography*. Madison: University of Wisconsin Press, 1961.

Karetzky, Stephen. *Reading Research and Librarianship: A History and Analysis.* Westport, Conn.: Greenwood Press, 1982.

Katz, Elihu, and Lazarsfeld, Paul F. *Personal Influence.* New York: Free Press, 1955.

Kelley, Grace O. *Woodside Does Read: A Survey of the Reading Interests and Habits of a Local Community.* Jamaica, N.Y.: Queens Borough Public Library, 1935.

Kelley, Mary. *Private Woman, Public Stage: Literary Domesticity in Nineteenth-Century America.* New York: Oxford University Press, 1984.

Kennedy, David M. *Over Here: The First World War and American Society.* New York: Oxford University Press, 1980.

Kerber, Linda K. *Women of the Republic: Intellect and Ideology in Revolutionary America.* Chapel Hill: University of North Carolina Press, 1980.

Kessler, Laureen. *The Dissident Press: Alternative Journalism in American History.* Beverly Hills, Calif.: Sage, 1984.

Kirsch, Irwin. *NAEP, Profiles of Literacy: An Assessment of Young Adults: Development Plan.* Princeton, N.J.: National Assessment of Educational Progress, 1985.

Kirsch, Irwin S., and Jungeblut, Ann. *Literacy: Profiles of America's Young Adults.* Princeton, N.J.: National Assessment of Educational Progress, Educational Testing Service, 1986.

———. *Literacy: Profiles of America's Young Adults. Final Report.* Princeton, N.J.: National Assessment of Educational Progress, Educational Testing Service, 1986.

Kitson, John W. "Profile of a Growth Industry: American Book Publishing at Mid-Century, with an Emphasis on the Integration and Consolidation Activity between 1959 and 1965." Ph.D. diss., University of Illinois, Urbana, 1968.

Klapper, Joseph T. *The Effects of Mass Communication.* Glencoe, Ill.: Free Press, 1960.

Kohl, Herbert. *Thirty-Six Children.* New York: Signet, 1967.

Kozol, Jonathan. *Illiterate America.* New York: Anchor/Doubleday, 1985.

Lamont, Thomas W. *My Boyhood in a Parsonage: Some Brief Sketches of American Life toward the Close of the Last Century.* New York: Harper and Brothers, 1946.

Larson, Magali Sarfatti. *The Rise of Professionalism: A Sociological Analysis.* Berkeley: University of California Press, 1977.

Lasch, Christopher. *The Culture of Narcissism: American Life in an Age of Diminishing Expectations.* New York: W. W. Norton, 1979.

———. *Haven in a Heartless World: The Family Besieged.* New York: Basic Books, 1977.

Lazarsfeld, Paul F.; Berelson, Bernard; and Gaudet, Hazel. *The People's Choice*. New York: Harper and Row, 1944.

Leavis, Q. D. *Fiction and the Reading Public*. London: Chatto and Windus, 1932.

Lee, Alfred M. *The Daily Newspaper in America: The Evolution of a Social Instrument*. New York: Macmillan, 1937.

Lehmann-Haupt, Hellmut; Wroth, Lawrence C.; and Silver, Rollo G. *The Book in America: A History of the Making and Selling of Books in the United States*. 2d ed. New York: R. R. Bowker, 1951.

Levine, Lawrence W. *Highbrow/Lowbrow: The Emergence of Cultural Hierarchy in America*. Cambridge: Harvard University Press, 1988.

Lewisohn, Ludwig. *Up Stream: An American Chronicle*. New York: Boni and Liveright, 1922.

Link, Henry C., and Hopf, Harry A. *People and Books: A Study of Reading and Book-Buying Habits*. New York: Book Industry Committee, 1946.

Lockridge, Kenneth. *Literacy in Colonial New England: An Enquiry into the Social Context of Literacy in the Early Modern West*. New York: W. W. Norton, 1974.

Lynes, Russell. *The Tastemakers*. New York: Grosset and Dunlap, 1949.

MacDonald, Betty. *The Egg and I*. Philadelphia: J. B. Lippincott, 1945.

Madison, Charles A. *Book Publishing in America*. New York: McGraw-Hill, 1966.

Magazine Advertising Bureau. *Magazine Reader Count for County, State, and Nation*. New York: Magazine Advertising Bureau, 1949.

Mailloux, Steven. *Interpretive Conventions: The Reader in the Study of American Fiction*. Ithaca: Cornell University Press, 1982.

Market Facts, Inc. *1983 Consumer Research Study on Reading and Book Purchasing: Focus on Adults*. New York: Book Industry Study Group, 1984.

Marvin, Carolyn. *When Old Technologies Were New: Thinking about Communications in the Late Nineteenth Century*. New York: Oxford University Press, 1988.

Marzolf, Marion Tuttle. *The Danish-Language Press in America*. New York: Arno Press, 1979.

Masche, W. Carl. "Factors Involved in the Consolidation and Suspension of Daily and Sunday Newspapers in the United States since 1900." M.A. thesis, University of Minnesota, 1932.

Mast, Gerald, ed. *The Movies in our Midst*. Chicago: University of Chicago Press, 1982.

Maynes, Mary Jo. *Schooling for the People: Comparative Local Studies of Schooling History in France and Germany, 1750–1850*. London: Holmes and Meier, 1984.

Melody, William H.; Salter, Liora; and Heyer, Paul, eds. *Culture, Communication, and Dependency: The Tradition of H. A. Innis.* Norwood, N.J.: Ablex, 1981.

Merry, Bruce. *Anatomy of the Spy Thriller.* London: Gill and Macmillan, 1977.

Mikulecky, Larry J.; Shanklin, Nancy Leavitt; and Caverly, David C. *Adult Reading Habits, Attitudes and Motivations: A Cross-Sectional Study.* Bloomington: Indiana University, School of Education, Monographs in Language and Reading Studies, 1979.

Mitford, Jessica. *A Fine Old Conflict.* New York: Alfred A. Knopf, 1977.

Monaghan, E. Jennifer. *A Common Heritage: Noah Webster's Blue-Black Speller.* Hamden, Conn.: Archon Books, 1983.

Morison, Samuel E. *The Intellectual Life of Colonial New England.* Ithaca: Cornell University Press, 1956. Originally published as *The Puritan Pronaos* (1936).

Mott, Frank Luther. *Golden Multitudes: The Story of Best Sellers in the United States.* New York: Macmillan, 1947.

———. *A History of American Magazines.* 5 vols. Cambridge: Harvard University Press, 1930–68.

Mullins, Ina V. S., and Jenkins, Lynn B. *The Reading Report Card, 1971–88: Trends from the Nation's Report Card.* Washington, D.C.: U.S. Department of Education, 1990.

Mumford, Lewis. *Technics and Civilization.* New York: Harcourt, Brace, 1934.

Murphy, Richard T. *Adult Functional Reading Study.* Princeton, N.J.: Educational Testing Service, 1973.

———. *Adult Functional Reading Study: Supplement to Final Report.* Princeton, N.J.: Educational Testing Service, 1975.

National Assessment of Educational Progress. *Changes in Mathematical Achievement, 1973–78.* Report no. 09-MA-01. Denver: Education Commission of the States, 1979.

National Commission on Excellence in Education. *A Nation at Risk: The Imperative for Educational Reform.* Washington, D.C.: Government Printing Office, 1983.

Neuman, W. Russell. *The Paradox of Mass Politics: Knowledge and Opinion in the American Electorate.* Cambridge: Harvard University Press, 1986.

Newsprint Information Committee. *A National Study of Newspaper Reading: Size and Characteristics of the Newspaper Reading Public.* New York: Audits and Surveys, 1961.

O'Neil, Robert M. *Classrooms in the Crossfire.* Bloomington: Indiana University Press, 1981.

Ong, Walter. *Orality and Literacy.* New York: Methuen, 1982.

———. *The Presence of the Word.* New Haven: Yale University Press, 1967.

Ormsbee, Hazel G. *The Young Employed Girl.* New York: Woman's Press, 1927.

O'Toole, J., et al. *Work in America: Report of a Special Task Force to the Secretary of Health, Education, and Welfare.* Cambridge: MIT Press, 1973.

Otto, Wayne, ed. *Reading Expository Materials.* New York: Academic Press, 1982.

Papashvily, Helen Waite. *All the Happy Endings: A Study of the Domestic Novel in America, the Women Who Wrote It, the Women Who Read It, in the Nineteenth Century.* New York: Harper and Row, 1956.

Parenti, Michael. *Inventing Reality: The Politics of the Mass Media.* New York: St. Martin's Press, 1986.

Park, Robert E. *The Immigrant Press and Its Control.* New York: Harper and Brothers, 1922.

Parsons, Rhey Boyd. "A Study of Adult Reading." Ph.D. diss., University of Chicago, 1923.

Peiss, Kathy. *Cheap Amusements: Working Women and Leisure in Turn-of-the-Century New York.* Philadelphia: Temple University Press, 1986.

Percy, William Alexander. *Lanterns on the Levee: Recollections of a Planter's Son.* Baton Rouge: Louisiana State University Press, 1941.

Peterson, Theodore. *Magazines in the Twentieth Century.* 2d ed. Urbana: University of Illinois Press, 1975.

Powell, Barry B. *Homer and the Origin of the Greek Alphabet.* Cambridge: Cambridge University Press, 1990.

Psychological Corporation. *Metropolitan Achievement Tests, 1978 Edition, Equivalent Grade Equivalent Scores for Metro '70 and Metro '78: Special Report No. 20, Revised.* New York: Harcourt Brace Jovanovich, 1978.

———. *Metropolitan Achievement Tests, 1978 Edition, Equivalent Grade Equivalent Scores between Metro '78 and the 1973 Stanford Achievement Test: Special Report No. 21.* New York: Harcourt Brace Jovanovich, 1978.

Purves, Alan C., and Beach, Richard. *Literature and the Reader: Research in Response to Literature, Reading Interests, and the Teaching of Literature.* Urbana, Ill.: National Council of Teachers of English, 1972.

Radway, Janice A. *Reading the Romance: Women, Patriarchy, and Popular Literature.* Chapel Hill: University of North Carolina Press, 1984.

Reilly, Mary L. *A History of the Catholic Press Association, 1911–1968.* Metuchen, N.J.: Scarecrow Press, 1971.

Reynolds, Bertha Caper. *An Uncharted Journey: Fifty Years Growth in Social Work.* New York: Citadel Press, 1972.

Rosenberg, Bernard, and White, David M., eds. *Mass Culture: The Popular Arts in America.* Glencoe, Ill.: Free Press, 1957.

Rucker, Bryce W. *The First Freedom.* Carbondale: Southern Illinois University Press, 1968.

Scheiber, Harry N. *The Wilson Administration and Civil Liberties, 1917–1921.* Ithaca: Cornell University Press, 1960.

Schick, Frank L. *The Paperbound Book in America: The History of Paperbacks and Their European Background.* New York: R. R. Bowker, 1958.

Schiller, Dan. *Objectivity and the News: The Public and the Rise of Commercial Journalism.* Philadelphia: University of Pennsylvania Press, 1981.

Schneiderman, Rose. *All for One.* New York: Paul S. Eriksson, 1967.

Schrader, William B. *Test Data as Social Indicators.* Princeton, N.J.: Educational Testing Service, 1968.

Schudson, Michael. *Advertising, the Uneasy Persuasion: Its Dubious Impact on American Society.* New York: Basic Books, 1984.

———. *Discovering the News: A Social History of American Newspapers.* New York: Basic Books, 1978.

Schulze, Lydia D. "Best-Sellers Evaluated for Readability and Portrayal of Female Characters." M.A. thesis, Rutgers University, 1976.

Schwarzlose, Richard A. *The American Wire Services: A Study of Their Development as a Social Institution.* New York: Arno Press, 1979.

Scribner, Sylvia S., and Cole, Michael M. *The Psychology of Literacy.* Cambridge: Harvard University Press, 1981.

Scripps, Charles E. *Economic Support of Mass Communication Media in the United States, 1929–1963.* Cincinnati, Ohio: Scripps-Howard Research, 1965.

Sharon, Amiel T. *Reading Activities of American Adults.* Princeton, N.J.: Educational Testing Service, 1972.

Shove, Raymond H. *Cheap Book Production in the United States 1870 to 1891.* Urbana: University of Illinois Library, 1937.

Silberman, Charles. *Crises in the Classroom.* New York: Vintage Books, 1970.

———, ed. *The Open Classroom.* New York: Vintage Books, 1973.

Simon, Ken A., and Grant, W. V. *Digest of Education Statistics.* Washington, D.C.: Government Printing Office, 1970.

Sklar, Robert. *Movie-Made America: A Cultural History of American Movies.* New York: Random House, 1975.

Smith, Henry Nash. *Democracy and the Novel: Popular Resistance to Classic American Writers.* New York: Oxford University Press, 1978.

Sollors, Werner. *Beyond Ethnicity: Consent and Descent in American Culture.* New York: Oxford University Press, 1986.

Soltes, Mordecai. *The Yiddish Press: An Americanizing Agency.* Philadelphia: Jewish Publication Society, 1925.

Soltow, Lee, and Stevens, Edward. *The Rise of Literacy and the Common School in the United States: A Socioeconomic Analysis to 1870.* Chicago: University of Chicago Press, 1981.

Some Comments on the Relationship between Scores on the 1973 and 1982 Editions of the Stanford Achievement Test: Stanford Special Report No. 4A. New York: Harcourt Brace Jovanovich, 1983.

Spufford, Margaret. *Small Books and Pleasant Histories: Popular Fiction and Its Readership in Seventeenth-Century England.* Cambridge: Cambridge University Press, 1981.

Stearns, Peter N. *Be a Man! Males in Modern Society.* New York: Holmes and Meier, 1979.

Stedman, Lawrence C., and Kaestle, Carl F. *An Investigation of Crude Literacy, Reading Performance, and Functional Literacy in the United States, 1880 to 1980.* Madison: Wisconsin Center for Education Research, Program Report 86-2, 1986.

Steel, Ronald. *Walter Lippmann and the American Century.* Boston: Little, Brown, 1980.

Steinberg, Salme Harju. *Reformer in the Marketplace: Edward W. Bok and the* Ladies' Home Journal. Baton Rouge: Louisiana State University Press, 1979.

Stephens, W. B. *Education, Literacy, and Society, 1830–70: The Geography of Diversity in Provincial England.* Manchester: Manchester University Press, 1987.

Sticht, Thomas G. *Basic Skills in Defense.* Alexandria, Va.: Human Resources Research Organization, 1982.

———, ed. *Reading for Working: A Functional Literacy Anthology.* Alexandria, Va.: Human Resources Research Organization, 1975.

Stock, Brian. *The Implications of Literacy: Written Language and Models of Interpretation in the Eleventh and Twelfth Centuries.* Princeton, N.J.: Princeton University Press, 1983.

Strunk, Mildred, comp. *Public Opinion, 1935–1946.* Princeton, N.J.: Princeton University Press, 1951.

Suleiman, Susan R., and Crossman, Inge. *The Reader in the Text: Essays on Audience and Interpretation.* Princeton, N.J.: Princeton University Press, 1980.

Sum, Andrew M.; Harrington, Paul E.; and Goedicke, William. *Basic Skills of America's Teens and Young Adults: Findings of the 1980 National ASVAB Testing and Their Implications for Education, Em-*

ployment and Training Policies and Programs. Boston: Northeastern University, 1986.

Tebbel, John. *The American Magazine: A Compact History*. New York: Hawthorne Books, 1969.

——. *George Horace Lorimer and the Saturday Evening Post*. Garden City, N.Y.: Doubleday, 1948.

——. *A History of Book Publishing in the United States*. 4 vols. New York: R. R. Bowker, 1972–81.

Thernstrom, Stephan. *Poverty and Progress: Social Mobility in a Nineteenth-Century City*. Cambridge: Harvard University Press, 1964.

Thurston, Carol. *The Romance Revolution: Erotic Novels for Women and the Quest for a New Sexual Identity*. Urbana: University of Illinois Press, 1987.

Tompkins, Jane P., ed. *Reader-Response Criticism: From Formalism to Post-Structuralism*. Baltimore: Johns Hopkins University Press, 1980.

Topp, Mildred Spurrier. *Smile Please*. Boston: Houghton Mifflin, 1948.

Trollinger, William Vance, Jr., and Kaestle, Carl F. *Difficulty of Text as a Factor in the History of Reading*. Madison: Wisconsin Center for Education Research, Program Report 86-13, 1986. ERIC: ED 312 625.

Turow, Joseph. *Media Industries: The Production of News and Entertainment*. New York: Longman, 1984.

Udell, John. *Economic Trends in the Daily Newspaper Business, 1946–1970*. Madison: University of Wisconsin, Bureau of Business Research and Service, 1970.

U.S. Bureau of the Census. *Ancestry and Language in the United States: November 1979*. Current Population Reports, ser. P-23, no. 116. Washington, D.C.: Government Printing Office, 1982.

——. *Educational Attainment in the United States: March 1979 and 1978*. Current Population Reports, ser. P-20, no. 356. Washington, D.C.: Government Printing Office, 1980.

——. *Educational Attainment in the United States, March 1982 to 1985*, by Rosalind R. Bruno. Current Population Reports, Population Characteristics, ser. P-20, no. 415. Washington, D.C.: Government Printing Office, 1987.

——. *Fourteenth Census of the United States*. Washington, D.C.: Government Printing Office, 1920.

——. *Historical Statistics of the United States, Colonial Times to 1970: Bicentennial Edition, Part 1*. Washington, D.C.: Government Printing Office, 1975.

——. *Illiteracy in the United States: November 1969*. Current Population Reports, ser. P-20, no. 217. Washington, D.C.: Government Printing Office, 1971.

———. *Illiteracy in the United States: October 1947*. Current Population Reports, ser. P-20, no. 20. Washington, D.C.: Government Printing Office, 1948.

———. *Literacy and Educational Attainment: March 1959*. Current Population Reports, ser. P-20, no. 99. Washington, D.C.: Government Printing Office, 1960.

———. *School Enrollment*. Current Population Reports, ser. P-20, no. 374. Washington, D.C.: Bureau of the Census 1981.

———. *School Enrollment, Educational Attainment, and Illiteracy: October, 1952*. Current Population Reports, ser. P-20, no. 45. Washington, D.C.: Government Printing Office, 1953.

———. *Statistical Abstract of the United States: 1982–83*. 103d ed. Washington, D.C.: Government Printing Office, 1982.

———. *Statistical Abstract of the United States: 1985*. 105th ed. Washington, D.C.: Government Printing Office, 1984.

———. *Consumer Expenditures and Income, Details of Expenditures and Income: Total United States, Urban and Rural, 1960–61*. Report no. 237-93, supplement 3, pt. A. Washington, D.C.: Government Printing Office, 1966.

U.S. Bureau of Labor Statistics. *Consumer Expenditure Survey: Diary Survey, 1980–81*. Bulletin 2173. Washington, D.C.: Department of Labor, 1983.

———. *Consumer Expenditure Survey: Interview Survey, 1972–73*. Bulletin 1997. Washington, D.C.: Department of Labor, 1978.

———. *Consumer Expenditure Survey: Interview Survey, 1980–81*. Bulletin 2225, Appendix C. Washington, D.C.: Department of Labor, 1985.

———. *Consumer Expenditure Survey: Interview Survey, 1982–83*. Bulletin 2246. Washington, D.C.: Department of Labor, 1986.

———. *Cost of Living in the United States*. Bulletin 357. Washington, D.C.: Government Printing Office, 1924.

———. *Economic Projections to 1990*. Bulletin 2121. Washington, D.C.: Department of Labor, 1982.

———. *Family Spending and Saving in Wartime*. Bulletin 822. Washington, D.C.: Government Printing Office, 1945.

———. *Money Disbursements of Wage Earners and Clerical Workers, 1934–36, Summary Volume*. Bulletin 638. Washington, D.C.: Government Printing Office, 1941.

———. *Study of Consumer Expenditures, Incomes, and Savings: Statistical Tables, Urban U.S. 1950. Vol. 9, Summary of Family Expenditures for Recreation, Reading, and Education*. Tabulated for the Wharton School of Finance and Commerce, University of Pennsylvania. Washington, D.C.: Department of Labor, 1957.

———. *Study of Consumer Expenditures, Incomes, and Savings: Statistical Tables, Urban U.S., 1950.* Vol. 13, *Summary of Family Incomes, Expenditures, and Savings; All Urban Areas Combined.* Tabulated for the Wharton School of Finance and Commerce, University of Pennsylvania, Washington, D.C.: Department of Labor, 1957.

———. *Study of Consumer Expenditures, Incomes, and Savings: Statistical Tables, Urban U.S., 1950.* Vol. 14, *Detailed Family Expenditures for Medical Care, Personal Care, Recreation, Transportation, and Miscellaneous Services.* Tabulated for the Wharton School of Finance and Commerce, University of Pennsylvania, Washington, D.C.: Department of Labor, 1957.

U.S. Commissioner of Labor. *Eighteenth Annual Report of the Commissioner of Labor, 1903: Document #23, Cost of Living and Retail Prices of Food.* Washington, D.C.: Government Printing Office, 1904.

———. *Seventh Annual Report of the Commissioner of Labor, 1891: Costs of Production: Textiles and Glass. Volume 2, Part III: Cost of Living.* Executive Documents of the House of Representatives, 52d Cong., vol. 2958, no. 232, pt. 2. Washington, D.C.: Department of Labor, 1891.

———. *Sixth Annual Report of the Commissioner of Labor, 1891: Costs of Production: Iron, Steel, Coal. Part III: Cost of Living.* Executive Documents of the House of Representatives, 51st Cong., vol. 2867, no. 265. Washington, D.C.: Department of Labor, 1891.

U.S. Congress. House. *Illiteracy and the Scope of the Problem in This Country: Hearing before the House Subcommittee on Post Secondary Education and Labor.* 97th Cong., 2d sess., 1982.

———. *Oversight on Illiteracy in the United States: Hearing before the House Subcommittee on Elementary, Secondary, and Vocational Education.* 99th Cong., 2d sess., 1983.

U.S. Congress. Office of Technology Assessment. *Technology and the American Economic Transition: Choices for the Future.* Washington, D.C.: Government Printing Office, 1988.

U.S. Department of Agriculture. *The Farmer's Standard of Living.* Bulletin 1466. Washington, D.C.: Government Printing Office, 1926.

———. *Rural Family Spending and Saving in Wartime.* Miscellaneous Publications, no. 520. Washington, D.C.: Government Printing Office, 1945.

U.S. Department of Commerce. *National Income and Product Account Data for 1929–1966.* Supplied by the Bureau of Economic Analysis. Washington, D.C.: Department of Commerce, 1986.

———. *The National Income and Product Accounts of the United States, 1929–76, Statistical Tables.* Washington, D.C.: Government Printing Office, 1981.

―――. *Survey of Current Business,* vol. 62, no. 7. Washington, D.C.: Government Printing Office, 1982.

―――. *Survey of Current Business,* vol. 64, no. 7. Washington, D.C.: Government Printing Office, 1984.

U.S. Department of Defense. *Counselor's Manual for the Armed Services Vocational Aptitude Battery Form 14.* Washington, D.C.: Office of the Assistant Secretary of Defense, 1984.

U.S. Department of Education. *The Condition of Education.* Washington, D.C.: National Center for Educational Statistics, 1979.

―――. *Update on Adult Illiteracy.* Washington, D.C.: Government Printing Office, 1986.

U.S. Department of Labor. *Cost of Living of Industrial Workers in the United States and Europe, 1888–1890.* 3d ed. Ann Arbor, Mich.: Inter-University Consortium for Political and Social Research, 1986.

―――. *Section II: Occupational Aptitude Pattern Structure: Manual for the USES General Aptitude Test Battery.* Washington, D.C.: Government Printing Office, 1979.

U.S. Department of Labor and U.S. Department of Education. *The Bottom Line: Basic Skills in the Workplace.* Washington, D.C.: Government Printing Office, 1988.

U.S. National Resources Committee. *Consumer Expenditures in the United States: Estimates for 1935–36.* Washington, D.C.: Government Printing Office, 1939.

U.S. Office of Education. *Statistics of Public, Society, and School Libraries.* Bulletin no. 25. Washington, D.C.: Government Printing Office, 1915.

van Dijk, Teun A., and Kintsch, Walter. *Strategies of Discourse Comprehension.* New York: Academic Press, 1983.

van Zuilen, A. J. *The Life Cycle of Magazines: A Historical Study of the Decline and Fall of the General Interest Mass Audience Magazine in the United States during the Period 1946–1972.* Vithoorn, Netherlands: Graduate Press, 1977.

Venezky, Richard L.; Kaestle, Carl F.; and Sum, Andrew M. *The Subtle Danger: Reflections on the Literacy Abilities of America's Young Adults.* Princeton, N.J.: Educational Testing Service, 1987.

Vogt, Dorothy K. *Literacy among Youths 12–17 Years: United States.* Rockville, Md.: National Center for Health Statistics, 1973.

Wainwright, Loudon. *The Great American Magazine: An Inside History of Life.* New York: Alfred A. Knopf, 1986.

Waples, Douglas. *Research Memorandum on Social Aspects of Reading in the Depression.* New York: Social Science Research Council, 1937.

Waples, Douglas, and Tyler, Ralph W. *What People Want to Read About.* Chicago: University of Chicago Press, 1931.

Watson, Elmo Scott. *A History of Newspaper Syndicates in the United States, 1865–1935*. Chicago: 1936.

Weibe, Robert H. *The Search for Order, 1877–1920*. New York: Hill and Wang, 1967.

Weisbrod, Vera Buch. *A Radical Life*. Bloomington: Indiana University Press, 1977.

Wells, Robert V. *Revolutions in Americans' Lives: A Demographic Perspective on the History of Americans, Their Families, and Their Society*. Westport, Conn.: Greenwood Press, 1980.

West, Jerry; Diodato, Louis; and Sandberg, Nancy. *A Trend Study of High School Offerings and Enrollments: 1972–73 and 1981–82*. Washington, D.C.: Government Printing Office, 1984. ERIC: ED 153 530.

Weyr, Thomas. *Reaching for Paradise: The Playboy Vision of America*. New York: Times Books, 1978.

Whiteside, Thomas. *The Blockbuster Complex: Conglomerates, Show Business, and Book Publishing*. Middletown, Conn.: Wesleyan University Press, 1980.

Wilder, Gita Z., and Powell, Kristin. *Sex Differences in Test Performance: A Survey of the Literature*. Report no. 89-3. New York: College Entrance Examination Board, 1989.

Williams, Raymond. *The Long Revolution*. London: Chatto and Windus, 1961.

————. *Marxism and Literature*. Oxford: Oxford University Press, 1977.

Wilson, Christopher P. *The Labor of Words: Literary Professionalism in the Progressive Era*. Athens: University of Georgia Press, 1985.

Wilson, Louis R. *The Geography of Reading*. Chicago: University of Chicago Press, 1938.

Winston, Sanford. *Illiteracy in the United States, from 1870 to 1920*. Chapel Hill: University of North Carolina Press, 1930.

Winter, Alan D. *The Gay Press: A History of the Gay Community and Its Publications*. Published by the author, 1976.

Wittke, Carl. *The German-Language Press in America*. Lexington: University of Kentucky Press, 1957.

Wood, James. *The Curtis Magazines*. New York: Ronald Press, 1971.

Wright, James D. *The Dissent of the Governed*. New York: Academic Press, 1976.

Yankelovich, Skelly, and White. *Consumer Research Study on Reading and Book Purchasing*. Darien, Conn.: Book Industry Study Group, 1978.

Yerkes, Robert M. *Psychological Examining in the United States Army*. Washington, D.C.: National Academy of Sciences, 1921.

Yoakum, Clarence S., and Yerkes, Robert M. *Army Mental Tests*. New York: Henry Holt, 1920.

Young, Sheryl. "A Theory and Simulation of Macrostructure." Ph.D. diss., University of Colorado, 1984.

ARTICLES, BOOK CHAPTERS, AND PAPERS

Acland, Henry. "If Reading Scores Are Irrelevant, Do We Have Anvthing Better?" *Educational Technology* (July 1976):25–29.

Amarel, Marianne. "Reader and the Text—Three Perspectives." In *Reading Expository Materials,* ed. Wayne Otto, 243–57. New York: Academic Press, 1982.

Asheim, Lester. "What Do Adults Read?" In *Adult Reading: The Fifty-fifth Yearbook of the National Society for the Study of Education,* ed. Nelson B. Henry, 5–28. Chicago: University of Chicago Press, 1956.

Auwers, Linda. "Reading the Marks of the Past: Exploring Female Literacy in Colonial Windsor, Connecticut." *Historical Methods* 13 (1980): 204–14.

Barganz, Jean C., and Dulin, Kenneth L. "Readability Levels of Selected Mass Magazines, 1925–1965." In *Reading: Process and Pedagogy, Nineteenth Yearbook of the National Reading Conference,* ed. George B. Schick and Merrill M. May. 2 vols. Milwaukee, Wis.: National Reading Conference, 1971.

Bauer, Raymond A., and Bauer, Alice H. "American Mass Society and Mass Media." *Journal of Social Issues* 16 (1960):3–66.

Beales, Ross W., Jr. "Studying Literacy at the Community Level: A Research Note." *Journal of Interdisciplinary History* 9 (1978):93–102.

Berelson, Bernard. "Review of Link and Hopf, *People and Books.*" *Library Quarterly* 17 (January 1947):71–73.

———. "What 'Missing the Newspaper' Means." In *Communication Research, 1948–9,* ed. Paul F. Lazarsfeld and Frank N. Stanton, 111–28. New York: Duell, Sloan and Pearce, 1949.

Bishop, John H. "Is the Test Score Decline Responsible for the Productivity Growth Decline?" *American Economic Review* 79 (March 1989):178–97.

Bloom, Benjamin S. "The 1955 Normative Study of the Tests of General Educational Development." *School Review* 64 (1956):110–24.

Blumler, Jay G.; Gurevitch, Michael; and Katz, Elihu. "Reaching Out: A Future for Gratifications Research." In *Media Gratifications Research: Current Perspectives,* ed. Karl E. Rosengren, Lawrence A. Wenner, and Philip Palmgreen, 255–74. Beverly Hills, Calif.: Sage, 1985.

Bok, Mary Louise Curtis. "Louisa Knapp Curtis." In *Notable Women of Pennsylvania.* Philadelphia: Pennsylvania Publishing, 1952.

Bormuth, John R. "Reading Literacy: Its Definition and Assessment." *Reading Research Quarterly* 1 (1973–74):7–66.

———. "The Value and Volume of Literacy." *Visible Language* 12 (1978):118–61.

Bowles, Samuel. "Second Thoughts on the Capitalism-Enlightenment Connection: Are Americans Over Educated or Are Jobs Dumb?" Address to Conference on Libraries and Literacy, National Commission on Libraries and Information Services, Washington, D.C., April 1, 1979.

Breland, Hunter M. "The SAT Score Decline: A Summary of Related Research." In Advisory Panel on the Scholastic Aptitude Test Score Decline, *On Further Examination,* appendix. New York: College Entrance Examination Board, 1977.

Britton, Bruce, et al. "Effects of Text Structure on Use of Cognitive Capacity during Reading." *Journal of Educational Psychology* 74 (1982):51–61.

Brooks, Van Wyck. "America's Coming of Age." In *Three Essays on America.* New York: E. P. Dutton, 1934.

Brown, Richard D. "From Cohesion to Competition." In *Printing and Society in Early America,* ed. William L. Joyce et al., 300–309. Worcester, American Antiquarian Society, 1983.

Bureau of Labor Statistics. "Expenditures and Savings of City Families in 1944." *Monthly Labor Review* 62 (January 1946).

Buros, Oscar. "Fifty years in Testing." In *Eighth Mental Measurements Yearbook,* ed. Oscar Buros, 1972–79. Highland Park, N.J.: Gryphon Press, 1978.

Carey, James W. "Harold Adams Innis and Marshall McLuhan." *Antioch Review* 27 (1967):5–39.

———. "The Problem of Journalism History." *Journalism History* 1 (Spring 1974):5–39.

Carey, James W., and Kreiling, Albert. "Popular Culture and Uses and Gratifications: Notes toward an Accommodation." In *The Uses of Mass Communications: Current Perspectives on Gratifications Research,* ed. Jay G. Blumler and Elihu Katz, 223–48. Beverly Hills, Calif.: Sage, 1974.

Carnovsky, Leon. "A Study of the Relationship between Reading Interests and Actual Reading." *Library Quarterly* 4 (1934):76–110.

Caughran, Alex, and Lindlof, John. "Should the 'Survival Literacy Study' Survive?" *Journal of Reading* 15 (March 1972):429–35.

Cervero, Ronald M. "Does the Texas Adult Performance Level Test Measure Functional Competence?" *Adult Education* 30 (1980):152–65.

"The Changes behind the CPI's New Look." *Business Week,* March 2, 1987.

Clanchy, Michael M. "Looking Back from the Invention of Printing." In *Literacy in Historical Perspective,* ed. Daniel Resnick, 7–22. Washington, D.C.: Library of Congress, 1983.

Cleary, T. A., and McCandless, S. A. "Summary of Score Changes (in Other Texts)." In Advisory Panel on the Scholastic Aptitude Test Score Decline, *On Further Examination,* appendix. New York: College Entrance Examination Board, 1977.

Coles, Gerald S. "U.S. Literacy Statistics: How to Succeed with Hardly Trying." *Literacy Work* 5 (1976):47–70.

Copperman, Paul. "The Achievement Decline of the 1970s." *Phi Delta Kappan* (June 1979):736–39.

Cuban, Larry. "Effective Schools: A Friendly but Cautionary Note." *Phi Delta Kappan* (June 1983):695–96.

Darnton, Robert. "Readers Respond to Rousseau." In *The Great Cat Massacre and Other Episodes in French Cultural History,* 215–56. New York: Vintage Books, 1974.

———. "What Is the History of Books?" *Daedalus* 111 (1982):65–83.

Dewey, John. Review of *Public Opinion,* by Walter Lippmann. *New Republic,* May 3, 1922, 286–88.

Diehl, William A., and Mikulecky, Larry. "The Nature of Reading at Work." *Journal of Reading* 24 (1980):221–28.

DiMaggio, Paul. "Cultural Capital and School Success: The Impact of Status Culture Participation on the Grades of U.S. High School Students." *American Sociological Review* 47 (1982):189–201.

———. "Cultural Entrepreneurship in Nineteenth-Century Boston: The Creation of an Organizational Base for High Culture in America." *Media, Culture and Society* 4 (1982):33–50.

———. "Cultural Entrepreneurship in Nineteenth-Century Boston, Part II: The Classification and Framing of American Art." *Media, Culture and Society* 4 (1982):303–22.

———. "Market Structure, the Creative Process, and Popular Culture: Toward an Organizational Reinterpretation of Mass-Culture Theory." *Journal of Popular Culture* 11 (1977):436–52.

DiMaggio, Paul, and Mohr, John. "Cultural Capital, Educational Attainment, and Marital Selection." *American Journal of Sociology* 90 (1985):1231–61.

Echternacht, Gary J. "A Comparative Study of Secondary Schools with Different Score Patterns." In Advisory Panel on the Scholastic Aptitude Test Score Decline, *On Further Examination,* appendix. New York: College Entrance Examination Board, 1977.

Elligett, Jane, and Tocco, Thomas S. "Reading Achievement in 1979 vs. Achievement in the Fifties." *Phi Delta Kappan* 62 (June 1980): 698–99.

Ellis, Donna Lloyd. "The Underground Press in America: 1955–1970." *Journal of Popular Culture* 5 (Summer 1971): 102–24.

Epstein, Jason. "The Decline and Rise of Publishing." *New York Review of Books*, March 1, 1990, 8–12.

Eurich, Alvin C., and Kraetsch, Gayla A. "A Fifty-Year Comparison of University of Minnesota Freshmen's Reading Performance." *Journal of Educational Psychology* 74 (1982):660–65.

Field, Alexander. "Industrialization and Skill Intensity: The Case of Massachusetts." *Journal of Human Resources* 15 (1980): 149–75.

Fine, Sidney A. "The Use of the *Dictionary of Occupational Titles* as a Source of Estimates of Educational and Training Requirements." *Journal of Human Resources* 3 (1968):363–75.

Fisher, Donald L. "Functional Literacy Tests: A Model of Question-Answering and an Analysis of Errors." *Reading Research Quarterly* 16 (1981):418–48.

Fishman, Joshua A., et al. "Ethnicity in Action: The Community Resources of Ethnic Languages in the United States." In *The Rise and Fall of the Ethnic Revival: Perspectives on Language and Ethnicity*, ed. Joshua A. Fishman et al., 195–282. New York: Mouton, 1985.

Fishman, Joshua A.; Hayden, Robert G.; and Warshauer, Mary E. "The Non-English and the Ethnic Group Press, 1910–1960." In *Language Loyalty in the United States: The Maintenance and Perpetuation of Non-English Mother Tongues by American Ethnic and Religious Groups*, 51–74. The Hague: Mouton, 1966.

Flanagan, John C. "Changes in School Levels of Achievement: Project Talent Ten and Fifteen Year Retests." *Educational Researcher* 5 (1976):9–12.

Flynn, James R. "The Mean I.Q. of Americans: Massive Gains, 1923 to 1978." *Psychological Bulletin* 95 (1984):29–51.

Folger, John K., and Nam, Charles B. "Educational Trends from Census Data." *Demography* 1 (1964):247–57.

Fox-Genovese, Elizabeth. "The New Female Literary Culture." *Antioch Review* 38 (Spring 1980):193–217.

Frase, Robert W. "Economic Trends in Trade Book Publishing." In *Books and the Mass Market*, ed. Harold K. Guinzberg, Robert W. Frase, and Theodore Waller, 21–42. Urbana: University of Illinois Press, 1953.

Freeman, Harold E., and Kassenbaum, Gene G. "The Illiterate in American Society: Some General Hypotheses." *Social Forces* 34 (1956):371–75.

Friedman, Susan Stanford. "Women's Autobiographical Selves: Theory and Practice." In *The Private Self: Theory and Practice of Women's Autobiographical Writings*, ed. Shari Benstock, 34–62. Chapel Hill: University of North Carolina Press, 1988.

Furet, François, and Ozouf, Jacques. "Literacy and Industrialization:

The Case of the Département du Nord in France." *Journal of European Economic History* 5 (1976):5–44.

Gabriel, Michael. "The Growth of the Small Publisher in the United States, 1960–1985." Research paper. University of Wisconsin, January 1986.

Gans, Herbert. "Diversity Is Not Dead." *New Republic,* April 3, 1961, 11–15.

––––––. "Symbolic Ethnicity: The Future of Ethnic Groups and Cultures in America." *Ethnic and Racial Studies* 2 (January 1979):1–18.

Garcia, Ofelia, et al. "The Hispanic Press in the United States: Content and Prospects." In *The Rise and Fall of the Ethnic Revival: Perspectives on Language and Ethnicity,* ed. Joshua A. Fishman et al., 343–59. New York: Mouton, 1985.

Gilmore, William J. "Elementary Literacy on the Eve of the Industrial Revolution: Trends in Rural New England, 1760–1830." *Proceedings of the American Antiquarian Society* 92 (1982):81–178.

––––––. "Literacy, the Rise of an Age of Reading, and the Cultural Grammar of Print Communications in America, 1735–1850." *Communication* 11 (1988):23–46.

Goody, Jack, and Watt, Ian. "The Consequences of Literacy." *Comparative Studies in Society and History* 5 (1963):304–45.

Gough, Kathleen. "Implications of Literacy in Traditional China and India." In *Literacy in Traditional Societies,* ed. Jack Goody, 70–84. Cambridge: Cambridge University Press, 1968.

Grafton, A. T. "The Importance of Being Printed." *Journal of Interdisciplinary History* 11 (1980):265–86.

Gray, William S. "How Well Do Adults Read?" In *Adult Reading: Fifty-fifth Yearbook of the National Society for the Study of Education,* ed. N. B. Henry. Chicago: University of Chicago Press, 1956.

––––––. "Catching Up with Literacy." *Journal of the Proceedings of the Seventy-first Annual Meeting of the National Education Association.* (1933): 280–81.

Greenberg, Bradley, and Dervin, Brenda. "Mass Communication among the Urban Poor." *Public Opinion Quarterly* 34 (1970):224–35.

Greer, Allan. "The Pattern of Literacy in Quebec, 1745–1899." *Histoire sociale* 44 (1978):293–335.

Griffith, William S., and Cervero, Ronald M. "The Adult Performance Level Program: A Serious and Deliberate Examination." *Adult Education* 27 (1977):209–24.

Gross, Robert A. "Much Instruction from Little Reading: Books and Librarians in Thoreau's Concord." *Proceedings of the American Antiquarian Society* 97 (1987):129–87.

Guthrie, John T., and Kirsch, Irwin S. "The Emergent Perspective on Literacy." *Phi Delta Kappan* 65 (1984):351–55.

Guthrie, John T.; Siefert, Mary; and Kirsch, Irwin S. "Effects of Education, Occupation, and Setting on Reading Practices." *American Educational Research Journal* 23 (1986):151–60.

Guttierez, Felix. "Spanish-Language Media in America: Background, Resources, History." *Journalism History* 4 (Summer 1977):34–41, 65–68.

Hale, Matthew. "History of Employment Testing." In *Ability Testing: Uses, Consequences, and Controversies.* Part 2, Documentation Section, ed. Alexandra K. Wigdor and Wendell R. Garner, 3–38. Washington, D.C.: National Academy Press, 1982.

Hall, David D. "The Uses of Literacy in New England, 1600–1850." In *Printing and Society in Early America*, ed. William L. Joyce et al., 1–47. Worcester: American Antiquarian Society, 1983.

Hall, G. Stanley. "The High School as the People's College." *Journal of the Proceedings of the Forty-first Annual Meeting of the National Education Association* (1902):260–68.

Handlin, Oscar. "Comments on Mass and Popular Culture." In *Culture for the Millions? Mass Media in Modern Society,* ed. Norman Jacobs, 63–70. Princeton, N.J.: D. Van Nostrand, 1959.

Harman, David. "Illiteracy: An Overview." *Harvard Educational Review* 40 (1970):226–43.

Hart, Harlow Irving. "Best Sellers in Fiction during the First Quarter of the Twentieth Century." *Publishers' Weekly,* February 14, 1925, 525–27.

Hawkes, Terence. "Taking It as Read." *Yale Review* 69 (1980):560–76.

Heath, Shirley Brice. "The Functions and Uses of Literacy." *Journal of Communication* 30 (1980):123–33.

———. "Social History and Sociolinguistics." *American Sociologist* 13 (1978):84–92.

Hohendahl, Peter U. "Introduction to Reception Aesthetics." *New German Critique* 10 (1977): 29–64.

Hoopes, Townshend. "Aliteracy and the Decline of the Language." In *Aliteracy: People Who Can Read but Won't*, ed. Nick Thimmesch, 36–39. Washington, D.C.: American Enterprise Institute for Public Policy Research, 1984.

Houston, R. A. "The Literacy Myth?" Illiteracy in Scotland, 1630–1760." *Past and Present* 96 (1982):82–102.

"The Iowa Tests of Educational Development: A Summary of Changes in the ITED Norms." University of Iowa, Iowa City, 1971. Mimeo.

Irwin, Judith W. "The Effect of Linguistic Cohesion on Prose Comprehension." *Journal of Reading Behavior* 12 (Winter 1980):325–32.

Isaac, Rhys. "Books and the Social Authority of Learning: The Case of Mid-Eighteenth-Century Virginia." In *Printing and Society in Early America,* ed. William L. Joyce et al., 228–49. Worcester: American Antiquarian Society, 1983.

Jameson, Fredric. "Ideology, Narrative Analysis, and Popular Culture." *Theory and Society* 4 (1977):543–59.

Jauss, Hans R. "Literary History as a Challenge to Literary Theory." In *New Directions in Literary History,* ed. Ralph Cohen, 11–41. Baltimore: Johns Hopkins University Press, 1974.

Jeffery, L. G. "Greek Alphabetic Writing." In *The Cambridge Ancient History,* ed. John Boardman et al., 3:819–33. 2d ed. Cambridge: Cambridge University Press, 1982.

Jencks, Christopher. "Declining Test Scores: An Assessment of Six Alternative Explanations." *Sociological Spectrum* (December 1980):1–15.

Johansson, Egil. "The History of Literacy in Sweden." In *Literacy and Social Development in the West: A Reader,* ed. Harvey Graff, 151–53. Cambridge: Cambridge University Press, 1981.

Kaestle, Carl F. "Moral Education and Common Schools in America: A Historian's View." *Journal of Moral Education* 13 (May 1984):101–11.

——. "'The Scylla of Brutal Ignorance and the Charybdis of a Literary Education': Elite Attitudes toward Mass Education in Early Industrial England and America." In *School and Society,* ed. Lawrence Stone, 177–91. Baltimore: Johns Hopkins University Press, 1976.

Katz, Elihu; Blumler, Jay; and Gurevitch, Michael. "Utilization of Mass Communication by the Individual." In *The Uses of Mass Communications: Current Perspectives on Gratifications Research,* ed. Jay G. Blumler and Elihu Katz, 19–32. Beverly Hills, Calif.: Sage, 1974.

Kelly, Robert G. "Literature and the Historian." *American Quarterly* 26 (1974):141–59.

Kemper, Susan. "Measuring the Inference Load of a Text." *Journal of Educational Psychology* 75 (1983):391–401.

Kintsch, Walter, and Vipond, Douglas. "Reading Comprehension and Readability in Educational Practice and Psychological Theory." In *Perspectives on Memory Research,* ed. Lars-Goran Nilsson, 329–65. Hillsdale, N.J.: Lawrence Erlbaum, 1979.

Kirsch, Irwin S., and Guthrie, John T. "Adult Reading Practices for Work and Leisure." *Reading Research Quarterly* 1 (1973–74):213–32.

——. "The Concept and Measurement of Functional Literacy." *Reading Research Quarterly* 13 (1977–78):485–507.

Klare, George R. "Assessing Readability." *Reading Research Quarterly* 10 (1974–75):62–102.

———. "Readability." In *Handbook of Reading Research,* ed. P. David Pearson et al., 681–744. New York: Longman, 1984.

Kleinfield, N. R. "The Supermarketer of Books." *New York Times Magazine,* November 9, 1986.

Laqueur, Thomas W. "Literacy and Social Mobility in the Industrial Revolution." *Past and Present* 64 (1974):96–107.

Lasswell, Harold. "The Structure and Function of Communication in Society." In *The Communication. of Ideas,* ed. Lyman Bryson. New York: Institute for Religious and Social Studies, 1948.

Leach, William R. "Transformations in the Culture of Consumption: Women and Department Stores, 1890–1925." *Journal of American History* 71 (September 1984):319–42.

Lerner, Barbara. "The Minimum Competence Testing Movement: Social, Scientific, and Legal Implications." *American Psychologist* 36 (1981): 1057–66.

Levin, Henry M., and Rumberger, R. "Hi-Tech Requires Few Brains." *Washington Post,* January 30, 1983.

Lichtenberger, J. P. "Negro Illiteracy in the United States." In *The Negro's Progress in Fifty Years,* ed. Emory R. Johnson. Annals of the American Academy of Political and Social Science, 49. Philadelphia, 1913.

McCombs, Maxwell E. "Mass Media in the Marketplace." *Journalism Monographs* 24 (August 1972):1–104.

McCombs, Maxwell E., and Eyal, Chaim H. "Spending on Mass Media." *Journal of Communication* 30 (Winter 1980):153–58.

McLeod, Jack M., and Becker, Lee B. "The Uses and Gratifications Approach." In *Handbook of Political Communications,* ed. D. Nimmo and K. Sanders, 67–99. Beverly Hills, Calif.: Sage, 1981.

Maynes, Mary Jo. "The Virtues of Archaism: The Political Economy of Schooling in Europe, 1750–1850." *Comparative Studies in Society and History* 21 (1979):611–25.

Mechling, Jay E. "Advice to Historians on Advice to Mothers." *Journal of Social History* 9 (Fall 1975):44–63.

Meier, Deborah. "'Getting Tough' in the Schools." *Dissent* (Winter 1984): 61–70.

———. "Why Reading Tests Don't Test Reading." *Dissent* (Fall 1981): 457–66.

Mikulecky, Larry. "Job Literacy: The Relationship between School Preparation and Workplace Activity." *Reading Research Quarterly* 17 (1982):400–419.

———. "The Mismatch between School Training and Job Literacy Demands." *Vocational Guidance Quarterly* 30 (1981):174–80.

Mikulecky, Larry, and Ehlinger, Jeanne. "The Influence of Metacognitive Aspects of Literacy on Job Performance of Electronics Technicians." *Journal of Reading Behavior* 18 (1986):41–62.

Mikulecky, Larry, and Winchester, Dorothy. "Job Literacy and Job Performance among Nurses at Varying Employment Levels." *Adult Education Quarterly* 34 (1983):1–15.

Miller, James R., and Kintsch, Walter. "Readability and Recall of Short Prose Passages: A Theoretical Analysis." *Journal of Experimental Psychology* 6 (1980):335–54.

Mills, C. Wright. "The New Left." In *Power, Politics and People,* ed. Irving Horowitz, 247–59. New York: Ballantine Books, 1963.

Modell, John. "Patterns of Consumption, Acculturation, and Family Income Strategies in Late Nineteenth-Century America." In *Family and Population in Nineteenth Century America,* ed. Tamara K. Hareven and Maris A. Vinovskis, 206–40. Princeton, N.J.: Princeton University Press, 1978.

Monaghan, E. Jennifer. "Literacy Instruction and Gender in Colonial New England." In *Reading in America: Literature and Social History,* ed. Cathy N. Davidson, 53–80. Baltimore: Johns Hopkins University Press, 1989.

Monteith, Mary K. "How Well Does the Average American Read? Some Facts, Figures, and Opinions." *Journal of Reading* (February 1980): 460–64.

Moran, Gerald F., and Vinovskis, Maris A. "The Great Care of Godly Parents: Early Childhood in Puritan New England." In *History and Research in Child Development,* Serial no. 211, vol. 50, ed. Alice Boardman Smuts and John W. Hagen, 24–37. Chicago: University of Chicago Monographs of the Society for Research in Child Development, 1986.

Murphy, Richard T. "Assessment of Adult Reading Competence." In *Reading and Career Education,* ed. Duane M. Nielsen and Howard F. Hjelm. Newark, Del.: International Reading Association, 1975.

Needham, Paul. Review of *The Printing Press as an Agent of Change: Communications and Cultural Transformations in Early-Modern Europe,* by Elizabeth Eisenstein. *Fine Print* 6 (1980):23–35.

Nixon, Raymond B. "The Problem of Newspaper Monopoly" (1948). Reprinted in *Mass Communications,* ed. Wilbur Schramm, 241–50. 2d ed. Urbana: University of Illinois Press, 1960.

Nord, David P. "Working Class Readers: Family, Community, and Reading in Late Nineteenth-Century America." *Communication Research* 13 (1986):156–81.

Northcutt, Norvell W. "Functional Literacy for Adults." In *Reading and Career Education,* ed. Duane M. Nielsen and Howard F. Hjelm. Newark, Del.: International Reading Association, 1975.

Olneck, Michael. "Terman Redux." *Contemporary Education Review* 3 (1984):297–314.

Olson, David R. "The Languages of Instruction: The Literate Bias of Schooling." In *Schooling and the Acquisition of Knowledge,* ed. R. C. Anderson, R. J. Spiro, and W. E. Montague, 65–89. Hillsdale, N.J.: Lawrence Erlbaum, 1977.

Palmgreen, Philip; Wenner, Lawrence A.; and Rosengren, Karl E. "Uses and Gratifications Research: The Past Ten Years." In *Media Gratifications Research: Current Perspectives,* ed. Karl E. Rosengren, Lawrence A. Wenner, and Philip Palmgreen, 11–37. Beverly Hills, Calif.: Sage, 1985.

Parker, Geoffrey. "An Educational Revolution? The Growth of Literacy and Schooling in Early Modern Europe." *Tijdschrift voor Geschiedenis* 93 (1980):210–20.

Perlmann, Joel. "Working Class Homeowning and Children's Schooling in Providence, R.I., 1880–1925." *History of Education Quarterly* 23 (Summer 1983):175–93.

Porter, Bruce. "B. Dalton: The Leader of the Chain Gang." *Saturday Review,* June 9, 1979, 53–57.

Real, Michael R. "Media Theory: Contributions to an Understanding of American Mass Communications." *American Quarterly* 32 (Bibliography issue, 1980):240–44.

Reed, Roy. "From the Campuses: Adventures in Publishing." *New York Times Book Review,* September 24, 1989.

Resnick, Daniel, and Resnick, Lauren. "The Nature of Literacy: An Historical Exploration." *Harvard Educational Review* 43 (1977):370–85.

———. "Standards, Curriculum, and Performance: Historical and Comparative Perspective." *Educational Researcher* 14 (1985):5–20.

Richek, Margaret A. "Effect of Sentence Complexity on the Reading Comprehension of Syntactic Structures." *Journal of Educational Psychology* 68 (1976):800–806.

Robinson, John. "The Changing Reading Habits of the American Public." *Journal of Communication* 30 (Winter 1980):141–52.

Robinson, John P., and Jeffres, Leo W. "The Changing Role of Newspapers in the Age of Television." *Journalism Monographs* 63, Association for Education in Journalism, 1979.

Rubin, Joan Shelley. "Self, Culture, and Self-Culture in Modern America: The Early History of the Book-of-the-Month Club." *Journal of American History* 71 (March 1985):782–806.

Sanderson, Michael. "Literacy and Social Mobility in the Industrial Revolution in England." *Past and Present* 56 (1972):75–104.

Schmandt-Besserat, Denise. "The Earliest Precursor of Writing." *Scientific American* 238 (June 1978):50–59.

Schofield, Roger S. "Dimensions of Illiteracy, 1750–1850." *Explorations in Economic History* 10 (1973):437–54.

———. "The Measurement of Literacy in Pre-Industrial England." In *Literacy in Traditional Societies,* ed. Jack Goody, 311–25. Cambridge: Cambridge University Press, 1968.

Schwarzlose, Richard Z. "Historical Dynamics of Technology and Social Values." *Prospects* 11 (1987):135–55.

Schweickart, Patrocinio P. "Reading Ourselves: Toward a Feminist Theory of Reading." In *Gender and Reading: Essays on Readers, Texts, and Contexts,* ed. Elizabeth A. Flynn and Patrocinio P. Schweickart, 35–39. Baltimore: Johns Hopkins University Press, 1986.

Selden, Ramsay. "On the Validation of the Original Readability Formulas." In *Text Readability: Proceedings of the March 1980 Conference,* ed. Alice Davison, Robert Lutz, and Ann Roalef, 10–30. Urbana: University of Illinois, Center for the Study of Reading, 1981.

Sharon, Amiel T. "What Do Adults Read?" *Reading Research Quarterly* 9 (1973–74):148–69.

Shils, Edward. "Daydreams and Nightmares: Reflections on the Criticism of Mass Culture." *Sewanee Review* 65 (1957):587–608.

———. "Mass Society and Its Culture." In *Culture for the Millions? Mass Media in Modern Society,* ed. Norman Jacobs, 1–27. Princeton, N.J.: D. Van Nostrand, 1959.

Smith, Henry Nash. "The Scribbling Women and the Cosmic Success Story." *Critical Inquiry* 1 (September 1974):47–70.

Smout, T. C. "Born Again at Cambuslang: New Evidence on Popular Religion and Literacy in Eighteenth-Century Scotland." *Past and Present* 97 (1982):114–27.

Spenner, Kenneth I. "Occupational Characteristics and Classification Systems." *Sociological Methods and Research* 9 (1980):239–64.

Spivey, Nancy Nelson. "Construing Constructivism: Reading Research in the United States." *Poetics* 16 (1987):169–92.

Spufford, Margaret. "First Steps in Literacy: The Reading and Writing Experiences of the Humblest Seventeenth-Century Spiritual Autobiographers." *Social History* 4 (1979):407–35.

Stephens, Walter. "Illiteracy and Schooling in the Provincial Towns, 1640–1870." In *Urban Education in the Nineteenth Century,* ed. David Reader, 27–47. London: Taylor and Francis, 1977.

Sticht, Thomas G., and McFann, Howard. "Reading Requirements for Career Entry." In *Reading and Career Education,* ed. Duane M. Nielsen and Howard F. Hjelm. Newark, Del.: International Reading Association, 1975.

Stone, Lawrence. "Literacy and Education in England, 1640–1900." *Past and Present* 42 (1969):69–139.

Strauss, Gerald. "Lutheranism and Literacy: A Reassessment." In *Religion and Society in Early Modern Europe, 1500–1800,* ed. Kaspar von Greyerz, 109–23. Boston: George Allen and Unwin, 1984.

Swanson, David L. "Political Communication Research and the Uses and Gratifications Model: A Critique." *Communication Research* 6 (1979): 37–53.

Szwed, John F. "The Ethnography of Literacy." In *Variation in Writing: Functional and Linguistic-Cultural Differences,* ed. Marcia Farr Whiteman, 13–23. Hillsdale, N.J.: Lawrence Erlbaum, 1981.

Tavris, Carol. "The End of I.Q. Slump." *Psychology Today,* April 1976, 69–74.

Thompson, E. P. "The Long Revolution." *New Left Review,* 9, 10 (May–June, July–August 1961):24–33, 34–39.

Thompson, Roger. "Illiteracy in America." *Editorial Research Reports,* June 24, 1983, 475–92.

Trabasso, Tom; Secco, Tom; and Van Den Broek, Paul. "Coherence in Narrative Text." In *Learning and Comprehension of Text,* ed. H. Mandell, Nancy Stein, and Tom Trabasso. Hillsdale, N.J.: Lawrence Erlbaum, 1983.

Trow, Martin. "The Democratization of Higher Education in America." *Archives européennes de sociologie* 3 (1962):231–62.

———. "The Second Transformation of American Secondary Education." *International Journal of Comparative Sociology* 2 (1961):144–66.

Tuddenham, Read D. "Soldier Intelligence in World Wars I and II." *American Psychologist* 3 (1948):54–56.

Tully, Alan. "Literacy Levels and Education Development in Rural Pennsylvania, 1729–1775." *Pennsylvania History* 39 (1972):302–12.

Tyler, Ralph W. "High School Pupils of Today." *Educational Research Bulletin* 9 (1930):409–10.

Venezky, Richard L. "The Development of Literacy in the Industrialized Nations of the West." In *Handbook of Reading Research,* ed. P. David Pearson. Newark, Del.: International Reading Association. In press.

———. "The Origins of the Present-Day Chasm between Adult Literacy Needs and School Literacy Instruction." *Visible Language* 16 (1982): 113–26.

Vinovskis, Maris A. "Horace Mann on the Economic Productivity of Education." *New England Quarterly* 43 (1970):550–71.

———. "Quantification and the History of Education: Observations on Antebellum Education Expansion, School Attendance and Educational Reform." *Journal of Interdisciplinary History* 14 (1983): 856–69.

Vinovskis, Maris A., and Bernard, Richard. "Beyond Catherine Beecher: Female Education in the Antebellum Period." *Signs* 3 (1978):856–69.

"Waldenbooks: Countering B. Dalton by Aping Its Computer Operations." *Business Week,* October 8, 1979, 116–21.

Waples, Douglas. "Relation of Subject Interests to Actual Reading." *Library Quarterly* 2 (January 1932):42–70.

Webb, R. K. "Working Class Readers in Early Victorian England." *English Historical Review* 65 (1950):333–51.

Wellborn, S. N. "Ahead: A Nation of Illiterates?" *U.S. News and World Report,* May 17, 1982, 53–57.

Werner, Leslie M. "13% of the U.S. Adults Are Illiterate in English, A Federal Study Finds." *New York Times,* April 21, 1986.

Witty, Paul, and Coomer, Ann. "How Successful Is Reading Instruction Today?" *Elementary English* 28 (December 1951):451–78.

Wood, Leonard A. "Book Reading, 1955–84; The Trend Is Up." *Publishers Weekly,* May 25, 1984.

Wood, William C. "Consumer Spending on the Mass Media: The Principle of Relative Constancy Reconsidered." *Journal of Communication* 36 (Spring 1986):39–51.

Youngren, J. Alan. "Christian Booksellers Find Happiness in Slow Growth." *Christianity Today,* September 4, 1981, 64–65.

Zajonc, Robert B., and Bargh, John. "Birth Order, Family Size, and Decline of SAT Scores." *American Psychologist* 35 (July 1980):662–68.

About the Authors

CARL F. KAESTLE is William F. Vilas Professor of Educational Policy Studies and History at the University of Wisconsin at Madison.

HELEN DAMON-MOORE teaches women's studies and education at Cornell College, Mount Vernon, Iowa.

LAWRENCE C. STEDMAN is assistant professor of education at the State University of New York at Binghamton.

KATHERINE TINSLEY teaches history at the Horace Mann School, Bronx, New York.

WILLIAM VANCE TROLLINGER, JR., is assistant professor of history at Messiah College, Grantham, Pennsylvania.

Index

Acland, Henry, 102, 103–4
Adult Functional Reading Study, 97–98, 103, 107, 108, 109, 110
Adult Performance Level Project, 98–99, 102, 104, 110, 126
Advertising, 249–51, 254–57, 259, 271
Aliteracy, 150
American College Test (ACT), 91, 130
Antin, Mary, 237–38, 240, 276
Armed Services Vocational Aptitude Battery, 112, 116
Atlantic Monthly, 206, 209, 212–18
Authorship, 68–69
Autobiography: as approach to history of literacy, xv, 243–44; analyzed, 225–43
Auwers, Linda, 22

Back-to-basics movement, 143–44
Bagdikian, Ben, 67
Bailyn, Bernard, 20–21
Baker, Josephine, 235–36
Berelson, Bernard, 39
Bible, 14, 27; Bible reading, 64, 232–33
Black Americans: and literacy, 25, 28, 31, 125–26; and publishing, 273, 288
Bloom, Benjamin, 86
Bloor, Ella Reeve, 231, 236–37
Bok, Edward, 252, 257–59
Bold, Christine, 70–71
Books: expansion of publication in early nineteenth century, 54–55; secondary literature, 65–66; formula fiction, 69–72; book buying trends, 149, 153–79; paperbacks, 166, 286, 290; frequency of book reading, 181, 183, 184–97, 200–201, 203, 205–6; book reading and education, 205; readability of bestsellers in *1920,* 207, 209–10, 212; book readers in the *1880s,* 278, 281–82; and standardization, 285; and diversity, 288. *See also* Novels
Bookstores, 37–38, 290
Boyer, Paul, 285
Brief Test of Literacy, 111–12, 126

Calvinism: and literacy, 15. *See also* Protestantism
Capitalism: as threat to diversity and freedom, 34–36, 274–75; and commercial development, 52–53; effects on consumer culture, 248–49, 250–51, 254–57, 260–62, 265–71, 290; effects on consolidation of publishing industries, 274. *See also* Industrialization
Carey, James W., 42, 50
Catholicism: and literacy, 13–14, 17–18
Cawelti, John, 70
Censorship, 285–86
Census, U.S.: literacy figures, 24, 76, 78–79, 110, 125; schooling a proxy for functional literacy, 92–94; English Language Proficiency Survey, 99
Centralization. *See* Consolidation; Standardization
Chamberlain, Hope Summerell, 229, 235, 236
Christian Booksellers Association, 287
Cipolla, Carlo, 13
Clanchy, Michael, 9, 10
Class. *See* Social class

Cohen, Rose, 230, 241
College Entrance Examination Board, Advisory Panel on the Scholastic Aptitude Test, 131, 132
Comics, 283, 289
Communication theory, 39–42
Consolidation: of culture, xvi, 35, 245, 272–93; of print industries, xvi, 66–67, 245, 283–85, 293
Constancy thesis. *See* McCombs, Maxwell
Constructivist model of reading, 42–43
Copperman, Paul, 90, 110, 131, 133, 138
Copyright law, 65, 282
Cremin, Lawrence A.: literacy as liberating, 4, 20–21, 54; literacy as breeding literacy, 53
Cressy, David, 16, 24
Culler, Jonathan, 43, 45
Cultural capital, 227–28, 237, 276–78
Curtis, Cyrus, 249, 250–56, 262, 267, 270
Curtis, Louisa Knapp, 249, 250–52, 270

Darnton, Robert, 36–37, 48–49, 53–54, 59
Davidson, Cathy N., 53, 57, 59, 62
Denning, Michael, 50, 57–59, 62
Deskilling, 120–21
DiMaggio, Paul, 272–73, 277
Diversity: in print, 51–52, 54, 65, 272–93; and literacy, 234; in autobiographies, 243
Dodd, Bella Visono, 241–42
Douglas, Ann, 63

Eisenstein, Elizabeth, 5, 10
Emporia (Kansas) Gazette, 68
Engelsing, Rolf, 53–55
England, 11, 13, 16, 17
English Language Proficiency Survey, 99, 100
Escarpit, Robert, 37, 40
Ethnicity, and literacy, 27. *See also* Immigration

Family budget studies, 151–52, 162–79
Farr, Roger, 76, 86, 88
Female literacy, 22, 23, 28, 30–31, 123–24, 197–98. *See also* Gender
Feminist press, 273, 288
Field, Alexander, 29
Fish, Stanley, 43, 45, 48
Fisher, Donald, 76, 102, 103, 111, 112
Flesch, Rudolf, 207–9, 211–13, 218
Flynn, Elizabeth Gurley, 230, 231, 233–34, 239–40

Foreign-language press, 69, 281, 287
France: literacy in, 13, 17–18, 19; bookstores in, 37
Franchise. *See* Politics
Freire, Paulo, 27
Functional literacy, 76, 78, 92–123, 128
Functionalism, 41
Furet, François, 17, 118

Gallup polls: 163, 183, 184–87, 190, 191, 233
Gates, Arthur, 87–88
Gay press, 273, 288
Gender: and magazines, xvi, 245–71; and literacy, 27; and early nineteenth-century novels, 57, 59, 62; and choice of books, 200. *See also* Female literacy
General Aptitude Test Battery (GATB), 116
General Educational Development (GED), 86, 119–20
Gilmore, William, 22–23, 55
Ginzburg, Carlo, 47–49
Goldman, Emma, 238–39
Goody, Jack, 5, 7, 8, 9
Graff, Harvey, 4, 5, 24–25, 29, 31
Gray, William S., 181
Griffith, Sally Foreman, 68

Hajda, Jan, 200–201
Hall, David, 56
Hamerow, Theodore, 11, 18
Havelock, Eric, 8
Heath, Shirley Brice, 38
Hoff, Harry A., 183, 190, 196, 197
Hohendahl, Peter, 50
Holland, Norman, 43, 46
Homogenization. *See* Standardization
Houston, Rab A., 14, 15, 31

Illiteracy. *See* Literacy
Immigration: and illiteracy, 25, 28; assimilation, 234–35, 245, 276; immigrant autobiographies, 237–43; and diverse print matter, 273; restricted, 283. *See also* Foreign-language press
Industrialization: and literacy, 17, 18, 28. *See also* Capitalism
Innis, Harold, 33–34, 35, 36, 274–75, 290
Intensive reading. *See* Reading
Iowa Tests of Basic Skills (ITBS), 129, 130
Iowa Tests of Educational Development (ITED), 90, 130
Iser, Wolfgang, 43, 45, 48

Jauss, Hans, 48, 59
Jencks, Christopher, 126, 139
Jobs. *See* Literacy and jobs

Kelley, Mary, 63–64
Kelly, Robert, 38
Kemper, Susan, 211, 216–19
Kirsch, Irwin, 98, 120, 126
Kreiling, Albert, 42, 50

Ladies' Home Journal, 246, 250–52,
253–54, 257–64, 267–68, 280
Laqueur, Thomas, 17
Lazarsfeld, Paul, 39
Levine, Lawrence, 60–62
Lewisohn, Ludwig, 47
Libraries, 181, 199–200, 238, 240, 245,
276
Life, 266–67
Link, Henry C., 183, 190, 196, 197
Lippmann, Walter, 67
Literacy: as a subject of study, xi–xii, 3;
major themes in history of, xvi; defined, 3, 77; in Greece, 4; and progress, 4, 27–28; expansion of, 5, 17, 26,
28, 51, 52, 54, 55, 127; causes of its
expansion, 5, 18, 19, 24, 28; and
schooling, 5–6, 19, 22, 30–31, 52–53,
55, 77, 121–23, 127, 205, 245, 276,
278, 283, 289; origins in ancient civilizations, 6; as a policy concern, 26, 31,
292–93; uses of, 27, 30, 227–43, 272;
and jobs, 29–30, 115–23, 134–35; and
the family, 31, 141, 142, 237, 243,
292; and politics, 292–93
Literacy rates, 10; as an approach to
history of literacy, xi–xii; in Europe,
1600–1850, 12–18; in Europe, *1850–
1900,* 18–19; in America, *1600–1900,*
19–25; differences among males and
females, 23, 123–24, 247; differences
among blacks and whites, 23, 125–26,
204–5; in America, twentieth century,
25–26, 31, 76, 291–92; in *1920,* 204–
5. *See also* Functional literacy
Lockridge, Kenneth, 20–21, 22
Lorimer, George Henry, 253–56
Luce, Henry, 67, 266

Magazines, 278, 279; magazine buying
trends, 149, 153–79; frequency of
magazine reading, 181, 183, 184–97,
201, 203, 205–6; romance adventure
magazines, 198, 199; readability in
1920, 206, 209, 212–18; and gender,
245–71; in the *1880s* and *1890s,* 278,
279, 280; and consolidation, 284–85
Mailloux, Steven, 45–46

Marvin, Carolyn, 35
Maynes, Mary Jo, 14
McCombs, Maxwell, xiv, 159, 178
Melville, Herman, 46, 63
Metropolitan Achievement Test (MAT),
131, 135, 137
Mikulecky, Larry, 119, 122–23, 184
Mini-Assessment of Functional Literacy
(MAFL). *See* National Assessment of
Educational Progress (NAEP)
Models, 36–38, 39, 42–43, 51–52
Moran, Gerald, 23, 247
Morison, Samuel E., 20
Ms., 268–70, 290
Munroe, Ruth, 181

National Assessment of Educational
Progress (NAEP): Young Adult Literacy Assessment, 31, 94, 99–100, 105,
106, 113, 126, 292; Mini- Assessment
of Functional Literacy (MAFL), 96–
97, 104–5, 106, 110, 118, 124; NAEP
achievement tests, 129, 130, 134,
136–37, 143
National Commission on Excellence in
Education (*A Nation at Risk* report),
76, 134, 139
National Reading Difficulty Index, 95–
96, 105–7, 111
New Criticism, 44–45
Newspapers: expanding circulation of,
54, 55, 278, 280; history of journalism, 65; newspaper buying trends,
149, 153–79; frequency of newspaper
reading, 181, 183, 184–97, 201, 203,
205–6; choice of, 199; readability, 209,
211–12; standardization, 283–84
Novels, 37, 53, 57–59, 63–64, 70–72,
247–48; dime novels, 57–58, 70; Westerns, 70–71

Occupations and occupational structure.
See Literacy and jobs
Ong, Walter, 8
Oral culture, 6–8, 34, 47–48
Ozouf, Jacques, 17, 18

Parsons, Rhey Boyd, 181, 190–95,
205–6
Peiss, Kathy, 61
Plato: and literacy, 7
Playboy, 265, 270
Politics, and school expansion, 18–19
Popular culture debate: *1950s,* 27, 275;
highbrow-lowbrow distinction, 56, 57,
60–62; and cultural consolidation,
245

Preliminary Scholastic Aptitude Test (PSAT), 90, 131, 137
Printing, 9, 288–89; impact of printing press, 5, 10, 13, 19
Protestantism: and literacy, 13–15, 17, 21

Quebec: literacy in, 14

Radical press, 281, 287–88
Radway, Janice, 59, 228
Readability, difficulty of text, 204, 205, 207–21
Readers, and texts, xiii, 39–50, 52, 59, 69–70; interests, 182
Reader-response theory, 43–46, 59
Reading: intensive vs. extensive, 53–55, 64, 232–33; and electronic media, 157–63; typology of purposes, 227–43; aloud, 230–32
Reading public: American, xii; diverging, 55, 64; stratified, 150, 203, 204, 211; trends in purchase of reading materials, 153–79; and age, 190–92; and education, 192–94, 200; and sex differences, 194–95, 200; and race, 195–96; and income, 196–97; in 1920, 204–7
Reading test scores. See Test scores
Religion: and printing press, 10, 13; and literacy rates, 15; religious publishing, 287. See also Catholicism; Protestantism
Robinson, John, 184, 191

Saturday Evening Post, 206, 209, 212–18, 246, 252–64, 266, 267
Schiller, Dan, 63
Schneiderman, Rose, 239
Schofield, Roger, 11, 12, 17
Scholastic Aptitude Test (SAT), 90–91, 124, 130, 131, 132, 134–35, 137, 139, 140
School and College Ability Tests (SCAT), 90
Schools. See Literacy and schooling
Schudson, Michael, 63
Science Research Associates (SRA) test, 133–34
Scotland: high literacy in, 15
Sex differences in literacy. See Female literacy; Gender; Literacy rates; Reading public
Signatures, as measure of literacy, 4, 11–12, 15, 23

Smith, Henry Nash, 56, 57
Smout, T. C., 15
Social class: and literacy, 13, 16, 24, 27, 102, 243; and divergent reading publics, 55, 56, 166–79; and divergent cultures, 62, 273; and cultural capital, 227–28, 237; middle-class reading before 1800, 246, 248
Sollors, Werner, 47
Soltow, Lee, 4, 23–25
Spufford, Margaret, 16
Standardization: of print matter content, xvi, 10, 51, 67, 272–93. See also Consolidation
Stanford Achievement Test, 135, 137
Stevens, Edward, 4, 23–25
Sticht, Thomas, 113, 114, 117–18
Stone, Lawrence, 17, 27
Survival Literacy Study, 95, 96, 106, 108, 111, 124, 125
Sweden: high literacy in, 15

Test scores, decline in 1970s, 26, 77, 89–91, 111, 129–45; reading test scores, then-and-now studies, 80–89; achievement test trends, 89–91, 127; reading grade level, 111–14; equating, renorming studies, 135–36
Then-and-now studies. See Test scores
Theory: and the history of literacy, 33–52
Thernstrom, Stephan, 29
Thompson, Edward P., 36
Tully, Alan, 21

Urbanization: and literacy, 13, 18
Uses and gratifications approach, 39–42

Vinovskis, Maris, 23, 29, 247

Waples, Douglas, 182
Watt, Ian, 5, 8, 9
Weisbrod, Vera, 240
White, William Allen, 68
Whiteside, Thomas, 67
Williams, Raymond, 34–36, 274–75, 290
Women and literacy. See Female literacy
Writing, development of, 6–9, 12

Young, Sheryl, 210–11, 214–16
Young Adult Literacy Assessment. See National Assessment of Education Progress (NAEP)